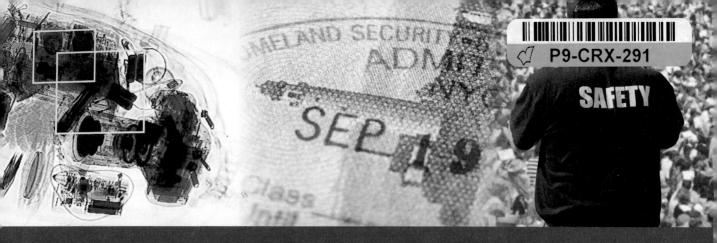

Introduction to
HOMELAND
SECURITY

Policy,
Organization,
and Administration

WILLARD M. OLIVER
Sam Houston State University
Huntsville, Texas

NANCY E. MARION
University of Akron
Akron, Ohio

JOSHUA B. HILL
Tiffin University
Tiffin, Ohio

JONES & BARTLETT
LEARNING

World Headquarters
Jones & Bartlett Learning
5 Wall Street
Burlington, MA 01803
978-443-5000
info@jblearning.com
www.jblearning.com

Jones & Bartlett Learning books and products are available through most bookstores and online booksellers. To contact Jones & Bartlett Learning directly, call 800-832-0034, fax 978-443-8000, or visit our website, www.jblearning.com.

Substantial discounts on bulk quantities of Jones & Bartlett Learning publications are available to corporations, professional associations, and other qualified organizations. For details and specific discount information, contact the special sales department at Jones & Bartlett Learning via the above contact information or send an email to specialsales@jblearning.com.

Production Credits

Executive Publisher: William Brottmiller
Publisher: Cathy L. Esperti
Senior Acquisitions Editor: Erin O'Connor
Editorial Assistant: Audrey Schwinn
Associate Production Editor: Rebekah Linga
Marketing Manager: Lindsay White
Manufacturing and Inventory Control Supervisor: Amy Bacus
Composition: diacriTech
Cover Design: Kristin E. Parker

Photo Research and Permissions Associate: Ashley Dos Santos
Cover Images: Luggage: © Khafizov Ivan Harisovich/ShutterStock, Inc.; Passport: © iStockphoto/Thinkstock.; Security: © egd/ShutterStock, Inc.; Twin Towers: © stockelements/ShutterStock, Inc.
Title Page Images: Luggage: © Khafizov Ivan Harisovich/ShutterStock, Inc.; Passport: © iStockphoto/Thinkstock.; Security: © egd/ShutterStock, Inc.; Twin Towers: © stockelements/ShutterStock, Inc.
Printing and Binding: Courier Companies
Cover Printing: Courier Companies

To order this product, use ISBN: 978-1-284-04583-3

Library of Congress Cataloging-in-Publication Data
Oliver, Willard M., author.
 Introduction to homeland security : policy, organization, and administration / Willard M. Oliver, Nancy E. Marion, and Joshua B. Hill.
    pages cm
 Includes bibliographical references and index.
 ISBN 978-1-4496-4544-1 (paper.)
 1. United States. Department of Homeland Security. 2. National security—United States. 3. Internal security—United States.
 4. Terrorism—United States—Prevention. I. Marion, Nancy E., author. II. Hill, Joshua B., author. III. Title.
 HV6432.4.O45 2015
 363.340973--dc23   2013038789

6048
Printed in the United States of America
18 17 16 15 14   10 9 8 7 6 5 4 3 2 1

Brief Contents

Contents

Courtesy of Leif Skoogfors/FEMA.

© ChameleonsEye/ShutterStock, Inc.

© infinity21/ShutterStock, Inc.

© Maksim Kabakou/ShutterStock, Inc.

Contents

© spirit of america/ShutterStock, Inc.

© spirit of america/ShutterStock, Inc.

© sakhorn/ShutterStock, Inc.

© twobee/ShutterStock, Inc.

© Stocksnapper/ShutterStock, Inc.

About the Authors

Willard M. Oliver is professor of criminal justice in the College of Criminal Justice at Sam Houston State University, Huntsville, Texas. He holds a PhD and MA in political science from West Virginia University and an MS and BS in criminal justice from Radford University. He is the author of numerous peer-reviewed journal articles and books, including *Homeland Security for Policing*, which is widely used in both criminal justice and homeland security courses. He is a retired Major from the U.S. Army Military Police Corps and is a decorated veteran of the Persian Gulf War. He is also a former police officer from the Washington, DC metropolitan area. Oliver holds a black belt in martial arts and is an avid marathon runner.

Nancy E. Marion is professor of political science and associate chair of the Department of Political Science at the University of Akron, Akron, Ohio. She holds a PhD and MA in political science from the State University of New York, an MS in criminal justice from American University, and a BS in administration of justice from Pennsylvania State University. She is the author of numerous peer-reviewed journal articles and books, including *The Public Policy of Crime and Criminal Justice*. Her research interests center around the interplay of politics and criminal justice/ homeland security policy. Most recently, she was awarded a research grant from the Canadian government to study border security issues and the "intermestic" nature of homeland security policies.

Joshua B. Hill is an assistant professor of Homeland Security and Terrorism at Tiffin University in Tiffin, Ohio. He holds a PhD in criminal justice, an MA in criminology and criminal justice from Sam Houston State University, and a BA in international relations from the University of Central Florida. His research interests include terrorism, international policing, and research methods. He has prior experience as a project manager with an NGO, the Institute for the Study of Violent Groups (ISVG), focusing on open-source collection of terrorist information. He most recently published an article examining terrorism culpability in the *Journal of Defense Modeling and Simulation*.

Reviewers

The authors and publisher wish to thank the following reviewers for their valuable input in the development of this text:

George Ackerman

Captain David M. Allender
Indianapolis Metropolitan Police Department

Edward T. Croissant
Tampa Police Department

Dustin A. Dorough
Brandman University

Camille Gibson
Prairie View A&M University

Sean Joiner
Augusta Technical College

Curtis Jones
Mississippi College

Keith Gregory Logan
Kutztown University of Pennsylvannia

Felix G. Mangual
University of Central Florida

John M. McCullough
South Hills School of Business and Technology

Mitchel P. Roth
Sam Houston State University

Jeffrey P. Rush
Austin Peay State University

Wojtek M. Wolfe
Rutgers University

Dominic D. Yin
City College of San Francisco

Introduction

On September 11, 2001, when Al Qaeda terrorists hijacked four planes and purposely flew two of them into the World Trade Towers in New York City, one into the Pentagon in Arlington, Virginia—the fourth crashed in Pennsylvania only because of the bravery of its passengers—America's world changed. Ushered in were both a new era and a new phrase in our vocabulary: *homeland security*. Despite the long hunt for the head of Al Qaeda, Osama bin Laden, and his eventual death at the hands of Navy Seal Team VI, the threat to America's homeland continues. As is evidenced by the over 50 terrorist attacks that have been thwarted since 9-11 and the one successful attack on Boston on April 15, 2013, America must remain ever vigilant and continue to work toward protecting the homeland.

In the immediate aftermath of 9-11, there was a call for an Office of Homeland Security in the White House, which eventually became the Department of Homeland Security (DHS). While the DHS is not the sole protector of America's homeland today, it has become the central player focused on the growing homeland security machinery for modern day civil defense. Yet, despite the strong federal nature of the DHS, most of the first-line responders—police, fire, and EMS—are local personnel, many from the criminal justice system. The primary methods for responding to future terrorist attacks and natural disasters, such as the Incident Command System, are all focused on these local responders. Thus, homeland security is, in many ways, an administrative and organizational response to both potential and real threats.

Homeland security has also grown in strength as an area of policy, which can be seen in the growth of oversight by all three branches of government—executive, legislative, and judiciary. The president manages the bureaucracy of homeland security, Congress the funding for and laws associated with it, and the Courts keep both in check for the constitutionality around the trade-off of more security versus less personal freedom. As a result of this ongoing policy activity, homeland security has also quickly become an area of academic study. It is for all of these reasons this book was written.

We felt it was important to take a broad view—to include all the various ideas, policies, and methods for addressing terrorist attacks and natural disasters—to provide a clear picture of what "homeland security" means in today's America. In order to present this picture realistically, we felt it was important to highlight homeland security policy, organization, and administration, as currently found in the field, study, and practice of homeland security. Thus, we have tried to incorporate the many perspectives of homeland security through our varied backgrounds and areas of expertise, including the administrative and organizational approaches (Oliver), the public policy perspectives (Marion), and the many aspects of terrorism and security (Hill).

Toward that end, this book is organized into 15 chapters, which lead the student of homeland security from the beginning to contemporary America. The book starts with a prologue detailing the tragic events of September 11, 2001, as a reminder of why we have created the field of homeland security in the first place. It then details the history of homeland security (Chapter 1), for although the term *homeland security* did not come about until 9-11, it was rooted in past concepts of civil defense and emergency management. The book then strives to define the concept of homeland security (Chapter 2) from its many and varied perspectives, particularly how it has developed conceptually, administratively, and organizationally over the past 12 years. The book then moves to discuss the two major concerns of homeland security, terrorism and natural disasters (Chapter 3).

This introduction to homeland security then proceeds to discuss how it developed in the aftermath of 9-11 (Chapter 4), and then describes its current status as a central federal organization—the Department of Homeland Security (Chapter 5). Chapter 6 moves beyond the federal bureaucracy to focus on the broader community. Chapter 7 looks at how this community, through anti-terrorism and counter-terrorism measures, works to address the terrorism side of homeland security.

The book then presents the National Strategy for Homeland Security (Chapter 8), the particular threats it attempts to address (Chapter 9), and how the homeland security cycle progresses (Chapter 10). In Chapter 11, it then looks at the local response mechanisms of the National Incident Management System (NIMS) and the Incident Command System (ICS).

The text then details the political (Chapter 12) and legal (Chapter 13) issues surrounding homeland security, and then deals with a wide array of issues that have evolved over the last 12 years, including communications and technology issues (Chapter 14), domain security issues (sea, land, and air, in Chapter 15), and then briefly discusses the future of homeland security in America (also Chapter 15).

Finally, as the book began with a prologue of the events of 9-11, it ends with the death of Osama bin Laden on May 1, 2011 (Epilogue), with the clear caveat that, with his death, the work is not finished, and the importance of continued vigilance is just as important today as it was in the immediate aftermath of September 11th.

Willard M. Oliver
Huntsville, Texas

Prologue

■ September 11, 2001

Tuesday, September 11, 2001, dawned temperate and nearly cloudless in the eastern United States.[1] Millions of men and women readied themselves for work. Some made their way to the Twin Towers, the signature structures of the World Trade Center complex in New York City. Others went to Arlington, Virginia, to the Pentagon. Across the Potomac River, the United States Congress was back in session. At the other end of Pennsylvania Avenue, people began to line up for a White House tour. In Sarasota, Florida, President George W. Bush went for an early morning run.

For those heading to an airport, weather conditions could not have been better for a safe and pleasant journey. Among the travelers were Mohamed Atta and Abdul Aziz al Omari, who arrived at the airport in Portland, Maine.

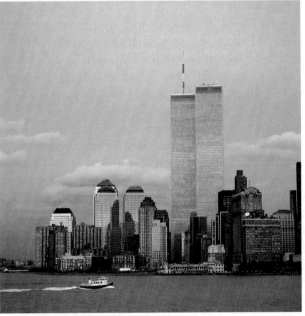

© robert paul van beets/ShutterStock, Inc.

Boston: American 11 and United 175

Atta and Omari boarded a 6:00 AM flight from Portland to Boston's Logan International Airport.

When he checked in for his flight to Boston, Atta was selected by a computerized prescreening system known as CAPPS (Computer Assisted Passenger Prescreening System), created to identify passengers who should be subject to special security measures. Under security rules in place at the time, the only consequence of Atta's selection by CAPPS was that his checked bags were kept off the plane until it was confirmed that he had boarded the aircraft. This did not hinder Atta's plans.

Atta and Omari arrived in Boston at 6:45. Seven minutes later, Atta apparently took a call from Marwan al Shehhi, a longtime colleague who was at another terminal at Logan Airport. They spoke for 3 minutes. It would be their final conversation.

Between 6:45 and 7:40, Atta and Omari—along with Satam al Suqami, Wail al Shehri, and Waleed al Shehri—checked in and boarded American Airlines Flight 11, bound for Los Angeles. The flight was scheduled to depart at 7:45 AM.

In another Logan terminal, Shehhi, joined by Fayez Banihammad, Mohand al Shehri, Ahmed al Ghamdi, and Hamza al Ghamdi, checked in for United Airlines Flight 175, also bound for Los Angeles. A couple of Shehhi's colleagues were obviously unused to travel; according to the United ticket agent, they had trouble understanding the standard security questions, and she had to go over them slowly until they gave the routine, reassuring answers. Their flight was scheduled to depart at 8:00.

The security checkpoints through which the passengers, including Atta and his colleagues, gained access to the American 11 gate were operated by Globe Security under a contract with American Airlines. In a different terminal, the single checkpoint through which passengers for United 175 passed was controlled by United Airlines, which had contracted with Huntleigh USA to perform the screening.

In passing through these checkpoints, each of the hijackers would have been screened by a walk-through metal detector calibrated to detect items with a minimum metal content of a .22-caliber handgun. Anyone who might have set off that detector would have been screened with a hand wand—a procedure requiring the screener to identify the metal item or items that caused the alarm. In addition, an x-ray machine would have screened the hijackers' carry-on belongings. The screening was in place to identify and confiscate weapons and other items prohibited from being carried onto a commercial flight. None of the checkpoint supervisors recalled the hijackers or reported anything suspicious regarding their screening.

While Atta had been selected by CAPPS in Portland, three members of his hijacking team—Suqami, Wail al Shehri, and Waleed al Shehri—were selected in Boston. Their selection affected only the handling of their checked bags, not their screening at the checkpoint. All five men cleared the checkpoint and made their way to the gate for American 11. Atta, Omari, and Suqami took their seats in first class (seats 8D, 8G, and 10B, respectively). The Shehri brothers had adjacent seats in row 2 (Wail in 2A, Waleed in 2B), in the first-class cabin. They boarded American 11 between 7:31 and 7:40. The aircraft pushed back from the gate at 7:40.

Shehhi and his team, none of whom had been selected by CAPPS, boarded United 175 between 7:23 and 7:28 (Banihammad in 2A, Shehri in 2B, Shehhi in 6C, Hamza al Ghamdi in 9C, and Ahmed al Ghamdi in 9D). Their aircraft pushed back from the gate just before 8:00.

Washington Dulles: American 77

Hundreds of miles southwest of Boston at Dulles International Airport in the Virginia suburbs of Washington, DC, five more men were preparing to take an early morning flight. At 7:15, Khalid al Mihdhar and Majed Moqed checked in at the American Airlines ticket counter for Flight 77, bound for Los Angeles. Within the next 20 minutes, they would be followed by Hani Hanjour and two brothers, Nawaf al Hazmi and Salem al Hazmi.

Hani Hanjour, Khalid al Mihdhar, and Majed Moqed were flagged by CAPPS. The Hazmi brothers were also selected for extra scrutiny by the airline's customer service representative at the check-in counter. The representative did so because one of the brothers did not have photo identification, nor could he understand English, and because the agent found both of the passengers to be suspicious. The only consequence of their selection was that their checked bags were held off the plane until it was confirmed that they had boarded the aircraft.

All five hijackers passed through the main terminal's west security screening checkpoint; United Airlines, which was the responsible air carrier, had contracted out the work to Argenbright Security. The checkpoint featured closed-circuit television that recorded all passengers, including the hijackers, as they were screened. At 7:18, Mihdhar and Moqed entered the security checkpoint.

Mihdhar and Moqed placed their carry-on bags on the belt of the x-ray machine and proceeded through the first metal detector. Both set off the alarm, and they were directed to a second metal detector. Mihdhar did not trigger the second alarm and was permitted through the checkpoint. After Moqed set it off, a screener used the hand wand on him. He passed this inspection.

About 20 minutes later, at 7:35, another passenger for Flight 77, Hani Hanjour, placed two carry-on bags on the x-ray belt in the main terminal's west checkpoint and proceeded, without alarm, through the metal detector. A short time later, Nawaf and Salem al Hazmi entered the same checkpoint. Salem al Hazmi cleared the metal detector and was permitted through; Nawaf al Hazmi set off the alarms for both the first and second metal detectors and was then hand-wanded before being cleared. In addition, his over-the-shoulder carry-on bag was swiped by an explosive trace detector and then passed. The video footage indicates that he was carrying an unidentified item in his back pocket, clipped to its rim.

When the local civil aviation security office of the Federal Aviation Administration (FAA) later investigated these security-screening operations, the screeners recalled nothing out of the ordinary. They could not recall that any of the passengers they screened were CAPPS selectees. Later, a screening expert reviewed the videotape of the hand-wanding, and he found the quality of the screener's work to have been "marginal at best." The screener should have "resolved" what set off the alarm, and in the case of both Moqed and Hazmi, it was clear he did not.

At 7:50, Majed Moqed and Khalid al Mihdhar boarded the flight and were seated in 12A and 12B in coach. Hani Hanjour, assigned to seat 1B (first class), soon followed. The Hazmi brothers, assigned to 5E and 5F, joined Hanjour in the first-class cabin.

Newark: United 93

Between 7:03 and 7:39, Saeed al Ghamdi, Ahmed al Nami, Ahmad al Haznawi, and Ziad Jarrah checked in at Newark's United Airlines ticket counter for Flight 93, going to Los Angeles. Two checked bags, two did not. Haznawi was selected by CAPPS. His checked bag was screened for explosives and then loaded on the plane.

The four men passed through the security checkpoint, owned by United Airlines and operated under contract by Argenbright Security. Like the checkpoints in Boston, it lacked closed-circuit television surveillance so there is no documentary evidence to indicate when the hijackers passed through the checkpoint, what alarms may have been triggered, or what security procedures were administered. The FAA interviewed the screeners later; none recalled anything unusual or suspicious.

The four men boarded the plane between 7:39 and 7:48. All four had seats in the economy-class cabin; their plane had no first-class section. Jarrah was in seat 1B, closest to the cockpit; Nami was in 3C, Ghamdi in 3D, and Haznawi in 6B.

The 19 men were aboard four transcontinental flights. They were planning to hijack these planes and turn them into large guided missiles, loaded with some 11,400 gallons of jet fuel. By 8:00 AM on the morning of Tuesday, September 11, 2001, they had defeated all the security layers that America's civil aviation security system then had in place to prevent a hijacking.

The Hijacking of American 11

American Airlines Flight 11 provided nonstop service from Boston to Los Angeles. On September 11th, Captain John Ogonowski and First Officer Thomas McGuinness piloted the Boeing 767, which carried its full capacity of nine flight attendants. Eighty-one passengers boarded the flight with them (including the five terrorists).

The plane took off at 7:59. Just before 8:14 it had climbed to 26,000 feet, not quite its initial assigned cruising altitude of 29,000 feet. All communications and flight profile data were normal. About this time the "Fasten Seatbelt" sign would usually have been turned off and the flight attendants would have begun preparing for cabin service.

At that same time, American 11 had its last routine communication with the ground when it acknowledged navigational instructions from the FAA's air traffic control (ATC) center in Boston. Sixteen seconds after that transmission, ATC instructed the aircraft's pilots to climb to 35,000 feet. That message and all subsequent attempts to contact the flight were not acknowledged. From this and other evidence, we believe the hijacking began at 8:14 or shortly thereafter.

Reports from two flight attendants in the coach cabin, Betty Ong and Madeline "Amy" Sweeney, tell us most of what we know about how the hijacking happened. As it began, some of the hijackers—most likely Wail al Shehri and Waleed al Shehri, who were seated in row 2 in first class—stabbed the two unarmed flight attendants who would have been preparing for cabin service.

It is unknown exactly how the hijackers gained access to the cockpit; FAA rules required that the doors remain closed and locked during flight. Ong speculated that they had "jammed their way" into the cabin. Perhaps the terrorists stabbed the flight attendants to get a cockpit key, to force one of them to open the cockpit door, or to lure the captain or first officer out of the cockpit. Or the flight attendants may just have been in their way.

At the same time or shortly thereafter, Atta—the only terrorist on board trained to fly a jet—would have moved to the cockpit from his first-class seat, possibly accompanied by Omari. As this was happening, passenger Daniel Lewin, who was seated in the row just behind Atta and Omari, was stabbed by one of the hijackers—probably Satam al Suqami, who was seated directly behind Lewin. Lewin had served 4 years as an officer in the Israeli military. He may have made an attempt to stop the hijackers in front of him, not realizing that another was sitting behind him.

The hijackers quickly gained control and sprayed Mace, pepper spray, or some other irritant in the first-class cabin, in order to force the passengers and flight attendants toward the rear of the plane. They claimed they had a bomb.

About 5 minutes after the hijacking began, Betty Ong contacted the American Airlines Southeastern Reservations Office in Cary, North Carolina, via an AT&T airphone to report an emergency aboard the flight. This was the first of several occasions on 9-11 when flight attendants took action outside the scope of their training, which emphasized that in a hijacking they were to communicate with the cockpit crew. The emergency call lasted approximately 25 minutes as Ong calmly and professionally relayed information about events taking place aboard the airplane to authorities on the ground.

At 8:19, Ong reported: "The cockpit is not answering, somebody's stabbed in business class—and I think there's Mace, that we can't breathe—I don't know, I think we're getting hijacked." She then told of the stabbings of the two flight attendants.

At 8:21, one of the American employees receiving Ong's call in North Carolina, Nydia Gonzalez, alerted the American Airlines operations center in Fort Worth, Texas, reaching Craig Marquis, the manager on duty. Marquis soon realized this was an emergency and instructed the airline's dispatcher responsible for the flight to contact the cockpit. At 8:23, the dispatcher tried unsuccessfully to contact the aircraft. Six minutes later, the air traffic control specialist in American's operations center contacted the FAA's Boston Air Traffic Control Center about the flight. The center was already aware of the problem.

The Boston Center knew of the problem in part because they overheard the hijackers attempting to communicate with the passengers. Just before 8:25, the in-flight microphone was keyed and one of the hijackers said, "Nobody move. Everything will be okay. If you try to make any moves, you'll endanger yourself and the airplane. Just stay quiet." Air traffic controllers heard the transmission, and Ong did not. The hijackers probably did not know how to operate the cockpit radio communication system correctly, and thus inadvertently broadcast their message over the air traffic control channel instead of the cabin public-address channel. Also at 8:25, and again at 8:29, Amy Sweeney (flight attendant) got through to the American Flight Services Office in Boston but was cut off after she reported someone was hurt aboard the flight. Three minutes later, Sweeney was reconnected to the office and began relaying updates to her manager, Michael Woodward.

At 8:26, Ong reported that the plane was "flying erratically." A minute later Flight 11 turned south. American also began getting identifications of the hijackers, as Ong and then Sweeney passed on some of the seat numbers of those who had gained unauthorized access to the cockpit.

Sweeney calmly reported that the plane had been hijacked, a man in first class had his throat slashed, two flight attendants had been stabbed—one was seriously hurt and on oxygen while the other's wounds seemed minor, a doctor had been requested, the flight attendants were unable to contact the cockpit, and there was a bomb in the cockpit. Sweeney told Woodward that she and Ong were trying to relay as much information as they could to people on the ground.

At 8:38, Ong told Gonzalez that the plane was flying erratically again. Around this time Sweeney told Woodward that the hijackers were Middle Eastern, naming three of their seat numbers. One spoke very little English and one spoke excellent English. The hijackers had gained entry to the cockpit, and she did not know how. The aircraft was in a rapid descent.

At 8:41, Sweeney told Woodward that passengers in coach were under the impression that there was a routine medical emergency in first class. Other flight attendants were busy with various activities, such as getting medical supplies, while Ong and Sweeney were reporting the events as they unfolded.

At 8:41, in American's operations center, a colleague told Marquis that the air traffic controllers declared Flight 11 a hijacking and "think he's [American 11] headed toward Kennedy [airport in New York City]. They're moving everybody out of the way. They seem to have him on primary radar. They seem to think that he is descending."

At 8:44, Gonzalez reported losing phone contact with Ong. About this same time Sweeney reported to Woodward, "Something is wrong. We are in a rapid descent … we are all over the place." Woodward asked Sweeney to look out the window to see if she could determine where they were. Sweeney responded: "We are flying low.

We are flying very, very low. We are flying way too low." Seconds later she said, "Oh my God, we are way too low." The phone call ended.

At 8:46:40, American 11 crashed into the North Tower of the World Trade Center in New York City. All on board, along with an unknown number of people in the tower, were killed instantly.

© Carmen Taylor/TAYLC/AP Images.

The Hijacking of United 175

United Airlines Flight 175 was scheduled to depart for Los Angeles at 8:00 AM. Captain Victor Saracini and First Officer Michael Horrocks piloted the Boeing 767, which had seven flight attendants. Fifty-six passengers boarded the flight.

United 175 pushed back from its gate at 7:58 and departed Logan Airport at 8:14. By 8:33, it had reached its assigned cruising altitude of 31,000 feet. The flight attendants would have begun their cabin service.

The flight had taken off just as American 11 was being hijacked, and at 8:42 the United 175 flight crew completed their report of a "suspicious transmission" overheard from another plane (which was Flight 11) just after takeoff. This was United 175's last communication with the ground.

The hijackers attacked sometime between 8:42 and 8:46. They used knives (as reported by two passengers and a flight attendant), Mace (reported by one passenger), and the threat of a bomb (reported by the same passenger). They stabbed members of the flight crew (reported by a flight attendant and one passenger). Both pilots had been killed (reported by one flight attendant). The eyewitness accounts came from calls made from the rear of the plane from passengers originally seated further forward in the cabin, a sign that passengers and perhaps crew had been moved to the back of the aircraft. Given similarities to American 11 in hijacker seating and in eyewitness reports of tactics and weapons, as well as the contact between the presumed team leaders, Atta and Shehhi, it is believed the tactics were similar on both flights.

The first operational evidence that something was abnormal on United 175 came at 8:47, when the aircraft changed beacon codes twice within a minute. At 8:51, the flight deviated from its assigned altitude, and a minute later New York air traffic controllers began repeatedly and unsuccessfully trying to contact it.

At 8:52 in Easton, Connecticut, a man named Lee Hanson received a phone call from his son Peter, a passenger on United 175. His son told him: "I think they've taken over the cockpit—an attendant has been stabbed—and someone else up front may have been killed. The plane is making strange moves. Call United Airlines. Tell them it's Flight 175, Boston to LA." Lee Hanson then called the Easton Police Department and relayed what he had heard.

Also at 8:52, a male flight attendant called a United office in San Francisco, reaching Marc Policastro. The flight attendant reported that the flight had been hijacked, both pilots had been killed, a flight attendant had been stabbed, and the hijackers were probably flying the plane. The call lasted about 2 minutes, after which Policastro and a colleague tried unsuccessfully to contact the flight.

At 8:58, the flight took a heading toward New York City.

At 8:59, Flight 175 passenger Brian David Sweeney tried to call his wife, Julie. He left a message on their home answering machine that the plane had been hijacked. He then called his mother, Louise Sweeney, told her the flight had been hijacked, and added that the passengers were thinking about storming the cockpit to take control of the plane away from the hijackers.

At 9:00, Lee Hanson received a second call from his son Peter:

It's getting bad, Dad—a stewardess was stabbed. They seem to have knives and Mace. They said they have a bomb. It's getting very bad on the plane. Passengers are throwing up and getting sick. The plane is making jerky movements. I don't think the pilot is flying the plane. I think we are going down. I think they intend to go to Chicago or someplace and fly into a building. Don't worry Dad. If it happens, it'll be very fast. My God, my God.

The call ended abruptly. Lee Hanson had heard a woman scream just before it cut off. He turned on a television, and in her home so did Louise Sweeney. Both then saw the second aircraft hit the World Trade Center.

At 9:03:11, United Airlines Flight 175 struck the South Tower of the World Trade Center. All on board, along with an unknown number of people in the tower, were killed instantly.

© SuperStock/age fotostock.

The Hijacking of American 77

American Airlines Flight 77 was scheduled to depart from Washington Dulles for Los Angeles at 8:10 AM. The aircraft was a Boeing 757 piloted by Captain Charles F. Burlingame and First Officer David Charlebois. There were four flight attendants. The flight carried 58 passengers.

American 77 pushed back from its gate at 8:09 and took off at 8:20. At 8:46, the flight reached its assigned cruising altitude of 35,000 feet. Cabin service would have begun. At 8:51, American 77 transmitted its last routine radio communication. The hijacking began between 8:51 and 8:54. As on American 11 and United 175, the hijackers used knives (reported by one passenger) and moved all the passengers (and possibly crew) to the rear of the aircraft (reported by one flight attendant and one passenger). Unlike the earlier flights, the Flight 77 hijackers were reported by a passenger to have box cutters. Finally, a passenger reported that an announcement had been made by the "pilot" that the plane had been hijacked. Neither of the firsthand accounts mentioned any stabbings or the threat or use of either a bomb or Mace, though both witnesses began the flight in the first-class cabin.

At 8:54, the aircraft deviated from its assigned course, turning south. Two minutes later the transponder was turned off and even primary radar contact with the aircraft was lost. The Indianapolis Air Traffic Control Center repeatedly tried and failed to contact the aircraft. American Airlines dispatchers also tried, without success.

At 9:00, American Airlines Executive Vice President Gerard Arpey learned that communications had been lost with American 77. This was now the second American aircraft in trouble. He ordered all American Airlines flights in the Northeast that had not taken off to remain on the ground. Shortly before 9:10, suspecting that American 77 had been hijacked, American headquarters concluded that the second aircraft to hit the World Trade Center might have been Flight 77. After learning that United Airlines was missing a plane, American Airlines headquarters extended their ground stop nationwide.

At 9:12, passenger Renee May called her mother, Nancy May, in Las Vegas. She said her flight was being hijacked by six individuals who had moved them to the rear of the plane. She asked her mother to alert American Airlines. Nancy May and her husband promptly did so.

At some point between 9:16 and 9:26, passenger Barbara Olson called her husband, Ted Olson, the Solicitor General of the United States. She reported that the flight had been hijacked, and the hijackers had knives and box cutters. She further indicated that the hijackers were not aware of her phone call, and that they had put all the passengers in the back of the plane. About a minute into the conversation, the call was cut off. Solicitor General Olson tried unsuccessfully to reach Attorney General John Ashcroft.

Shortly after the first call, Barbara Olson reached her husband again. She reported that the pilot had announced that the flight had been hijacked, and she asked her husband what she should tell the captain of the flight to do. Ted Olson asked for her location and she replied that the aircraft was then flying over houses. Another passenger told her they were traveling northeast. The Solicitor General then informed his wife of the two previous hijackings and crashes. She did not display signs of panic and did not indicate any awareness of an impending crash. At that point, the second call was cut off.

At 9:29, the autopilot on American 77 was disengaged; the aircraft was at 7,000 feet and approximately 38 miles west of the Pentagon. At 9:32, controllers at the Dulles Terminal Radar Approach Control "observed a primary radar target tracking eastbound at a high rate of speed." This was later determined to have been Flight 77.

At 9:34 Ronald Reagan Washington National Airport advised the Secret Service of an unknown aircraft heading in the direction of the White House. American 77 was then 5 miles west-southwest of the Pentagon and began a 330-degree turn. At the end of the turn, it was descending through 2,200 feet, pointed toward the Pentagon and downtown Washington. The hijacker pilot then advanced the throttles to maximum power and dove toward the Pentagon.

At 9:37, American Airlines Flight 77 crashed into the Pentagon, traveling at approximately 530 miles per hour. All on board, as well as many civilian and military personnel in the building, were killed.

© Fotosearch/age fotostock.

The Battle for United 93

At 8:42 AM, United Airlines Flight 93 took off from Newark (New Jersey) Liberty International Airport bound for San Francisco. The aircraft was piloted by Captain Jason Dahl and First Officer Leroy Homer and there were five flight attendants. Thirty-seven passengers, including the hijackers, boarded the plane. Scheduled to depart the gate at 8:00, the Boeing 757's takeoff was delayed because of the airport's typically heavy morning traffic.

The September 11th hijackers had planned to take flights scheduled to depart at 7:45 (American 11), 8:00 (United 175 and United 93), and 8:10 (American 77). Three of the flights had actually taken off within 10–15 minutes of their planned departure times. United 93 would ordinarily have taken off about 15 minutes after pulling away from the gate. When it left the ground at 8:42, the flight was running more than 25 minutes late.

As United 93 left Newark, the flight's crew members were unaware of the hijacking of American 11. Around 9:00, the FAA, American, and United were facing the staggering realization of apparent multiple hijackings. At 9:03, they would see another aircraft strike the World Trade Center. Crisis managers at the FAA and the airlines did not yet act to warn other aircraft. At the same time, Boston Center realized that a message transmitted just before 8:25 by the hijacker pilot of American 11 included the phrase, "We have some planes."

No one at the FAA or the airlines that day had ever dealt with multiple hijackings. Such a plot had not been carried out anywhere in the world in more than 30 years and never in the United States. As news of the hijackings filtered through the FAA and the airlines, it does not seem to have occurred to their leadership that they needed to alert other aircraft in the air that they too might be at risk.

United 175 was hijacked between 8:42 and 8:46, and awareness of that hijacking began to spread after 8:51. American 77 was hijacked between 8:51 and 8:54.

By 9:00, FAA and airline officials began to comprehend that attackers were going after multiple aircraft. American Airlines' nationwide ground stop began between 9:05 and 9:10 and was followed by a United Airlines ground stop. FAA controllers at Boston Center, which had tracked the first two hijackings, requested at 9:07 that Herndon Command Center "get messages to airborne aircraft to increase security for the cockpit." There is no evidence that Herndon took such action. Boston Center immediately began speculating about other aircraft that might be in danger, leading them to worry about a transcontinental flight (Delta 1989) that, in fact, was not hijacked. At 9:19, the FAA's New England regional office called Herndon and asked that Cleveland Center advise Delta 1989 to use extra cockpit security.

Several FAA air traffic control officials later explained it was the air carriers' responsibility to notify their planes of security problems. One senior FAA air traffic control manager said that it was simply not the FAA's place to order the airlines what to tell their pilots. The 9-11 Commission noted that such statements do not reflect an adequate appreciation of the FAA's responsibility for the safety and security of civil aviation.

The airlines bore responsibility, too. They were facing an escalating number of conflicting and, for the most part, erroneous reports about other flights, as well as a continuing lack of vital information from the FAA about the hijacked flights. The 9/11 Commission found no evidence, however, that American Airlines sent any cockpit warnings to its aircraft on 9-11. United's first decisive action to notify its airborne aircraft to take defensive action did not come until 9:19, when a United flight dispatcher, Ed Ballinger, took the initiative to begin transmitting warnings to his 16 transcontinental flights: "Beware any cockpit intrusion. Two a/c [aircraft] hit World Trade Center." One of the flights that received the warning was United 93. Because Ballinger was still responsible for his other flights as well as Flight 175, his warning message was not transmitted to Flight 93 until 9:23.

By all accounts, the first 46 minutes of Flight 93's cross-country trip proceeded routinely. Radio communications from the plane were normal. Heading, speed, and altitude ran according to plan. At 9:24, Ballinger's warning to United 93 was received in the cockpit. Within 2 minutes, at 9:26, the pilot, Jason Dahl, responded with a note of puzzlement: "Ed, confirm latest mssg plz. Jason."

The hijackers attacked at 9:28. While traveling 35,000 feet above eastern Ohio, United 93 suddenly dropped 700 feet. Eleven seconds into the descent, the FAA's air traffic control center in Cleveland received the first of two radio transmissions from the aircraft. During the first broadcast, the captain or first officer could be heard declaring "Mayday!" amid the sounds of a physical struggle in the cockpit. The second radio transmission, 35 seconds later, indicated that the fight was continuing. The captain or first officer could be heard shouting: "Hey, get out of here! Get out of here! Get out of here!"

On the morning of 9-11, there were only 37 passengers on United 93—33 in addition to the 4 hijackers. This was below the norm for a Tuesday morning during the summer of 2001. But there is no evidence that the hijackers manipulated passenger levels or purchased additional seats to facilitate their operation.

The terrorists who hijacked three other commercial flights on 9-11 operated in five-man teams. They initiated their cockpit takeover within 30 minutes of takeoff. On Flight 93, however, the takeover took place 46 minutes after takeoff and there were only four hijackers. The operative likely intended to round out the team for this flight, Mohamed al Kahtani, had been refused entry by a suspicious immigration inspector at Florida's Orlando International Airport in August.

Because several passengers on United 93 described three hijackers on the plane, not four, some have wondered whether one of the hijackers had been able to use the cockpit jump seat from the outset of the flight. FAA rules allow use of this seat by documented and approved individuals, usually air carrier or FAA personnel. There is no evidence indicating that one of the hijackers, or anyone else, sat there on this flight. All the hijackers had assigned seats in first class, and they seem to have used them. It is more likely that Jarrah, the crucial pilot-trained member of their team, remained seated and inconspicuous until after the cockpit was seized; and once inside, he would not have been visible to the passengers.

At 9:32, a hijacker, probably Jarrah, made or attempted to make the following announcement to the passengers of Flight 93: "Ladies and gentlemen: Hear the captain, please sit down keep remaining sitting. We have a bomb on board. So, sit." The flight data recorder (also recovered) indicates that Jarrah then instructed the plane's autopilot to turn the aircraft around and head east.

The cockpit voice recorder data indicates that a woman, most likely a flight attendant, was being held captive in the cockpit. She struggled with one of the hijackers who killed or otherwise silenced her.

Shortly thereafter, the passengers and flight crew began a series of calls from GTE airphones and cellular phones. These calls between family, friends, and colleagues took place until the end of the flight and provided those on the ground with firsthand accounts. They enabled the passengers to gain critical information, including the news that two aircraft had slammed into the World Trade Center.

At 9:39, the FAA's Cleveland Air Route Traffic Control Center overheard a second announcement indicating that there was a bomb on board, that the plane was returning to the airport, and that they should remain seated. While it apparently was not heard by the passengers, this announcement, like those on Flight 11 and Flight 77, was intended to deceive the passengers. Jarrah, like Atta earlier, may have inadvertently broadcast the message because he did not know how to operate the radio and the intercom. According to the 9-11 Commission, none of them had ever flown an actual airliner before.

At least two callers from the flight reported that the hijackers knew that passengers were making calls but did not seem to care. It is quite possible Jarrah knew of the success of the assault on the World Trade Center. He could have learned of this from messages being sent by United Airlines to the cockpits of its transcontinental flights, including Flight 93, warning of cockpit intrusion and telling of the New York attacks. But even without them, he would certainly have understood that the attacks on the World Trade Center would already have unfolded, given Flight 93's tardy departure from Newark. If Jarrah did know that the passengers were making calls, it might not have occurred to him that they were certain to learn what had happened in New York, thereby defeating his attempts at deception.

At least 10 passengers and two crew members shared vital information with family, friends, colleagues, or others on the ground. All understood the plane had been hijacked. They said the hijackers wielded knives and claimed to have a bomb. The hijackers were wearing red bandanas, and they forced the passengers to the back of the aircraft.

Callers reported that a passenger had been stabbed and that two people were lying on the floor of the cabin, injured or dead—possibly the captain and first officer. One caller reported that a flight attendant had been killed.

One of the callers from United 93 also reported that he thought the hijackers might possess a gun, but none of the other callers reported the presence of a firearm. One recipient of a call from the aircraft recounted specifically asking her caller whether the hijackers had guns. The passenger replied that he did not see one. No evidence of firearms or of their identifiable remains was found at the aircraft's crash site, and the cockpit voice recorder gives no indication of a gun being fired or mentioned at any time. We believe that if the hijackers had possessed a gun, they would have used it in the flight's last minutes as the passengers fought back.

Passengers on three flights reported the hijackers' claim of having a bomb. The FBI said they found no trace of explosives at the crash sites. One of the passengers who mentioned a bomb expressed his belief that it was not real. Lacking any evidence that the hijackers attempted to smuggle such illegal items past the security screening checkpoints, it is believed the bombs were probably not real.

During at least five of Flight 93's passengers' phone calls, information was shared about the attacks that had occurred earlier that morning at the World Trade Center. Five calls described the intent of passengers and surviving crew members to revolt against the hijackers. According to one call, they voted on whether to rush the terrorists in an attempt to retake the plane. They decided and acted.

At 9:57, the passenger assault began. Several passengers had terminated phone calls with loved ones in order to join the revolt. One of the callers ended her message as follows: "Everyone's running up to first class. I've got to go. Bye."

The cockpit voice recorder captured the sounds of the passenger assault muffled by the intervening cockpit door. Some family members who later listened to the recording report that they can hear the voice of a loved one among the din. The 9/11 Commission could not identify the specific voices.

In response, Jarrah immediately began to roll the airplane to the left and right, attempting to knock the passengers off balance. At 9:58:57, Jarrah told another hijacker in the cockpit to block the door. Jarrah continued to roll the airplane sharply left and right, but the assault continued. At 9:59:52, Jarrah changed tactics and pitched the nose of the airplane up and down to disrupt the assault. The recorder captured the sounds of loud thumps, crashes, shouts, and breaking glasses and plates. At 10:00:03, Jarrah stabilized the airplane.

Five seconds later, Jarrah asked, "Is that it? Shall we finish it off?" A hijacker responded, "No. Not yet. When they all come, we finish it off." The sounds of fighting continued outside the cockpit. Again, Jarrah pitched the nose of the aircraft up and down. At 10:00:26, a passenger in the background yelled, "… in the cockpit. If we don't, we'll die!" Sixteen seconds later, a passenger yelled, "Roll it!" Jarrah stopped the violent maneuvers at about 10:01:00 and said, "Allah is the greatest! Allah is the greatest!" He then asked another hijacker in the cockpit, "Is that it? I mean, shall we put it down?" to which the other replied, "Yes, put it in it, and pull it down."

The passengers continued their assault and at 10:02:23, a hijacker yelled, "Pull it down! Pull it down!" The hijackers remained at the controls but must have judged that the passengers were only seconds from overcoming them. The airplane headed down; the control wheel was turned hard to the right. The airplane rolled onto its back, and one of the hijackers began shouting "Allah is the greatest! Allah is the greatest!" With the sounds of the passenger counterattack continuing, the aircraft plowed into an empty field in Shanksville, Pennsylvania, at 580 miles per hour, about 20 minutes' flying time from Washington, DC.

Jarrah's objective was to crash his airliner into symbols of the American Republic, the U.S. Capitol or the White House. He was defeated by the unarmed passengers of United 93.

■ Endnotes

1. The prologue is based on the *9/11 Commission Report*. See National Commission on Terrorist Attacks Upon the United States. (2004). *The 9/11 Commission Report: Final Report of the National Commission on Terrorist Attacks Upon the United States (Authorized Edition)*. New York, NY: W.W. Norton & Company, Inc.

A History of Homeland Security

Chapter Outline

- Introduction
- History of Domestic Security
  - Early History: 1776–1916
  - Civil Defense and Two Hot Wars: 1917–1945
  - Civil Defense and the Cold War: 1946–1991
  - Emergency Management: 1979–2001
- Chapter Summary

Chapter Objectives

- Understand the context of 9-11 from a historical perspective

- Learn how domestic security has developed in the 20th century

- Understand the concepts of civil defense, emergency management, and homeland security and how they are similar/different

■ Introduction

On the morning of February 22, 1974, "a burly middle-aged man" by the name of Samuel Byck entered the Baltimore–Washington International (BWI) Airport with a briefcase in hand.[1] He walked to the front of the line at Gate C. The people in line were waiting to board Delta Flight 523 bound for Atlanta, Georgia. A security guard by the name of George Ramburg stood nearby, his back turned to the passenger line. Byck pulled a .22 caliber pistol from underneath his raincoat and fired twice into the security guard's back, killing him instantly. As Ramburg's body crumpled to the ground, people began screaming and running in all directions. Byck leaped over the security chain, ran down the boarding ramp, and boarded the airplane. Delta Flight 523 had just been hijacked, and its destination was the White House. Samuel Byck intended to use the plane as a missile, flying it into the White House, in order to assassinate the President, Richard M. Nixon.[2]

Samuel Byck was born on January 30, 1930 in South Philadelphia. His parents were poor, and Byck dropped out of high school in the ninth grade in order to help support the family. After a series of odd jobs, he enlisted in the U.S. Army in 1954, and was honorably discharged 2 years later. He married and had four children, but he struggled with employment, attempting to start several businesses, all of which failed. While working as a tire salesman, he applied for a Small Business Administration loan to start yet another business, but was turned down. He became depressed and blamed his troubles on President Nixon.[3]

His depression led to marital troubles, which led to divorce, and finally he ended up in a psychiatric clinic. A year later, in 1973, he began plotting to assassinate President Nixon. Byck began a series of tape recordings threatening the president, which he mailed to various public officials. The Secret Service was notified and they investigated, but after speaking with Byck's psychiatrist, they determined he was harmless. By late 1973, Byck had formulated a plan to assassinate the president. Then, on February 20, 1974, he wrote his last will and testament, writing, "I will each of my children . . . the sum of one dollar each. They have each other and they deserve each other."[4] Since he knew he would not be able to purchase a gun, he stole a .22 caliber pistol from a friend, and on the morning of February 22, 1974, he drove to BWI. Along the way, he tape recorded his complaints against President Nixon and explained that his plans were to hijack a plane, fly it into the White House, and assassinate the president. Byck even gave his mission a name: Operation Pandora's Box.

As Byck entered the plane, he fired one round inside the cabin of the plane and then entered the cockpit through the open door. He screamed at the pilot, "Fly this plane out of here!"[5] The pilot, after regaining his composure, explained that he could not roll back from the gate until the ground crew removed the wheel blocks. Byck became enraged and shot the copilot in the stomach. He then turned back to the pilot and screamed, "The next one will be in the head."[6] Byck then went into the passenger cabin and grabbed a female passenger, dragged her into the cockpit, telling her to help the pilot fly the plane. At this point, two shots from outside of the plane exploded through the windshield, causing Byck to shove the woman out of the cockpit. He then turned back into the cockpit and fired twice. One bullet struck the already wounded copilot in the eye, and the other entered the pilot's right shoulder.[7]

The pilot then radioed ground control: "Emergency, emergency, we're all shot . . . ah . . . can you get another pilot here to the airplane . . . ah . . . this fellow has shot us both."[8] The pilot also asked that the wheel blocks be removed so the plane could taxi away from the gate. He then passed out.

His rage now growing, Byck grabbed another female passenger, dragged her into the cockpit, and ordered her to fly the plane. He then fired two more shots in anger, one into the copilot and another into the pilot. The woman became hysterical after seeing the two pilots shot and tried to flee the cockpit. Two more shots rang out and the cockpit windows again shattered, as two more bullets entered from outside of the plane. Byck began firing wildly at the windows, which made him more of a visible target to the snipers outside. They fired two more shots. The first one of these entered Byck's stomach, the second his chest. He fell to the floor.[9]

When Byck fell, he lost hold of his pistol. While on the floor, he frantically searched for the lost gun. He found it, sat up, and put the .22 pistol to his temple and fired. The carnage was over.

Police entered the airplane and found Byck dying. He only lived a few more minutes. They found the briefcase he had carried aboard the plane. Inside was an improvised gasoline bomb with an igniter.

The media reported on the hijacking, but did not disclose Byck's intent of flying the plane into the White House to assassinate President Nixon. They wanted to avoid any potential copycats. Apparently, no one had ever thought about hijacking an airplane and using it as a missile, and it was not something anyone wanted to share.

In 1987, an FAA Report titled *Troubled Passage: The Federal Aviation Administration During the Nixon–Ford Term 1973–1977*, revealed Byck's intent.[10] It chillingly predicted, "though Byck lacked the skill and self-control to reach his target, he had provided a chilling reminder of the potential of violence against civil aviation. Under a more relaxed security system, his suicidal rampage might have begun when the airline was aloft."[11]

Fourteen years later, on September 11, 2001, Byck's suicidal intent was realized when the four airplanes were aloft. In the wake of the attacks that day, many remarked that no one had ever thought this possible.[12]

History knows better.

History of Domestic Security

In the aftermath of September 11, 2001, a recurring lament by the media was the fact that no one had imagined that a small group of men would be able to commandeer a passenger jet and use it as a missile to target American icons such as the World Trade Towers, the U.S. Capitol, the Pentagon, or the White House. In fact, even a number of government officials made the same statement, including the acting Chairman of the Joint Chiefs of Staff at the time, Air Force General Richard Myers, who said, "You hate to admit it, but we hadn't thought about this."[13] The reality, however, as history will show, is very different. History demonstrates through the previous short vignette that the idea had already been considered by Samuel Byck in 1974. While it is recognized that the reasons for Byck's attack on the passenger airline that morning were concealed for some time from the public, the concept had been considered. Twenty years later, Frank Eugene Corder, a 38-year-old truck driver who faced mental and financial issues, and suffered from both alcohol and drug addictions, flew a Cessna 150 into the White House on September 12, 1994.[14] Although he was only successful in killing himself, it highlighted the potential threat that an aircraft could have on the American government. It is also interesting to note that bestselling author Tom Clancy, 1 month prior to Corder's plane crash into the White House, released the book *Debt of Honor*, in which a plane is deliberately crashed into the U.S. Capitol during the State of the Union speech.

This chapter covers the history of homeland security. It does so by reaching further back into American history, both before the terrorist attacks on September 11, 2001, and before the term **homeland security** entered the American lexicon. It does so to highlight the reality that homeland security was not created in a vacuum in the wake of 9-11, but rather developed across all of American history: from the early threats to American settlers and the quandary of what level of government was responsible for responding to natural disasters, through changes wrought by two world wars and the birth of the term **civil defense**, and into the

KEY TERMS
Homeland security—1) an effort to prevent, mitigate, respond, and recover from natural and man-made disasters, including terrorist attacks; 2) a department within the Federal Government focused on prevention, mitigation, responding to and recovering from both natural and man-made disasters.

KEY TERMS
Civil defense—an effort to protect the citizens of the United States from a military attack.

modern age when Americans saw the multi-decade Cold War come to end, only to be replaced by terroristic threats from both rogue nations and organizations. The focus of the chapter will remain on our federalist system, assessing how the national and state governments responded to threats and then dealt with both terrorism and natural disasters prior to 9-11.

Early History: 1776–1916

The Founding Fathers had to deal with issues of America's defense, both foreign and domestic, from the very beginning. After declaring itself free of England, the new government was forced to deal with the British government while operating under the Articles of Confederation. After winning the Revolutionary War and settling into the new system of government, it became clear that the Articles were no longer

© North Wind Picture Archives/Alamy.

working, and a Constitutional Convention was convened in Philadelphia in the summer of 1787. While the right of the national government to deal with foreign enemies was readily accepted by all, an issue arose over how to deal with domestic insurrections. If there are internal threats, does that fall under the purview of the states or the national government? The question was an important one for Shays' Rebellion (see **Box 1.1**) was still present on the minds of those in attendance that summer.[15]

In 1786, the U.S., still operating under the Articles of Confederation, was suffering a monetary crisis.[16] Many farmers were grossly in debt, and more than 4,000 were being forced to enter debtors' prisons until their debts could be paid. The rebellion started with petitions to the government for paper currency, lower taxes, and judicial reform. When this failed, the farmers in western Massachusetts united under the reluctant leadership of Daniel Shays, a bankrupt farmer and former captain in the Revolutionary War. Shays and his followers, many of whom were also veterans, donned their

---

BOX 1.1   George Washington on Shays' Rebellion

Letter to Henry Knox

....

Mount Vernon, 25th Feb. 1787
. . . On the prospect of the happy termination of this insurrection I sincerely congratulate you; hoping that good may result from the cloud of evils which threatened not only the hemisphere of Massachusetts but by spreading its baneful influence, the tranquility of the Union. Surely Shays must be either a weak man—the dupe of some characters who are yet behind the curtain—or has been deceived by his followers.

Or which may yet be more likely, he did not conceive that there was energy enough in the Government to bring matters to the crisis to which they have been pushed. It is to be hoped the General Court of that State concurred in the report of the Committee that a rebellion did actually exist. This would be decisive, and the most likely means of putting the finishing stroke to the business . . .

....

George Washington

old uniforms and began marching on Massachusetts courts to prevent them from holding session and throwing more of their own into prison. After 11 rebellion leaders were arrested and indicted on disorder charges, approximately 1,200 farmers went to the Springfield Court House to prevent the Massachusetts Supreme Judicial Court from holding session. These types of protests continued until January of 1787, when the protesters made their boldest move, seizing the federal arsenal in Springfield. Within 2 weeks, the governor of Massachusetts sent in the militia, some 4,000 strong, to rout the 2,000 members of Shays' Rebellion. Several were killed and the leadership, including Shays, was arrested. They were then tried and sentenced to death for treason. Two of these men, John Bly and Charles Rose, were hung, but with the election of a new governor, John Hancock, the rest were granted pardons.[17]

Shays' Rebellion was not unique, but its timing it the utmost importance. That summer, in Philadelphia, members of the Constitutional Convention considered the implications of Shays' Rebellion, for it "reminded everyone attending in Philadelphia that the Confederation, as it stood, was powerless to protect itself, or any of the states, from large-scale domestic violence, and that this absence of a central power was itself a limitation on state sovereignty."[18] As a result, the framers, in Article 4, Section 4, of the U.S. Constitution, would resolve this issue by stating that "the United States shall guarantee to every State in this Union a Republican form of Government, and shall protect each of them against Invasion; and on Application of the Legislature, or the Executive (when the Legislature cannot be convened) against domestic Violence."[19] This particular article and the concerns of the Constitutional Convention did not take long to make real the problems foreseen.

Another group of farmers, this time in western Pennsylvania during Washington's first term in office, protested the tax his administration imposed on whiskey.[20] The protests began in 1791 and reached a climax in July of 1794 when a U.S. Marshal came with warrants to arrest tax derelicts and was attacked, followed by an attack on the local tax assessor in his own home. As Pennsylvania could not get the rebellion under control, a request was made to President Washington for the national government to assist, who responded with 12,000 military soldiers. The Whiskey Rebellion quickly fell apart, but its legacy would be everlasting, for it demonstrated the centralized power of the new government to suppress not only foreign threats, but domestic threats as well (see **Box 1.2**).

While the national government's role in foreign threats was primary, and against domestic threats secondary, only after the state government (which includes local

---

BOX 1.2 Whiskey Rebellion Proclamation

By the President of the United States of America

A Proclamation, August 7, 1794

I, George Washington, President of the United States, do hereby command all persons, being insurgents, as aforesaid, and all others whom it may concern, on or before the 1st day of September next to disperse and retire peaceably to their respective abodes. And I do moreover warn all persons whomsoever against aiding, abetting, or comforting the perpetrators of the aforesaid treasonable acts; and do require all officers and other citizens, according to their respective duties and the laws of the land, to exert their utmost endeavors to prevent and suppress such dangerous proceedings.

G. Washington,
By the President, Edm. Randolf

© North Wind Picture Archives/Alamy.

government) had exhausted its capabilities, what was unclear was the government's role in responding to natural disasters. The U.S. Constitution has no clause stating that it is the role of the government to assist states in recovery from natural disasters. In fact, the 9th and 10th amendments subsume this notion, meaning that since the power is not delegated to the United States by the Constitution, it would be reserved for the states. However, because it was not prohibited, it raised a reasonable question regarding the federal government's role in helping with recovery.

No less a man than the "Father of the Constitution" would, on several occasions, have the opportunity to address this particular issue. In 1794, while James Madison was serving in the U.S. House, Congress had appropriated $15,000 in relief for French refugees who had fled from an insurrection in Santo Domingo to both Baltimore and Philadelphia. Madison voted against the bill and noted, "I cannot undertake to lay my finger on that article of the Constitution which granted a right to Congress of expending, on objects of benevolence, the money of their constituents."[21] While this was relief being granted to foreign refugees, the question raised was whether he would offer the same response when it was Americans. In 1803, when serving as Secretary of State, a bill came before Congress to provide relief for the victims of a major Christmas (1802) fire in Portsmouth, New Hampshire. Madison railed against the idea, and Madison's replacement in the House of Representatives, William Giles, wrote that it was not the role of Congress to "attend to what generosity and humanity require, but to what the Constitution and their duty require."[22] The legislation passed, allowing for the payment of local bonds to be delayed by 1 year.[23]

Similar resolutions would arise occasionally throughout the 19th century, but they tended to be the exception and not the rule. One particular exception, however, was the American Civil War. After America split into the Union versus the Confederacy, many people remaining in the north were southern sympathizers. Realizing the dangers to the Union of subversive activity and sabotage, President Lincoln authorized the suspension of habeas corpus, meaning that people deemed a threat to the U.S. government could be arrested and kept in jail indefinitely without a hearing. Although the constitutionality of the suspension was challenged, it was not resolved until after the war, finding in the case *Ex Parte Milligan* (1866) that neither Congress nor the president had the right under the U.S. Constitution to impose martial law and suspend habeus corpus when civilian courts were functioning.

The Civil War also generated another issue regarding the powers of the national government and states in times of insurrection. After the Civil War, during Reconstruction, when the southern states were undergoing the process of rejoining the union, the states were often patrolled by the U.S. military. In part the issue had to do with the rise of the Ku Klux Klan and its acts of terrorism on southern blacks, but it also had to do with the national government using the military as a police force, which weighed against the U.S. Constitution.

After a compromise, the military was removed, and in order to prevent such future transgressions, the U.S. Congress passed the Posse Comitatus Act in 1878 (see **Box 1.3**). The act requires that any use of the military for purposes of local law enforcement or to maintain "law and order" must be "expressly authorized by the Constitution or act of Congress."[24]

Between the end of the Civil War (1865) and before the U.S. entry into World War I (1917), a number of natural disasters helped to shape America's response to future events, both man-made and natural. One of the worst disasters in American history came on May 31, 1889, with the Johnstown Flood.[25] A catastrophic failure of a dam 14 miles above Johnstown, Pennsylvania, after several days of heavy rain swept down on the unsuspecting town and nearly wiped out the entire town. The estimated damages were $17 million, and 2,209 people lost their lives. In the aftermath, a relatively new organization, the American Red Cross (see **Box 1.4**), led by its founder Clara Barton, descended upon Johnstown and handled the disaster recovery. The Red Cross was there for 5 months.

Another major disaster, the Great San Francisco Earthquake and Fire of 1906, would also highlight America's future, for, in this case, despite local response, the military unit located at the Presidio decided to take over the response (in violation of Posse Comitatus) to fight the fires, prevent looting, provide relief, and to police the streets.[26] In addition, the American Red Cross once again responded, serving alongside the army as a relief agency. In fact, as a result of the San Francisco Earthquake, the American Red Cross, now chartered by Congress, began to serve as the primary relief agency in catastrophic events, freeing the military to engage in those duties necessary to reestablish order—a symbiotic relationship that continues to this day.

BOX 1.3   The Posse Comitatus Act

Section 15 of chapter 263, of the Acts of the 2nd session of the 45th Congress.

Sec. 15. From and after the passage of this act it shall not be lawful to employ any part of the Army of the United States, as a posse comitatus, or otherwise, for the purpose of executing the laws, except in such cases and under such circumstances as such employment of said force may be expressly authorized by the Constitution or by act of Congress; and no money appropriated by this act shall be used to pay any of the expenses incurred in the employment of any troops in violation of this section and any person willfully violating the provisions of this section shall be deemed guilty of a misdemeanor and on conviction thereof shall be punished by fine not exceeding ten thousand dollars or imprisonment not exceeding 2 years or by both such fine and imprisonment.

BOX 1.4   American Red Cross Congressional Charter, 1905

To continue and carry on a system of national and international relief in time of peace and to apply the same in mitigating the sufferings caused by pestilence, famine, fire, floods, and other great national calamities, and to devise and carry on measures for preventing the same.

▦ Civil Defense and Two Hot Wars: 1917–1945

Prior to World War I, the United States was largely an isolationist country, protected by the great expanse of two great oceans. There was one occasion on American soil that raised the issue of America's defenses just prior to the war, and that was when Pancho Villa and his *Villistas* bandits crossed into the United States on March 9, 1916 and entered the town of Columbus, New Mexico.[27] They attacked the American 13th Cavalry, looted houses, and fought with civilians. Eight American soldiers and 10 civilians died, raising not only a military response but also a concern for establishing some form of civil defense along the U.S.–Mexico Border. General "Black Jack" Pershing was sent into Mexico to pursue Villa, while additional consideration was given to enhancing the mounted watchmen of the United States Immigration Service, although it was not until May 28, 1924 that this group would form into the United States Border Patrol.[28]

At the time that Pancho Villa attacked the United States, the world had already been at war for several years. World War I began on July 28, 1914 and very quickly came to include all the major empires at the time, including the German, Austro-Hungarian, Ottoman, Russian, and British empires.[29] President Woodrow Wilson took a strong noninterventionist stance, and the United States remained on the sidelines trying to broker a peace settlement. After his reelection in 1916, the sinking of seven U.S. merchant ships and the interception of the famous Zimmerman telegram (where Germany encouraged Mexico to join the war as an ally against the United States[30]), Wilson asked for a declaration of war. Congress deliberated for several months, but declared war on April 6, 1917. Pershing was recalled from his hunt for Pancho Villa and was established as the commander of the American Expeditionary Force (AEF). America was about to step onto the world stage.

During this time, there was concern back home about the safety of the American people. While the United States did not have to fear the aerial bombardments that European citizens now suffered, there was a perceived need to protect the general public from future attacks. In fact, consideration had already been given to this possibility. Tucked into an army appropriations bill, on August 29, 1916 the federal government established the Council of National Defense.[31] The council was a presidential advisory board that included the Secretaries of War, Navy, Interior, Agriculture, Commerce, and Labor, and assisted by an Advisory Committee appointed by the president. Its responsibilities included "coordinating resources and industries for national defense" and "stimulating civilian morale."[32]

When the United States declared war in 1917, the work of the council escalated. The federal government asked state governors to create their own councils in order to support the National Council's efforts. Every state responded by organizing its own state-level council of defense, and by the end of the war 182,000 local civil defense councils had been formed across the United States. These local councils conducted civil defense patrols, funded and deployed air raid sirens, and practiced safety drills. After the war ended on November 11, 1918, the National Council switched its focus to demobilization efforts until their operations were suspended in June of 1921. Although the National Council ceased operations, many of the local councils continued to operate over the next decade (see FIGURE 1.1.).

For that next decade, the federal government did little in regard to civil defense, but after Hitler came to power in 1933, the White House became concerned. That

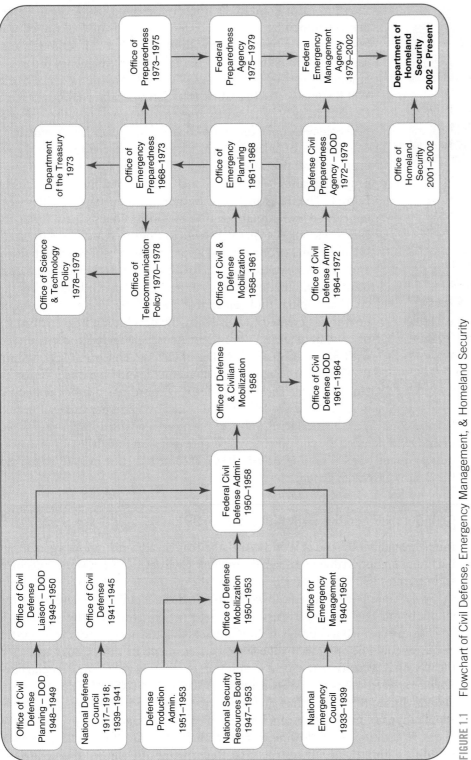

FIGURE 1.1 Flowchart of Civil Defense, Emergency Management, & Homeland Security

Data from: Defense Civil Preparedness Agency. (1975). Significant Events in United States Civil Defense History. Washington, D.C.: Defense Civil Preparedness Agency; Homeland Security National Preparedness Task Force. (2006). Civil Defense and Homeland Security: A Short History of National Preparedness Efforts. Washington, D.C.: U.S Department of Homeland Security.

AMERICA CALLING

Take your place in
CIVILIAN DEFENSE
CONSULT YOUR NEAREST DEFENSE COUNCIL

© Courtesy Everett Col/age fotostock.

year, President Franklin D. Roosevelt created the National Emergency Council by executive order. The focus of the council was essentially war preparation without calling it that, and only one aspect of its mission was the coordination of emergency programs among all agencies involved in national preparedness.[33] Once World War II ignited in Europe, Roosevelt resurrected the National Defense Council in 1939, and shortly after in 1940, converted the National Emergency Council into the Office of Emergency Management.[34]

An issue of federalism quickly arose between the national government and the states. The federal funding for civil defense was only for dealing with attacks such as the bombing of civilians in Europe. The states and many of the large metropolitan cities were concerned with nonattack disaster preparedness. New York City Mayor Fiorello La Guardia wrote to Roosevelt and argued, "there is a need for a strong Federal Department to coordinate activities, and not only to coordinate but to initiate and get things done. Please bear in mind that up to this war and never in our history, has the civilian population been exposed to attack. The new technique of war has created the necessity for developing new techniques of civilian defense."[35] President Roosevelt agreed and responded with the creation of the Office of Civilian Defense (OCD) within the Office for Emergency Management, and he named Mayor La Guardia as the Director.[36] The OCD coordinated attack preparedness between the federal and state governments and established defense councils at the local level. Some of the more renowned initiatives related to the OCD included the creation of civil defense plans, air raid drills, urban blackouts, and sand bag stockpiling. As World War II came to a close in 1945, so too did the Office of Civilian Defense.

Civil Defense and the Cold War: 1946–1991

Immediately after the end of World War II, the Truman administration began bringing troops home and drawing down the military. Civil defense was no longer deemed an important issue. That was the case until the beginning of the Cold War, when the Soviet Union turned hostile toward the United States and began developing the atomic bomb. The War Department's Civil Defense Board reviewed the issue of civil defense and deemed it a local issue, but did note that the majority of the necessary resources could be provided by the federal government. In 1947, Congress passed the National Security Act, which, in addition to creating the Central Intelligence Agency, created the National Security Resources Board (NSRB). The NSRB was tasked with mobilizing civilian and military support and maintaining adequate supplies for use in the event of a war, specifically a nuclear attack on the United States. In addition, the following year Truman created the Office of Civil Defense Planning within the newly restructured Department of Defense (also created by the National Security Act of 1947).

At this point, the Truman administration had a hodgepodge of organizations focused on civil defense, state and local governments demanding more assistance, and a public growing ever more concerned with national security. The NSRB was tasked with coming up with a plan that was finally released in 1950 and became known as the *Blue Book*.[37] The overall recommendation was to create one agency to deal with coordinating civil defense in America. In response, Congress enacted the Federal Civil Defense Act of 1950, which placed most of the civil defense burden on the states and created the Federal Civil Defense Administration (FCDA) as the one agency to formulate national policy to guide the states' efforts.[38] The FCDA throughout the 1950s led shelter-building programs, sought to improve federal and state coordination, established an attack warning system, stockpiled supplies, and started a well-known national civic education campaign, which included Bert the Turtle in "Duck and Cover."[39]

In 1953, when former World War II General Dwight D. Eisenhower was sworn in as President of the United States, the new president realized that civil defense would be an expensive venture on the part of the federal government, and so he minimized the responsibility and requested less funding for the FCDA.[40] Then, in 1958, to highlight the diminished role the federal administration would play in Eisenhower's second term, the FCDA was downgraded to the Office of Defense and Civilian Mobilization. Then, as if to highlight the greater emphasis on *civil* defense, the name of the office was changed again to the Office of Civil Defense and Mobilization.

In 1961, when President John F. Kennedy took office, he had a different approach and embraced federal involvement in emergency planning. He proposed a "nation-wide long-range program of identifying present fallout shelter capacity and providing shelter in new and existing structures."[41] To accomplish these goals, Kennedy issued Executive Order 10952 on July 20, 1961, which divided the Office of Civil Defense and Mobilization into two new organizations: The Office of Emergency Planning (OEP) and the Office of Civil Defense (OCD). OEP was part of the president's Executive Office and tasked with advising and assisting the president in determining policy for all nonmilitary emergency preparedness, including civil defense. OCD was part of the Office of the Secretary of Defense and was tasked with overseeing the nation's civil defense program. Although the creation of fall-out shelters was initiated during the Kennedy administration, adequate funding began to dwindle during the Johnson administration due to funding needs for both his Great Society programs and the Vietnam War. The influence of civil defense and emergency planning had been greatly diminished.

In 1969, President Richard M. Nixon entered office, and shortly thereafter a series of natural disasters struck, with the most devastating coming from Hurricane Camille.[42] Nixon charged the Office of Emergency Planning to conduct a review, which released its results in 1970. As a result, several new federal agencies arose. The Office of Civil Defense would fold into the Defense Civil Preparedness Agency under the Department of Defense. This agency was responsible for a military response to natural and man-made disasters. The Office of Emergency Planning became the Office of Emergency Preparedness, which was to handle the civilian side of these events. However, a number of tasks were given to other agencies, including the Office of Science and Technology Policy, the Department of the Treasury, and the Federal Disaster Assistance Administration under Housing and Urban Development (HUD). While the decentralization of the planning did allow each agency to concentrate on its area of expertise, coordination between these agencies was lacking and there was an inordinate amount of overlap, leading to wasteful spending.[43]

▪ Emergency Management: 1979–2001

President Jimmy Carter entered office in 1977 with the goal of reining in federal government bureaucracy by making it more efficient. Carter ordered a review of civil defense agencies and programs, and the review found an enormous amount of duplication of effort and wasteful spending. The recommendation was to consolidate all civil defense spending under one agency in order to better coordinate the federal response to natural disasters. The result was Executive Order 12148, dated July 20, 1979, which created the Federal Emergency Management Agency (FEMA) as the lead agency for coordinating federal disaster relief. FEMA also absorbed a number of agencies such as the Federal Insurance Administration, the National Fire Prevention and Control Administration, and the National Weather Service Community Preparedness Program. At the time, the creation of FEMA represented the single largest consolidation of civil defense efforts in U.S. history.[44]

> **KEY TERMS**
>
> **Emergency management**—the preparation for and the carrying out of all emergency functions, other than functions for which military forces are primarily responsible, to minimize injury and repair damage resulting from emergencies or disasters caused by enemy attack, sabotage or other hostile action, by fire, flood, earthquake, storm or other natural causes, or by technological or man-made catastrophes.

Although civil defense had now given way to **emergency management** under the Carter administration, the sole purpose of FEMA was to respond to natural disasters, not man-made attacks. When President Ronald Reagan entered office, he changed that and made FEMA a dual-use agency, enabling all future emergency management funds to be used for natural disasters as well as attacks on the homeland.[45] FEMA then began working toward the development of a full all-hazard preparedness plan at the federal level known as the Integrated Emergency Management System (IEMS). Despite all of the efforts by FEMA to launch this all-hazards plan, Congress would not fund the system and the idea was shelved.

Courtesy of Jocelyn Augustino/FEMA.

After President George H.W. Bush (Bush I) took office in 1989, a number of disasters occurred that once again galvanized the emergency management community. The *Exxon Valdez* oil spill, Hurricane Hugo (which struck the Virgin Islands, Puerto Rico, and South Carolina), and the Loma Prieta earthquake (which hit southern California) all struck in 1989, and the federal response was criticized as poor. FEMA dusted off the IEMS plan and developed the Federal Response Plan (FRP) as a means of improving performance. Drawing from the Incident Command System and Incident Management System Framework, the FRP defined how 27 federal agencies and the American Red Cross would respond to the needs of state and local governments when they were overwhelmed by a disaster. The national government now had an all-hazards plan.

Just prior to the 1992 presidential election, Hurricane Andrew struck South Florida and once again highlighted the poor performance of the government in its response. As one report noted, "government at all levels was slow to comprehend the scope of the disaster."[46] Arkansas Governor Bill Clinton won the election and entered office in 1993. Clinton brought with him from Arkansas James Lee Witt, who had been the Director of Emergency Management for the State of Arkansas (see **Box 1.5**). He was really the first appointee to the position who had an emergency management background. He created three functional directorates corresponding to the major phases of emergency management: mitigation, preparedness, and response and recovery. These three directorates were all then focused on creating and implementing an all-hazards plan.

BOX 1.5 James Lee Witt Biography

Courtesy of FEMA News Photo.

James Lee Witt is founder and Chairman of the Board of Directors of Witt Associates, a public safety and crisis management consulting firm based in Washington, D.C. Witt Associates provides disaster recovery and mitigation management services to state and local governments, educational institutions, the international community, and corporations.

Mr. Witt most recently served as a special advisor to the state of Louisiana, assisting with the nation's largest long-term recovery effort in the aftermath of Hurricanes Katrina and Rita.

In 2003–2006, Mr. Witt served as the Chief Executive Officer of the International Code Council (ICC), a 50,000-member association dedicated to building safety by developing the codes used to construct residential and commercial buildings, including homes and schools. The majority of U.S. cities, counties, and states that adopt codes, choose building and fire safety codes developed by the ICC.

James Lee Witt has over 25 years of disaster management experience, culminating in his appointment as the Director of the Federal Emergency Management Agency, where he served from 1993–2001. In this capacity, he is credited with turning FEMA from an unsuccessful bureaucratic agency to an internationally lauded, all-hazards disaster management agency. His leadership abilities have been praised by nationally recognized organizations, including the Council for Excellence in Government, Harvard University's Kennedy School of Government, and the National Association of Broadcasters.

Mr. Witt was appointed by President Clinton and confirmed by the U.S. Senate as Director of the Federal Emergency Management Agency in April 1993. In February 1996, President Clinton elevated Mr. Witt to cabinet status, a first for a FEMA director. As FEMA director, Mr. Witt coordinated federal disaster relief on behalf of President Clinton, including the response and recovery activities of 28 federal agencies and departments, the American Red Cross, and other volunteer agencies. He also oversaw the National Flood Insurance Program, the U.S. Fire Administration, and other proactive mitigation activities that help reduce loss of life and property from all types of hazards. Mr. Witt directed 2,500 employees located in Washington, D.C. and 10 regional offices.

From 1993 to 2000, Mr. Witt oversaw more than 350 disasters. More importantly, he was responsible for response and recovery operations for some of the most devastating disasters of all time, including the most costly flood disaster in the nation's history, the most costly earthquake, and a dozen highly destructive hurricanes.

As Director of FEMA, Mr. Witt was the architect of national government programs related to emergency preparedness and mitigation, response, and recovery. In addition to his experience in emergency management on the state and local level, Mr. Witt has expertise integrating community-based disaster management with national emergency management strategy. He initiated Project Impact, the innovative disaster prevention program implemented in over 240 communities to make communities disaster resistant at the local level.

Mr. Witt integrated flood mitigation, control, and protection into FEMA's policy. After the devastating Midwest floods of 1993, Mr. Witt pursued an aggressive flood-prone property acquisition and relocation program. By purchasing properties that were repeatedly flooded, he saved taxpayers millions of dollars when floods ravaged the same Midwest area again in 1995.

Mr. Witt's professional career includes the formation of Witt Construction, a commercial and residential construction company. After 12 years as a successful businessman and community leader, he was elected County Judge for Yell County, serving as the chief elected official for the county with judicial responsibilities for county and juvenile court. At age 34, he was the youngest elected county judge in Arkansas and was later honored for his accomplishments by the National Association of Counties. After being re-elected six times to the position, Mr. Witt was tapped by then-Governor Bill Clinton to assume leadership of the Arkansas Office of Emergency Services (OES). He served as the Director of the Arkansas OES for 4 years.

Mr. Witt and his wife, Lea Ellen, reside in Alexandria, Virginia, a suburb of Washington, D.C., and Dardanelle, Arkansas.

The implementation of the plan would prove necessary for one bombing, and fortuitous in the wake of a second. The first bombing was of the World Trade Center by international terrorists on February 26, 1993, and the second was of the Alfred P. Murrah Federal Building in Oklahoma City by domestic terrorists on April 19, 1995. As a result of these two truck bombings in America, in 1996 Clinton elevated the FEMA directorship to Cabinet-level status, improving the line of communication between the director and the president. What then followed was a series of Congressional hearings, commissions, and recommended policies for dealing with domestic preparedness and national security.

One of the more influential commissions was formed by the Clinton administration and was known formally as the Advisory Panel to Assess Domestic Response Capabilities for Terrorism Involving Weapons of Mass Destruction. Virginia Governor Jim Gilmore was appointed as the commission chair, hence the commission became known more simply as the Gilmore Commission. It developed a series of five reports to the president and Congress, starting in 1999, which made numerous recommendations, including the creation of a fusion center to integrate and analyze all intelligence pertaining to terrorism and counter-terrorism and the creation of a civil liberties oversight board. In the commission's first several years, most of the recommendations were considered, but very few were acted upon.

Another influential commission was The U.S. Commission on National Security in the 21st century, chartered by the Department of Defense, and known as the Hart–Rudman Commission. It began a comprehensive re-examination of U.S. national security policies. One of the commission's recommendations was the creation of a Cabinet-level National Homeland Security Agency responsible for planning, coordinating, and integrating various U.S. government activities involved in "homeland security." The commission defined homeland security as "the protection of the territory, critical infrastructures, and citizens of the United States by federal, state, and local government entities from the threat or use of chemical, biological, radiological, nuclear, cyber, or conventional weapons by military or other means."[47] Legislation toward this end was actually introduced on March 29, 2001, but hearings continued through April of 2001 without the passage of any legislation.

Then came September 11, 2001, and the concept of emergency management in the United States would quickly give way to the concepts of homeland security.

■ Chapter Summary

Although the United States has always been concerned with securing the homeland, it is evident from the historical record that this effort has gone through many stages. Initially, it would appear that under the strict constructs of federalism, states were seen as being responsible for dealing with all natural disasters themselves, and that resources from the national government would only be applied when Article 4, Section 4 of the U.S. Constitution was invoked (see **Box 1.6**). Two World Wars would subtly begin to change that mindset in the first half of the 20th century, when the national government embraced a cooperative, albeit limited, response in the name of civil defense. As the U.S. shifted to a Cold War in the fight against communism, a more cooperative response evolved with a division between civil and military responses. In 1979, a consolidated approach under the Federal Emergency Management Agency (FEMA) saw civil defense evolve into emergency management, and eventually a dual response policy for responding to natural and man-made disasters. As emergency management

BOX 1.6   U.S. Constitution Article 4, Section 4

The United States shall guarantee to every State in this Union a Republican Form of Government, and shall protect each of them against Invasion; and on Application of the Legislature, or of the Executive (when the Legislature cannot be convened) against domestic Violence.

evolved in the 1990s, its elevation to a Cabinet-level status marked its significant rise as a policy issue and the importance the federal government now paid to the issue.

Most of the evolution from civil defense to emergency management has been marked as a reactionary response to some natural or man-made disaster. World War I brought about civil defense. The World Trade Center and Oklahoma City bombings brought about the elevation of FEMA to a Cabinet-level agency. Yet, it should also be noted that the ideas for these changes tended to exist prior to the events; it was only after the natural or man-made disasters that these changes came about. The ultimate evidence for this is the 21st-Century Commission's ideas about creating a "Cabinet-level National Homeland Security Agency," which did not come about until after September 11, 2001. And finally, it would seem that the federal government apparatus has waffled between strong centralization and consolidation, to a more decentralized and multi-agency response.

In brief, the evolution of the homeland security apparatus (call it also civil defense or emergency management) has generally resulted from disasters (natural and man-made) but was based on ideas that existed prior to these events.

Review/Discussion Questions

1. In the aftermath of September 11, 2001 it was said that no one had ever thought planes could be used as weapons. Why is this not the case?
2. Describe domestic security in the 18th and 19th centuries. Why was domestic security not so much an issue?
3. Detail the development of civil defense, especially describing the development during both World War I and World War II.
4. What is emergency management, how did it develop, and how is it different from civil defense?
5. What were the antecedents to the development of homeland security in America prior to the terrorist attacks on September 11?

Additional Readings

Defense Civil Preparedness Agency. (1975). *Significant Events in United States Civil Defense History.* Washington, DC: Defense Civil Preparedness Agency.

Homeland Security National Preparedness Task Force. (2006). *Civil Defense and Homeland Security: A Short History of National Preparedness Efforts.* Washington, DC: U.S. Department of Homeland Security.

Maxwell, Bruce. (2004). *Homeland Security: A Documentary History.* Washington, DC: CQ Press.

■ Endnotes

1. Melanson, P.H. & P.D. Stevens. (2002). *The Secret Service: The Hidden History of an Enigmatic Agency.* New York, NY: Carrol & Graff, p. 107.

2. Oliver, W.M. & N. Marion. (2010). *Killing the President: Assassinations, Attempts, and Rumored Attempts on U.S. Commanders-in-Chief.* Santa Barbara, CA: Praeger.

3. Sifakis, C. (2001). *Encyclopedia of Assassinations.* New York, NY: Checkmark.

4. Melanson, P.H. & P.D. Stevens. (2002). *The Secret Service: The Hidden History of an Enigmatic Agency.* New York, NY: Carrol & Graff, p. 109.

5. Clarke, J.W. (1982). *American Assassins: The Darker Side of Politics.* Princeton, NJ: Princeton University Press, p. 128.

6. Clarke, J.W. (1982). *American Assassins: The Darker Side of Politics.* Princeton, NJ: Princeton University Press, p. 128.

7. Oliver, W.M. & N.E. Marion. (2010). *Killing the President: Assassinations, Attempts, and Rumored Attempts on U.S. Commanders-in-Chief.* Santa Barbara, CA: Praeger.

8. Melanson, P.H. & P.D. Stevens. (2002). *The Secret Service: The Hidden History of an Enigmatic Agency.* New York, NY: Carrol & Graff, p. 108.

9. Oliver, W.M. & N.E. Marion. (2010). *Killing the President: Assassinations, Attempts, and Rumored Attempts on U.S. Commanders-in-Chief.* Santa Barbara, CA: Praeger.

10. Preston, E. (1987). *Troubled Passage: The Federal Aviation Administration During the Nixon-Ford Term, 1973–1977.* Washington, DC: U.S. Government Printing Office.

11. Preston, E. (1987). *Troubled Passage: The Federal Aviation Administration During the Nixon-Ford Term, 1973–1977.* Washington, DC: U.S. Government Printing Office.

12. National Commission on Terrorist Attacks Upon the United States. (2004). *The 9/11 Commission Report: Final Report of the National Commission on Terrorist Attacks Upon the United States (Authorized Ed.).* New York: W.W. Norton & Company, Inc.

13. Pinkerton, J. (2002). "Our Homeland Securitizers Should Read More." *New American Foundation.* Retrieved from http://www.newamerica.net/publications/articles/2002/our_homeland_securitizers_should_read_more

14. Oliver, W.M. & N.E. Marion. (2010). *Killing the President: Assassinations, Attempts, and Rumored Attempts on U.S. Commanders-in-Chief.* Santa Barbara, CA: Praeger.

15. Szatmary, D.P. (2002). *Shays' Rebellion: The Making of an Agrarian Insurrection.* Boston: University of Massachusetts Press.

16. Oliver, W.M. & J.F. Hilgenberg, Jr. (2010). *A History of Crime and Criminal Justice in America.* 2nd ed. Durham, NC: Carolina Academic Press.

17. Richards, L.L. (2002). *Shays' Rebellion: The American Revolution's Final Battle.* Philadelphia: University of Pennsylvania Press.

18. Johnson, P. (1997). *A History of the American People.* New York: HarperCollins, p. 188.

19. Article 4, Section 4, United States Constitution.

20. Hogeland, W. (2006). *The Whiskey Rebellion.* New York: Scribner; Slaughter, T.P. (1986). *The Whiskey Rebellion: Frontier Epilogue to the American Revolution.* New York: Oxford University Press.

21. As quoted in Williams, W.E. (2006). "Constitution Day." Ideas on Liberty. Retrieved from http://econfaculty.gmu.edu/wew/articles/fee/constitution.html

22. As quoted in Williams, W.E. (2006). "Constitution Day." Ideas on Liberty. Retrieved from http://econfaculty.gmu.edu/wew/articles/fee/constitution.html

23. Sauter, M.A. & J.J. Carafano. (2012). *A Complete Guide: Homeland Security.* 2nd ed. New York: McGraw Hill.

24. The Posse Comitatus Act of 1878, Section 1385 of Title 18, United States Code.

25. McCullough, D. (1968). *The Johnstown Flood.* New York: Simon & Schuster.

26. Barker, M. E. (1998). *Three Fearful Days: San Francisco Memoirs of the 1906 Earthquake & Fire.* San Francisco, CA: Londonborn Publications; Thomas, G. & M.M. Witts. (1971); *The San Francisco Earthquake.* New York: Stein and Day.

27. Welsome, E. (2007). *The General and the Jaguar: Pershing's Hunt for Pancho Villa.* Lincoln, NE: Bison Books.

28. Bumgarner, J.B. (2006). *Federal Agents: The Growth of Federal Law Enforcement in America.* Westport, CT: Praeger Publishers.

29. Keegan, J. (2000). *The First World War.* New York: Vintage; Meyer, G.J. (2007). *A World Undone: The Story of the Great War, 1914 to 1918.* New York: A Delta Book.

30. Tuchman, B.W. (1985). *The Zimmerman Telegram.* New York: Ballantine Books.

31. Homeland Security National Preparedness Task Force. (2006). *Civil Defense and Homeland Security: A Short History of National Preparedness Efforts.* Washington, DC: U.S. Department of Homeland Security.

32. Homeland Security National Preparedness Task Force. (2006). *Civil Defense and Homeland Security: A Short History of National Preparedness Efforts.* Washington, DC: U.S. Department of Homeland Security, p. 5.

33. Homeland Security National Preparedness Task Force. (2006). *Civil Defense and Homeland Security: A Short History of National Preparedness Efforts.* Washington, DC: U.S. Department of Homeland Security.

34. Defense Civil Preparedness Agency. (1975). *Significant Events in United States Civil Defense History.* Washington, DC: Defense Civil Preparedness Agency.

35. Homeland Security National Preparedness Task Force. (2006). *Civil Defense and Homeland Security: A Short History of National Preparedness Efforts.* Washington, DC: U.S. Department of Homeland Security, p. 5.

36. Defense Civil Preparedness Agency. (1975). *Significant Events in United States Civil Defense History.* Washington, DC: Defense Civil Preparedness Agency.

37. Defense Civil Preparedness Agency. (1975). *Significant Events in United States Civil Defense History.* Washington, DC: Defense Civil Preparedness Agency; Homeland Security National Preparedness Task Force. (2006). *Civil Defense and Homeland Security: A Short History of National Preparedness Efforts.* Washington, DC: U.S Department of Homeland Security.

38. Kerr, T. (1983). *Civil Defense in the U.S.: Bandaid for a Holocaust.* Denver, CO: Westview Press.

39. Homeland Security National Preparedness Task Force. (2006). *Civil Defense and Homeland Security: A Short History of National Preparedness Efforts.* Washington, DC: U.S. Department of Homeland Security. See Duck and Cover (1951). Available online at http://archive.org/details/DuckandC1951

40. Homeland Security National Preparedness Task Force. (2006). *Civil Defense and Homeland Security: A Short History of National Preparedness Efforts.* Washington, DC: U.S. Department of Homeland Security.

41. Homeland Security National Preparedness Task Force. (2006). *Civil Defense and Homeland Security: A Short History of National Preparedness Efforts.* Washington, DC: U.S. Department of Homeland Security, p. 12.

42. Hearn, P.D. (2004). *Hurricane Camille: Monster Storm of the Gulf Coast.* Jackson, MS: University of Mississippi Press.

43. Lanouette, W. (1978). "The Best Civil Defense May Be the Best–Or Worst– Offense." *The National Journal*, September 9.

44. Homeland Security National Preparedness Task Force. (2006). *Civil Defense and Homeland Security: A Short History of National Preparedness Efforts.* Washington, DC: U.S. Department of Homeland Security.

45. Blanchard, B.W. (1986). "American Civil Defense 1945-1984: The Evolution of Programs and Policies." *Federal Emergency Management Agency Monograph Series, 2,* 1–29.

46. Homeland Security National Preparedness Task Force. (2006). *Civil Defense and Homeland Security: A Short History of National Preparedness Efforts.* Washington, DC: U.S. Department of Homeland Security, p. 22.

47. Homeland Security National Preparedness Task Force. (2006). *Civil Defense and Homeland Security: A Short History of National Preparedness Efforts.* Washington, DC: U.S. Department of Homeland Security, p. 24.

Homeland Security Defined

Chapter Objectives

- To understand that there is no commonly accepted definition of homeland security and why that is the case

- To understand common themes of homeland security as found through the homeland security bureaucracy, concepts, strategy, mission, goals, and areas of emphasis

- To consider the importance of having an acceptably shared definition of homeland security

Chapter Outline

- Introduction
- What Is Homeland Security?
  - Definition by Homeland Security Bureaucracy Evolution
  - Definition by the Homeland Security Concept Evolution
  - Definition by Homeland Security Strategic Documents
  - Definition by Homeland Security Mission and Goals
  - Definition by Homeland Security Areas of Emphasis
- Whither a Definition?
- Chapter Summary

■ Introduction

Dawn broke cold and brisk as coffee pots began to percolate and people stirred to life that January morning in the northern Virginia suburbs. Soon, the traffic was as heavy as ever in Fairfax and neighboring Arlington County, as people made their way down side streets and highways on their way to work. Police officers responded to a variety of traffic fender-benders, moving them off to the side of the road in order to keep the flow of traffic from backing up on the main arteries into the nation's capital, Washington, D.C. With each passing minute, traffic became heavier and heavier.

One location that always backed up was Dolley Madison Boulevard, Route 123, heading eastbound toward the George Washington Parkway, the "G.W." in local parlance. At what appeared to be a typical traffic intersection, cars began backing up in the two left-turn lanes, waiting for the light to turn red. The road they were waiting to turn left onto appeared to lead into just another northern Virginia suburb. Only it was not a suburb at all. Nor was it typical. It was the entrance to the headquarters of the Central Intelligence Agency.

It was January 25, 1993. The time was approximately 8:00 AM.

In one of the left-hand turn lanes was a brown 1970s Datsun station wagon, waiting behind several other vehicles stopped at the light.[1] The two turn lanes behind the Datsun were full, and the left travel lane was also backed up with people waiting to turn left into CIA headquarters. Suddenly, the door of the Datsun opened and a man in his late 20s exited the vehicle. He was short in stature with olive skin and a thick mustache. As he exited the vehicle, he pulled from the car an AK-47 semi-automatic rifle and he began walking down the median strip. He raised the AK-47 and began firing shots into the cars stopped behind him, aiming toward the drivers. He fired eight rounds as he walked along the median, ultimately hitting five men: Frank Darling, Lansing Bennett, Nicholas Starr, Calvin Morgan, and Stephen Williams.[2]

As the shooter reached a certain point on the median, he stopped, turned, and began walking back. As he reached the first car he had fired into, the one immediately behind his car, he raised the AK-47 and shot Frank Darling in the head two more times. He then climbed back into the driver's seat of the Datsun and proceeded to drive east toward the G.W. Parkway, then headed south into Arlington County.

A police officer in Arlington County heard two tones on his radio and was told to check his on-board computer for an important message.[3] The screen read that there was a shooting at the CIA headquarters, several people were injured from an AK-47, and the suspect was heading toward the G.W. Parkway. He began making his way toward the parkway as it followed along the Potomac River, heading south to George Washington's Mount Vernon. As he traveled the G.W. Parkway, he was informed to be on the lookout for a 1970s model station wagon. He started to drive into one of the many parks along the Parkway but was called to Arlington Hospital to guard one of the shooting victims who had been transported there by ambulance.

It turns out the suspect was one Aimal Kasi, born in Pakistan in the mid-1960s, who had entered the United States in 1991.[4] He stayed in Reston, Virginia with a friend and found work as a courier, driving by the entrance to the CIA almost on a daily basis. He knew that all of the people turning left at the intersection worked for the CIA, so he purchased the AK-47 and began planning his attack.

After the shooting, he drove to a nearby park and waited for about an hour and a half. As no one approached his car, he traveled back to Reston, hid the weapon under a sofa and left the house.[5] He purchased lunch at McDonalds, checked into a hotel, and watched the news about his attack. He then flew home to Pakistan the following morning.[6]

Two of the shooting victims, Frank Darling and Lansing Bennett, died from their wounds. The other three survived. A joint investigation between the FBI and local police was launched, and Kasi was eventually identified as the shooter.[7] He was listed on the FBI's Most Wanted Fugitives[8] list. The search turned international

© Virginia Department of Corrections/Getty Images.

What Happened After the CIA Shooting?

At the time of the shootings, U.S. officials knew nothing of Kasi's identity or affiliations. Authorities identified Kasi as the shooter several days later, after his roommate filed a missing person's report with local police. Soon after, the FBI placed Kasi on their Most Wanted List, while the State Department posted a $2 million dollar reward for his capture; it was later increased to $3.5 million. Yet, for 4 years various plans to locate, track, and capture Kasi failed.

As the years passed, Kasi assumed the United States had forgotten about him and began leaving Afghanistan to visit friends in Pakistan. On June 15, 1997, acting on an informant's tip, a combined FBI and CIA team lured Kasi to a meeting in the Dera Ghazi Khan District of Punjab, Pakistan to work out details of a supposed business venture involving smuggled arms and electronics. As the plan unfolded, CIA headquarters established radio contact with a Chevy Suburban containing a joint CIA–FBI team sitting outside a Chinese restaurant and hotel where Kasi waited to meet his alleged new business partners.

The appointed 4 PM meeting time came and went, as Acting DCI George Tenet anxiously awaited word. At 4:30,

according to one account, the radio cracked "Base, base, this is Red Rover. The package is aloft, the package is aloft." Kasi was in American hands. Within minutes, Tenet phoned the families of Kasi's victims.

Tenet made a public announcement of the arrest 2 days later praising the 4-year effort—and ultimate success—of the CIA, FBI, and State Department.

The Justice Department decided that local authorities in Fairfax County should try Kasi on capital murder charges since federal law did not then provide for the death penalty for terrorist acts. In court, Kasi acknowledged his role in the shootings, but pleaded not guilty. Convicted after a jury trial, Kasi received the death penalty, carried out by lethal injection at the Virginia State Penitentiary in Jarratt on November 14, 2002.

A permanent memorial to Frank Darling and Lansing Bennett was erected in May 2002 near the site of the shootings on Route 123.

as it was discovered Kasi had returned to Pakistan (see **Box 2.1**). Eventually, a source identified his whereabouts; he was captured and smuggled back into the United States. He was placed on trial, found guilty of murder, and executed on November 4, 2002.[9]

What Is Homeland Security?

The killing of two CIA employees and the wounding of three others was the first attack in the 1990s that suggested the possibility of international terrorism coming to the United States. The case of Aimal Kasi, however, was treated as an isolated incident, and in many ways as nothing more than a domestic crime. Although both the FBI and local police worked together to solve the case, when it was discovered that Kasi had fled back to Pakistan, the operation became a joint effort between the CIA and the FBI. He was captured and, in an early use of rendition, was brought back to the United States without going through diplomatic channels. Once he returned to the United States, however, he was tried as a criminal in a Virginia Court, charged with two counts of capital murder. Found guilty of these crimes, he was executed in Virginia's death chamber, as Virginia has and uses death penalty statutes.

The question that arises from this short case study is whether this was an act of terrorism (see text elsewhere for further discussion on terrorism), and if so, was this an early example of America defending the homeland? Kasi, by all accounts, acted alone out of hatred that arose from watching CNN and seeing "Americans kill Muslims."[10] He had no accomplices, represented no terrorist group per se, and was simply driven by his personal hatred toward Americans being in the Middle East. Hence, the murders were criminal acts. However, Kasi was not born in the United States, came from a country where many people tend to foster a hatred for America, and may have grown up among many of the radical Mullahs preaching violence against Americans. Given this scenario, was this an act of terrorism?

Regardless, the following month, the United States would witness the first bombing of the World Trade Center, this time through a conspiracy among terrorists with Al Qaeda ties. Yet even this attack was treated more as a crime than as an act of terrorism. Interestingly when, 2 years later, the Oklahoma City bombing was perpetrated by Americans, this act was generally considered more of an act of terrorism than the first World Trade Center bombing, albeit it was domestic terrorism not international terrorism. It was the attacks on 9-11, however, that brought the concept of terrorism to the forefront of the minds of most Americans. It was also this event that brought the concept of **homeland security** to life, but has left us to beg the question: What exactly is homeland security?

Bellavita, in his article about defining homeland security, noted that people often ask, "What is homeland security? Is it a program, an objective, a discipline, an agency, an administrative activity, another word for emergency management? Is it about terrorism? All hazards? Something completely different?"[11] Logan and Ramsay explained in their book on homeland security that "Although the United States was familiar with terrorism long before September 11, 2001, the term *homeland security* was not commonly used until the aftermath of the 2001 terrorist attacks on New York and Washington, D.C.," and that even though the new agency was called the Department of Homeland Security by the Bush Administration, "the lack of definition of what is meant by *homeland security* and how it related to existing civilian agencies and their missions resulted in challenges for the new department, for agencies that combined in it, and for state government counterparts."[12] Even 10 years after the September 11 attacks, Reese, in an analysis of emergency management and homeland security policy for Congress, observed that "the U.S. government does not have a single definition for 'homeland security.'"[13]

Recognizing that there is no generally accepted definitive definition of homeland security, it is important to understand that the current and varied definitions come from various sources. The first is from a historical perspective, as primarily detailed in the following text. The second is also from a historical perspective, but related more to the evolution of governmental usage of the term as found in documents such as presidential directives and commission reports. A third source, and closely related to the second, is found in federal strategic documents attempting to wrestle with the definition, but in a post 9-11 environment. A fourth source comes not from abstract strategy but instead from a focus on the mission and **goals of homeland security** in this same post-9-11 world. Finally, we can return to Bellavita's analysis, in which he argues that the definition has actually developed in eight different areas and has not yet reached a shared definition, although some of the definitions do share certain elements. It is to these four perspectives that we now turn.

Definition by Homeland Security Bureaucracy Evolution

As detailed elsewhere in this text, civil defense arose out of fears during World War I, but responsibility was largely relegated to the states. In World War II, the idea

KEY TERMS
Homeland security—an effort to prevent, mitigate, respond, and recover from natural and man-made disasters, including terrorist attacks.

KEY TERMS
Homeland security goals—those key tasks that must be accomplished in order for the homeland security mission to be accomplished.

KEY TERMS
Homeland security bureaucracy—the various federal, state, and local agencies that are directly or indirectly involved in the protection of America's homeland.

of civil defense was resurrected, and although initially under state responsibility, the states were given direction through federal coordination. During the Cold War, at least at first, civil defense became more centralized under the federal government and, more specifically, coordinated out of the White House.[14] During the Nixon administration, the move was toward a centralized, independent agency, eventually the Federal Emergency Management Agency (FEMA), with a decentralized execution. FEMA became the primary means for emergency management policies and practices throughout the 1990s. In the wake of 9-11, however, the emphasis was on a much broader federal government response in which emergency preparedness and response, essentially FEMA's role, was only a part. FEMA would then be absorbed as only one component, or directorate, under the Department of Homeland Security.

In this quick historical review, it is evident that the true nature and development of homeland security, and hence its eventual definition, is primarily a response to cataclysmic events and an evolving bureaucratic organization to best deal with such events. World Wars I and II were events that called for a response, and civil defense was that bureaucratic response. Throughout the Cold War and a number of serious natural disasters, changes to the bureaucracy were the usual response to these events. Hence the creation of the Department of Homeland Security (DHS) was simply a response to the events of September 11th, and merely the next step in an evolutionary development of bureaucratic changes (See FIGURE 2.1).[15] After 9-11, "homeland security" could be loosely defined as a wider-reaching, bureaucratic response (and organization) to better prepare and respond to future terrorist attacks against the United States. Although charged to include natural disasters, early on DHS was heavily focused on terrorist attacks. It was not until Hurricane Katrina (2005) that it came to focus also on natural disasters (as in an "all-hazard" organization).

In this sense, the term homeland security is part of a historical evolution that is embodied by the federal bureaucracy created in the wake of the various cataclysmic events. As a result, the definition would simply be however the reigning bureaucracy, today the Department of Homeland Security, defines the concept.

FIGURE 2.1　　The Evolution of Homeland Security.

Reproduced from: U.S. Department of Homeland Security. (2010). Quadrennial Homeland Security Review Report: A Strategic Framework for a Secure Homeland. Washington, D.C.: U.S. Department of Homeland Security, p. 14. Courtesy of the DHS.

▦ Definition by the Homeland Security Concept Evolution

Rather than developing as a bureaucratic reaction to events over time, the concept of homeland security can be thought of evolving from the policy experts in the decade prior to September 11, 2001. While most Americans were not focused on the issue of terrorism in the 1990s, many government entities and researchers/think-tanks were. For instance, in Presidential Directive Number 62, dated May 22, 1998, President Clinton addressed the issue of "Protection Against Unconventional Threats to the Homeland and Americans Overseas."[16] On the same day, Clinton also issued Presidential Directive Number 63, regarding Critical Infrastructure Protection, and while not using the term homeland security, discussed what could be considered the preliminary plans for a Department of Homeland Security.

In 1999, a number of interested government agencies, including defense, justice, and energy, along with the Director of FEMA, entered into a contract with the RAND Corporation's National Defense Research Institute to establish a federally funded advisory panel. It was officially known as the U.S. Congressional Advisory Panel to Assess Domestic Response Capabilities for Terrorism Involving Weapons of Mass Destruction. Informally it was known as the Gilmore Commission, named for its chair, former Virginia Governor Jim Gilmore. In the Advisory Panel's first official report, published December 15, 1999, it speaks of "federal funding for domestic preparedness and homeland defense programs."[17]

Another commission formed the year before was the U.S. Commission on National Security/21st Century, also known as the Hart–Rudman Task Force on Homeland Security, which was developed at the request of Secretary of Defense William Cohen. The goal of the task force was to assess the emerging international security environment and to develop possible responses. In one document, released on February 15, 2001, the task force noted that "mass-casualty terrorism directed against the U.S. homeland was of serious and growing concern," and that "it recommends a new National Homeland Security Agency to consolidate and refine the missions of the nearly two dozen disparate departments and agencies that have a role in U.S. homeland security today."[18] The task force's recommendations actually found their way into a bill, House Resolution 1158 in the 107th Congress, titled the National Homeland Security Agency Act.[19] The bill was introduced into the House on March 21, 2001 and was referred to committee, where it subsequently died.

In this case, the term homeland security developed not so much as a bureaucratic response to attacks or disasters, but rather bureaucratic policy development within the federal government focused on changing the bureaucracy to meet future attacks. In this case, it is clear the concept of homeland security was being circulated among policy experts concerned with the issue of terrorism and they had developed a plan for evolving the bureaucratic response to future attacks.

Courtesy of Donna Burton, Defense Information Systems Agency.

The only problem was that while the policy experts had identified a legitimate problem (international terrorism attacks on the U.S.) and they created a possible plan for better dealing with this problem (the creation of the National Homeland Security Agency), they were missing serious public concern in order to galvanize the issue to force passage through Congress. That would not come until the events of September 11, 2001.

In this historical sense, the development of homeland security, and hence its definition, was placed in the hands of the federal policy makers, developing plans based on perceived problems, rather than as merely a reaction to them.

Definition by Homeland Security Strategic Documents

Reese has explained that homeland security has been defined in several strategic documents post 9-11.[20] The first homeland security strategy document issued by the Bush Administration was the 2003 *National Strategy for Homeland Security,* which was revised in 2007. In 2008, the Department of Homeland Security issued *Strategic Plan—One Team, One Mission, Securing Our Homeland.* The 2007 *National Strategy for Homeland Security* primarily focused on terrorism, whereas the 2008 *Strategic Plan* included references to all-hazards and border security. Arguably, the 2003 and 2007 *National Strategies for Homeland Security* specifically addressed terrorism, due to such incidents as the 9-11 terrorist attacks and the attempted bombing of American Airlines Flight 93, by Richard Reid, named the "Shoe Bomber" for disguising the bomb within his shoe (see **Box 2.2**). In contrast, the 2008 *Strategic Plan* addressed terrorism and all-hazards due to natural disasters such as Hurricanes Katrina and Rita in 2005. These documents were superseded by several documents, which are now considered the principal homeland security strategies.

Today, the White House and the Department of Homeland Security have advanced the homeland security strategies in the 2010 *National Security Strategy,* which addresses all-hazards and is not primarily terrorism focused. DHS's strategic

---

BOX 2.2   Richard Reid—"The Shoe Bomber"

Richard Reid, a British citizen and self-proclaimed follower of Osama bin Laden, boarded a plane in December of 2001, flying from Paris, France to Miami, Florida. While in flight across the Atlantic Ocean, Reid was seen by fellow passengers lighting matches and trying to touch them to his shoe. He was subdued by a combination of passengers and flight attendants and, after an emergency landing in Boston, turned over to the FBI. Reid was found to have had enough explosives in his shoe to damage the plane, but he could not get the fuse to light. Reid was dubbed the "Shoe Bomber" by the media and was eventually tried and found guilty of terrorism charges. He is serving a term of life in prison.

Reproduced from: Carafano, James Jay. (2007). "U.S. Thwarts 19 Terrorists Attacks Against America Since 9/11." *Backgrounder.* Washington, DC: The Heritage Foundation.

© ELISE AMENDOLA/AP Images.

documents are the 2010 *Quadrennial Homeland Security Review*, the 2010 *Bottom-Up Review*, and the 2012 *Strategic Plan*. DHS states that these documents are nested in the 2010 *National Security Strategy*. At the national level, the 2010 *National Security Strategy* guides not just DHS's homeland security activities, but it also guides the homeland security missions of all federal government agencies.

TABLE 2.1 provides a summary of the various homeland security definitions along with the specific documents they originated from. Some of the common themes that can be found among these definitions include: 1) the **homeland security enterprise** (see **Box 2.3**), encompasses a federal, state, local, and tribal government and private sector approach that requires coordination; 2) homeland security can involve securing against and responding to both hazard-specific and all-hazards threats, and: 3) homeland security activities do not imply total protection or complete threat reduction. Each of these documents highlights the importance of coordinating homeland security missions and activities. However, individual federal, state, local,

KEY TERMS

Homeland security enterprise—the collective efforts and shared responsibilities of federal, state, local, tribal, territorial, nongovernmental, and private-sector partners—as well as individuals, families, and communities—to maintain critical homeland security capabilities.

TABLE 2.1 Summary of Homeland Security Definitions

Document	Definition
2007 National Strategy for Homeland Security (White House)	A concerted, national effort to prevent terrorist attacks within the United States, reduce America's vulnerability to terrorism, and minimize the damage and recovery from attacks that do occur.
2008 U.S. Department of Homeland Security Strategic Plan, Fiscal Years 2008–2013 (DHS)	A unified, national effort to prevent and deter terrorist attacks, protect and respond to hazards, and to secure the national borders.
2010 National Security Strategy (White House)	A seamless coordination among federal, state, and local governments to prevent, protect against, and respond to threats and natural disasters.
2010 Quadrennial Homeland Security Review (DHS)	A concerted, national effort to ensure a homeland that is safe, secure, and resilient against terrorism and other hazards where American interests, aspirations, and ways of life can thrive.
2010 Bottom-Up Review (DHS)	Preventing terrorism, responding to and recovering from natural disasters, customs enforcement and collection of customs revenue, administration of legal immigration services, safety and stewardship of the nation's waterways and marine transportation system, as well as other legacy missions of the various components of DHS.
2011 National Strategy for Counterterrorism (White House)	Defensive efforts to counter terrorist threats.
2012 Strategic Plan (DHS)	Efforts to ensure a homeland that is safe, secure, and resilient against terrorism and other hazards.

Reproduced from: Reese, Shawn. (2012). "Defining Homeland Security: Analysis and Congressional Considerations." Congressional Research Service. Retrieved online at http://www.fas.org/sgp/crs/homesec/R42462.pdf

BOX 2.3   The Homeland Security "Enterprise"

The homeland security "enterprise" refers to the collective efforts and shared responsibilities of federal, state, local, tribal, territorial, nongovernmental, and private-sector partners—as well as individuals, families, and communities—to maintain critical homeland security capabilities. It connotes a broad-based community with a common interest in the safety and well-being of America and American society.

Reproduced from: U.S. Department of Homeland Security. (2010). *Quadrennial Homeland Security Review Report: A Strategic Framework for a Secure Homeland*. Washington, DC: U.S. Department of Homeland Security, p. 12.

and tribal government efforts are not identified in the documents. Homeland security, according to these documents, is preventing, responding to, and recovering from natural and man-made disasters, especially terrorist attacks, which is consistent with evolving homeland security policy after 9-11.

The focus of the definition of homeland security communicated in these strategy documents differs in two areas that may be considered substantive. Natural disasters are specifically identified as an integral part of homeland security in only four of these six documents, but are not mentioned in the 2007 *National Strategy for Homeland Security* and the 2011 *National Strategy for Counterterrorism*.[21] Only one document—the *Bottom-Up Review*—specifically includes border and maritime security and immigration in its homeland security definition.[22] The 2012 *Strategic Plan* uses the encompassing terms "other hazards" to define any threat other than terrorism.[23] These "other hazards" are obviously significant and require substantial funding. An absence of consensus about the inclusion of these policy areas may result in unintended consequences for national homeland security operations. For example, not including maritime security in the homeland security definition may result in policymakers, Congress, and stakeholders inadequately addressing maritime homeland security threats, or, more specifically, being unable to prioritize federal investments in border versus intelligence activities.[24]

The varied and sometimes competing definitions in these documents indicates that there is no generally accepted and succinct **homeland security concept**.[25] Without a definitive homeland security concept, policymakers and others with homeland security responsibilities may not successfully coordinate activities well or focus on the most necessary activities. Coordination is especially essential to homeland security because of the multiple federal agencies and the state and local partners with whom they interact. Coordination may be difficult if these entities do not operate with the same understanding or set of priorities. For example, definitions that do not specifically include immigration or natural disaster response and recovery may result in homeland security stakeholders and federal entities not adequately resourcing and focusing on these activities. Additionally, an absence of a consensus definition may result in Congress funding a homeland security activity that DHS does not consider a priority. For example, Congress may appropriate funding for a counterterrorism program such as the State Homeland Security Grant Program when DHS may have identified an all-hazards grant program, such as the Emergency Management Performance Grant Program, as a priority. It is, however, possible that a consensus definition and overall concept exists among policymakers and federal entities, but that it isn't communicated in the strategic documents.

KEY TERMS
Homeland security concepts— fundamental aspects of homeland security that are common to all responses whether they are natural disasters or terrorist attacks, such as preparedness.

Finally, former DHS Deputy Secretary Jane Lute recently stated that homeland security "… is operation, it's transactional, it's decentralized, it's bottom-driven," and influenced by law enforcement, emergency management, and the political environment. Conversely, Lute stated that national security "… is strategic, it's centralized, it's top-driven," and influenced by the military and the intelligence community.[26] Some see in these comments an attempt by DHS to establish a homeland security definition that is more operational than strategic. If nothing else, these comments serve as a fine illustration of the difficulty of reaching a common understanding of homeland security and its associated missions.[27]

Definition by Homeland Security Mission and Goals

Another means by which to assess a common definition of homeland security is through the mission and goals of homeland security as articulated by the many sources detailed previously. These varied homeland security definitions, in numerous documents, result in the homeland security stakeholders identifying and executing varied strategic missions.[28] Homeland security stakeholders include federal departments and agencies, state and local governments, and nonprofit and nongovernmental organizations. The strategic documents specifically identify numerous homeland security missions such as terrorism prevention; response and recovery; critical infrastructure protection and resilience; federal, state, and local emergency management and preparedness; and border security. As noted earlier, none of these documents specifically task one federal entity with the overall homeland security responsibilities. TABLE 2.2 details the various missions and goals that have been articulated by these government documents.

The federal documents all identify specific missions as essential to securing the nation. All of the documents state that the nation's populace, critical infrastructure, and key resources need protection from terrorism and natural disasters. Protection from both terrorism and natural disasters is a key strategic **homeland security mission**.

Some, but not all, of the documents include missions related to border security, immigration, the economy, and general resilience. Members of Congress and congressional committees have sometimes criticized these documents.[29]

Senator Susan Collins (R-ME), at the time a ranking member of the Committee on Homeland Security and Governmental Affairs, expressed disappointment in the *Quadrennial Homeland Security Review* and *Bottom-Up Review* because they did not communicate priorities and stated that they did not compare favorably to the most recent *Quadrennial Defense Review*.[30] According to Collins, the *Quadrennial Defense Review* identifies national security and U.S. military priorities through a process "… from objectives to capabilities and activities to resources."[31] Furthermore, the *Quadrennial Homeland Security Review* missions are different from the 2007 *National Strategy for Homeland Security* missions, and neither identifies priorities or resources for DHS or other related federal agencies. Since the *National Strategy for Homeland Security* and the *Quadrennial Homeland Security Review* missions are differing and varied, and because the *Quadrennial Homeland Security Review* does not specifically identify a strategic process to achieve its mission, one may assume that these documents serve solely as operational guidance (see **Box 2.4**). Additionally, some critics found the *Bottom-Up Review* lacking in detail and failing to meet its intended purpose.[32]

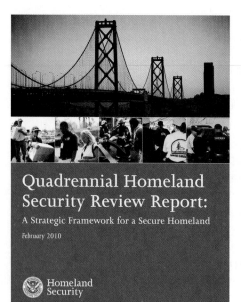

Quadrennial Homeland Security Review Report:

A Strategic Framework for a Secure Homeland

February 2010

Homeland Security

Courtesy of the DHS.

TABLE 2.2 Summary of Homeland Security Missions and Goals

Document	Mission and Goals
2007 National Strategy for Homeland Security (White House)	• Prevent and disrupt terrorist attacks • Protect the American people, critical infrastructure, and key resources • Respond to and recover from incidents that do occur • Strengthen the foundation to ensure long term success
2008 U.S. Department of Homeland Security Strategic Plan, Fiscal Years 2008–2013 (DHS)	• Protect the nation from dangerous people • Protect the nation from dangerous goods • Protect critical infrastructure • Strengthen the nation's preparedness and emergency response capabilities • Strengthen and unify the department's operations and management
2010 National Security Strategy (White House)	• Strengthen national capacity • Ensure security and prosperity at home • Secure cyberspace • Ensure American economic prosperity
2010 Quadrennial Homeland Security Review (DHS)	• Prevent terrorism and enhance security • Secure and manage our borders • Enforce and administer our immigration laws • Safeguard and secure cyberspace • Ensure resilience to disasters • Provide essential support to national and economic security.
2010 Bottom-Up Review (DHS)	• Prevent terrorism and enhance security • Secure and manage borders • Enforce and manage immigration laws • Safeguard and secure cyberspace • Ensure resilience to disasters • Improve departmental management and accountability
2011 National Strategy for Counterterrorism (White House)	• Protect the American people, homeland, and American interests • Eliminate threats to the American people's, homeland's, and interests' physical safety • Counter threats to global peace and security • Promote and protect U.S. interests around the globe
2012 Strategic Plan (DHS)	• Prevent terrorism and enhance security • Secure and manage our borders • Enforce and administer our immigration laws • Safeguard and secure cyberspace • Ensure resilience to disasters • Provide essential support to national and economic security

BOX 2.4   The 5 Core Missions of the U.S. Department of Homeland Security and Their Goals

Core Mission #1—Preventing Terrorism and Enhancing Security

Goal 1.1: Prevent Terrorist Attacks: Malicious actors are unable to conduct terrorist attacks within the United States.

Objectives:

- Understand the threat: Acquire, analyze, and appropriately share intelligence and other information on current and emerging threats.
- Deter and disrupt operations: Deter, detect, and disrupt surveillance, rehearsals, and execution of operations by terrorists and other malicious actors.
- Protect against terrorist capabilities: Protect potential targets against the capabilities of terrorists, malicious actors, and their support networks to plan and conduct operations.
- Stop the spread of violent extremism: Prevent and deter violent extremism and radicalization that contributes to it.
- Engage communities: Increase community participation in efforts to deter terrorists and other malicious actors and mitigate radicalization toward violence.

Goal 1.2: Prevent the Unauthorized Acquisition or Use of Chemical, Biological, Radiological, and Nuclear Materials and Capabilities: Malicious actors, including terrorists, are unable to acquire or move dangerous chemical, biological, radiological, and nuclear materials or capabilities within the United States.

Objectives:

- Anticipate emerging threats: Identify and understand potentially dangerous actors, technologies, and materials.
- Control access to CBRN: Prevent terrorists and other malicious actors from gaining access to dangerous materials and technologies.
- Control movement of CBRN: Prevent the illicit movement of dangerous materials and/or technologies.
- Protect against hostile use of CBRN: Identify the presence of and effectively locate, disable, or prevent the hostile use of CBRN.

Goal 1.3: Manage Risks to Critical Infrastructure, Key Leadership, and Events: Key sectors actively work to reduce vulnerability to attack or disruption.

Objectives:

- Understand and prioritize risks to critical infrastructure: Identify, attribute, and evaluate the most dangerous threats to critical infrastructure and those categories of critical infrastructure most at risk.
- Protect critical infrastructure: Prevent high-consequence events by securing critical infrastructure assets, systems, networks, or functions—including linkages through cyberspace—from attacks or disruption.
- Make critical infrastructure resilient: Enhance the ability of critical infrastructure systems, networks, and functions to withstand and rapidly recover from damage and disruption and adapt to changing conditions.
- Protect government leaders, facilities, and special events. Preserve continuity of government and ensure security at events of national significance.

Core Mission #2—Securing and Managing Our Borders

Goal 2.1: Effectively Control U.S. Air, Land, and Sea Borders: Prevent the illegal flow of people and goods across U.S. air, land, and sea borders while expediting the safe flow of lawful travel and commerce.

Objectives:

- Prevent illegal entry: Prevent the illegal entry of people, weapons, dangerous goods, and contraband, and protect against cross-border threats to health, food, environment, and agriculture, while facilitating the safe flow of lawful travel and commerce.
- Prevent illegal export and exit: Prevent the illegal export of weapons, proceeds of crime, and other dangerous goods, and the exit of malicious actors.

Goal 2.2: Safeguard Lawful Trade and Travel: Ensure security and resilience of global movement systems.

Objectives:

- Secure key nodes: Promote the security and resilience of key nodes of transaction and exchange within the global supply chain.
- Secure conveyances: Promote the safety, security, and resilience of conveyances in the key global trading and transportation networks.
- Manage the risk posed by people and goods in transit.

Goal 2.3: Disrupt and Dismantle Transnational Criminal Organizations: Disrupt and dismantle transnational organizations that engage in smuggling and trafficking across the U.S. border.

Objectives:

- Identify, disrupt, and dismantle transnational criminal and terrorist organizations: Disrupt transnational criminal or terrorist organizations involved in cross-border smuggling, trafficking, or other cross-border crimes, dismantle their infrastructure, and apprehend their leaders.
- Disrupt illicit pathways: Identify, disrupt, and dismantle illicit pathways used by transnational criminal and terrorist organizations.

Core Mission #3—Enforcing and Administering Our Immigration Laws

Goal 3.1: Strengthen and Effectively Administer the Immigration System: Promote lawful immigration, expedite administration of immigration services, and promote the integration of lawful immigrants into American society.

Objectives:

- Promote lawful immigration: Clearly communicate to the public information on immigration services and procedures.
- Effectively administer the immigrations services system: Create a user-friendly system that ensures fair, consistent, and prompt decisions.
- Promote the integration of lawful immigrants into American society: Provide leadership, support, and opportunities to immigrants to facilitate their integration into American society and foster community cohesion.

Goal 3.2: Prevent Unlawful Immigration: Reduce conditions that encourage foreign nationals to illegally enter and remain in the United States, while identifying and removing those who violate our laws.

Objectives:

- Reduce demand: Eliminate the conditions that encourage illegal employment.
- Eliminate systemic vulnerabilities: Prevent fraud, abuse, and exploitation, and eliminate other systemic vulnerabilities that threaten the integrity of the immigration system.

- Prevent entry or admission: Prevent entry or admission of criminals, fugitives, other dangerous foreign nationals, and other unauthorized entrants.
- Arrest, detain, prosecute, and remove: Arrest, detain, prosecute, and remove criminal, fugitive, dangerous, and other unauthorized foreign nationals consistent with due process and civil rights protections.

Core Mission #4—Safeguarding and Securing Cyberspace

Goal 4.1: Create a Safe, Secure, and Resilient Cyber Environment: Ensure malicious actors are unable to effectively exploit cyberspace, impair its safe and secure use, or attack the Nation's information infrastructure.

Objectives:

- Understand and prioritize cyber threats: Identify and evaluate the most dangerous threats to Federal civilian and private-sector networks and the Nation.
- Manage risks to cyberspace: Protect and make resilient information systems, networks, and personal and sensitive data.
- Prevent cyber crime and other malicious uses of cyberspace: Disrupt the criminal organizations and other malicious actors engaged in high-consequence or wide-scale cyber crime.
- Develop a robust public-private cyber incident response capability: Manage cyber incidents from identification to resolution in a rapid and replicable manner with prompt and appropriate action.

Goal 4.2: Promote Cybersecurity Knowledge and Innovation: Ensure that the Nation is prepared for the cyber threats and challenges of tomorrow.

Objectives:

- Enhance public awareness: Ensure that the public recognizes cybersecurity challenges and is empowered to address them.
- Foster a dynamic workforce: Develop the national knowledge base and human capital capabilities to enable success against current and future threats.
- Invest in innovative technologies, techniques, and procedures: Create and enhance science, technology, governance mechanisms, and other elements necessary to sustain a safe, secure, and resilient cyber environment.

Core Mission #5—Ensuring Resilience to Disasters

Goal 5.1: Mitigate Hazards: Strengthen capacity at all levels of society to withstand threats and hazards.

Objectives:

- Reduce the vulnerability of individuals and families: Improve individual and family capacity to reduce vulnerabilities and withstand disasters.
- Mitigate risks to communities: Improve community capacity to withstand disasters by mitigating known and anticipated hazards.

Goal 5.2: Enhance Preparedness: Engage all levels and segments of society in improving preparedness.

Objectives:

- Improve individual, family, and community preparedness: Ensure individual, family, and community planning, readiness, and capacity-building for disasters.
- Strengthen capabilities: Enhance and sustain nationwide disaster preparedness capabilities, to include life safety, law enforcement, information sharing, mass evacuation and shelter-in-place, public health, mass care, and public works.

Goal 5.3: Ensure Effective Emergency Response: Strengthen response capacity nationwide.

Objectives:

- Provide timely and accurate information to the public: Establish and strengthen pathways for clear, reliable, and current emergency information, including effective use of new media.
- Conduct effective disaster response operations: Respond to disasters in an effective and unified manner.
- Provide timely and appropriate disaster assistance: Improve governmental, nongovernmental, and private-sector delivery of disaster assistance.

Goal 5.4: Rapidly Recover: Improve the Nation's ability to adapt and rapidly recover.

Objectives:

- Enhance recovery capabilities: Establish and maintain nationwide capabilities for recovery from major disasters.
- Ensure continuity of essential services and functions: Improve capabilities of families, communities, private-sector organizations, and all levels of government to sustain essential services and functions.

Reproduced from: U.S. Department of Homeland Security. (2010). *Quadrennial Homeland Security Review Report: A Strategic Framework for a Secure Homeland.* Washington, DC: U.S. Department of Homeland Security.

Further congressional criticism includes an observation of the absence of a single DHS strategy. At a recent House Homeland Security Committee's Subcommittee on Oversight, Investigations, and Management hearing, Chairman Michael McCaul (R-TX) stated that "… DHS needs a single strategic document, which subordinate agencies can follow and make sure the strategy is effectively and efficiently implemented. This single document should conform to the National Security Strategy of the United States of America. If the agencies do not have clearly established list of priorities, it will be difficult to complete assigned missions."[33]

Other criticism includes the Council on Foreign Relations' (CFR) discussion of the 2010 National Security Strategy (NSS). CFR states that the "… one thing that the NSS discussion of resilience omits, but which the Deputy National Security Adviser John Brennan has emphasized, is that despite all the homeland security precautions, there is likely to be a successful attack. When that happens, real resilience will entail a calm, deliberate response and confidence in the durability of the country's institutions."[34] In summary, as Reese has noted, "Multiple definitions, missions, and an absence of prioritization results in consequences to the nation's security."[35]

Definition by Homeland Security Areas of Emphasis

One further means of coming to a consensus on a definition of homeland security has been articulated by Naval Postgraduate School Instructor Christopher Bellavita.[36] He advances the idea that rather than focusing on historical evolution, government definitions, or homeland security missions, the best way to define homeland security is by focusing on various **areas of emphasis in homeland security**. He argues there are essentially seven areas of focus: 1) Terrorism, 2) All Hazards, 3) Terrorism and Catastrophes, 4) Jurisdictional Hazards, 5) Meta Hazards, 6) National Security, and 7) Security *Über Alles*.[37]

> **KEY TERMS**
>
> Homeland security areas of emphasis—various ways of perceiving homeland security as detailed by Homeland Security expert Christopher Bellavita.

In the first instance, homeland security is about terrorism, hence it is focused on the prevention of, response to, and recovery from future terrorist attacks.[38] Terrorism, in this case, is both foreign and domestic, and the mechanisms to deal with terrorism are located at the federal, state, local, and tribal levels of government, while also including the private sector. The focus on homeland security in this regard is aimed at mitigating the impact these attacks may have on the United States.

In the second area of focus, homeland security is about all hazards; thus, it is not limited solely to terroristic attacks, but encompasses terrorism, natural disasters such as hurricanes, floods, and earthquakes, and other issues such as border security, illegal immigration, and cyber attacks. It is a concerted effort by national, state, local, and tribal agencies to prevent and disrupt terrorism, protect against man-made and natural disasters, and respond to and recover from such incidents.

The third area of Terrorism and Catastrophes appears to be little different from either the first or the second. Bellavita argues here that the Department of Homeland Security often details homeland security as either including both terrorism and natural disasters, and sometimes just terrorism. In this case it is not just a focus on terrorism (as in area one), or on everything, but whatever the Department of Homeland Security sets as a priority, which state, local, and tribal governments tend to follow. Therefore, the focus is on what DHS sets as a priority and the other agencies then follow to prepare for, respond to, and recover from either a terrorist attack or a catastrophe.

The fourth area of focus, according to Bellavita, is Jurisdictional Hazards. In this case, the concept of homeland security is really contingent upon the jurisdiction one is talking about and the specific hazards they may face. Washington, D.C. and New York City both face unique challenges because of their size and importance to the nation; San Diego, and El Paso face different issues in that they are border cities; Houston and Boston face unique challenges as major port cities; while New Orleans and Miami face the threat of hurricanes. In other words, homeland security means different things to different people based upon the environment in which they live, and what is most likely to threaten the safety and security of the local citizens.

The fifth area, Meta Hazards, takes on a much larger focus. Moving beyond terrorism and natural disasters, or even such terror threats as cyber attacks, meta hazards begin to look at threats they may affect any aspect of the American way of life. In this case, things such as the growing federal debt, global warming, or America's dependence on foreign oil, may be cause for future threats to the United States, and thus warrant a broad homeland security response.

The sixth area sounds more confined, National Security, as when government efforts to define homeland security are solely focused on threats to our national security. The goal here is to use the instruments of national power to protect the sovereignty, territory, domestic population, and critical infrastructure of the United States against threats and aggression. In many ways, this area of focus is rooted in the development of our 20th century national security apparatus, and homeland security is the evolution from earlier concepts of civil defense, as discussed elsewhere in this text.

The last area, according to Bellavita, is what he calls Security *Über Alles,* which translates from German as being "security above all." In other words, homeland security is about protecting the United States, no matter what, even if it means curtailing American civil liberties, taking away personal freedoms, and to defer to government to have the best interest of American citizens in mind. This concept of homeland security emphasizes process over outcomes.

In the end, when asking the larger question, "What is homeland security?" Bellavita avoids answering the question, because depending upon the emphasis of the seven areas he details, one would end up with various definitions. Still further, it matters whether one is trying to develop a pragmatic and usable definition, an objective reality definition, or simply a coherent definition, all of which further exacerbates reaching a commonly shared definition of homeland security.

Whither a Definition?

Policymakers are faced with an extremely complex list of potential threats to security, for which they then attempt to plan. However, failure to anticipate and respond to just one of those threats may lead to significant human and financial costs.[39] Homeland security is essentially about managing risks.[40] The purpose of a strategic process is to develop missions to achieve that end. Before risk management can be accurate and effective, policymakers must coordinate and communicate. That work depends to some degree on developing a foundation of common definitions of key terms and concepts in order to ensure stakeholders are aware of, trained for, and prepared to meet assigned missions. At the national level, there does not appear to be an attempt to align definitions and missions among disparate federal entities. DHS is, however, attempting to align its definitions and missions, but does not prioritize its missions. Because of this, funding may drive priorities rather than priorities driving the funding.

DHS is aligning its definitions and missions in the *Quadrennial Homeland Security Review,* the *Bottom-Up Review*, and the 2012 *Strategic Plan*; however, DHS does not prioritize the missions. DHS prioritizes specific goals, objectives, activities, and specific initiatives within the missions, and prioritizes initiatives across the missions. However, there still exists no single national homeland security definition, nor is there a prioritization of national homeland security or DHS missions.

There is no evidence in the existing homeland security strategic documents that supports the alignment and prioritization of the varied missions, nor do any of the documents convey how national, state, or local resources are to be allocated to achieve these missions. Without prioritized resource allocation to align missions, proponents of prioritization of the nation's homeland security activities and operations maintain that plans and responses may be haphazard and inconsistent.

Congress may decide to address the issues associated with **homeland security strategy**, definitions, and missions, in light of the potential for more significant events to occur similar to the 9-11 terrorist attacks and Hurricane Katrina. Many observers assert that these outstanding policy issues result from the varied definitions and missions identified in numerous national strategic documents. Additionally, they note that these documents do not consistently address risk mitigation associated with the full range of homeland security threats. From this perspective, one piece missing from these documents is a discussion of the resources and fiscal costs associated with preparing for low risk, but high-consequence, threats.

Specifically, Congress may choose to consider a number of options to address the apparent lack of a consensus regarding definitions, missions, and priorities by requiring the development of a clearer and more comprehensive national homeland security strategy. One of these options might be a total rewrite of the national homeland security strategy. This option would be similar to the Bush Administration's issuance of national homeland security strategies in 2002 and 2007. Such a strategy could include a definitive listing of mission priorities based on an encompassing definition that not only includes DHS specific responsibilities, but all federal department and agency responsibilities. A strategy that includes priorities could improve Congress's and other policymakers' ability to make choices between competing homeland security missions. This option would also be a departure from the current administration's practice of including national homeland security guidance in the National Security Strategy.

Another option would be to build upon the current approach by requiring the administration to develop the National Security Strategy that succinctly identifies homeland security missions and priorities. Alternatively, Congress may determine that the present course of including national homeland security guidance in the National Security Strategy is adequate, and may focus strictly on DHS activities. This option would entail DHS further refining its *Quadrennial Homeland Security Review* and the 2012 *Strategic Plan*.

It has been argued that homeland security, at its core, is about coordination because of the disparate stakeholders and risks.[41] Many observers assert that homeland security is not only about coordination of resources and actions to counter risks; it is also about the coordination of the strategic process policymakers use in determining the risks, the stakeholders and their missions, and the prioritization of those missions.

Without a general consensus on the physical and philosophical definition and missions of homeland security, achieved through a strategic process, some believe there will continue to be disjointed and disparate approaches to securing the nation. From this perspective, general consensus on the homeland security concept necessarily starts with a consensus definition and an accepted list of prioritized missions that are constantly reevaluated to meet the many risks of the new paradigm that is homeland security in the 21st century.

KEY TERMS
Homeland security strategy—the overarching plan for dealing with all hazards that focuses on shared goals and responsibilities for protecting and defending the homeland.

◾ Chapter Summary

In the aftermath of the September 11, 2001 terrorist attacks, the term "Homeland Security" entered America's lexicon. While the Office of Homeland Security stood up and was later replaced by the Department of Homeland Security, those working in the field, at all levels of government and academia, have attempted to create an acceptable definition of what homeland security encompasses. The desire is to avoid the "all things to all people" problem and to reach a shared, unified definition. However, definitions have greatly varied for a number of reasons. The first set of definitions appear to have developed based on the bureaucratic structure moving from civil defense in the early 20th century to emergency management in the late 20th century. This was then further refined in the wake of 9-11. Another set of definitions is related more directly to how quickly the homeland security response occurred after 9-11 and are rooted in the contemporary post-9-11 responses. Yet another set of definitions draws upon strategic documents, some on the missions and goals of homeland security, while still others emphasize specific areas of focus or attention. In all, while there does not yet appear yet to be a consensus on the definition, there are common themes that appear throughout these varied definitions.

■ Review/Discussion Questions

1. Trace the origins of the term homeland security and articulate how that has affected the bureaucratic perspective in defining this term. Give consideration to the chapter review of civil defense and emergency management.
2. Provide a definition of homeland security based on homeland security concepts. Justify your definition.
3. What is the homeland security enterprise? Does it help define homeland security or does it just muddy the waters?
4. When reviewing the various homeland security strategies, missions, and goals, do these clarify our definition of homeland security?
5. Provide a definition of homeland security based on Bellavita's "areas of emphasis." Justify your definition.

■ Additional Readings

Bellavita, C. (2008). "Changing Homeland Security: What is Homeland Security?" *Homeland Security Affairs, 4.* Retrieved online at http://www.hsaj .org/?fullarticle=4.2.1

Reese, S. (2012). "Defining Homeland Security: Analysis and Congressional Considerations." *Congressional Research Service.* Retrieved online at http:// www.fas.org/sgp/crs/homesec/R42462.pdf

■ Endnotes

1. Kessler, R. (2003). *The CIA at War: Inside the Secret Campaign Against Terror.* New York: St. Martin's Press.
2. *Kasi v. Commonwealth of Virginia* (1998). Record Nos. 980797, 980798, November 06, 1998. Retrieved online at http://caselaw.findlaw.com/ va-supreme-court/1206379.html
3. That police officer was the lead author of this book (Oliver).

4. Kessler, R. (2003). *The CIA at War: Inside the Secret Campaign Against Terror.* New York: St. Martin's Press.

5. The lead author (Oliver) has always wondered if he would have found Kasi in the park. It is unlikely, however, as the description given to officers that morning was wrong and no one had thought to look at the license plate number.

6. *Kasi v. Commonwealth of Virginia* (1998). Record Nos. 980797, 980798, November 06, 1998. Retrieved online at http://caselaw.findlaw.com/va-supreme-court/1206379.html

7. Lengel, A. (2006). "Celebrated FBI Agent Will Retire Haunted By Those Who Got Away." *The Washington Post.* Retrieved online at http://www.washingtonpost.com/wp-dyn/content/article/2006/08/27/AR2006082700923.html

8. *Kasi v. Commonwealth of Virginia* (1998). Record Nos. 980797, 980798, November 06, 1998. Retrieved online at http://caselaw.findlaw.com/va-supreme-court/1206379.html

9. CNN Justice. (2002). "Pakistani Man Executed for CIA Killings." *CNN.* Retrieved online at http://articles.cnn.com/2002-11-14/justice/cia.killings.execution_1_cia-employees-mir-aimal-kasi-cia-killings?_s=PM:LAW

10. *Kasi v. Commonwealth of Virginia* (1998). Record Nos. 980797, 980798, November 06, 1998. Retrieved online at http://caselaw.findlaw.com/va-supreme-court/1206379.html

11. Bellavita, C. (2008). "Changing Homeland Security: What is Homeland Security?" *Homeland Security Affairs, 4.* Retrieved online at http://www.hsaj.org/?fullarticle=4.2.1

12. Logan, K.G. & Ramsay, J.D. (2012). *Introduction to Homeland Security.* Boulder, CO: Westview Press, pp. 24–25.

13. Reese, S. (2012). "Defining Homeland Security: Analysis and Congressional Considerations." *Congressional Research Service.* Retrieved online at http://www.fas.org/sgp/crs/homesec/R42462.pdf

14. Hogue, H.B. & Bea, K. (2006). "Federal Emergency Management and Homeland Security Organization: Historical Developments and Legislative Options." *Congressional Research Service.* Retrieved online at http://www.fas.org/sgp/crs/homesec/RL33369.pdf

15. The 9/11 Commission presents this evolution of how counterterrorism has evolved through the adaptation (and nonadaptation) of the law enforcement community, the Federal Aviation Administration, the intelligence community, the State Department, Department of Defense, the White House, and Congress. See: National Commission on Terrorist Attacks Upon the United States. (2004). *The 9/11 Commission Report: Final Report of the National Commission on Terrorist Attacks Upon the United States (Authorized Ed.).* New York: W.W. Norton & Company, Inc.

16. The majority of PDD 62 is a classified document, but elements of it are found through a White House Fact Sheet, dated May 22, 1998, titled "Combatting Terrorism: Presidential Decision Directive 62." Retrieved online at http://www.fas.org/irp/offdocs/pdd-62.htm

17. Advisory Panel to Assess Domestic Response Capabilities for Terrorism Involving Weapons of Mass Destruction. (1999). *Assessing the Threat.* Retrieved online at http://www.rand.org/content/dam/rand/www/external/nsrd/terrpanel/terror.pdf

18. The United States Commission on National Security/21st Century. (2001). *Road Map for National Security: Imperative for Change.* Retrieved online at http://govinfo.library.unt.edu/nssg/PhaseIIIFR.pdf

19. See H.R. 1158 (107th): National Homeland Security Agency Act. Retrieved online at http://www.govtrack.us/congress/bills/107/hr1158

20. This section is based on Reese, Shawn. (2012). "Defining Homeland Security: Analysis and Congressional Considerations." *Congressional Research Service.* Retrieved online at http://www.fas.org/sgp/crs/homesec/R42462.pdf

21. Office of the President, Homeland Security Council. (2007). *The National Homeland Security Strategy.* Washington, DC: White House; Office of the President. (2011). *National Strategy for Counterterrorism.* Washington, DC: White House.

22. U.S. Department of Homeland Security. (2010). *Bottom-Up Review.* Washington, DC: U.S. Department of Homeland Security, p. 3.

23. U.S. Department of Homeland Security. (2012). *Department of Homeland Security Strategic Plan: Fiscal Years 2012–2016.* Washington, DC: U.S. Department of Homeland Security, p. 2.

24. Reese, S. (2012). "Defining Homeland Security: Analysis and Congressional Considerations." *Congressional Research Service.* Retrieved online at http://www.fas.org/sgp/crs/homesec/R42462.pdf

25. Reese, S. (2012). "Defining Homeland Security: Analysis and Congressional Considerations." *Congressional Research Service.* Retrieved online at http://www.fas.org/sgp/crs/homesec/R42462.pdf

26. Bellavita, C. (2011). "A New Perspective on Homeland Security?" *Homeland Security Watch.* Retrieved online at http://www.hlswatch.com/2011/12/20/a-new-perspective-on-homeland-security/

27. Reese, S. (2012). "Defining Homeland Security: Analysis and Congressional Considerations." *Congressional Research Service.* Retrieved online at http://www.fas.org/sgp/crs/homesec/R42462.pdf

28. Reese, S. (2012). "Defining Homeland Security: Analysis and Congressional Considerations." *Congressional Research Service.* Retrieved online at http://www.fas.org/sgp/crs/homesec/R42462.pdf

29. Reese, S. (2012). "Defining Homeland Security: Analysis and Congressional Considerations." *Congressional Research Service.* Retrieved online at http://www.fas.org/sgp/crs/homesec/R42462.pdf

30. U.S. Congress, Senate Committee on Homeland Security and Governmental Affairs. (2011). *Charting a Path Forward: The Homeland Security Department's Quadrennial Review and Bottom-Up Review.* 111th Cong., 2nd sess., July 21, 2010.

31. U.S. Department of Defense. (2010). *Quadrennial Defense Review.* Washington, DC: U.S. Department of Defense, p. iii.

32. Petes, K.M. (2010). "DHS Bottom-Up Review is Long on Ambition, Short on Detail." *Government Executive.* Retrieved online at http://www.govexec.com/defense/2010/07/dhs-bottom-up-review-is-long-on-ambition-short-on-detail/31939/

33. U.S. Congress, House Committee on Homeland Security, Subcommittee on Oversight, Investigations, and Management. (2011). *Is DHS Effectively Implementing a Strategy to Counter Emerging Threats?* 112th Cong., 2nd sess., February 3, 2011.

34. Biddle, S., Garrett, L., & Lindsay, J.M., et al. (2010). "Obama's NSS: Promise and Pitfalls." Council on Foreign Relations. Retrieved from http://www.cfr.org/defensehomeland-security/obamas-nss-promise-pitfalls/p22240

35. Reese, S. (2012). "Defining Homeland Security: Analysis and Congressional Considerations." *Congressional Research Service.* Retrieved online at http://www.fas.org/sgp/crs/homesec/R42462.pdf

36. Bellavita, C. (2008). "Changing Homeland Security: What is Homeland Security?" *Homeland Security Affairs, 4,* 1-30. Retrieved online at http://www.hsaj.org/?fullarticle=4.2.1

37. Bellavita, C. (2008). "Changing Homeland Security: What is Homeland Security?" *Homeland Security Affairs, 4,* 1-30. Retrieved online at http://www.hsaj.org/?fullarticle=4.2.1

38. This section is based on the article: Bellavita, C. (2008). "Changing Homeland Security: What is Homeland Security?" *Homeland Security Affairs, 4,* 1–30. Retrieved online at http://www.hsaj.org/?fullarticle=4.2.1

39. Kettl, D.F. (2007). *System Under Stress: Homeland Security and American Politics.* 2nd Ed. Washington, DC: CQ Press.

40. Reese, S. (2012). "Defining Homeland Security: Analysis and Congressional Considerations." *Congressional Research Service.* Retrieved online at http://www.fas.org/sgp/crs/homesec/R42462.pdf

41. Kettl, D.F. (2007). *System Under Stress: Homeland Security and American Politics.* 2nd Ed. Washington, DC: CQ Press.

Modern Terrorism and Natural Disasters

Chapter Objectives

- To understand the definitional issues surrounding the study of terrorism and why they are relevant

- To understand the components of terrorism and what differentiates it from regular crime

- To understand the relationship between terrorism and natural disasters as they relate to homeland security

Chapter Outline

■ Introduction

The bombs detonated almost simultaneously at 10:36 AM. The first, in Nairobi, Kenya, was hidden in a truck driven towards the United States embassy, probably with the intent to park it in the underground garage beneath the embassy.[1] The second, in Dar es Saalam, Tanzania, was hidden in a similar manner to the first.[2] The first bomb, the driver of which managed to get it closer to the building, ripped through the building, killing 212 people and wounding around 4,000. The second bomb, which was stopped at the security perimeter, killed 10 people and injured 77. Of the total number of people killed, only 11 were Americans, despite the extensive damage to both embassies and the destruction of a nearby facility in Nairobi.[3] The bombs were large enough to register as small earthquakes, and the bomb in Nairobi shattered windows as far as 1 km away from the actual blast.[4]

The American response to the attacks was swift, with the U.S. engaging in Operation Infinite Reach, sending cruise missiles into Sudan and Afghanistan to attack those responsible for the bombings.[5] The FBI quickly identified several of the perpetrators and one of them made the Ten Most Wanted list.[6] Terrorist organizations such as Egyptian Islamic Jihad and Al Qaeda were linked to the attack, and discussions among the terrorists took place in countries as far away as Azerbaijan.[7]

While this sounds like an attack that happened recently, this attack was on August 7, 1998, approximately 15 years ago. For the first time, it introduced the figures of Osama bin Laden and Ayman al-Zawahiri to the American people, who would have such a profound impact on the American psyche 3 years later on September 11, 2001.[8] Already, the "new" nature of **terrorism** was seen—a loosely networked affiliation of individuals, hard to track, with a presence in countries around the world. The increasing emphasis on the number of casualties too can be seen in hindsight.[9]

Why, then, was the U.S. unprepared for the attack 3 years later, which would thrust terrorism onto the American public as the most important problem facing our country? Why, despite our response to the attacks in Africa, were the terrorists undeterred from attacking the U.S. homeland?

KEY TERM
Terrorism—the use of violence and intimidation in the pursuit of political aims.

The answers to these questions are unclear, and much of any plausible answer depends on the position of the person trying to answer it. This chapter is one attempt to understand the reasons. It approaches the topic of terrorism holistically, by examining what terrorism is and how we can distinguish it from regular crime, looking at terrorism in a historical context and identifying potential reasons that individuals engage in terrorist behavior. Additionally, it examines the reason that terrorism can be effective, particularly the psychological impact it can have, and, in that light, also examines the role of natural disasters on the American public.

It is no surprise that there was a general perception that government needed to be changed after the events of September 11, 2001. The aftermath of the 9-11 attacks was the worst man-made disaster on U.S. soil since the bombing of Pearl Harbor, over 50 years earlier. The subsequent development of the Department

© Justin Guariglia/age fotostock.

of Homeland Security represented the largest change in government structure since the development of the Department of Defense.[10] However, just 4 years after the worst terrorist attack in United States history, Hurricane Katrina demonstrated that even a major overhaul in the nation's security apparatus was insufficient to deal with all hazards. In addition to the human cost, these two events combined caused over $3.4 trillion dollars in economic damage,[11] displaced 400,000 people,[12] and had profound effects on the national psyche.[13] Even so, the U.S. remains predominately focused on the security threat that terrorism represents and expends a great deal of money to avoid another 9-11-like event. This chapter covers the hazards of terrorism and natural disasters with a particular focus on the development and causes of terrorism.

Brief History of Terrorism

Terrorism is by no means a new phenomenon. Scholars have identified attacks that can be classified as terrorism from as far back as 32 A.D.[14] While today we tend to think of terrorism in religious terms, largely as a result of the amount of emphasis placed on the terrorist organization Al Qaeda after the 9-11 attacks, this has not always been the case.[15] Terrorists have a variety of motivations, ranging from religious beliefs to socio-political objectives to single issues such as animal rights or abortion. Partly because of this wide range of motivations, terrorism has been very hard to define and there remains no agreed-upon definition that spans even the agencies within the U.S. government.[16]

Acts that could be called terrorism have been going on since at least the first century. Religious groups such as the Zealots used close-range attacks to deliver bloody political messages to the Romans and Jewish sympathizers, and by the 17th century, groups were regularly utilizing bombings to deliver their messages. The development of terrorism can be broken up, broadly, into five periods, each distinguished by the predominant motivating factor for terrorism present during the respective eras. Each of these periods has important distinctions that have added elements to what we call terrorism today. Importantly, when examining the different eras of terrorism, the time periods are not mutually exclusive; they frequently overlap. In fact, as seen in the following example, sometimes individual groups can span several different eras of terrorism.

While modern religious terrorism brings to mind planes flying into buildings, religious terrorism is not new.[17] In fact, in terms of what we would consider terrorism today, religious terrorism is the oldest type, ranging back to at least the first century A.D.[18] Ancient religious sects such as the Zealots, a 3rd century Jewish group, used public acts of violence, including some of the first recorded acts of chemical warfare, to send a message to their enemies. Other groups also used this type of violence to intimidate rivals, as in the case of the Assassins (a Shi'a Muslim sect) and even used religiously motivated killings as the basis for entire subcultures, such as the Thugee, a Hindu religious group dedicated to the Goddess Kali.[19]

As with modern religious terrorism, the primary distinction of ancient religious terrorism is the motivating factor behind the attacks. These groups provide, in many ways, excellent models of comparison for modern religious terrorist organizations, discussed elsewhere.

BOX 3.1   "Regime de la Terreur"

© HultonArchive/iStockphoto.

Perhaps most important in terms of the development of what we consider modern terrorism is the period during the French Revolution known as the "Reign of Terror." This period of history was marked by citizen tribunals dedicated to the eradication of what was left of the aristocracy in France after the revolution.[20] These tribunals would receive secret testimony about individuals in the population who were supposedly a part of the aristocracy or supporting it. The goal, which was considered positive at first, was to create a spectacle out of the execution of those individuals found guilty in order to influence others to not support the monarchy or become counter-revolutionary.[21] This was also known as la terreur,

and those who carried it out were terrorists. It is estimated that 40,000 people were killed during the Reign of Terror.[22] Eventually, the leader of the revolution, Robespierre, was accused and executed in the same way that he oversaw so many others, by guillotine.[23] As mentioned earlier, though it was originally considered a positive term, "terrorist" eventually came to mean an excess of violence and abuse of power. Over time, it developed into the term "terrorism" that we have today.[24]

The Reign of Terror is important insofar as it added the word "terrorism" to modern language usage. Additionally, it reinforced the political nature of terrorism, something now recognized as essential to our understanding of the concept.[25] Further, because of the excesses of the revolution, the word terrorism gained a negative connotation, an aspect that remains with the word today. This negative view is partially what makes terrorism so difficult to define, as no groups wish to be labeled as a terrorist group and actively seek to change how their image is defined.[26]

In addition, like groups in other eras of terrorism, the Regime de la Terreur was successful, if only for a time. Robespierre and his compatriots were in charge of France, and despite their later ousting, it proved that terrorism could be an effective means of control. This lesson was well learned by later dictators such as Hitler, Mussolini, and Stalin, who while not considered terrorists in the sense we mean it today, certainly used terror to control their populations' behavior.[27]

The era of "state terrorism" is fundamentally different from the previous era and the eras that came after it, because those who committed the terrorist acts during this era were nation-states (a country, or state, that has a unified culture and belief system). Beginning during the Reign of Terror (see **Box 3.1**) during the French Revolution and continuing off-and-on throughout World War II, the era of state terrorism was characterized by high levels of violence carried out by states to control their own populations. Hitler, Mussolini, Stalin, and other dictators of that era are prime examples of those who engaged in this type of terrorism.[28] While modern terrorism is usually thought to be carried out by subnational actors, state terrorism is carried out by the political entities in control of the country. This, through separating state terrorism from what we generally would consider terrorism today, is important as it demonstrates the ineluctable political nature of terrorism.[29]

Early Political Terrorism

Early political terrorism was accompanied by the increasing use of propaganda in conjunction with the rise of the anarchist political view.[30] The groups that utilized violence to achieve their goals also frequently used the printed word to more specifically communicate goals and effect change. However, much of the violence was unorganized, given the nature of the anarchist world view. This is not to say violence during this period was without effect. Incidents like the 1886 Haymarket bombing in Chicago by anarchists and perhaps most importantly, the assassination of Archduke Franz Ferdinand (one of the precipitating factors of World War I) by Serbian nationalists, did have lasting societal impact.[31] Subsequent to the anarchist and nationalist attacks was increasing violence supported by the Soviet Union. Specifically, left-wing political organizations like the Red Army Faction and the Baader-Meinhoff Group who, during the 1960s, utilized violence for political ends, were often given money and arms by the Soviets.[32] Additionally, it is during this period that we first begin to see cooperation between organizations, notably the Baader-Meinhoff Group and the Palestinian Liberation Organization, a precursor to modern religious terrorist organizations. Trading arms for training, the groups established an important bridge, despite the fact that their goals were quite different.[33] This "networked" nature of terrorism has become a hallmark in the modern age of terrorist attacks.[34]

Two major events preceded the re-emergence of religious terrorism in the late 20th century: the Iranian Revolution of 1979 and the collapse of the Soviet Union in 1991. Combined, these two factors led to both a weakening of the structural system in these countries, keeping religious groups from gaining prominence, and it gave individuals an alternative system to motivate their actions.[35] More specifically, before the Cold War ended, religious groups found themselves under-supported, with most effort going towards political organizations at the direction of either Soviet or Western powers. With the loss of financial and political support beginning in the mid 1980s, and the total collapse of support in the 1990s, religious groups were free to take up the mantle of political change that had been dominated by the political groups.[36] Additionally, individuals who were relying on the promise of communism to provide them with better living circumstances had wearied of promises unkept, so with the rise of the alternative Iranian model, individuals were poised to support groups who adopted a similar **strategy**. Further, Iran had an explicit goal to export the revolution to other countries, specifically in the Middle East, but also worldwide.

Like ancient religious terrorism, many of the groups engaging in terrorism today have multiple goals, but retain their religious motivation.[37] Unfortunately, with the increase in technology, their ability to kill those whom they feel are their enemies has grown, and so has their willingness to do so. Scholars like Bruce Hoffman[38] have argued that because terrorists have no earthly constituency—in other words, no one to please here on earth, because their primary allegiance is to God alone—there is very little to stop them from utilizing even weapons of mass destruction against their enemies. Combined with the idea that anyone opposing their viewpoint is an enemy of God, it provides modern religious terrorist organizations with powerful incentives to commit devastating acts of terrorism.[39]

KEY TERM
Strategy—a plan of action or policy designed to achieve a major overall goal.

■ Modern International Terrorism

KEY TERM

International terrorism—the use of violence and intimidation in the pursuit of political aims committed by those from outside of one's own state/country.

KEY TERM

Domestic terrorism—the use of violence and intimidation in the pursuit of political aims committed by those from within one's own state/country.

Modern international terrorism is less defined by its motivation or tactics, as in previous eras of terrorism, as it is by the nature of modernity. The first attack generally considered modern international terrorism took place in 1968, an important year technologically speaking, as the first news satellite was launched. This first modern terrorist act, a hijacking by a PLO-related group, was modern because it made use of both wide media coverage, as well as a potent symbol of Israel, as the plane hijacked belonged to El-Al, Israel's national airline. Perhaps more importantly, it was the first hijacking where the specific purpose was to force negotiation with the terrorists, who had previously been ignored by Israel.[40] This combination of elements has come, in large part, to define what terrorism means in the modern era (see **Box 3.2**). Attacks are designed to be widely broadcast, affecting a large audience, and frequently are designed to be deadly. Modern terrorism has redefined the

---

BOX 3.2   Typologies of Terrorism

Typologies of terrorism, or ways to categorize attacks, are important to the study of terrorism as a phenomenon and specifically to homeland security. Because terrorism is an incredibly wide-ranging phenomenon, with motivations by terrorists being as diverse as saving animals to bringing about Armageddon, it is important to understand the "rationale" for a terrorist attack in order to be able to stop it and attacks like it in the future. It is important to understand that while groups usually fall primarily into one type of terrorism or another, groups can frequently be classified as more than one type (e.g., right-wing nationalist). Additionally, as is the case with most issues regarding terrorism, there is no agreed-upon typology for terrorist groups. The sections following detail frequently used 'types' of groups in the terrorism literature.

Domestic/International

Perhaps the most widely used typology within the context of government counter-terrorism operations is the distinction between domestic and international terrorists and terrorist groups.[41] While the difference is simple, with **international terrorism** originating from outside the borders of the country in which the attack takes place and **domestic terrorism** originating from within the country where the attack happens, it is important because of the division of labor within the United States government. Organizations like the FBI are almost exclusively focused on domestic terrorism because of their limited overseas reach (though this has changed somewhat since 9-11) and organizations like the Central

Intelligence Agency (CIA) are focused almost exclusively on international terrorism.[42]

Even with a generally simple distinction, however, the difference between a domestic and international terrorist attack is not always easy to determine. If an attack is carried out by citizens from within the country, but directed from outside the country, a decision has to be made on who has primary jurisdiction, and designation of the attack as domestic or international becomes difficult and sometimes controversial. Especially large attacks, such as 9-11, frequently have elements of both domestic and international terrorism involved, making investigations complex. Nevertheless, the distinction between the two remains important both for those responsible for responding to terrorism as well as those who study it.

Left-wing/Right-wing

One of the most frequently utilized typologies in the literature on terrorism is based on the historical political difference in the United States. Left-wing terrorist groups focus on the destruction of the state, with the usual justification that the state is not representative of the people and needs to be replaced with a socialist, anarchist, or communist government (or lack of government in the case of anarchists). Right-wing groups tend to be more authoritarian in nature and frequently operate in support of the government, or even argue for additional government control—particularly of groups that they believe threaten the state. The FBI still regularly uses this terminology (i.e., left-wing and right-wing) to describe terrorist organizations.[43]

Though this typology has been used frequently, especially in the context of domestic terrorism, there are limits to its relevance. While the left/right distinction is useful in the context of the United States and in some places in Western Europe, there are many places where this dichotomy does not hold. Further, even in the U.S., there are good reasons to believe that the distinction is more historically relevant than currently so. While there is no doubt that a political divide still exists within the U.S. that falls along these ideological lines, there is less terrorism that corresponds to these lines directly. In fact, more domestic terrorism appears to be stemming from a religious or nativist orientation, similar to the rest of the world during this era of modern international terrorism.

Nationalist

Nationalist terrorism is focused on the national aspirations of a group of people, usually defined along ethnic boundaries. Historically, groups such as the Palestinian Liberation Organization (PLO) and the Irish Republican Army (IRA) can be considered nationalist in orientation.[44] Even in the United States there have been nationalist groups, particularly those organizations dedicated to the independence of Puerto Rico and groups who refuse to recognize the legitimacy of the current government. Internationally, these groups are more prominent and have had more success. National independence movements, such as the Algerian movement for independence, have even met with reasonable success in the international arena.

Single-issue

Single-issue terrorist organizations are those organizations without a broad ideological or political agenda, but rather those who focus on a specific issue of interest to members of those groups. Anti-abortion groups who bomb clinics, while having perhaps a religious background, are only engaging in terrorism against those who they believe are responsible for abortions. Similarly, animal rights and environmental terrorists engage selectively against those who they believe harm animals or the environment. Groups like the Animal Liberation Front (ALF), Earth Liberation Front (ELF) and the Army of God (AOG) only engage those whom they believe to be in violation of their moral standards on a single issue.[45]

Like other forms of terrorism, single-issue terrorism is frequently found in association with other ideological underpinnings. As mentioned earlier, groups who bomb abortion clinics frequently have a religious motivation, and those who attack animal labs sometimes have political motivation beyond saving animals. Nevertheless, the groups that engage in this type of terrorism largely focus their violence on the individuals they feel are responsible for their specific issue of choice.

Religious

Terrorist organizations that have religion as their motivation are some of the most dangerous. This is because, unlike nationalist groups for instance, they usually do not cater to a constituency. Instead, these groups and individuals feel that their primary duty is to God, and frequently this means they are willing to go to greater lengths in terms of the amount of destruction and death they are willing to cause. This is primarily because, while groups with a constituency must have support to achieve their goals, the religious group's goals are frequently transcendental in nature and will only be achieved through the group's actions. Additionally, those who do not support the groups are frequently considered apostates or enemies of God, and are therefore subject to the same treatment as those whom the group opposes.[46]

As mentioned earlier, religious groups are perhaps the primary type of organization now engaging in terrorism worldwide. This perhaps accounts for the increase in the number of deaths seen post 9-11, though attacks on military and police forces in Iraq and Afghanistan have no doubt inflated that number. Even so, moving forward, it is likely that religious terrorism will remain the most frequently encountered type of terrorism and will also remain one of the most difficult to defeat.

Summary

Typologies of terrorism allow us to separate one type of group from another. This is essential for both operations against terrorists as well as research regarding terrorists and their organizations. While many of the "types" of terrorism are not mutually exclusive, distinguishing between types allows for comparison between organizations and assists with a variety of practical tasks necessary for combating terrorists. While the preceding is only a small sample of the potential types of terrorism, understanding the most frequently used types is essential to understanding both the literature on terrorism and the groups that carry it out.

relationship between the media and terrorism as well. Coverage of major terrorist events comes in real-time, with the goals of the groups taking responsibility communicated along with the carnage they create. Perhaps the best example of this type of terrorism is September 11, 2001, discussed more elsewhere.

The history of terrorism has much to teach about what we recognize as terrorism today. Throughout each era, groups with different motivations and capabilities used violent tactics to communicate a message to a target audience. While several of the eras overlap, it is important to note the progression of terrorism from a politically/religiously motivated activity through the time where it was used as a method of control by states, to the modern era of terrorism, which in many ways resembles the earliest days of terrorism.

Terrorism, for instance, stands in contrast to criminal acts such as robbery and murder, the sole purpose of which is contained within the act itself. As will be seen in the following section, the elements differentiating terrorism from regular crime are important to understand, as without them it would be difficult to combat the phenomenon. However, the definition of terrorism has also proven perhaps the most difficult part of both studying and understanding terrorism.[47]

■ Political and Social Foundations

The political and social foundations for terrorism are complex. There is no clear agreement on the definition of terrorism, while the concept of "crime" is more generally agreed upon.[48] In the sections following, definitional issues of terrorism are explored along with some of the psychological and sociological explanations for terrorism. The response to terrorism in a homeland security context is at least partially dependent on the way the concept (of terrorism) is defined, and what is believed to cause it.

Terrorism: The Term

Definitions of terrorism have varied widely among scholars and practitioners.[49] Definitions have been suggested from the very basic, such as, "you know it when you see it," to complex definitions put together by committees that are essentially impractical.[50] Even various agencies within the U.S. government have definitions of terrorism that scarcely resemble one another. For instance, compare the definition used by the FBI and the one used by the U.S. Department of State. The FBI's definition:

> The unlawful use of force or violence against persons or property to intimidate or coerce a government, the civilian population, or any segment thereof in furtherance of political or social objectives.[51]

Important elements in this definition include the use of force, the fact that it can be against persons or property, and that the goal is to coerce a government or civilian population for social or political reasons. Compare this to the Department of State's definition of terrorism: "premeditated, politically motivated violence perpetrated against noncombatant targets by sub-national groups or clandestine agents."[52]

In the Department of State's definition we see different areas of emphasis with some commonalities to the FBI definition. Specifically, the requirement of premeditation, the sub-national status of the attackers, and the noncombatant nature of the targets represent important differences between these two definitions; the use of violence and the political nature of the attacks represent common areas. This same overlap and difference is also found in the Department of Defense (DOD) as well as the National Counter-Terrorism Center (NCTC) definitions.

Significantly, the definition utilized by the Department of Homeland Security (DHS) (18 USC § 2331—Definitions) for terrorism is quite broad, encompassing both domestic and international terrorism as well as defining who can be a terrorist and what acts might constitute an act of terrorism. Of particular interest is the acts defined as terrorism do not necessarily need to be violent; they need only be considered dangerous to human life while containing the other elements listed in the definition. **Box 3.3** offers a comprehensive discussion of the DHS definition of terrorism.

BOX 3.3   DHS Definition of Terrorism

Definitions of terrorism are frequently complicated as they have to take into account the requirements of both the agency (or agencies) coping with it as well as the multifaceted aspects of the phenomenon itself. The Department of Homeland Security's definition is a good example of this and can serve as a paradigm for examining other government definitions.

DHS Definition

1. the term "international terrorism" means activities that:
   A. involve violent acts or acts dangerous to human life that are a violation of the criminal laws of the United States or of any State, or that would be a criminal violation if committed within the jurisdiction of the United States or of any State;
   B. appear to be intended:
      i.   to intimidate or coerce a civilian population;
      ii. to influence the policy of a government by intimidation or coercion; or
      iii. to affect the conduct of a government by mass destruction, assassination, or kidnapping; and
   C. occur primarily outside the territorial jurisdiction of the United States, or transcend national boundaries in terms of the means by which they are accomplished, the persons they appear intended to intimidate or coerce, or the locale in which their perpetrators operate or seek asylum;
2. the term "national of the United States" has the meaning given such term in section 101(a)(22) of the Immigration and Nationality Act;
3. the term "person" means any individual or entity capable of holding a legal or beneficial interest in property;

4. the term "act of war" means any act occurring in the course of:
   A. declared war;
   B. armed conflict, whether or not war has been declared, between two or more nations; or
   C. armed conflict between military forces of any origin; and
5. the term "domestic terrorism" means activities that:
   A. involve acts dangerous to human life that are a violation of the criminal laws of the United States or of any State;
   B. appear to be intended:
      i.   to intimidate or coerce a civilian population;
      ii. to influence the policy of a government by intimidation or coercion; or
      iii. to affect the conduct of a government by mass destruction, assassination, or kidnapping; and
   C. occur primarily within the territorial jurisdiction of the United States.[53]

Summary

The DHS definition of terrorism is from the U.S. Code and encompasses a variety of elements that the other definitions presented in this text do not. Most interestingly, it provides not only definitions for domestic and international terrorism, but also include elements describing who is to be considered a terrorist. In some ways, despite its length, it is a very broad definition of terrorism as it does not specify who the targets necessarily are (can be government or civilian) and does not include violence as a necessary element; only actions that are dangerous to human life. When examining other definitions of terrorism, it is instructive to consider what elements they have in common with this definition and what elements are different.

Finally, aside from the general definitions of terrorism, there are also specific acts that further muddy the waters. For instance, the Animal Enterprise Terrorism Act (AEPA) of 2006 (18 USC § 43—Force, Violence, And Threats Involving Animal Enterprises) states that interfering with or damaging the property of an "animal enterprise" (including testing facilities, circuses, etc.) can be constituted as an act of terrorism. This is fundamentally different from other definitions of terrorism as it is specific to one type of terrorism and bases the criminality of the act on the identity of the victim, not the motivation of the attackers.

These differences of definition is by no means limited to government agencies, however. Academics studying the phenomenon of terrorism have also been unable to reach consensus on what definitively constitutes an act of terrorism. In fact, Alex P. Schmid[54] attempted to reconcile the 100-plus definitions found in the academic literature into a single, comprehensive definition and found it was impossible. Others have referred to the definitional issue in terrorism as the "black hole of terrorism studies."[55]

A further complication is the fact that some terrorists themselves seek to redefine what they are called. In general, even perpetrators of terrorist acts do not want to be defined as "terrorists." Instead they would rather be labeled "freedom fighters" or "insurgents." In fact, many terrorist organizations actively argue their cases in the media that they are not terrorists, in some instances even arguing that a government constitutes the "real" terrorists (see for example, Osama bin Laden's claim of responsibility for 9-11). This debate is not idle talk; how we define terrorism is important on several levels. A clear definition makes prosecution much easier, and it also allows academics to study phenomenon more efficiently so that the problem can be better understood and addressed.[56] Without a comprehensive, cohesive definition of terrorism, this is made much more difficult.

What Is Terrorism?

Despite the differences in definitions, of which there are many, there are some common themes that arise regularly. In fact, there seem to be five generally agreed-upon attributes to attacks that are termed terrorist.[57] These are by no means universally acknowledged. However, these elements are present within most definitions of terrorism:

- Political (social or religious) motivation
- Violence or the credible threat of violence
- Sub-national actors
- Instrumental in nature
- Victim/target separation

These five elements are usually straightforward and can be used to determine whether an event is a terrorist attack or a different form of crime. The first element, the political nature of the act, is the most important. It is the element that most clearly distinguishes an act of terrorism from the merely criminal. Second, any act of terrorism has to be violent, or at least credibly threaten violence. In this case, violence is construed broadly to include destruction of property, as in the FBI definition earlier, as well as in specific designation, such as the AEPA. Third, acts of terrorism are carried out by sub-national actors. If the actors conducting an attack were part of a recognized nation-state, it would be an act of war, not an act of terrorism. The last two elements of terrorism—the instrumental nature of an attack and the separation of the victim and target—are closely linked. Any act of terrorism must be instrumental insofar as the goal of the attack is not the violence itself, but rather to motivate change. This is closely linked to the final element, which is victim/target separation. Specifically, while terrorists kill victims, the victims represent a means to an end: the influence on the actual target. More concretely, terrorists kill individuals (their victims) to influence their target (whomever they wish to influence). This is distinct from murder where the victim and target are the same.

In short, terrorism is a complex phenomenon encompassing a wide variety of acts and actors. An agreed-upon and comprehensive definition has been hard to come by, even within the federal government. Individuals who conduct terrorist attacks actively seek to change who the public perceives as "terrorists" and frequently are referred to in terms other than "terrorist" by the media, who wish to appear unbiased. However, despite these differences, there are five basic elements that make up what most people generally consider terrorism: political motivation, violence, sub-national actors, instrumental in nature, and victim/target separation.

Political and Social Theories of Terrorism

Just as there are ongoing disagreements about the definition of terrorism, there are strong differences among academics and others as to what causes terrorism. Those engaging in this argument have generally fallen into two camps, though the arguments each camp is making are not necessarily mutually exclusive.[58] The first group argues along the lines of traditional criminological/sociological/psychological theory, suggesting certain psychological and/or sociological factors cause individuals to become terrorists. The second focuses on the rationality of terrorism as a choice among many for furthering a political or religious objective.

Individual and Group-Level Theories

There have been a great number of theories posited for why individuals engage in terrorism. Many of these have a basis in psychological or sociological explanations of behavior. Ted Robert Gurr,[59] for example, examines the idea of relative deprivation, or the view of a particular group feeling underserved or undervalued in comparison to other groups. Other scholars have looked directly at poverty, type of government, and even childhood trauma as reasons people join terrorist organizations. One of the most frequently attempted efforts in terrorism studies is, in fact, the development of a psychological "profile" of a terrorist. All such attempts at this have failed, thus far. In fact, the majority of psychological studies done on known terrorists (usually those who have been captured and imprisoned) suggest that terrorists do not differ in noticeable psychological ways from the general population.[60]

This fact, that terrorists are essentially the same as everyone else, is difficult for people in the general population to accept. It is much easier and comforting to think of terrorists as "loony" or "crazy." While there has been no success at developing a psychological profile of terrorists, there has been some interesting work done regarding the psychology of terrorism itself. John Horgan,[61] particularly, has focused his work on psychological factors that lead to the individual ability to carry out acts of terrorism. Additionally, scholars such as Drake[62] have focused attention on those elements of terrorist attacks that are influenced by not only the psychology of the perpetrator, but the psychology of the victims as well, in order to understand how they are related. For instance, analyzing how the 2013 Boston Marathon bombers selected their target may focus on not only the psychology of the two brothers (Dzhokhar and Tamerlan Tsarnaev), as well as the behavior of the marathon runners and spectators (individuals focused on running or watching the runners, not security).

Psychology is, of course, not the only social science that has been applied to the understanding of terrorism. Sociology and political science have also affected our understanding, particularly through an emphasis on power dynamics within groups and between groups and countries, as well as examining new techniques, like social network analysis, that allow for the disruption of terrorist cells around the world. The bulk of the research in these fields, however, has been at the country level of analysis, examining the factors that make a country more or less likely to be the victim of terrorism, or to produce terrorists. An exception to this is the work done in political economy, which has focused on terrorist decision-making. Work by scholars such as Enders and Sandler[63] have revolutionized the way that terrorism as a phenomenon is examined, and others, like Bueno de Mesquita,[64] have helped us understand why some terrorist organizations are more deadly than others.

The implications for deterministic research such as that found in the fields of psychology, political science, and criminology has led to important developments in our understanding of terrorism.[65] Our understanding of terrorist targeting, psychological motivation, socio-economic background factors, and power dynamics allows for ever-increasing effectiveness in the fight against terrorist organizations, both in the United States and abroad. However, many of these factors, obviously, are difficult to change externally. The U.S. has little ability to alter socio-economic factors or individual psychology, for instance. There is, however, a research perspective that suggests the ability to affect terrorist behavior and (perhaps) even the decision to become a terrorist in the first place.

■ Terrorism as Strategic Choice

While psychology and the other social sciences look at factors that determine whether or not someone is likely to become a terrorist, there is another area that examines terrorism and terrorists from a different perspective.[66] It assumes that, rather than background factors causing someone to become a terrorist, individuals make a conscious choice to engage in terrorism. It assumes that individuals who are interested in political (or social or religious) change can choose to go about creating the change in a variety of ways. One of those choices, among many, is to engage in terrorism.[67]

This is a novel approach as it has some implications that differ if background factors are assumed to be causal. For instance, if individuals are compelled to become terrorists, say by some individual-level psychological factor, then it makes little sense to negotiate with said terrorist. If, on the other hand, the terrorist is making a conscious choice to engage in terrorism, instead of running for office for instance, then perhaps it is possible to change the terrorist's mind by engaging in cooperative negotiation.

The implications for adopting this strategic model of terrorism are broad. The ability to convince terrorists to change their behavior through negotiation or some other means would clearly alter our view of the problem of terrorism. If terrorists are rational decision-makers interested in achieving specific goals, providing alternative methods of achieving these goals may deter them from their original plans. Additionally, actions like "target-hardening" (the strengthening of the security of a building or location in order to protect it from future attack) may change the terrorists' decision calculus and deter them from attacking specific targets. Further, by opening opportunities for political participation, it may be possible to give terrorists other means by which to achieve their goals, making their violent intentions unnecessary.

While the goals of terrorists usually are made clear by the terrorists themselves, their underlying motivation is not always clear. Methods that help us understand terrorism include different social science disciplines that can all be useful in determining why terrorists carry out attacks, and can also help determine where and how terrorists might attack next. The strategic-choice approach to terrorism also gives homeland security practitioners additional methods to influence terrorist decision-making and provides new opportunities to change terrorist behavior.

Modern Global Terrorism, U.S. Terrorist Attacks, 9-11 Attacks

Modern global terrorism is unique in the history of terrorism because of both the level of violence and the reach of the terrorist acts.[68] Terrorists have learned how to use the media to communicate their messages to an incredibly wide audience, especially with the advent of the Internet.[69] In addition, modern terrorists have become much more sophisticated in their cooperation with one another and in their use of financial networks and communication.[70] This has made combating terrorism more difficult and more complex.

While the focus of the world has been on global terrorism, it is important to note that even terrorists operating domestically have utilized many of these same increases in capability. The wide availability of information for creating weapons, establishing secure communications, and the ability to plan and coordinate attacks have made so-called "home grown" terrorists sometimes just as threatening as global organizations with a great deal more funding and organization.[71]

U.S. Terrorist Attacks

While it is easy to focus on the recent events of September 11, 2001 as the "beginning" of terrorism in the U.S., it is important to remember that even well before that horrific attack, America had suffered devastating attacks from terrorists.[72] Importantly, while some of these attacks were by terrorist organizations that might be considered international, like the 1993 World Trade Center bombing, many have been by groups entirely from the U.S. Perhaps the most significant home-grown terrorist attack, the Oklahoma City bombing in 1995, was carried out by an individual who most would consider a "low risk" for terrorist activities, judging by today's standards.[73] Other entities, like The Order in the 1970s and more recently the Unabomber, have also carried out successful attacks in the United States that captivated and terrorized the nation.[74]

▦ 9-11

Of course the most significant terrorist attack in U.S. history is September 11th. This attack, aside from being the largest single loss-of-life from a terrorist act, is also a paragon of modern terrorism.[75] Not only was it a mass-casualty event, but it took full advantage of the media, both during the attack and after, and targeted specific, recognizable symbols of American and Western power.[76] The attack is considered by many to be the benchmark that other terrorist organizations may try to reach and exceed.[77]

In addition to the direct loss of life and financial losses incurred, 9-11 also motivated an incredible overhaul of our national government. The creation of the Department of Homeland Security was a direct response to the 9-11 Commission Report,[78] and its creation suggested that poor information-sharing was, in large part, to blame for the success of the attacks. This change in government structure fundamentally changed how we view security in the United States, as well as how we combat threats such as terrorism.

■ Understanding Terrorism—Organization and Threat

Terrorism is a difficult problem to solve, given its wide variety of motivations, its relative ease of attack, and the wide publicity given to even unsuccessful operations.[79] Understanding how terrorism is organized, both domestically and internationally, is essential to combating the threat. One way to do this is to create a typology of terrorism, which allows academics and practitioners alike to understand a group's motivations, attack strategies, and goals, and additionally, allows for comparison between groups. One of the most commonly used typologies of terrorism is also one of the simplest: international versus domestic terrorism.[80]

▦ International Terrorism

International terrorism, as outlined in the DHS definition of terrorism (taken from the U.S. Code) earlier, is terrorism that originates partially or substantially in a jurisdiction outside of the United States. Despite the relative simplicity of the distinction between international and domestic terrorism, it is not always easy to determine which an attack is. Other times, such as with the Oklahoma City bombing in 1995, determining whether an attack is domestic or international is less challenging. Making the determination is essential, however, to determining jurisdiction for the investigation. An agency such as the CIA has a much larger international reach than the FBI and takes a much larger role in cases of international terrorism.

One of the important aspects of international terrorism as it relates to the United States is that the attack does not have to take place within the borders of the United States. Attacks like the Beirut bombing, a truck bomb at the U.S. Marine Corps barracks in Beirut, Lebanon in 1982, have targeted U.S. interests and property abroad.[81] One of Al Qaeda's first large-scale attacks was against the U.S. embassies in Kenya and Tanzania, killing citizens of those countries and U.S. citizens alike.

The threat posed by international terrorism to the United States is obviously large. This was one of the significant lessons learned from the 9-11 attacks on New York City and the Pentagon.[82] Since 9-11 there has been a concerted effort to thwart international terrorist attacks that include many international partners. Thus far, these prevention efforts have been largely successful. However, even with the death of Osama bin Laden, there remains an international movement with significant support that will continue to attempt attacking the United States. This is clearly indicated in the 2011 National Intelligence Estimate, released by the Director of National Intelligence:[83]

Courtesy of Colonel Emerson Begolly.

> We judge the U.S. Homeland will face a persistent and evolving terrorist threat over the next 3 years. The main threat comes from Islamic terrorist groups and cells, especially al-Qa'ida, driven by their undiminished intent to attack the Homeland and a continued effort by these terrorist groups to adapt and improve their capabilities.

Domestic Terrorism

Domestic terrorism, or terrorism originating within the United States, is a continuing threat to homeland security.[84] While the 9-11 attacks, because of their dramatic nature, have focused attention on international terrorism, domestic terrorism has a potent history in the United States and continues to be actively carried out by various organizations within the nation, stemming from a variety of motivations. Anti-government attacks, such as the Oklahoma City bombing in 1995, the Olympics bombing in 1996, which was motivated by anti-abortion sentiments, and the Vail, Colorado arson that was motivated by animal rights ideology all demonstrate this variety in motivation.[85]

Domestic terrorism remains one of the principal threats to homeland security.[86] The form this threat takes is varied, including eco-terrorism and animal rights terrorism, militia extremism, anarchist extremism, white supremacy, anti-abortion terrorism, and other forms. The FBI has stated that they consider eco-terrorism the most threatening form of domestic terrorism, and has documented over 2,000 attacks resulting in over $110 million in damages since 1979.[87] Similarly, as recently as February 2012, white supremacist terrorists have been arrested and charged with transporting explosive devices and firebombing the home of an interracial couple.[88]

In addition to the "normal" domestic threats such as eco-terrorism and white supremacy, there is the additional problem of home-grown terrorists with religious motivations. Particularly, there is a significant concern that international organizations, such as Al Qaeda, may attempt to support, but not direct, domestic terrorist organizations. The National Intelligence Estimate suggests,

> Although we have discovered only a handful of individuals in the United States with ties to al-Qa'ida senior leadership since 9-11, we judge that al-Qa'ida will intensify its efforts to put operatives here… We assess that the spread of radical—especially Salafi—Internet sites, increasingly aggressive anti-U.S. rhetoric and actions, and the growing number of radical, self-generating cells in Western countries indicate that the radical and violent segment of the West's Muslim population is expanding, including in the United States. The arrest and prosecution by U.S. law enforcement of a small number of violent Islamic extremists inside the United States—who are becoming more connected ideologically, virtually, and/or in a physical sense to the global extremist movement—points to the possibility that others may become sufficiently radicalized that they will view the use of violence here as legitimate.[89]

Like 9-11 for international terrorism, many of these attacks, and particularly Oklahoma City, indicate the potential threat that domestic attacks presented for the U.S. and have led to widespread efforts of cooperation between local and federal law enforcement agencies to attempt to combat them. These efforts, though generally successful, have not been able to halt domestic terrorist activity in the United States.

In short, terrorism has been and continues to be a significant threat for the United States. Additionally, despite large-scale efforts, particularly regarding international terrorism, there remain dedicated groups who wish to attack the U.S. Domestically, these groups range in motivation from single-issues like abortion and animal rights, to home-grown religious terrorist organizations modeled on Al Qaeda. Internationally, the threat remains largely religious in nature, with Al Qaeda, and groups inspired by them, seeking to make large-scale attacks within the U.S.

■ Natural Disasters

Natural disasters, like terrorism, are one of the major threats the United States experiences on a regular basis.[90] Events like Hurricane Katrina, and more recently a series of tornadoes in the Midwest, remind us that while we face human-made threats regularly, natural hazards remain equally deadly and happen with much more frequency. As with terrorism, there are methods by which the government can mitigate the threat of, and cope with the results of, natural disasters. The sections following cover the difference between natural hazards and threats, and some of the governmental responses to natural disasters when they happen at each level: national, state, and local.

▦ Hazards

Hazards, in the context of natural phenomenon, are potential harms to humans or the environment caused by natural events. Hazards can be caused by hydrological, meteorological, seismic, geologic, volcanic, and mass-movement processes that occur in nature.[91] Though frequently used interchangeably with the concept of threat, the two ideas are distinct. In the United States, there are a wide variety of natural hazards including earthquakes, tornadoes, hurricanes, wildfires, floods, lightning strikes, landslides, sink holes, drought, and others. These hazards cause a tremendous amount of damage nation-wide each year. Floods alone accounted for $8.4 billion dollars in damage to the economy in 2011 and were responsible for 114 deaths, and the decade leading up was more costly in terms of lives than previous decades.[92] Additionally, though not usually given as much media attention as terrorist attacks, natural hazards occur with more frequency and result in a great deal more loss-of-life than man-made hazards, over time.[93]

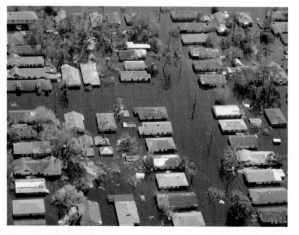

Courtesy of the NOAA.

▦ Risks

Risks are hazards when combined with their probability of happening. For instance, while an earthquake is always a hazard, it poses little threat to states in the Southeast and is, therefore, not considered a significant **risk** in that location. More concretely, risks are more contextually specific than hazards, even if they are comprised of the same phenomenon. Hazard risks, therefore, are always examined within their respective locations. There are frequently hazards that pose little risk, but never risks that do not consist of a hazard.[94]

The process of developing methods to deal with hazards, including determining how probable the risk of a hazard is, is called risk management. Risk management in regards to natural events is one of the primary responsibilities of government, and there has been a long history of risk management at all levels of government.[95] Risk management includes both qualitative and quantitative methodologies, and knowledge of an area's history of hazards and disasters is critical to risk management.

Types

Natural disasters are what happens when a threat comes to fruition and overwhelms the ability of a single agency to deal with it. Examples from history abound. Perhaps the most memorable **natural disaster** in recent memory is Hurricane Katrina. This, however, was not the largest natural disaster in the history of the United States when measured by relative cost, nor even the deadliest hurricane when measured by loss of life. That title belongs to the Galveston Hurricane of 1900, during which 8,000 individuals died.[96] In fact, there are usually several dozen declared disasters every year. In 2011 alone there were 99 major declared disasters in the U.S. totaling over $80 billion dollars in damage. [97]

Different types of disasters occur with different frequency in various locations around the country. Floods, for instance, affect many sections of the nation and are one of the most costly types of disaster. Even relatively rare events, such as tsunamis, can cause huge amounts of damage, and therefore must be taken into account when generating response plans. Further, many disasters compound when they occur. Again, taking earthquakes as an example, related disasters like fires, floods and others may happen at the same time.[98] This is clearly illustrated by the recent nuclear disaster caused by a tsunami in Japan.[99] Within this context, government has a series of responsibilities: mitigation or the reduction of the probability of disasters happening; preparedness or preparing for when disasters happen; response during the disaster event; and recovery, for after the disaster has passed.

Over the course of the United States' history, there have been a variety of major natural disasters, and the methods by which these disasters have been addressed have changed with the rise of emergency management as a professional discipline and academic discipline. Despite this improvement in our ability to deal with disasters when they happen, natural disasters continue to deeply affect both property and life throughout the nation in a variety of ways. In **Box 3.4**, the most frequently occurring types of disaster are examined.[100]

Natural disasters are much more frequently occurring, but receive less attention, than terrorist attacks. This is surprising not just because of the difference in the number of occurrences, but also because the combined monetary cost of natural disasters dwarfs that of terrorism in most years. In any event, both terrorism and natural disasters require a large response effort, and many times, the recovery requires similar elements. This closely ties the two types of events together, even though their causes are distinct.

BOX 3.4   Frequently Occurring Disasters

Floods

Floods affect nearly every area of the country and can be among the most damaging types of natural disasters. While floods technically are defined as any time a significant amount of water overwhelms land that is normally dry, larger floods can not only cause extensive damage but may persist for significant periods of time. Floods have a variety of causes including torrential rain, dam breaks, and frequently for large floods, hurricanes.[101] According to the Federal Emergency Management Agency's flood statistics, the most costly flood in U.S. history was caused by Hurricane Katrina in Louisiana and surrounding states, and resulted in over $16 billion dollars in damage as well as at least 1,836 deaths.[102]

Wildfires

Wildfires, sometimes known as brush or forest fires, are fires that surpass the ability of local fire suppression groups to contain them. They can burn huge amounts of acreage, destroy property, and frequently result in deaths. These fires are usually caused by humans, but can also be caused by lightning strikes if weather conditions are dry enough. They are becoming a more significant problem across the country as people build their homes in more wooded areas.[103]

Tornadoes

Tornadoes are frequently occurring, powerful storms that appear as rotating, funnel-shaped clouds. They are among the most destructive types of natural disasters, with winds sometimes reaching 300 miles per hour and damage trailing up to 50 miles. In the largest tornadoes, the path of destruction can reach a mile wide. Tornadoes usually develop as part of a larger storm system, but occasionally tornadoes develop so rapidly that there is little advanced warning. Nearly every state in the country is at risk for these severe storms.[104]

Hurricanes

Hurricanes are large, powerful storms that develop in the open ocean and move onto coastal areas. The Atlantic hurricane season lasts from June to November while storms in the Pacific tend to develop between May and November. These storms can be hundreds of miles wide and frequently spawn other significant weather events such as tornadoes and flooding. In order to be classified as a hurricane, wind speeds much reach a minimum sustained level of 74 miles per hour [105] but winds can reach up to 200 miles per hour in the most severe storms. Coastal communities are most at risk, but even areas far inland sometimes sustain significant damage from large hurricanes.[106]

■ Chapter Summary

The attacks on 9-11 motivated the modern change of homeland security in America and marked one of the seminal events of the early 21st century. The attacks were as devastating as they were because of the fear generated by Al Qaeda, something they were practiced at achieving through events like the Bali bombing. Terrorism generally is designed to generate fear to motivate change in the individuals and groups targeted by it, and in some respects, September 11th was a success for the terrorists.

However, despite the fact that America and the rest of the world are now familiar with terrorism in an everyday context, there is no agreed upon definition of the term. History, however, gives us several elements that have remained consistent with the concept of terrorism over time. It is politically, socially, or religiously motivated, violent, is carried out by sub-national actors to achieve some goal, and the victims and targets are rarely the same. Nearly all definitions, despite their variations, carry most or all of these elements.

Natural disasters, like terrorism, can be physically and emotionally devastating. Unlike catastrophic terrorism, however, natural disasters occur with frequency in nearly every part of the country. Wildfires and floods are the most frequent types

© PA Photos/Landov.

of natural disasters in the U.S., but many other types, such as hurricanes and tornadoes, also cause a significant amount of damage each year.

Both terrorism and natural disasters require response from every level of government when an event occurs. These responses are frequently similar, especially in the immediate aftermath of an event. Thus, terrorism and natural disasters are linked directly in the context of homeland security. As homeland security develops in its "all-hazards" approach to disaster management, there will be closer ties across these types of events—despite their different and disparate causes.

■ Review/Discussion Questions

1. What are the components of terrorism, and why are each of them important for differentiating terrorism from crime?

2. Explain the importance of the development of terrorism over time. What elements have remained the same throughout, and which ones have changed over time?

3. Compare and contrast the psychological explanations for terrorism to strategic explanations of terrorism. Which approach is more effective in explaining terrorism and why?

4. What is the difference between hazard and risk? Which should we use for planning purposes and why?

5. Why is there more focus on terrorism than natural disasters despite the latter's more frequent occurrence and higher cost?

■ Additional Readings

Hoffman, B. (2006). *Inside Terrorism* (2nd ed.). New York: Columbia University Press.

Sageman, M. (2004). *Understanding Terror Networks*. Philadelphia, PA: University of Pennsylvania Press.

Sloan, S. (2006). *Terrorism: The Present Threat in Context*. New York: Berg.

■ Endnotes

1. U.S. Department of State, Bureau of Diplomatic Security. (1998). *Political Violence Against Americans, 1998*.

2. U.S. Department of State, Bureau of Diplomatic Security. (1998). *Political Violence Against Americans, 1998*.

3. U.S. Department of State, Bureau of Diplomatic Security. (1998). *Political Violence Against Americans, 1998*.

4. Koper, K.D., Wallace, T.C., Reinke, R.E., & Leverette, J.A. (2002). "Empirical Scaling Laws for Truck Bomb Explosions Based on Seismic and Acoustic Data." *Bulletin of the Seismological Society of America 92*(2), 527–542.

5. Machon, M.J. (2006). *Targeted Killing as an Element of U.S. Foreign Policy in the War on Terror: A Monograph*. Fort Leavenworth, KS: School of Advanced Military Studies. Retrieved from http://www.fas.org/irp/eprint/machon.pdf

6. *NBC News*. "Al Qaeda Timeline: Plots and Attacks." Retrieved from http://www.msnbc.msn.com/id/4677978/ns/world_news-hunt_for_al_qaida/t/al-qaida-timeline-plots-attacks/#.UJviK8WHKSo

7. Nikoghosyan, H. (2010). Book review: "Mercenaries, Extremists, and Islamist Fighters in Karabagh War." *The Armenian Weekly*. Retrieved from http://www.armenianweekly.com/2010/12/21/book-review-mercenaries-extremists-and-islamist-fighters-in-karabagh-war/

8. National Commission on Terrorist Attacks Upon the United States. (2004). *The 9/11 Commission Report: Final Report of the National Commission on Terrorist Attacks Upon the United States (Authorized Ed.)*. New York: W.W. Norton & Company, Inc.

9. Hoffman, B. (2006). *Inside Terrorism* (2nd ed.). New York: Columbia University Press; Sloan, S. (2006). *Terrorism: The Present Threat in Context*. New York: Berg; Sageman, M. (2004). *Understanding Terror Networks*. Philadelphia, PA: University of Pennsylvania Press.

10. *Washington Post*. (2010). "The Department of Homeland Security." Retrieved on August 23, 2012 from http://www.washingtonpost.com/politics/homeland-security-department/gIQALxPx4O_topic.html

11. *New York Times*. (n.d.). "One 9-11 Tally: $3.3 Trillion." Retrieved on August 15, 2012 from http://www.nytimes.com/interactive/2011/09/08/us/sept-11-reckoning/cost-graphic.html

12. *PBS NewsHour*. (2006). "Hurricane Katrina Displaced over 400,000, Report Says." Retrieved on August 15, 2012 from http://www.pbs.org/newshour/updates/social_issues/jan-june06/census_06-07.html

13. Siliver, R.C., Holman, A., McIntosh, D.N., Poulin, M., & Gil-Rivas, V. (2002). "Nationwide Longitudinal Study of Psychological Responses to September 11." *Journal of the American Medical Association, 288*, 1235-1244.

14. Hoffman, B. (2006). *Inside Terrorism* (2nd ed.). New York: Columbia University Press.

15. Sloan, S. (2006). *Terrorism: The Present Threat in Context*. New York: Berg.

16. Hoffman, B. (2006). *Inside Terrorism* (2nd ed.). New York: Columbia University Press.

17. Anderson, S., & Sloan, S. (2003). *Terrorism: Assassins to Zealots*. Landham, MD: Scarecrow Press; Hoffman, B. (2006). *Inside Terrorism* (2nd ed.). New York: Columbia University Press; Sloan, S. (2006). *Terrorism: The Present Threat in Context*. New York: Berg.

18. Anderson, S., & Sloan, S. (2003). *Terrorism: Assassins to Zealots*. Landham, MD: Scarecrow Press.

19. Anderson, S., & Sloan, S. (2003). *Terrorism: Assassins to Zealots*. Landham, MD: Scarecrow Press.

20. Hoffman, B. (2006). *Inside Terrorism* (2nd ed.). New York, NY: Columbia University Press.

21. Hoffman, B. (2006). *Inside Terrorism* (2nd ed.). New York, NY: Columbia University Press; Gough, H. (1998). *The Terror in the French Revolution*. New York, NY: Palgrave Macmillan.

22. Gough, H. (1998). *The Terror in the French Revolution*. New York, NY: Palgrave Macmillan.

23. Hoffman, B. (2006). *Inside Terrorism* (2nd ed.). New York: Columbia University Press; Gough, H. (1998). *The Terror in the French Revolution*. New York, NY: Palgrave Macmillan.

24. Sloan, S. (2006). *Terrorism: The Present Threat in Context*. New York: Berg.

25. Hoffman, B. (2006). *Inside Terrorism* (2nd ed.). New York: Columbia University Press.

26. Norris. P, Montague, K., & Just, M. (2003). *Framing Terrorism: The News Media, the Government, and the Public*. New York, NY: Routledge.

27. Hoffman, B. (2006). *Inside Terrorism* (2nd ed.). New York: Columbia University Press.

28. Hoffman, B. (2006). *Inside Terrorism* (2nd ed.). New York, NY: Columbia University Press.

29. Hoffman, B. (2006). *Inside Terrorism* (2nd ed.). New York, NY: Columbia University Press.

30. Hoffman, B. (2006). *Inside Terrorism* (2nd ed.). New York: Columbia University Press; Sloan, S. (2006). *Terrorism: The Present Threat in Context*. New York, NY: Berg.

31. Hoffman, B. (2006). *Inside Terrorism* (2nd ed.). New York: Columbia University Press.

32. Smith, J., & Moncourt, A. (2009). *The Red Army Faction: A Documentary History—Volume 1: Projectiles for the People*. Quebec, Canada: Kersplebedeb Publishing.

33. Hoffman, B. (2006). *Inside Terrorism* (2nd ed.). New York, NY: Columbia University Press.

34. Sageman, M. (2004). *Understanding Terror Networks*. Philadelphia, PA: University of Pennsylvania Press.

35. Hoffman, B. (2006). *Inside Terrorism* (2nd ed.). New York, NY: Columbia University Press.

36. Hoffman, B. (2006). *Inside Terrorism* (2nd ed.). New York, NY: Columbia University Press.

37. Sloan, S. (2006). *Terrorism: The Present Threat in Context*. New York, NY: Berg.

38. Hoffman, B. (1995). "'Holy Terror': The Implication of Terrorism Motivated by a Religious Imperative." *Studies in Conflict and Terrorism, 18*(4), 271-284.

39. Sloan, S. (2006). *Terrorism: The Present Threat in Context*. New York, NY: Berg.

40. Hoffman, B. (2006). *Inside Terrorism* (2nd ed.). New York, NY: Columbia University Press.

41. Hoffman, B. (2006). *Inside Terrorism* (2nd ed.). New York, NY: Columbia University Press; E.g., Crimes and Criminal Procedure § 2331, 18 USC 113B (2012).

42. Hoffman, B. (2006). *Inside Terrorism* (2nd ed.). New York, NY: Columbia University Press.

43. Jarboe, J.F. (2002). Testimony Before the House Subcommittee on Forests and Forest Health. Retrieved on August 23, 2012 from http://www.fbi.gov/news/testimony/the-threat-of-eco-terrorism

44. Flemming, P., Stohl, M., & Schmidt, A.P. (1985). "The Theoretical Utility of Typologies of Terrorism: Lessons and Opportunities" in Stohl, M. (Ed.), *The Politics of Terrorism*. New York: CRC Press.

45. Monaghan, R. (2000). "Single-issue Terrorism: A neglected Phenomenon?" *Studies in Conflict and Terrorism, 23*, 255-265.

46. Hoffman, B. (2006). *Inside Terrorism* (2nd ed.). New York, NY: Columbia University Press; E.g., Crimes and Criminal Procedure § 2331, 18 USC 113B (2012).

47. Schmid, A. P. (1984). *Political Terrorism: A Research Guide*. New Brunswick, NJ: Transaction Books.

48. Sloan, S. (2006). *Terrorism: The Present Threat in Context*. New York, NY: Berg.

49. Hoffman, B. (2006). *Inside Terrorism* (2nd ed.). New York, NY: Columbia University Press; Sloan, S. (2006). *Terrorism: The Present Threat in Context*. New York: Berg.

50. Sloan, S. (2006). *Terrorism: The Present Threat in Context*. New York, NY: Berg.

51. Federal Bureau of Investigation, n.p.

52. Department of State, n.p.

53. Crimes and Criminal Procedure § 2331, 18 USC 113B (2012).

54. Schmid, A. P. (1984). *Political Terrorism: A Research Guide*. New Brunswick, NJ: Transaction Books.

55. Charters, D. (2004). "What Has Been the Impact of the Anti-Terrorism Act on Canada?" in *The Views of Canadian Scholars on the Impact of the Anti-Terrorism Act*. Ottawa, Canada: Canadian Department of Justice.

56. Hoffman, B. (2006). *Inside Terrorism* (2nd ed.). New York, NY: Columbia University Press.

57. Sloan, S. (2006). *Terrorism: The Present Threat in Context*. New York, NY: Berg.

58. Reich, W.S. (ed.) (1998). *Origins of Terrorism*. Washington, DC: The Woodrow Wilson Center Press.

59. Gurr, T.R. (2006). Economic Factors. In Richardson, L. (Ed.). *The Roots of Terrorism (Democracy and Terrorism)*. New York, NY: Routledge.

60. Horgan, J. (2005). *The Psychology of Terrorism*. New York, NY: Routledge.

61. Horgan, J. (2005). *The Psychology of Terrorism*. New York, NY: Routledge.

62. Drake, C.J.M (1998). *Terrorists' Target Selection*. New York, NY: Palgrave.

63. Enders, W., and Sandler, T. (2011). *The Political Economy of Terrorism* (2nd ed.). Cambridge, UK: Cambridge University Press.

64. Bueno de Mesquita, E. (2005). "Conciliation, Counterterrorism, and Patterns of Terrorist Violence." *International Organization, 59*, 145–176.

65. Reich, W.S. (ed.) (1998). *Origins of Terrorism*. Washington, DC: The Woodrow Wilson Center Press.

66. Reich, W.S. (ed.) (1998). *Origins of Terrorism*. Washington, DC: The Woodrow Wilson Center Press.

67. Crenshaw, M. (1998). "The Logic of Terrorism: Terrorist Behavior as a Product of Strategic Choice." In Reich, W. A. (Ed.), *The Origins of Terrorism*, 7-24. Washington, DC: Woodrow Wilson Center Press.

68. Hoffman, B. (2006). *Inside Terrorism* (2nd ed.). New York, NY: Columbia University Press; Sloan, S. (2006). *Terrorism: The Present Threat in Context*. New York: Berg.

69. Norris. P, Montague, K., & Just, M. (2003). *Framing Terrorism: The News Media, the Government, and the Public*. New York, NY: Routledge.

70. Sageman, M. (2004). *Understanding Terror Networks*. Philadelphia, PA: University of Pennsylvania Press.

71. Federal Bureau of Investigation (2009). *Domestic Terrorism*. Retrieved on August 23, 2012 at http://www.fbi.gov/news/stories/2009/september/domterror_090709

72. National Commission on Terrorist Attacks Upon the United States. (2004). *The 9/11 Commission Report: Final Report of the National Commission on Terrorist Attacks Upon the United States (Authorized Ed.)*. New York: W.W. Norton & Company, Inc.

73. Sloan, S. (2006). *Terrorism: The Present Threat in Context*. New York, NY: Berg.

74. Anderson, S., & Sloan, S. (2003). *Terrorism: Assassins to Zealots*. Landham, MD: Scarecrow Press; Hoffman, B. (2006). *Inside Terrorism* (2nd ed.). New York, NY: Columbia University Press.

75. National Commission on Terrorist Attacks Upon the United States. (2004). *The 9/11 Commission Report: Final Report of the National Commission on Terrorist Attacks Upon the United States (Authorized Ed.)*. New York: W.W. Norton & Company, Inc.; Hoffman, B. (2006). *Inside Terrorism* (2nd ed.). New York, NY: Columbia University Press; Sloan, S. (2006). *Terrorism: The Present Threat in Context*. New York: Berg; Sageman, M. (2004). *Understanding Terror Networks*. Philadelphia, PA: University of Pennsylvania Press.

76. Hoffman, B. (2006). *Inside Terrorism* (2nd ed.). New York, NY: Columbia University Press.

77. Hoffman, B. (2006). *Inside Terrorism* (2nd ed.). New York, NY: Columbia University Press; Sloan, S. (2006). *Terrorism: The Present Threat in Context*. New York, NY: Berg; Sageman, M. (2004). *Understanding Terror Networks*. Philadelphia, PA: University of Pennsylvania Press.

78. National Commission on Terrorist Attacks Upon the United States. (2004). *The 9/11 Commission Report: Final Report of the National Commission on Terrorist Attacks Upon the United States (Authorized Ed.)*. New York: W.W. Norton & Company, Inc.

79. Sloan, S. (2006). *Terrorism: The Present Threat in Context*. New York, NY: Berg.

80. Federal Bureau of Investigation (2009). *Domestic Terrorism*. Retrieved on August 23, 2012 at http://www.fbi.gov/news/stories/2009/september/domterror_090709

81. Hoffman, B. (2006). *Inside Terrorism* (2nd ed.). New York, NY: Columbia University Press.

82. National Commission on Terrorist Attacks Upon the United States. (2004). *The 9/11 Commission Report: Final Report of the National Commission on Terrorist Attacks Upon the United States (Authorized Ed.)*. New York: W.W. Norton & Company, Inc.

83. National Intelligence Council. (2007). *National Intelligence Estimate: The Terrorist Threat to the US Homeland*, p. 5. Retrieved on August 27, 2012 from http://www.c-span.org/pdf/nie_071707.pdf

84. Federal Bureau of Investigation (2009). *Domestic Terrorism*. Retrieved on August 23, 2012 at http://www.fbi.gov/news/stories/2009/september/domterror_090709

85. Federal Bureau of Investigation (2009). *Domestic Terrorism*. Retrieved on August 23, 2012 at http://www.fbi.gov/news/stories/2009/september/domterror_090709

86. Federal Bureau of Investigation (2009). *Domestic Terrorism*. Retrieved on August 23, 2012 at http://www.fbi.gov/news/stories/2009/september/domterror_090709

87. Jarboe, J.F. (2002). Testimony Before the House Subcommittee on Forests and Forest Health. Retrieved on August 23, 2012 from http://www.fbi.gov/news/testimony/the-threat-of-eco-terrorism

88. Federal Bureau of Investigation. (2012). *Arkansas Man Sentenced for his Role in Firebombing Residence of Interracial Couple*. Retrieved on August 23, 2012 from http://www.fbi.gov/littlerock/press-releases/2012/

arkansas-man-sentenced-for-his-role-in-firebombing-residence-of-interracial-couple

89. National Intelligence Council. (2007). *National Intelligence Estimate: The Terrorist Threat to the US Homeland*, p. 5. Retrieved on August 27, 2012 from http://www.c-span.org/pdf/nie_071707.pdf

90. Haddow, G.D., Bullock, J.A., & Coppola, D.P. (2011). *Introduction to Emergency Management*. Burlington, MA: Elsiver.

91. Haddow, G.D., Bullock, J.A., & Coppola, D.P. (2011). *Introduction to Emergency Management*. Burlington, MA: Elsevier.

92. Reliefweb. *Annual Disaster Statistical Review* (2011). Retrieved from http://reliefweb.int/report/world/annual-disaster-statistical-review-2011-numbers-and-trends on March 12, 2013.

93. Haddow, G.D., Bullock, J.A., & Coppola, D.P. (2011). *Introduction to Emergency Management*. Burlington, MA: Elsevier.

94. Canadian Center for Occupational Health and Safety. (n.d.). *Hazard and Risk*. Retrieved from htp://www.ccohs.ca/oshanswers/hsprograms/hazard_risk.html on March 12, 2013.

95. Haddow, G.D., Bullock, J.A., & Coppola, D.P. (2011). *Introduction to Emergency Management*. Burlington, MA: Elsevier.

96. National Oceanic and Atmospheric Administration. (n.d.). *Galveston Storm of 1900*. Retrieved from http://www.history.noaa.gov/stories_tales/cline2.html on March 12, 2013.

97. Federal Emergency Management Agency. (2012). *Disasters by Year*. Retrieved from http://www.fema.gov/disasters/grid/year

98. Haddow, G.D., Bullock, J.A., & Coppola, D.P. (2011). *Introduction to Emergency Management*. Burlington, MA: Elsevier.

99. Demetriou, D. (2011). "Japan Earthquake, Tsunami and Fukushima Nuclear Disaster: 2011 Review." *The Telegraph*. Retrieved from http://www.telegraph.co.uk/news/worldnews/asia/japan/8953574/Japan-earthquake-tsunami-and-Fukushima-nuclear-disaster-2011-review.html on March 12, 2013.

100. Haddow, G.D., Bullock, J.A., & Coppola, D.P. (2011). *Introduction to Emergency Management*. Burlington, MA: Elsevier.

101. Federal Emergency Management Agency. (2012). *Floods*. Retrieved from http://www.ready.gov/floods on March 12, 2013.

102. National Oceanic and Atmospheric Administration. (n.d.). *Hurricane Katrina: Most Destructive Storm Ever to Hit the US*. Retrieved from http://www.katrina.noaa.gov/ on March 12, 2013.

103. Federal Emergency Management Agency. (2012). *Wildfires*. Retrieved from http://www.ready.gov/wildfires on March 12, 2013.

104. Federal Emergency Management Agency (2012). *Tornadoes*. Retrieved from http://www.ready.gov/tornadoes on March 12, 2013.

105. National Hurricane Center. (2012). *Saffir-Simpson Hurricane Wind Scale*. Retrieved from http://www.nhc.noaa.gov/aboutsshws.php

106. Federal Emergency Management Agency (2012). *Hurricanes*. Retrieved from http://www.ready.gov/hurricanes on March 12, 2013.

The Development of Homeland Security

Chapter Outline

- Introduction
- Office of Homeland Security
- USA PATRIOT Act
- The Homeland Security Act of 2002
- Homeland Security Presidential Directives
- Chapter Summary

Introduction

President George W. Bush was in Sarasota, Florida, visiting a class of children at Emma Booker Elementary School.[1] The President was seated in a classroom when, at 9:05 AM, Andrew Card (Chief of Staff) whispered to him: "A second plane hit the second tower. America is under attack."[2]

The President later explained that his first instinct was to project calm, not to have the country see an excited reaction from him at a moment of crisis. The press was standing behind the children; he saw their phones and pagers start to ring. The President felt he should project strength and calm until he could better understand what was happening.[3]

The President remained in the classroom for another 5–7 minutes, while the children continued reading. He then returned to a holding room shortly before 9:15, where he was briefed by staff and saw television coverage. He next spoke to Vice President Dick Cheney, National Security Advisor Condoleezza Rice, New York Governor George Pataki, and FBI Director Robert Mueller (who assumed the

© Doug Mills/AP Images.

directorship on September 4, 2001). He decided to make a brief statement from the school before leaving for the airport. The Secret Service later explained their priority was to move the President to a safer location, but they did not think it imperative to run him out the door.

Between 9:15 and 9:30, the staff was busy arranging a return to Washington, while the President consulted his senior advisers about his remarks. No one in the Bush party had any information during this time that other aircraft were hijacked or missing. Staff was in contact with the White House Situation Room, but no one was in contact with the Pentagon. The focus was on the President's statement to the nation. The only decision made during this time was to return to Washington. The President then briefly addressed the nation (see **Box 4.1**).

The President's motorcade then departed at 9:35 and arrived at the airport between 9:42 and 9:45. During the ride, the President learned about the attack on the Pentagon. He boarded the aircraft, asked the Secret Service about the safety of his family, and called the Vice President. According to notes of the call, at about 9:45 the President told the Vice President: "Sounds like we have a minor war going on here. I heard about the Pentagon. We're at war ... somebody's going to pay."[4]

About this time, Card, the lead Secret Service agent, the President's military aide, and the pilot were conferring on a possible destination for Air Force One. The Secret Service agent felt strongly that the situation in Washington was too unstable for the President to return there, and Card agreed. The President strongly wanted to return to Washington and only grudgingly agreed to go elsewhere. The issue was still undecided when the President conferred with the Vice President at about the time Air Force One was taking off. The Vice President recalled urging the President not to return to Washington. Air Force One departed at about 9:54 without any fixed destination. The objective was to get up in the air—as fast as possible—and then decide where to go.

BOX 4.1 Remarks in Sarasota, Florida, on the Terrorist Attack on New York City's World Trade Center, September 11, 2001

Today we've had a national tragedy. Two airplanes have crashed into the World Trade Center in an apparent terrorist attack on our country. I have spoken to the Vice President, to the Governor of New York, to the Director of the FBI and have ordered that the full resources of the Federal Government go to help the victims and their families and to conduct a full-scale investigation to hunt down and to find those folks who committed this act.

Terrorism against our Nation will not stand.

And now if you would join me in a moment of silence.

[*A moment of silence was observed.*]

May God bless the victims, their families, and America. Thank you very much.

Reproduced from: Bush, George W. (2001). "Remarks in Sarasota, Florida, on the Terrorist Attack on New York City's World Trade Center." Public Papers of the Presidents of the United States. Washington, D.C.: U.S. G.P.O.

In the meantime, the White House was notified that an unauthorized plane was heading toward Washington, D.C., and it was not communicating. The Vice President was rushed into the tunnels underneath the White House to a protective bunker. He stopped at one point in the tunnel where a bench, television, and phone were available. After verification of the missing plane and the attack on the Pentagon, Vice President Cheney contacted the President and advised him not to return to Washington. After the call ended, Mrs. Cheney and the Vice President moved from the tunnel to the shelter conference room.

President Bush reluctantly acceded to this advice, and at about 10:10 Air Force One changed course and began heading due west. The immediate objective was to find a safe location, not too far away, where the President could land and speak to the American people. The Secret Service was also interested in refueling the aircraft and paring down the size of the traveling party. The President's military aide, an Air Force officer, quickly researched the options and, sometime around 10:20, identified Barksdale Air Force Base, Louisiana, as an appropriate interim destination.

When Air Force One landed at Barksdale at about 11:45, personnel from the local Secret Service were still en route to the airfield. The motorcade consisted of a military police lead vehicle and a van; the proposed briefing theater had no phones or electrical outlets. Staff scrambled to prepare another room for the President's remarks. The President completed his statement, which for security reasons was taped and not broadcast live, and the traveling party returned to Air Force One. At 2:30 PM, the President's address was released to the nation (see **Box 4.2**).

The next destination was discussed. Once again, the Secret Service recommended against returning to Washington, and the Vice President agreed. Offutt Air Force Base in Nebraska was chosen because of its elaborate command and control facilities, and because it could accommodate overnight lodging for 50 persons. The Secret Service wanted a place where the President could spend several days, if necessary.

BOX 4.2 Remarks at Barksdale Air Force Base, Louisiana, on the Terrorist Attacks, September 11, 2001

Freedom itself was attacked this morning by a faceless coward, and freedom will be defended. I want to reassure the American people that the full resources of the Federal Government are working to assist local authorities to save lives and to help the victims of these attacks. Make no mistake: The United States will hunt down and punish those responsible for these cowardly acts.

I've been in regular contact with the Vice President, the Secretary of Defense, the national security team, and my Cabinet. We have taken all appropriate security precautions to protect the American people. Our military at home and around the world is on high-alert status, and we have taken the necessary security precautions to continue the functions of your Government.

We have been in touch with the leaders of Congress and with world leaders to assure them that we will do whatever is necessary to protect America and Americans.

I ask the American people to join me in saying a thanks for all the folks who have been fighting hard to rescue our fellow citizens and to join me in saying a prayer for the victims and their families.

The resolve of our great Nation is being tested. But make no mistake: We will show the world that we will pass this test. God bless.

Reproduced from: Bush, George W. (2001). "Remarks at Barksdale Air Force Base, Louisiana, on the Terrorist Attacks." Public Papers of the Presidents of the United States. Washington, D.C.: U.S.

Air Force One arrived at Offutt at 2:50 PM. At about 3:15, President Bush met with his principal advisers through a secure video teleconference. Rice said President Bush began the meeting with the words, "We're at war," and that Director of Central Intelligence George Tenet said the agency was still assessing who was responsible, but the early signs all pointed to Al Qaeda.[5]

The Secretary of Defense directed the nation's armed forces to Defense Condition 3, an increased state of military readiness. For the first time in history, all nonemergency civilian aircraft in the United States were grounded, stranding tens of thousands of passengers across the country. Contingency plans for the continuity of government and the evacuation of leaders had been implemented. The Pentagon had been struck; the White House or the Capitol had narrowly escaped direct attack. Extraordinary security precautions were put in place at the nation's borders and ports.

In the late afternoon, the President overruled his aides' continuing reluctance to have him return to Washington and ordered Air Force One back to Andrews Air Force Base. He was flown by helicopter to the White House, passing over the still-smoldering Pentagon. At 8:30 that evening, President Bush addressed the nation from the White House (see **Box 4.3**). Following his speech, President Bush met again with his National Security Council, expanded to include Secretary of Transportation Norman Mineta and Joseph Allbaugh, the Director of the Federal Emergency Management Agency. Secretary of State Colin Powell, who had returned from Peru after hearing of the attacks, joined the discussion. They reviewed the day's events.

It is important to understand that President Bush and his administration now had numerous tasks to perform all at once. Among these tasks included moving America to a war footing and responding militarily to the attack; organizing federal

---

BOX 4.3   Address to the Nation on the Terrorist Attacks, September 11, 2001

© Doug Mills/AP Images.

Good evening. Today our fellow citizens, our way of life, our very freedom came under attack in a series of deliberate and deadly terrorist acts. The victims were in airplanes or in their offices: secretaries, business men and women, military and Federal workers, moms and dads, friends and neighbors. Thousands of lives were suddenly ended by evil, despicable acts of terror.

The pictures of airplanes flying into buildings, fires burning, huge structures collapsing have filled us with disbelief, terrible sadness, and a quiet, unyielding anger. These acts of mass murder were intended to frighten our Nation into chaos and retreat, but they have failed. Our country is strong.

A great people has been moved to defend a great nation. Terrorist attacks can shake the foundations of our biggest buildings, but they cannot touch the foundation of America. These acts shattered steel, but they cannot dent the steel of American resolve. America was targeted for attack because we're the brightest beacon for freedom and opportunity in the world. And no one will keep that light from shining.

Today our Nation saw evil, the very worst of human nature. And we responded with the best of America, with the daring of our rescue workers, with the caring for strangers and neighbors who came to give blood and help in any way they could.

Immediately following the first attack, I implemented our Government's emergency response plans. Our military is powerful, and it's prepared. Our emergency teams are working in New York City and Washington, DC, to help with local rescue efforts.

Our first priority is to get help to those who have been injured and to take every precaution to protect our citizens at home and around the world from further attacks.

assistance, especially to New York City; determining when civil aviation could be restored, borders and ports reopened, as well as financial markets; and to find some means of responding domestically to the attack, which would become the **Office of Homeland Security**. While there were multiple tasks at hand, each was not created in a vacuum, but in concert with each other, although when it came to the reviewing domestic capabilities a temporary "domestic consequences" group had to be quickly developed.[6]

The process of reviewing these issues during this time of crisis underscored an absence of an effective government organization dedicated to assessing domestic vulnerabilities and handling problems of protection and preparedness. Though a number of agencies had some part of the task, none had security as its primary mission. What then developed in the months ahead were a number of responses to this deficiency. The first was the development of the Office of Homeland Security within the White House, which would assume these responsibilities. The second was the development of new tools for protection and preparedness that within 6 weeks became the **USA PATRIOT Act**. Third, was the implementation of a series of presidential directives to begin implementing changes in the way America protected itself against future terrorist attacks. And, finally, the even greater task of creating a **Department of Homeland Security**, a new cabinet level bureaucracy that would deal more directly with assessing vulnerabilities and handling the problems of protection and preparedness through an aggregate of multiple agencies and various agency components. These four actions, which all followed the 9-11 attacks, occurred quite rapidly: September 20, October 26, October 29, and November 25, 2002 respectively, forming the basis for modern-day homeland security in America.

> **KEY TERM**
> **Office of Homeland Security**—the office inside of the White House (Executive Branch) led by former Governor Tom Ridge, charged with securing the homeland, and which served as the nucleus for the Department of Homeland Security.

> **KEY TERM**
> **USA PATRIOT Act**—a ten-letter acronym for federal legislation formally titled Uniting and Strengthening America by Providing Appropriate Tools Required to Intercept and Obstruct Terrorism Act of 2001.

> **KEY TERM**
> **Department of Homeland Security**—a federal cabinet-level agency created in 2002 by taking various pre-existing agencies and placing them under one federal bureaucracy charged with protecting America's homeland.

The functions of our Government continue without interruption. Federal agencies in Washington which had to be evacuated today are reopening for essential personnel tonight and will be open for business tomorrow. Our financial institutions remain strong, and the American economy will be open for business as well.

The search is underway for those who are behind these evil acts. I've directed the full resources of our intelligence and law enforcement communities to find those responsible and to bring them to justice. We will make no distinction between the terrorists who committed these acts and those who harbor them.

I appreciate so very much the Members of Congress who have joined me in strongly condemning these attacks. And on behalf of the American people, I thank the many world leaders who have called to offer their condolences and assistance.

America and our friends and allies join with all those who want peace and security in the world, and we stand together to win the war against terrorism.

Tonight I ask for your prayers for all those who grieve, for the children whose worlds have been shattered, for all whose sense of safety and security has been threatened. And I pray they will be comforted by a power greater than any of us, spoken through the ages in Psalm 23: "Even though I walk through the valley of the shadow of death, I fear no evil, for You are with me."

This is a day when all Americans from every walk of life unite in our resolve for justice and peace. America has stood down enemies before, and we will do so this time. None of us will ever forget this day. Yet, we go forward to defend freedom and all that is good and just in our world.

Thank you. Good night, and God bless America.

Reproduced from: Bush, George W. (2001). "Address to the Nation on the Terrorist Attacks." Public Papers of the Presidents of the United States. Washington, D.C.: U.S. G.P.O.

■ Office of Homeland Security

In the aftermath of the attacks on September 11, 2001, the following day, President Bush toured the damage at the Pentagon in Arlington, Virginia. He gave a short speech noting that, "Coming here makes me sad, on the one hand; it also makes me angry. Our country will, however, not be cowed by terrorists, by people who don't share the same values we share, by people who are willing to destroy people's lives because we embrace freedom. The nation mourns, but our government will go on; the country will function. We are on high alert for possible activity."[7] Several days later, on September 14th, Bush toured the remains of the World Trade Center site in New York City. There he had a memorable exchange with the rescue workers. He began to speak, but an audience member yelled, "Can't hear you."[8] The President said, "I can't get any louder," and the audience laughed.[9]

He then began with his prepared speech stating that the nation mourned the loss of thousands of lives. Several people surrounding the president shouted, "I can't hear you."[10] And President Bush, in an impromptu statement shouted back, "I can hear you. I can hear you. The rest of the world hears you. And the people who knocked these buildings down will hear from us soon!"[11] The crowd cheered and broke into a chant of "USA! USA! USA!"[12]

The President returned to Washington, D.C. and worked on the development of a proper response to the attacks, both militarily and domestically. On September 20, 2001, President Bush appeared before a joint session of Congress to speak to the American people about the tragic events of 9-11 and his administration's response (see **Box 4.4**). In this speech, Bush announced the creation of an Office of Homeland Security and he named former Pennsylvania Governor Tom Ridge as the new office's first director (see **Box 4.5**).

© The White House/Getty Images.

| **BOX 4.4** | Address Before a Joint Session of the Congress of the United States Proposing New Office of Homeland Security, September 20, 2001 |

Our Nation has been put on notice: We are not immune from attack. We will take defensive measures against terrorism to protect Americans. Today dozens of Federal departments and agencies, as well as State and local governments, have responsibilities affecting homeland security. These efforts must be coordinated at the highest level.

So tonight I announce the creation of a Cabinet-level position reporting directly to me, the Office of Homeland Security. And tonight I also announce a distinguished American to lead this effort to strengthen American security, a military veteran, an effective Governor, a true patriot, a trusted friend, Pennsylvania's Tom Ridge. He will lead, oversee, and coordinate a comprehensive national strategy to safeguard our country against terrorism and respond to any attacks that may come.

These measures are essential. But the only way to defeat terrorism as a threat to our way of life is to stop it, eliminate it, and destroy it where it grows. Many will be involved in this effort, from FBI agents to intelligence operatives to the reservists we have called to active duty. All deserve our thanks, and all have our prayers. And tonight, a few miles from the damaged Pentagon, I have a message for our military: Be ready. I've called the Armed Forces to alert, and there is a reason. The hour is coming when America will act, and you will make us proud …

Reproduced from: Bush, George W. (2001). "Address Before a Joint Session of the Congress on the United States Response to the Terrorist Attacks of September 11. September 20, 2001." Public Papers of the Presidents of the United States. Washington, D.C.: U.S. G.P.O.

BOX 4.5 Tom Ridge, Homeland Security Secretary, 2003–2005

On January 24, 2003, Tom Ridge became the first Secretary of the Department of Homeland Security. Ridge worked with more than 180,000 employees from combined agencies to strengthen our borders, provide for intelligence analysis and infrastructure protection, improve the use of science and technology to counter weapons of mass destruction, and to create a comprehensive response and recovery division.

Tom Ridge was sworn in as the first Director of the Office of Homeland Security in October 2001, following the tragic events of September 11. The charge to the nation's new director of homeland defense was to develop and coordinate a comprehensive national strategy to strengthen the United States against terrorist threats or attacks. In the words of President George W. Bush, he had the strength, experience, personal commitment, and authority to accomplish this critical mission. Ridge stepped down as Secretary in February 2005.

Ridge was twice elected Governor of Pennsylvania, serving from 1995 to 2001. He kept his promise to make Pennsylvania "a leader among states and a competitor among nations." Governor Ridge's aggressive technology strategy helped fuel the state's advances in the priority areas of economic development, education, health, and the environment.

Born Aug. 26, 1945, in Pittsburgh's Steel Valley, Governor Ridge was raised in a working class family in veterans' public housing in Erie. He earned a scholarship to Harvard, graduating with honors in 1967. After his first year at The Dickinson School of Law, he was drafted into the U.S. Army, where he served as an infantry staff sergeant in Vietnam, earning the Bronze Star for Valor. After returning to Pennsylvania, he earned his law degree and was in private practice before becoming assistant district attorney in Erie County. He was elected to Congress in 1982. He was the first Congressman to have served as an enlisted man in the Vietnam War, and was overwhelmingly re-elected five times.

Reproduced from: Department of Homeland Security. (2012). "Tom Ridge, Homeland Security Secretary 2003-2005." Department of Homeland Security.

In the days following the speech, President Bush and his administration crafted an Executive Order that created not only the Office of Homeland Security, but also a Homeland Security Council. The Executive Order was signed on October 8, 2001, and put into motion the beginning of what became the largest major bureaucratic restructuring of the federal government since World War II.

The mission of the Office of Homeland Security was to "develop and coordinate the implementation of a comprehensive national strategy to secure the United States from terrorist threats or attacks."[13] The functions of the office were intended to "coordinate the executive branch's efforts to detect, prepare for, prevent, protect against, respond to, and recover from terrorist attacks within the United States."[14] More specifically, the functions of the new office were spelled out in more detail under ten areas of focus: (1) the development of a *national strategy* working with executive departments and agencies, state and local governments, as well as private entities; (2) the *detection* of terroristic threats through the collection and analysis of information; (3) *preparedness* for and mitigation of the consequences of terrorist threats and attacks; (4) *protection* of critical infrastructure; (5) *response and recovery* from terrorist attacks; (6) *incident management*; (7) *continuity of government*; (8) *public affairs*; (9) *review of legal authorities* and *development of legislative proposals*; and (10) *budget review*.

Essentially, it was intended that the new Director of Homeland Security would work as an adviser to the President for domestic threats, much in the same way that the National Security Adviser (Dr. Condoleezza "Condi" Rice at the time) advises the President on international threats. In fact, the Chief of Staff to the President,

Andrew H. Card, Jr., explained it this way: "If you take a look at what Condi Rice does so effectively, you'll get an idea what Governor Ridge will be doing just as effectively."[15]

The position of National Security Adviser had been created in 1947 in the aftermath of World War II and the beginning of the Cold War. The purpose of the

position was to have one adviser to the President who worked through a council that coordinated national defense, intelligence, and diplomatic relations in order to advise on international threats to the United States. Thus, the second half of the Executive Order on the Office of Homeland Security emulated the National Security Council with its own Homeland Security Council. The Director of Homeland Security would oversee this new council, being responsible for "advising and assisting the President with respect to all aspects of homeland security" and the council "shall serve as the mechanism for ensuring coordination of homeland security-related activities of executive departments and agencies and effective development and implementation of homeland security policies."[16] Director Tom Ridge and his new council, barely formed, hit the ground running and began carrying out the various charges of his new office.

© Gerald L. Nino/DHS/AP Images.

On March 21, 2002, another Executive Order was issued related to the Homeland Security Council. In this case, a Senior Advisory Committee to the Homeland Security Council was created. This was a committee of 21 presidential appointees who could provide advice directly to the President and the Director of Homeland Security, and would be composed of state and local officials, academics, private sector personnel, emergency services personnel, and first responders. The official title of the new committee was the President's Homeland Security Advisory Council (PHSAC).[17]

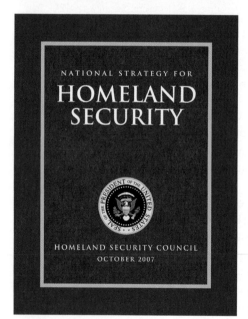

NATIONAL STRATEGY FOR
HOMELAND SECURITY

HOMELAND SECURITY COUNCIL
OCTOBER 2007

The formation of the Office of Homeland Security within the White House with its Homeland Security Director and Council, as well as the Advisory Council, proved to be a very important element in the eventual development of the Department of Homeland Security. It was the first step in a very rapid process for changing the federal bureaucracy that eventually evolved into the cabinet-level Department of Homeland Security.[18] In addition, it also provided the first *National Strategy for Homeland Security*, once again emulating the National Security Council's *National Security Strategy* document. This document was important for it outlined the coordinated plan for homeland security.

Courtesy of the DHS.

■ USA PATRIOT Act

In the immediate aftermath of the tragedy of 9-11, the United States Congress also went to work. The gravity of the situation called for action. The debates over whether to allow certain bills to move forward, such as the Combating Terrorism Act, which gave more power to the government for investigative purposes, were over. The bills that had languished in committee or had failed passage prior to September 11, 2001 were now dusted off, introduced, and passed within hours. Congress was on a war footing, despite not yet knowing with whom, exactly, America was at war.

In the public policy literature, there are a number of scholars who can explain this phenomenon. Anthony Downs had described the "issue attention cycle" where various public problems go through a five-stage cycle.[19] The first stage is the pre-problem stage, where the policymakers, academics, and other interested experts recognize a problem, but the overall majority of Americans do not, hence the problem and its policy solution are not at the forefront of concern. The second stage is alarmed discovery and euphoric enthusiasm, where an event occurs and people instantly become concerned. The policy issue instantly moves to the forefront of people's attention. September 11 was clearly the American public's alarmed discovery of terrorism and the threat Al Qaeda posed to the United States. It is in this stage that policies are rapidly passed and a flurry of activity develops to confront the problem. Then Downs' cycle moves to the third stage, where the realization of the costs cause us to give pause, which moves us into the fourth stage where there is a decline in public interest, and finally to the fifth stage or "post-problem," where the issue fades to the background and only the experts give the issue any attention. In the case of the 9-11 attacks, the public became instantly concerned and there was, as Downs explains, a "euphoric enthusiasm" to pass policies to protect America.[20]

Another public policy scholar, John W. Kingdon, explains the passage of polices with more detail.[21] Kingdon argues that there are three separate factors that have to come together in order for public policy to pass. He describes these as three "streams" that flow independently of one another but which intersect at some point in order to open up a window of opportunity for passage. There is the problem stream, the solutions stream, and the political stream. The problem stream is the most basic involving a widespread problem, one that most people would identify as a significant problem, that necessitates a governmental response. There must be a solution to the problem, generally created by those in the federal bureaucracy, private sector, or academia. These solutions are generally created by the experts in the area of concern. Finally, there is the political stream, in which both the politicians and the public are paying attention to the problem. When these three streams converge, there is a window of opportunity for the passage of new public policy.

In the case of 9-11, the terrorist attacks by Al Qaeda on American soil were clearly the problem, one in which nearly all of America agreed. The political stream was also present, for the public demanded action and the politicians knew they had to respond. The solution stream then came out of largely everything that had been previously considered by stakeholders as possible solutions to the threat of terrorism, but had either not reached the attention of the politicians or had simply not been passed in the U.S. House or Senate. In short, the attacks and public concern caused politicians to find any and every proposal even remotely related to protecting America against terrorism to be part of the solution—especially anything that would make investigations of terrorists easier in order to protect American against future attacks.

What happened next was a political fight that had long centered around the issue of security versus privacy.[22] On the one hand, many Democrats and the American Civil Liberties Union were concerned that if these bills were all introduced and passed, they would take away the civil liberties of many Americans, encroach upon the Fourth Amendment rights against unreasonable searches and seizures, and thus potentially violate the Constitutional rights of Americans. On the other hand, the Republicans and many think-tanks focused on anti-terrorism legislation. They were concerned that without these laws, federal law enforcement's ability to investigate terroristic threats and conduct counter-terrorism operations against potential terrorist threats would be severely limited. Members of the U.S. Senate came together and discussed what should be in the bill on September 19th, and from there the bill began to be crafted. In reality it was a catch-all bill; many proposals that had been previously entertained and failed, plus many new proposals, were all cobbled together into what became the Uniting and Strengthening America by Providing Appropriate Tools Required to Intercept and Obstruct Terrorism Act of 2001—the USA PATRIOT Act.

The Democrats realized they were in a weak position, for there was a clear need that Congress act decisively, and that it should act with solidarity. In other words, anyone who voted against the new proposal would be seen as anti-American and not overly concerned with responding to the attacks of 9-11. Democrats worked to ensure that all of the proposals that gave more authority to federal law enforcement would have court oversight. In many instances, this type of oversight was included in the bill, but in others it was rejected as being redundant, as oversight was already granted to the courts. What hampered this political wrangling, however, turned out to be a new terroristic threat—anthrax.

© Ron Thomas/AP Images.

One week after September 11, 2001, on September 18, someone began mailing letters containing anthrax spores to various media outlets such as ABC, CBS, and NBC News, as well as Senators Tom Daschle (D-SD) and Patrick Leahy (D-VT). Anthrax spores are a biological agent that appears as a white powder and can enter the body through inhalation, cutaneous contact, as well as ingestion. It causes a skin reaction and lesions and can lead to death.

In the case of the anthrax mailing, 5 people died and 17 others were infected. No one knew at the time if this was another Al Qaeda attack or an act of domestic terrorism (although one individual, Steven Hatfill, was suspected, the investigation shifted later to Bruce Ivins, who then committed suicide. No one was ever held accountable for these biological attacks). The result of the anthrax attacks, however, was to enhance the need to pass the USA PATRIOT Act. The act was introduced into the U.S. House of Representatives on October 23rd and passed 357 to 66 on October 24, 2001. The following day, October 25th, the Senate passed the bill 98 to 1 (Russ Feingold [D-WI] was the lone dissenter), and on October 26, 2001 President George W. Bush signed it into law (see **Box 4.6**).

The bill, which had integrated numerous earlier proposals and several other bills that had been previously introduced into both the House and Senate, were organized around ten titles (see **Box 4.7**). Each of these titles consisted of numerous sections (numbering more than 1,000 in total) that detailed the new laws and modifications to previous laws. In fact, more than 15 previous acts, some dating as far back as 1934, were amended by the USA PATRIOT Act (see **Box 4.8**). As a result, the bill was comprehensive and sweeping in scope. In order to protect against the possibility of too much power being included in the legislation, many of the act's provisions had a sunset clause, meaning that within a certain timeframe the law would no longer be on the books unless the provision was reauthorized by Congress. Most of these were set to expire on December 31, 2005.

Proponents of the USA PATRIOT Act found that it enhanced the sharing of information between intelligence and law enforcement agencies, tearing down the wall that separated them and allowing them to "connect the dots."[23] It has also been

---

BOX 4.6   Remarks on Signing the USA PATRIOT Act of 2001, October 26, 2001

… one thing is for certain: These terrorists must be pursued; they must be defeated; and they must be brought to justice. And that is the purpose of this legislation. Since the 11th of September, the men and women of our intelligence and law enforcement agencies have been relentless in their response to new and sudden challenges.

We have seen the horrors terrorists can inflict. We may never know what horrors our country was spared by the diligent and determined work of our police forces, the FBI, ATF agents, Federal marshals, custom officers, Secret Service, intelligence professionals, and local law enforcement officials. Under the most trying conditions, they are serving this country with excellence and often with bravery.

They deserve our full support and every means of help that we can provide. We're dealing with terrorists who operate by highly sophisticated methods and technologies, some of which were not even available when our existing laws were written. The bill before me takes account of the new realities and dangers posed by modern terrorists. It will help law enforcement to identify, to dismantle, to disrupt, and to punish terrorists before they strike.

For example, this legislation gives law enforcement officials better tools to put an end to financial counterfeiting,

smuggling, and money laundering. Secondly, it gives intelligence operations and criminal operations the chance to operate not on separate tracks but to share vital information so necessary to disrupt a terrorist attack before it occurs.

As of today, we're changing the laws governing information sharing. And as importantly, we're changing the culture of our various agencies that fight terrorism. Countering and investigating terrorist activity is the number one priority for both law enforcement and intelligence agencies …

This legislation is essential not only to pursuing and punishing terrorists but also preventing more atrocities in the hands of the evil ones. This Government will enforce this law with all the urgency of a nation at war. The elected branches of our Government and both political parties are united in our resolve to find and stop and punish those who would do harm to the American people.

It is now my honor to sign into law the USA PATRIOT Act of 2001.

Reproduced from: Bush, George W. (2001). "Remarks on Signing the USA PATRIOT ACT of 2001." Public Papers of the Presidents of the United States. Washington, D.C.: U.S. G.P.O.

BOX 4.7   USA PATRIOT Act (2001)—Ten Titles

Title I	Enhancing Domestic Security Against Terrorism		Title VII	Increased Information Sharing for Critical Infrastructure Protection
Title II	Surveillance Procedures		Title VIII	Terrorism Criminal Law
Title III	Anti-Money Laundering to Prevent Terrorism		Title IX	Improved Intelligence
Title IV	Border Security		Title X	Miscellaneous
Title V	Removing Obstacles to Investigating Terrorism			
Title VI	Victims and Families of Victims of Terrorism			

Reproduced from: P.L. 107-56, 115 Stat. 272 (2001), The Uniting and Strengthening America by Providing Appropriate Tools Required to Intercept and Obstruct Terrorism (USA PATRIOT ACT).

BOX 4.8   Federal Statutes Amended by the USA PATRIOT Act, 2001

Bank Holding Company Act of 1956   12 USC 1841

Communications Act of 1934   47 USC 151

Controlled Substances Import and Export Act   21 USC 951

Controlled Substances Act   21 USC 826

Electronic Communication Privacy Act of 1986   18 USC 2510

Fair Credit Reporting Act   15 USC 1681

Federal Deposit Insurance Act   12 USC 1811

Federal Wiretap Statute   18 USC 119

Foreign Assistance Act of 1961   22 USC 2291

Foreign Intelligence Surveillance Act   50 USC 1805

Intelligence Reform and Terrorism Prevention Act of 2004   118 Stat. 3742

National Security Act   50 USC 401

Omnibus Crime Control and Safe Streets Act of 1968   42 USC 3797

Right to Financial Privacy Act of 1978   12 USC 3401

Violent Crime Control and Law Enforcement Act of 1994   49 USC 46502

Reproduced from: P.L. 107-56, 115 Stat. 272 (2001), The Uniting and Strengthening America by Providing Appropriate Tools Required to Intercept and Obstruct Terrorism (USA PATRIOT ACT).

noted that the act gave investigators the same tools to go after terrorists that it already had to go after criminals, particularly those involved in organized crime and drug trafficking, thus allowing law enforcement to conduct investigations without tipping off terrorists. The act was also seen as updating the law to reflect not only the new threats to America but the new technologies that existed, such as cell phones and the Internet. In addition, there was much praise for the enhanced penalties for those who committed terroristic acts, allowing stiffer penalties for those who harbor terrorists, enhancing punishments for those conspiring against the government, and to punish bioterrorists. Finally, the act provided for both judicial and congressional oversight of these new laws and their enforcement to ensure that civil liberties would not be violated.

Opponents of the bill have noted that the law went too far in authorizing indefinite detentions of immigrants for purposes of investigations. They also pointed out that the ability of law enforcement to search homes and businesses without the owner's permission, or even their knowledge, went far beyond what similar legislation for organized crime and drug trafficking ever provided. Opponents also argued against the use of National Security Letters (NSLs), which allowed federal law enforcement, in the name of national security, to search telephone, cell phone, email, and financial records without a court order. Still further, the ability of law enforcement to request business records, cell phone logs, library records, and other financial records without even the National Security Letter was too much power and not enough protection for Americans' civil liberties. In addition, many argued that the oversight by the judiciary and Congress did not reach far enough.

Judicial challenges did surface, although these cases took time to work their way through the legal system. Several of the provisions were found unconstitutional and were struck down by federal judges, including the use of the National Security Letters to circumvent the need for court orders, as well as the warrantless searches into various records, including personal library records. Then, when the first authorization of the USA PATRIOT Act reached its first sunset period, the U.S. Congress amended the act, adding in enhanced security at seaports and new powers for the U.S. Secret Service, but did not reauthorize two provisions within Title II related to roving wiretaps and access to business records, in part because of the court rulings.

There is no doubt that the USA PATRIOT Act gave federal law enforcement more power to track down, surveil, and investigate potential terrorists and terroristic threats. Yet there is also little doubt that the ability given to the government has come at a cost of Americans' civil liberties. Anytime government is given more power and authority, it encroaches upon the freedom of the people. Whether that encroachment is worth the price is an issue people continue to debate to this day.

■ The Homeland Security Act of 2002

Although President Bush had created the Office of Homeland Security within the White House, he initially opposed the idea of creating a cabinet-level bureaucracy. Members of the 107th Congress (2001–2002), however, wanted to create a more stable organization geared toward protecting the United States. A number of proposals were made by various members of Congress over the early months of 2002. One of those was by Senators Joseph Lieberman (D-CT) and Arlen Specter (R-PA) who introduced the Department of National Homeland Security Act of 2001 (S 1534) that would create a cabinet-level Department of National Homeland Security.

At the same time, in the U.S. House, Representative Richard K. Armey (R-TX) proposed the National Homeland Security Act of 2002 (HR 5005). This proposal sought to establish a Department of Homeland Security, an executive department that would be headed by a Secretary that was appointed by the President with the advice and consent of the Senate. The new department would be responsible for: (1) overseeing policies for preventing terrorist attacks within the United States; (2) passing new laws that reduce the vulnerability of the United States to terrorism; (3) minimizing the damage done during a terrorist attack and assisting in the recovery from such attacks; (4) carrying out all functions of those agencies transferred to DHS; (5) ensuring that the functions of the agencies within DHS not related directly to protecting the country are not diminished; (6) ensuring that the overall economic security of the United States is not diminished by any activities related to protecting the United States; and (7) monitoring possible connections between illegal drug trafficking and terrorism.[24] Under Armey's proposal, the new department would be comprised of the U.S. Customs Service, the Transportation Security Administration, the Federal Protective Service of the General Services Administration, the Federal Law Enforcement Training Center, and the Office for Domestic Preparedness within the Office of Justice Programs of the Department of Justice.[25]

The Bush administration initially resisted both proposals to develop a cabinet-level department with the responsibility of overseeing homeland security. Bush argued that the job could best be handled out of the White House Office of Homeland Security, which former Governor Tom Ridge was already at work in advancing based upon President Bush's Executive Order. After Congressional support seemed to be gaining for the idea of a new department, the White House abruptly reversed its position and proposed its own plan. On June 6th, President Bush announced his proposal for a new Department of Homeland Security. In a speech before a joint session of Congress, Bush noted that "We've got to get used to the fact that they want to come again,"[26] and that "… our government must be reorganized to deal most effectively with the new threats of the 21st century."[27] Bush went on to announce a plan to create a new cabinet-level department that would coordinate national efforts to prevent terrorism (see text of speech, **Box 4.9**). This new department would consist of entire agencies or portions of over 40 agencies and departments that already played a role in protecting the United States.

The majority of Congressional members supported the proposal for reorganizing the federal agencies to enable the country to fight terrorism more effectively. Nonetheless, there was much discussion and heated deliberations about the President's proposal. On a number of occasions, proposals were put forth to bring the CIA, the FBI, and the National Security Agency (NSA) under the Department of Homeland Security, but after numerous debates and avid support against such plans, the legislation failed. Some Democrats in the House were worried that Bush's plan was inadequate and possibly even counterproductive. They thought it would

---

BOX 4.9   President Bush's Statement Proposing Department of Homeland Security

… So tonight I ask the Congress to join me in creating a single, permanent department with an overriding and urgent mission—securing the homeland of America and protecting the American people. Right now as many as a 100 different government agencies have some responsibilities for homeland security, and no one has final accountability. For example, the Coast Guard has several missions, from search and rescue to maritime treaty enforcement. It reports to the Transportation Department, whose primary responsibilities are roads, rails, bridges, and the airways. The Customs Service, among other duties, collects tariffs and prevents smuggling, and it is part of the Treasury Department, whose primary responsibility is fiscal policy, not security.

Tonight I propose a permanent Cabinet-level Department of Homeland Security to unite essential agencies that must work more closely together, among them, the Coast Guard, the Border Patrol, the Customs Service, Immigration officials, the Transportation Security Administration, and the Federal Emergency Management Agency. Employees of this new agency will come to work every morning knowing their most important job is to protect their fellow citizens. The Department of Homeland Security will be charged with four primary tasks. This new agency will control our borders and prevent terrorists and explosives from entering our country.

It will work with state and local authorities to respond quickly and effectively to emergencies. It will bring together our best scientists to develop technologies that detect biological, chemical, and nuclear weapons, and to discover the drugs and treatments to best protect our citizens; and this new department will review intelligence and law enforcement information from all agencies of government and produce a single daily picture of threats against our homeland. Analysts will be responsible for imagining the worst and planning to counter it. The reason to create this department is not to [increase] the size of government but to increase its focus and effectiveness. The staff of this new department will be largely drawn from the agencies we are combining. By ending duplication and overlap, we will spend less on overhead and more on protecting America. This reorganization will give the good people of our government their best opportunity to succeed by organizing our resources in a way that is thorough and unified.

What I am proposing tonight is the most extensive reorganization of the federal government since the 1940s. …

only result in a larger bureaucracy without making the "parts" work together more effectively. Other argued that the Bush proposal was not "budget neutral" and would inflate the cost of doing business far beyond what the current agency structure spent on an annual basis.[28]

Ultimately, after the fall mid-term elections in 2002, there was enough support and the proposal passed Congress. The House of Representatives voted in favor 299 to 121 on November 13, 2002, and the U.S. Senate passed the bill 90 to 9 on November 19, 2002. The new Department of Homeland Security was established when President Bush signed the Homeland Security Act of 2002 on November 25, 2002 (see **Box 4.10**).[29]

Former Pennsylvania Governor Tom Ridge, who was then serving as the Director of the Office of Homeland Security, was nominated to serve as the first Secretary of Homeland Security. Once confirmed by the U.S. Senate, he was charged with carrying out the organizational planning that ultimately joined more than 179,000 federal employees from 22 existing federal agencies (often in multiple components from one agency) to report to one single, cabinet-level organization. The Department of Homeland Security officially opened on January 24, 2003.

BOX 4.10   Remarks on Signing the Homeland Security Act of 2002, November 25, 2002

The new department will analyze threats, will guard our borders and airports, protect our critical infrastructure, and coordinate the response of our nation to future emergencies. The Department of Homeland Security will focus the full resources of the American government on the safety of the American people …

Dozens of agencies charged with homeland security will now be located within one Cabinet department, with the mandate and legal authority to protect our people. America will be better able to respond to any future attacks, to reduce our vulnerability and, most important, prevent the terrorists from taking innocent American lives.

The Department of Homeland Security will have nearly 170,000 employees, dedicated professionals … When the Department of Homeland Security is fully operational, it will enhance the safety of our people in very practical ways. First, this new department will analyze intelligence information on terror threats collected by the CIA, the FBI, the National Security Agency, and others … Second, the department will gather and focus all our efforts to face the challenge of cyberterrorism and the even worse danger of nuclear, chemical, and biological terrorism. This department will be charged with encouraging research on new technologies that can detect these threats in time to prevent an attack. Third, state and local governments will be able to turn for help and information to one federal domestic security agency, instead of more than 20 agencies that currently divide these responsibilities. This will help our local governments work in concert with the federal government for the sake of all the people of America. Fourth, the new department will bring together the agencies responsible for border, coastline, and transportation security. There will be a coordinated effort to safeguard our transportation systems and to secure the border so that we're better able to protect our citizens and welcome our friends. Fifth, the department will work with state and local officials to prepare our response to any future terrorist attack that may come. We have found that the first hours and even the first minutes after the attack can be crucial in saving lives, and our first-responders need the carefully planned and drilled strategies that will make their work effective.

◼ Homeland Security Presidential Directives

As previously mentioned, President George W. Bush, not long after the creation of the Office of Homeland Security, created the President's Homeland Security Advisory Council and Senior Advisory Committee for Homeland Security. He did this through an Executive Order 13260, which he signed on March 19, 2002.[30] This was the first of a number of presidential executive orders Bush signed related to homeland security. The next was an Executive Order 13311, pertaining to homeland security information sharing, and then another entitled Strengthening the Sharing of Terrorism Information to Protect Americans (#13356), both of which allowed intelligence agencies to share information related to potential domestic terrorism threats with other federal agencies.[31] Previously, intelligence agencies generally could not share this information with other federal agencies due to its high-level classification. Finally, Executive Order 13407, Public Alert and Warning System, created the often ridiculed and derided color-coded warning system that signified to the U.S. public the current terrorist threat level.[32] These executive orders, which have the full force of law, are a means by which the president can direct certain officers and agencies within the executive branch of government. In these instances, President Bush was directing federal agencies on new practices they would implement, such as high-level information sharing, the creation of a Homeland Security Advisory Council, and the use of a public alert and warning system.

© Joshua Roberts/AFP/Getty Images.

There is another means by which presidents can also issue directives to executive branch officers and agencies, and that is through what are known as presidential directives. These directives are a form of executive orders, but are usually created through the advice and consent of a particular council. In the past, the main council for these directives has almost always been the National Security Council, and the topics have been related to national security. Bush wanted to develop the same relationship between the president and his Homeland Security Council as existed between the president and the National Security Council. Therefore, like the issuance of National Security Presidential Directives, Bush would issue **Homeland Security Presidential Directives**. During his two terms in office, President Bush issued 25 such directives (see **Box 4.11**).

The first two Homeland Security Presidential Directives (HSPDs) were issued on October 29, 2001 and were related to the organization and operation of the Homeland Security Council (HSPD-1) and Combating Terrorism Through Immigration Policies (HSPD-2). Additional Homeland Security Presidential Directives included the management of domestic incidents (HSPD-5) and how federal agencies needed to prepare for certain emergencies (HSPD-8). These two directives, in particular, became critical to the development of the National Incident Management System (later called the National Incident Management Framework), which was focused on developing a national response to both natural disasters and terroristic attacks, and the creation of the Incident Command System (ICS) as the primary means for carrying out such responses at the federal, state, and local levels. Other Homeland Security

BOX 4.11 Homeland Security Presidential Directives

HSPD-1 Organization and Operation of the Homeland Security Council   Oct. 1, 2001

HSPD-2 Combating Terrorism Through Immigration Policies   Oct. 1, 2001

HSPD-3 Homeland Security Advisory System   Mar. 11, 2002

HSPD-4 National Strategy to Combat Weapons of Mass Destruction   Dec. 11, 2002

HSPD-5 Management of Domestic Incidents   Feb. 28, 2003

HSPD-6 Integration and Use of Screening Information   Sep. 16, 2003

HSPD-7 Critical Infrastructure Identification, Prioritization, and Protection   Dec. 17, 2003

HSPD-8 National Preparedness   Dec. 17, 2003

HSPD-9 Defense of United States Agriculture and Food   Feb. 3, 2004

HSPD-10 Biodefense for the 21st Century   Apr. 28, 2004

HSPD-11 Comprehensive Terrorist-Related Screening Procedures   Aug. 27, 2004

HSPD-12 Common ID Standard for Federal Employees/Contractors   Aug. 27, 2004

HSPD-13 Maritime Security Policy   Dec. 21, 2004

HSPD-14 Domestic Nuclear Detection Office   Apr. 15, 2005

HSPD-15 U.S. Strategy and Policy in the War on Terror (Classified)   Classified

HSPD-16 National Strategy for Aviation Security   Jun. 22, 2006

HSPD-17 Nuclear Materials Information Program   Aug. 28, 2006

HSPD-18 Medical Countermeasures Against Weapons of Mass Destruction   Jan. 31, 2007

HSPD-19 Combating Terrorist Use of Explosives in the United States   Feb. 12, 2007

HPSD-20 National Continuity Policy   Apr. 4, 2007

HSPD-21 Public Health and Medical Preparedness   Oct. 18, 2007

HSPD-22 Domestic Chemical Defense   Classified

HSPD-23 Cyber Security and Monitoring   Jan. 8, 2008

HSPD-24 Biometrics for ID and Screening to Enhance National Security   Jun. 5, 2008

HSPD-25 Arctic Region Policy   Jan. 9, 2009

Reproduced from: Bush, George W. (2001-2009). Homeland Security Presidential Directives.

Presidential Directives were related to domestic nuclear detection (HSPD-14), maritime security (HSPD-13), and the last Bush-issued directive was related to security in the Arctic region (HSPD-25). Several of these HSPDs remain classified, due to the nature of the directive, but the majority are unclassified and available to the public.

■ Chapter Summary

The terrorist attacks on September 11, 2001 called for an American response both overseas and domestically. In the immediate aftermath, to more effectively deal with future attacks as well as natural disasters, the President created the Office of Homeland Security in the White House, issued executive orders and Homeland Security Presidential Directives. The U.S. Congress passed the USA PATRIOT Act of 2001 and the Homeland Security Act of 2002, the former a wide array of laws giving federal law enforcement more investigatory powers for purposes of anti-terrorism and counter-terrorism, while the latter set in motion the creation of a new cabinet-level Department of Homeland Security. Once the new Secretary of Homeland Security, Tom Ridge, was confirmed, the new department came into existence and began consolidating all of the agencies and agency components that made up the new department. This represented the largest organizational shift in federal bureaucracy since World War II.

■ Review/Discussion Questions

1. Explain the different between the White House/Executive Branch Office of Homeland Security and the Department of Homeland Security.
2. How was the USA PATRIOT Act, a comprehensive piece of legislation, passed so quickly in just 6 weeks? Where did all of the provisions within the bill come from?
3. What is the Homeland Security Act of 2002, how did it come about, and what did it do?
4. What is a Homeland Security Presidential Directive, how many have there been, and how have they contributed to homeland security in the United States?

■ Additional Readings

The Homeland Security Act of 2002. HR 5005; PL 107-296; 116 Stat. 2135. Retrieved online at http://www.dhs.gov/xlibrary/assets/hr_5005_enr.pdf

National Commission on Terrorist Attacks Upon the United States. (2004). *The 9/11 Commission Report: Final Report of the National Commission on Terrorist Attacks Upon the United States (Authorized Ed.).* New York: W.W. Norton & Company, Inc.

O'Harrow, R., Jr. (2002). "Six Weeks in Autumn." *The Washington Post.* Retrieved online at http://www.washingtonpost.com/wp-dyn/content/article/2006/05/09/AR2006050900961.html

U.S. Department of Justice. (2013). USA PATRIOT Act. Retrieved online at http://www.justice.gov/archive/ll/highlights.htm

■ Endnotes

1. Portions of the introduction are based on the 9/11 Commission Report. See National Commission on Terrorist Attacks Upon the United States. (2004). *The 9/11 Commission Report: Final Report of the National Commission on Terrorist Attacks Upon the United States (Authorized Ed.).* New York: W.W. Norton & Company, Inc.
2. National Commission on Terrorist Attacks Upon the United States. (2004). *The 9/11 Commission Report: Final Report of the National Commission on Terrorist Attacks Upon the United States (Authorized Ed.).* New York: W.W. Norton & Company, Inc., p. 38.

3. The authors recognize that the reactions of President George W. Bush on September 11, 2001 are not without controversy, and while there is a wide debate on the Internet, much of it is presented from a wide array of perspectives, often with emotion, and sometimes in conspiratorial tones. The 9/11 Commission details President Bush's reactions and provides justifications for the decisions made in a historical (not ahistorical) manner. Therefore, the 9/11 Commission's findings are relied upon to track the President's movements on 9/11.

4. National Commission on Terrorist Attacks Upon the United States. (2004). *The 9/11 Commission Report: Final Report of the National Commission on Terrorist Attacks Upon the United States (Authorized Ed.)*. New York: W.W. Norton & Company, Inc., p. 39.

5. National Commission on Terrorist Attacks Upon the United States. (2004). *The 9/11 Commission Report: Final Report of the National Commission on Terrorist Attacks Upon the United States (Authorized Ed.)*. New York: W.W. Norton & Company, Inc., p. 326.

6. National Commission on Terrorist Attacks Upon the United States. (2004). *The 9/11 Commission Report: Final Report of the National Commission on Terrorist Attacks Upon the United States (Authorized Ed.)*. New York: W.W. Norton & Company, Inc.

7. Bush, G.W. (2001). "Remarks While Touring Damage at the Pentagon in Arlington, Virginia. September 12, 2001." *Public Papers of the Presidents of the United States*. Washington, DC: U.S. G.P.O.

8. Bush, G.W. (2001). "Remarks to Police, Firemen, and Rescueworkers at the World Trade Center Site in New York City. September 14, 2001." *Public Papers of the Presidents of the United States*. Washington, DC: U.S. G.P.O.

9. Bush, G.W. (2001). "Remarks to Police, Firemen, and Rescueworkers at the World Trade Center Site in New York City. September 14, 2001." *Public Papers of the Presidents of the United States*. Washington, DC: U.S. G.P.O.

10. Bush, G.W. (2001). "Remarks to Police, Firemen, and Rescueworkers at the World Trade Center Site in New York City. September 14, 2001." *Public Papers of the Presidents of the United States*. Washington, DC: U.S. G.P.O.

11. Bush, G.W. (2001). "Remarks to Police, Firemen, and Rescueworkers at the World Trade Center Site in New York City. September 14, 2001." *Public Papers of the Presidents of the United States*. Washington, DC: U.S. G.P.O.

12. Bush, G.W. (2001). "Remarks to Police, Firemen, and Rescueworkers at the World Trade Center Site in New York City. September 14, 2001." *Public Papers of the Presidents of the United States*. Washington, DC: U.S. G.P.O.

13. Bush, G.W. (2001). "Executive Order Establishing Office of Homeland Security. October 8, 2001." Retrieved online at http://georgewbush-whitehouse.archives.gov/news/releases/2001/10/print/20011008-2.html

14. Bush, G.W. (2001). "Executive Order Establishing Office of Homeland Security. October 8, 2001." Retrieved online at http://georgewbush-whitehouse.archives.gov/news/releases/2001/10/print/20011008-2.html

15. Becker, E. & Weiner, T. (2001). "A Nation Challenged: Homeland Security; New Office to Become a White House Agency." *New York Times*, September 28, p. A1.

16. Bush, G.W. (2001). "Executive Order Establishing Office of Homeland Security. October 8, 2001." Retrieved online at http://georgewbush-whitehouse.archives.gov/news/releases/2001/10/print/20011008-2.html

17. Bush, G.W. (2001). "Executive Order Establishing the President's Homeland Security Advisory Council and Senior Advisory Committees for Homeland Security. March 21, 2001." Retrieved online at http://georgewbush-whitehouse.archives.gov/news/releases/2002/03/20020321-9.html

18. Scardale, M. & Spencer, J. (2002). "Federal Homeland Security Policy." The Heritage Foundation. Retrieved online at http://www.heritage.org/research/reports/2002/06/federal-homeland-security-policy

19. Downs, A. (1972). "Up and Down with Ecology: The 'Issue-Attention Cycle.'" *The Public Interest, 28,* 38-50.

20. Petersen, K.K. (2009). "Revisiting Downs' Issue-Attention Cycle: International Terrorism and U.S. Public Opinion." *Journal of Strategic Security, 2,* 1-16.

21. Kingdon, J.W. (2011). *Agendas, Alternatives, and Public Policies.* 2nd ed. Boston, MA: Longman.

22. O'Harrow, R., Jr. (2002). "Six Weeks in Autumn." *The Washington Post.* Retrieved online at http://www.washingtonpost.com/wp-dyn/content/article/2006/05/09/AR2006050900961.html

23. See, for instance, the U.S. Department of Justice. (2012). "The USA PATRIOT Act: Preserving Life and Liberty." Retrieved online at http://www.justice.gov/archive/ll/highlights.htm, or Sauter, M.A. & Carafano, J.J. (2012). *A Complete Guide to Homeland Security.* New York, NY: McGraw Hill.

24. "Bill Summary and Status: 107th Congress" http://thomas.loc.gov/cgi-bin/bdquery/z?d107:HR05005:@@@D&summ2=m&

25. "New Security Office Scrutinized" in *CQ Almanac 2001* 57th ed., 10-4-10-5. Washington, DC: Congressional Quarterly, 2002. http://library.cqpress.com/cqalmanac/cqal01-106-6372-328132

26. Bush, G.W. "Remarks at the World Pork Expo in Des Moines, Iowa," June 7, 2002, Online by Peters, G. & Woolley, J.T. *The American Presidency Project,* http://www.presidency,ucsb.edu/ws/?pid=73027

27. Bush, G.W. "The President's Radio Address" June 8, 2002, Online by Peters, G. & Woolley, J.T. *The American Presidency Project,* http://www.presidency.ucsb.edu/ws/?pid=25064

28. "Homeland Department Created," in *CQ Almanac 2002* 58th ed., 7-3-7-8. Washington, DC: Congressional Quarterly, 2003. http://library.cqpress.com/cqalmanac/cqal02-236-10378-664466

29. The Homeland Security Act of 2002. HR 5005; PL 107-296; 116 Stat. 2135. Retrieved online at http://www.dhs.gov/xlibrary/assets/hr_5005_enr.pdf

30. Bush, G.W. (2002). Executive Order 13260 of March 19, 2002. Establishing the President's Homeland Security Advisory Council and Senior Advisory Committee for Homeland Security. Retrieved online at http://www.fas.org/irp/offdocs/eo/eo-13260.htm

31. Bush, G.W. (2003). Executive Order 13311 of July 29, 2003, Homeland Security Information Sharing. Retrieved online at http://www.fas.org/irp/offdocs/eo/eo-13311.htm; Bush, G.W. (2004). Executive Order 13356 of August 27, 2004, Strengthening the Sharing of Terrorism Information To Protect Americans. Retrieved online at http://www.fas.org/irp/offdocs/eo/eo-13356.htm

32. Bush, G.W. (2006). Executive Order 13407 of June 26, 2006, Public Alert and Warning System. Retrieved online at http://www.fas.org/irp/offdocs/eo/eo-13407.htm

The Department of Homeland Security

Chapter Outline

Chapter Objectives

- To develop an overview of the Department of Homeland Security (DHS)

- To understand the organizational structure of DHS

- To understand the missions and goals of DHS

■ Introduction

About a month after the 9-11 terrorist attacks, President George W. Bush used his power of executive order to establish the Office of Homeland Security, which would be responsible for coordinating all homeland security efforts geared toward preventing another terrorist attack similar to that of 9-11.[1] The office was given five basic responsibilities, the first of which was to work with federal, state, and local agencies to prepare for a possible terrorist event. Second, the office was to mitigate the consequences of terrorist threats and attacks. Third, personnel from the office were to coordinate efforts between federal agents as well as other agencies to prevent terrorist attacks within the U.S. Protecting critical infrastructure from terrorist attacks was the fourth responsibility, and the last was providing incident management, continuity of government, and the development of programs geared toward educating the public about preventing terrorism.

President Bush immediately appointed Tom Ridge, the former governor of Pennsylvania and a Vietnam Veteran and past member of the House of Representatives, as the head of the new office and gave him the title of Assistant to the President for Homeland Security. According to the White House, Ridge's job would be similar to that of the National Security Advisor; he would be responsible for making policy and advising the president on homeland security measures. Joining Ridge in advising the president was a new Homeland Security Council, also created in the president's executive order. The Council was comprised of representatives of the executive branch, including the Attorney General of the United States, the Secretaries of Defense, Treasury, Agriculture, and Health and Human Services, and the directors of the FBI and the Federal Emergency Management Agency (**FEMA**).[2]

Although the **Office of Homeland Security** was a first step in creating a consistent federal policy to protect America from terrorism, many members of Congress sought a more permanent agency for overseeing homeland security policies. This resulted in a new agency: the **Department of Homeland Security**.

■ New Department—DHS

The intent of the Homeland Security Act was to realign government operations and communications into one organization by moving agencies responsible for national security into one group. The law consolidated all (or portions of) 22 existing federal agencies and departments that had some responsibility for homeland security into the new Department of Homeland Security (DHS). This was the largest reorganization of the federal government since the beginning of the Cold War.[3] The agencies relocated into DHS included FEMA, the Bureau of Alcohol, Tobacco and Firearms (BATF), the U.S. Coast Guard, U.S. Border Patrol, U.S. Customs Service, and the Transportation Security Administration (TSA).[4] Another federal agency, the Secret Service, would report directly to the Secretary of Homeland Security and retain its primary mission to protect the President and other government leaders.[5] The Immigration and Naturalization Service was split into two separate components, including an Immigration Enforcement Bureau (to protect borders and keep out illegal immigrants) and a Citizenship Bureau (to handle immigration services).[6] A list of the agencies reorganized into DHS is provided in TABLE 5.1.

The new Department was assigned three critical objectives, which were to (1) prevent terrorist attacks within the U.S., (2) reduce America's vulnerability to terrorism, and (3) minimize the damage from potential attacks and natural disasters.[7] Additionally, four goals were identified for the new department. The first of the goals concerned border and transportation security. As President Bush described, "We must closely monitor who is coming into and out of our country to help prevent foreign terrorists from entering our country and bringing in their instruments of terror ... we must expedite the legal flow of people and goods on

KEY TERM

FEMA—the Federal Emergency Management Agency, an agency charged with providing federal assistance to citizens and first responders in all-hazard events declared as necessitating a federal response.

KEY TERM

Office of Homeland Security—the office inside of the White House (executive branch) lead by former Governor Tom Ridge, charged with securing the homeland, and which served as the nucleus for the Department of Homeland Security.

KEY TERM

Department of Homeland Security—a federal cabinet-level agency created in 2002 by taking various pre-existing agencies and placing them under one federal bureaucracy charged with protecting America's homeland.

TABLE 5.1 Reorganization of Agencies into DHS	
New Agency	**Old Agency**
U.S. Customs and Border Protection	Justice and Treasury
Immigration and Customs Enforcement	Justice and Treasury
Federal Protective Service	General Services Administration
Transportation Security Administration	Transportation
Federal Law Enforcement Training Center	Treasury
Animal and Plant Health Inspection Service (Part)	Agriculture
Office for Domestic Preparedness	Justice
Federal Emergency Management Agency	None
Strategic National Stockpile National Disaster Medical System	Health and Human Services
Nuclear Incident Response Team	Energy
Domestic Emergency Support Teams	Justice
National Domestic Preparedness Office	FBI
CBRN Countermeasures Programs	Energy
Environmental Measurements Laboratory	Energy
National Biological Warfare Defense Analysis Center	Defense
Plum Island Animal Disease Center	Agriculture
Federal Computer Incident Response Center	General Services Administration
National Communications System	Defense
National Infrastructure Protection Center	FBI
Energy Security and Assurance Program	Energy
U.S. Coast Guard	Transportation
U.S. Secret Service	Treasury

Data from: Department of Homeland Security. (2013). "Who Joined DHS?" Retrieved online at http://www.dhs.gov/who-joined-dhs

which our economy depends." In other words, the department was to find a way to prevent terrorists from entering the country, while at the same time allowing for trade to continue.[8] Another goal focused on emergency preparedness and response. It was important that the country prepare for possible attacks and minimize the damage if one does occur. It was also necessary to be able to recover quickly from attacks. A third DHS goal was to prepare countermeasures for possible chemical, biological, radiological, and nuclear attacks. The last goal was to increase the country's ability to collect and analyze information while protecting critical infrastructures.

The department was organized into four primary divisions. The first was Border and Transportation Security, which was comprised of border control and transportation agencies. This division was given the responsibility for setting U.S. visa policy and securing U.S. borders and transportation systems. The second became the Emergency Preparedness and Response division, which included FEMA and the functions of other agencies charged with preparing for and responding to terror attacks. The third division was Science and Technology, which was comprised of different programs and efforts related to science and technology and was given the task of developing countermeasures against terror attacks involving weapons of mass destruction such as chemical, biological, radiological, and nuclear. The final division was the Information Analysis and Infrastructure Protection section, which was responsible for analyzing all intelligence information on potential terrorist action against the country and for evaluating critical U.S. infrastructure for vulnerabilities to terrorism. Each division was headed by an undersecretary.[9]

Relations between the federal, state, and local governments were streamlined in the new department. A new Intergovernmental Affairs group would coordinate federal homeland security programs with state and local officials. This would give state and local officials one primary contact in the federal government for issues concerning training, equipment, planning, emergency response, or other critical needs.

The law provided for a 1-year extension for airports to install equipment to screen baggage at airports to detect explosives. It also limited the legal liability for airport screening companies and provided that noncitizen U.S. nationals could work as airport passenger and baggage screeners. Related to this were provisions to require the TSA to create a program for training commercial airline pilots to carry weapons aboard aircraft. Those pilots who volunteer will be trained, and if they achieve proficiency comparable to that for air marshals and meet other TSA requirements, they may be deputized as federal flight deck officers and then allowed to carry firearms.[10]

Leadership

Tom Ridge was named Secretary of the new Department of Homeland Security on January 24, 2003. Upon his swearing-in, he said his job is "to develop the organizational framework needed to refocus and reorganize the department's workforce to accomplish the unified mission of protecting America."[11] Following the re-election of President Bush, Ridge resigned. Admiral James Milton Loy then became the Acting Secretary of Homeland Security serving from February 1, 2005 to February 15, 2005. During this time, Bush nominated the former Commissioner of the New York City Police Department, Bernard Kerik, to replace Ridge. Kerik was forced to withdraw his nomination on December 10, citing personal reasons (he explained that he had hired an illegal immigrant as a nanny for his children). On January 11, 2005, Bush then nominated federal judge Michael Chertoff to serve as the second Homeland Security secretary. Chertoff was confirmed on February 15, 2005 by a vote of 98-0 in the U.S. Senate. He was sworn in the same day.

The third head of the Department of Homeland Security was Janet Napolitano (see **Box 5.1**). Nominated by President Obama, the Senate confirmed Napolitano's appointment on January 20, 2009. In order to assist in the transition, Chertoff did not resign until January 21, 2009.

BOX 5.1   Janet Napolitano: Secretary of Homeland Security

Janet Napolitano was sworn in on January 21, 2009 as the third Secretary of the Department of Homeland Security, and she stepped down on August 31, 2013 to become the President of the University of California. Prior to joining the Obama Administration, Napolitano was mid-way through her second term as Governor of the State of Arizona. While governor, Napolitano became the first woman to chair the National Governors Association, where she was instrumental in creating the Public Safety Task Force and the Homeland Security Advisors Council. She also chaired the Western Governors Association. Napolitano previously served as the Attorney General of Arizona and the U.S. Attorney for the District of Arizona.

Napolitano's homeland security background is extensive. As U.S. Attorney, she helped lead the domestic terrorism investigation into the Oklahoma City Bombing. As Arizona Attorney General, she helped write the law to break up human smuggling rings. As governor, she implemented one of the first state homeland security strategies in the nation, opened the first state counter-terrorism center and spearheaded efforts to transform immigration enforcement. She's also been a pioneer in coordinating federal, state, local and bi-national homeland security efforts, and presided over large-scale disaster relief efforts and readiness exercises to ensure well-crafted and functional emergency plans.

Napolitano graduated from Santa Clara University in 1979, where she won a Truman Scholarship, and received her Juris Doctor (J.D.) in 1983 from the University of Virginia School of Law. After law school, she served as a law clerk for Judge Mary M. Schroeder of the U.S. Court of Appeals for the Ninth Circuit before joining the law firm of Lewis and Roca.

Reproduced from: Department of Homeland Security. (2013). "Secretary Janet Napolitano." Retrieved online at http://www.dhs.gov/xabout/structure/gc_1232568253959.shtm

Secretary Napolitano gave the first "State of America's Homeland Security" speech on January 27, 2011. Like the President's State of the Union address, Napolitano provided the nation with an update of the country's homeland security, which she reported as "more secure than it was 10 years ago, and, indeed, more secure than it was 2 years ago."[12] In the address (see **Box 5.2**), the Secretary noted that the country's security is not solely the responsibility of the Department of Homeland Security, but rather a shared responsibility that requires "engagement of our entire society, with government, law enforcement, the private sector, and the public all playing their respective roles."[13] She said that communities play a vital role by forging strong partnerships with local law enforcement.

In that speech, Secretary Napolitano announced the end of the color-coded alert system, replacing it with the **National Terrorism Advisory System**, a two-tiered system that included an "imminent threat" or "elevated threat." This was bolstered by the new "If You See Something, Say Something" campaign whereby citizens are asked to report suspicious activities to law enforcement. The Secretary reported on Project Global Shield, a program with other countries to prevent the theft of precursor chemicals that could be used by terrorist groups to make explosive devices. Napolitano described the expansion of E-Verify that help businesses ensure their workforce is legal, and the development of another new program, Einstein 2, a threat detection system to detect and disrupt malicious cyber activity.[14]

KEY TERM

National Terrorism Advisory System— a new general threat level system that replaced the old color-coded system that was much derided by the public and the media.

Courtesy of the DHS.

Statement by Secretary of Homeland Security Janet Napolitano, July 12, 2013

For more than four years I have had the privilege of serving President Obama and his Administration as the Secretary of Homeland Security. The opportunity to work with the dedicated men and women of the Department of Homeland Security, who serve on the frontlines of our nation's efforts to protect our communities and families from harm, has been the highlight of my professional career. We have worked together to minimize threats of all kinds to the American public. The Department has improved the safety of travelers; implemented smart steps that make our immigration system more fair and focused while deploying record resources to protect our nation's borders; worked with states to build resiliency and make our nation's emergency and disaster response capabilities more robust; and partnered with the private sector to improve our cybersecurity. After four plus years of focusing on these challenges, I will be nominated as the next President of the University of California to play a role in educating our nation's next generation of leaders. I thank President Obama for the chance to serve our nation during this important chapter in our history, and I know the Department of Homeland Security will continue to perform its important duties with the honor and focus that the American public expects.

Reproduced from: Department of Homeland Security. (2012). Secretary of Homeland Security Janet Napolitano's 2nd Annual Address on the State of America's Homeland Security: Homeland Security and Economic Security. Retrieved online at http://www.dhs.gov/news/2012/01/30/secretary-homeland-security-janet-napolitanos-2nd-annual-address-state-americas

Organization and Mission

DHS is currently the third largest cabinet-level department within the federal government, and is headed by the Secretary of Homeland Security, who is nominated by the President and confirmed by the Senate. The Secretary is assisted by a Deputy Secretary (see FIGURE 5.2), and the headquarters are in Washington, D.C. in a former naval facility, with many other offices located throughout the city. The department will eventually be consolidated into one location, about 5 miles from the Capitol building in a facility built in 1855 that once housed the Government Hospital for the Insane.[15]

The mission of DHS is to protect the U.S. and American territories from terrorist attacks, man-made accidents, and natural disasters. To do this effectively, DHS was organized into different offices (see FIGURE 5.1). The department is headed by the Secretary, who is responsible for overseeing the department's activities and assistance to state and local governments and to ensure a comprehensive approach to homeland security. Within this office are the Office of the General Counsel, Office of Inspector General, the Federal Law Enforcement Training Center (FLETC), the Directorates for Science and Technology, and the Office of Intelligence and Analysis.

© Jim Lo Scalzo/EPA/Landov.

Budget

In 2003, Congress passed a homeland security appropriations bill allocating $30.4 billion for fiscal year 2004. This was the first appropriations for the new department. Bush requested the money to enable the department to protect the nation's

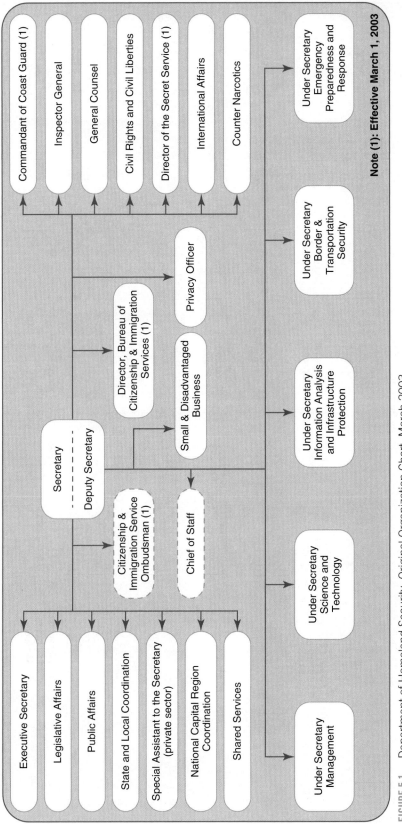

FIGURE 5.1 Department of Homeland Security: Original Organization Chart, March 2003

Courtesy of the DHS.

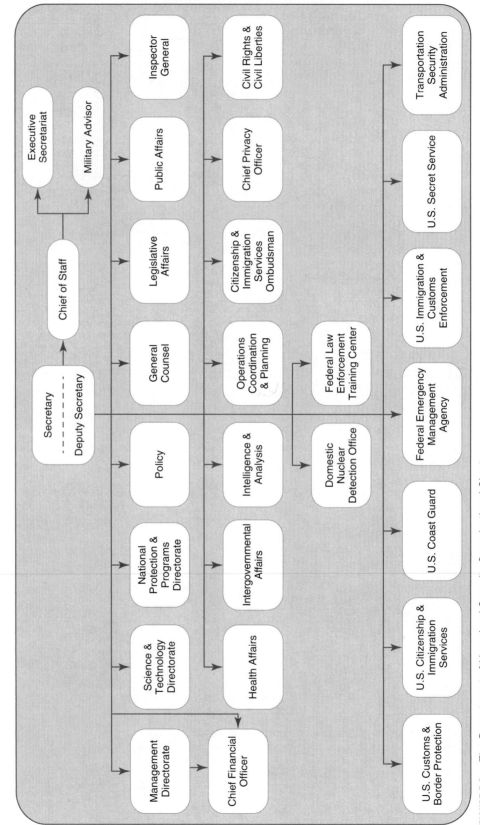

FIGURE 5.2   The Department of Homeland Security Organizational Chart

Courtesy of the DHS.

ports, airports, borders, and infrastructure from terrorism.[16] Since that time, the department's allocation has grown, as shown in TABLE 5.2. In order to understand how the money is allocated within the Department of Homeland Security, TABLE 5.3 shows the percentage of the budget going to the various agencies within DHS. Note that Customs Border Protection, FEMA, and the U.S. Coast Guard receive the largest amounts. It should also be noted that while the U.S. Secret Service appears to have a small percentage, much of their budget is classified and not part of the budget allocations of DHS.

TABLE 5.2 Yearly Budgets for Department of Homeland Security

Year	Dollar Amount
FY 2009 Enacted	$52.7 billion
FY 2010 Enacted	$56.0 billion
FY 2011 Enacted	$54.8 billion
FY 2012 Enacted	$59.7 billion
FT 2013 Presidential Request	$59.0 billion

Data from: Department of Homeland Security. (2012). "Fiscal Year 2011 Budget in Brief." Retrieved online at http://www.dhs.gov/xlibrary/assets/budget_bib_fy2011.pdf; Department of Homeland Security. (2012). "Fiscal Year 2012 Budget in Brief." Retrieved online at http://www.dhs.gov/xlibrary/assets/budget_bib_fy2012.pdf; Department of Homeland Security. (2013). "Fiscal Year 2013 Budget in Brief." Retrieved online at http://www.dhs.gov/xlibrary/assets/mgmt/dhs-budget-in-brief-fy2013.pdf

TABLE 5.3 2013 Department of Homeland Security Budget Allocations

Organization	Percent of Budget
FEMA	17%
FEMA Grant Program	5%
NPPD	4%
U.S. Secret Service	3%
U.S. Coast Guard	17%
TSA	13%
ICE	10%
Customs Border Protection	21%
A&O	1%
Dept. Ops	1%
DNDO	1%
S&T	1%
FLETC, OIG, OHA	1%
USCIS	5%

Data from: Department of Homeland Security. (2013). "Fiscal Year 2013 Budget in Brief." Retrieved online at http://www.dhs.gov/xlibrary/assets/mgmt/dhs-budget-in-brief-fy2013.pdf

■ DHS's Role Today

The Department of Homeland Security has five major mission areas (see FIGURE 5.3):

1. Counter-terrorism
2. Security of U.S. borders, be they land, sea, or air
3. Enforcement of our nation's immigration laws
4. Protection of cyberspace
5. Prepare in advance for and then respond quickly to any type of emergency that might occur.[17]

Each of these areas is described in the following text.

Counter-terrorism

Aviation Security

This mission area of Homeland Security seeks to guarantee the safety of air travel. One important aspect of aviation security is the Federal Air Marshal Service that helps to detect, deter, and defeat potential acts against U.S. air carriers, airports, passengers, and crews. Air marshals blend in with passengers on flights as a way to protect those on the plane. Air marshals often work with other law enforcement agencies such as the National Counterterrorism Center, the National Targeting Center, and the FBI's Joint Terrorism Task Forces.[18]

Another part of aviation security is Secure Flight, a program operated by TSA that works in conjunction with the existing Terrorism Watch List (a database of potential terrorists maintained by the government). It is a matching process for those who fly. Under the program, all airlines must provide each passenger's name as it appears on a government-issued ID, their date of birth, gender, and redress number (assigned in relation to a passenger's complaint).[19] If a passenger's name appears on the list, that passenger is unable to board the plane.

TSA works to keep passengers safe through screening programs in airports. TSA currently screens every passenger and every piece of luggage taken onto commercial aircraft.

Security officers are assigned to over 700 security checkpoints (located throughout the airports) and carry out nearly 7,000 baggage screening areas each day (located at the airport entry point for all ticketed customers).[20] The Air Cargo Security Program helps to ensure the safety of cargo on all modes of transportation. Since October 2008, 100% of the cargo on 96% of the flights that begin in the United States is now screened. TSA also requires background checks on employees who screen cargo, those who have knowledge of how it is going to be transported, and those who actually transport the cargo.[21]

Chemical Security

The chemical industry is a key component of the U.S. economy,[22] so DHS has established a number of programs to ensure safety of chemical storage, use, and transportation. For example, the department

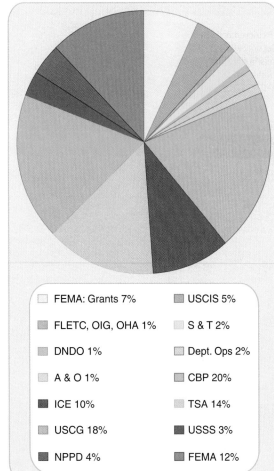

FEMA: Grants 7%   USCIS 5%

FLETC, OIG, OHA 1%   S & T 2%

DNDO 1%   Dept. Ops 2%

A & O 1%   CBP 20%

ICE 10%   TSA 14%

USCG 18%   USSS 3%

NPPD 4%   FEMA 12%

FIGURE 5.3   U. S. Department of Homeland Security
Courtesy of the DHS.

created the Chemical Facility Anti-Terrorism Standards for any U.S. facility that manufactures, uses, stores, or distributes certain chemicals at or above a specified quantity.[23]

At the same time, DHS recognizes that responsibility for chemical security is shared among federal, state, and local governments, as well as the private sector. Government and industry officials must work cooperatively to guarantee the security of America's chemical facilities, while at the same time not harming the nation's economy.

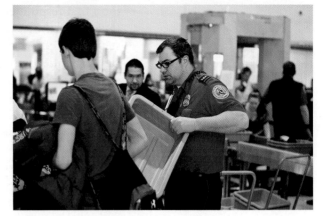

Courtesy of the Barry Bahler/DHS.

Fraud and Counterfeit

The Secret Service, as part of DHS, oversees the integrity of the nation's financial infrastructure. They implement programs geared to preventing electronic crime and other computer-related fraud. Because the Internet is worldwide, many of the investigations by the Secret Service are international in scope and involve international law enforcement agencies and other federal, state, and local agencies. These investigations cover counterfeiting of U.S. currency, food stamps, and postage stamps; counterfeiting of foreign currency; identity crimes (identity theft, false identification fraud, credit card fraud, bank fraud, and check fraud; passport/visa fraud); telemarketing fraud; telecommunications fraud (cellular and hard wire); computer fraud; investigations of forgery or impersonations of U.S. Saving Bonds, U.S. Treasury Notes, Bonds and Bills; and electronic funds transfer (EFT).

As part of the USA PATRIOT Act, the Secret Service was required to establish Electronic Crimes Task Forces and Electronic Crimes Working Group Initiatives. These task forces are comprised of law enforcement (from federal, state, and local agencies), as well as prosecutors, private industry, and academia, and are geared toward preventing, detecting, mitigating, and investigating possible attacks on the nation's financial systems. They provide support and resources for investigating crimes that have significant economic or community impact, that involve organized criminal groups with multiple districts or transnational organizations, and/or the use of schemes involving new technology.[24]

The Secret Service also established the Electronic Crimes Special Agent Program (ECSAP), which conduct examinations on computers and other electronic devices. Those serving in the program are agents with computer investigative skills.

Information Sharing

One primary goal of DHS was to increase communication and sharing of intelligence between law enforcement agencies. To do this, DHS has developed the Automated Critical Asset Management System (ACAMS), an online database to help state and local governments (law enforcement, public safety, and emergency response personnel) collect and use asset data, assess asset vulnerabilities, develop all-hazards incident response and recovery plans, and build public-private partnerships. It is available at no cost through Homeland Security's Office of Infrastructure Protection.[25]

Another way DHS is attempting to increase information sharing is through their Critical Infrastructure and Key Resources (CIKR) Asset Protection Technical Assistance Program (CAPTAP). This program is intended to assist state and local first responders, emergency managers, and homeland security officials to understand the basic tenets of the National Infrastructure Protection Plan and the steps required to develop and implement the plan. CAPTAP also provides tools to support critical infrastructure protection programs and provide information on the resources available to state and local agencies to build effective infrastructure protection programs.[26]

The Homeland Security Information Network (HSIN) is a national secure website for law enforcement at all levels to share information and collaborate on issues pertaining to homeland security. HSIN is comprised of a network of communities, called Communities of Interest (COI), such as emergency management, law enforcement, critical sectors, and intelligence. HSIN provides a 24/7 virtual meeting space for instant messaging and document sharing, allowing members to communicate and collaborate with each other instantly, regardless of their location.[27]

Infrastructure

Protecting America's critical infrastructure (i.e., the underlying facilities and systems necessary to run a country, such as roads, power grids, communications systems, and water supplies) is key because such attacks could be very disruptive and have lasting effects far beyond the initial target. DHS has many programs to help protect these critical systems. One of those is the Critical Infrastructure Learning Series, 1-hour Web-based seminars for local law enforcement agencies and others in charge of infrastructure with tools, trends, issues, and best practices for infrastructure protection. They are conducted by senior critical infrastructure (CI) protection experts and are provided at no cost.[28]

The Critical Infrastructure Sector Partnerships is another way DHS seeks to develop protection programs between the public and private sectors. This is crucial because the private sector owns and operates approximately 85% of the nation's critical infrastructure.[29]

FEMA, as part of DHS, has created the Emergency Management and Response–Information Sharing and Analysis Center (EMR–ISAC) to promote awareness of all-hazards threats and provide other information to help protect critical infrastructure. They collect, analyze, and disseminate information into concise reports on credible threats and disseminate them to the appropriate owners and operators. Databases are maintained to increase information sharing and provide assistance if needed. They provide Critical Infrastructure Protection (CIP) notices that contain vital information regarding threats that may affect operations. These documents are sent only to key individuals who have been validated as having the "need to know." They also distribute "infograms" containing articles about trends, bulletins containing homeland security information distributed as needed for the interest of ESS personnel, and other things such as job aids, DVDs, and guides.[30]

Law Enforcement

Immigration and Customs Enforcement (ICE) is a bureau of DHS designed to enter into partnerships with state and local law enforcement organizations to assist them with immigration enforcement within their jurisdictions.[31] ICE also helps local police deal with issues concerning human trafficking.[32]

Nuclear Security

DHS has established efforts to protect the nation against a possible act of radiological or nuclear terrorism. The department coordinates efforts with other agencies both inside and outside of the United States in order to prevent such materials or weapons from entering the United States to be used in an attack. The Domestic Nuclear Detection Office (DNDO) in DHS is developing technologies to detect nuclear threats.[33] One of these is the Intelligent Radiation Sensing System (IRSS), which will provide law enforcement better means to protect communities from radiological or nuclear threats. The IRSS uses a networked system to determine the presence, location, and type of radiological material in a specific area more quickly and accurately than a group of individual detectors.[34]

DHS also has a Shielded Nuclear Alarm Resolution (SNAR) program that allows DHS officials to work with governments and companies around the world to strengthen the security of nuclear materials. To help further this mission, DHS's DNDO is developing technology that can identify radiological and nuclear threats at ports without disrupting the flow of commerce. The SNAR program allows for efficient scanning of cargo containers to locate potential nuclear material.[35]

Secure Identification

It is important that DHS ensure accurate identification of people travelling into the U.S. One way they do that is through their Secure Flight Program, described previously. Another way is through the US–VISIT program, which provides biometric identification services (i.e., fingerprints and photographs) to federal, state, and local government decision-makers to help them identify people and determine risk. This information also helps immigration officers determine whether a person should be given a visa or enter the U.S.

Border Security

DHS is concerned with the security of all borders, while at the same time not interrupting travel and trade. One way this is accomplished is through the Container Security Initiative (CSI), a program intended to help increase security for maritime containerized cargo shipped to the United States from around the world. CSI addresses the threat to border security and global trade posed by the potential for terrorist use of a maritime container to deliver a weapon.[36]

Immigration

The Department of Homeland Security is responsible for providing immigration-related services and benefits such as naturalization and work authorization as well as investigative and enforcement responsibilities for enforcement of federal immigration laws, customs laws, and air security laws. This is done through ICE.

Cybersecurity

The Department of Homeland Security plays an important role in countering threats against cyberspace. DHS seeks to develop ways to keep our federal networks and critical infrastructure secure by protecting against all forms of cyber attacks. In 2004, DHS created the National Cyber Security Division (NCSD), which has partnered with government, industry, and academia as well as the international community to make cybersecurity a national and shared priority.

The National Security Presidential Directive 54/Homeland Security Presidential Directive 23 established the Comprehensive National Cybersecurity Initiative (CNCI) that formalizes a series of efforts to safeguard the federal systems from cyber-attacks. On the federal level the CNCI focuses on three key areas: to establish a defense that will reduce any vulnerabilities and prevent intrusions; to defend against all threats through use of intelligence and strengthening supply chain security; and to shape the future technological environment through research, development, and education as well as investing in technology.

As part of its role overseeing the CNCI, DHS has responsibility for ensuring the security of the nation's information technology (IT) and communications infrastructure. DHS has attempted to improve technology to prevent future attacks by hiring additional personnel for the Computer Emergency Readiness Team (US–CERT), the department's watch and warning center for the federal government's Internet infrastructure. US–CERT is charged with providing response support and defense against cyber-attacks for the Federal Civil Executive Branch while providing information sharing and collaboration with state and local government, industry, and international partners.

US-CERT is working to expand the Einstein Program to all federal departments and agencies as a way to provide an early warning system to identify malicious cyber activity. The Einstein Program helps identify unusual network traffic patterns and trends which signal unauthorized network traffic so that security personnel can identify and respond to potential threats. NCSD is in the process of deploying Einstein 2.

DHS is also attempting to thwart cyber-terrorism by forming the National Cybersecurity Center that will focus on coordinating intelligence about cyber threats between the many agencies. Additionally, DHS has expanded the National Cyber Investigative Joint Task Force (NCIJTF) so that it will include representatives from many federal agencies, including the Secret Service. This organization will also aid in the coordination and information sharing of information on cyber threats.[37]

Recently, DHS has begun a new national campaign called "Stop. Think. Connect." aimed at increasing the public's understanding of cyber threats and empowering the public to be safer and more secure online. The main objective is to help citizens become more aware of threats and arm people with the tools needed to protect themselves and their families.[38]

Preparedness, Response, and Recovery

If a terrorist attack occurs or a natural disaster or other emergency, DHS will provide a coordinated and comprehensive federal response and begin a fast and effective recovery effort. The department assumes primary responsibility for ensuring that all emergency response professionals are prepared for any situation.

To prepare for various types of emergencies, DHS/FEMA/Citizen Corps has created a Community Preparedness Webinar Series that provides information on community preparedness topics and resources available to citizens, community organizations, and Citizen Corps Councils. These webinars are available several times each month and are free to the public.[39] FEMA also has a program known as Ready (see www.ready.gov) that involves being informed (what to do before, during, and after an emergency), making a plan (prepare, plan, and stay informed for emergencies), building a kit (build a kit for disasters and be prepared), and getting involved (find opportunities to get involved to promote community preparedness).

There are also numerous agencies within the Department of Homeland Security that have very specific functions. Each of these agencies and a brief description follows:

Transportation Security Administration: Protects the nation's transportation system to ensure freedom of movement for people and commerce; includes airport security, inspection of rail cars, patrol of subways; strives to make all modes of transportation safe.

U.S. Customs and Border Protection: One of DHS's largest and most complex agencies, with a priority mission of keeping terrorists and their weapons out of the U.S. It also has a responsibility for securing and facilitating trade and travel while enforcing hundreds of U.S. regulations, including immigration and drug laws and guarding the nation's borders.

U.S. Citizenship and Immigration Services: Secures America's promise as a nation of immigrants by providing accurate and useful info to immigrants, granting immigration and citizenship benefits, promoting an awareness and understanding of citizenship, and ensuring the integrity of our immigration system.

U.S. Immigration and Customs Enforcement: Promotes homeland security and public safety through the criminal and civil enforcement of federal laws governing border control, customs, trade, and immigration.

U.S. Secret Service: Safeguards the nation's financial infrastructure and payment systems to preserve the integrity of the economy; also protects national leaders, visiting heads of state, and designated sites and National Special Security Events.

Federal Emergency Management Agency (FEMA): Supports U.S. citizens and first responders to ensure that the nation can work together to build, sustain, and improve its capability to prepare for, protect against, respond to, recover from, and mitigate all hazards.

U.S. Coast Guard: One of the five armed forces of the U.S. and the only military organization within the DHS. The Coast Guard protects the maritime economy and the environment, defends U.S. maritime borders, and saves those in peril at sea.

■ Chapter Summary

The Department of Homeland Security, formed by President Bush and Congress in the days after 9-11, was developed to help protect the country from any more terrorist attacks. The department was formed by a reorganization and consolidation of many other federal agencies, or portions of agencies, that had some role in homeland security. Since its formation, DHS has continued to collect and analyze intelligence about terrorism as a way to understand terrorist groups and break up any potential plots against the U.S. DHS has also helped states and local governments prepare for another attack, if it happens. President Obama and Congress have continued to support the department and its activities.

■ Review/Discussion Questions

1. How and why was the Department of Homeland Security established?
2. What is the organizational structure of DHS?
3. What are some of the components of DHS?
4. What agencies were transferred to DHS upon its creation?
5. Who was the first leader of DHS and who is the current Secretary?

■ Additional Readings

Bush, G.W. (2002). *The Department of Homeland Security*. Washington, D.C.: Office of the President.

Department of Homeland Security. (2013). *Creation of the Department of Homeland Security*. Retrieved online at http://www.dhs.gov/creation-department-homeland-security

Department of Homeland Security. (2013). *Who Joined DHS*. Retrieved online at http://www.dhs.gov/who-joined-dhs

■ Endnotes

1. Bush, G.W. (2001). Executive Order 13228: Establishing the Office of Homeland Security and the Homeland Security Council. *The American Presidency Project*. Retrieved online at http://www.presidency.ucsb.edu/ws/?pid=61509

2. CQ Almanac. (2002). New Security Office Scrutinized. *CQ Almanac 2001* 57th ed. Retrieved online at http://library.cqpress.com/cqalmanac/cqal01-106-6372-328132

3. CQ Almanac. (2003). Homeland Department Created. *CQ Almanac 2002* 58th ed. Retrieved online at http://library.cqpress.com/cqalmanac/cqal02-236-10378-664466

4. CQ Almanac. (2003). Homeland Department Created. *CQ Almanac 2002* 58th ed. Retrieved online at http://library.cqpress.com/cqalmanac/cqal02-236-10378-664466

5. Bush, G.W. (2002). Message to the Congress Transmitting Proposed Legislation to Create the Department of Homeland Security. *The American Presidency Project*. Retrieved online at http://www.presidency,ucsb.edu/ws/?pid=64050

6. CQ Almanac. (2003). Immigration and Naturalization Service (INS) Abolished, With Border Security, Immigration Services Divided at Department of Homeland Security (DHS). *CQ Almanac 2002*, 58th ed. Retrieved online at http://library.cqpress.com/cqalmanac/cqal02-236-10366-664138

7. Bush, G.W. (2002). Memorandum on the Establishment of the Department of Homeland Security. *The American Presidency Project*. Retrieved online at http://www.presidency,ucsb.edu/ws/?pid=73352

8. Bush, G.W. (2002). Remarks to Federal Employees on the Proposed Department of Homeland Security. *The American Presidency Project.* Retrieved online at http://www.presidency,ucsb.edu/ws/?pid=73054

9. CQ Almanac. (2003). Homeland Security Provisions. *CQ Almanac 2002* 58th ed. Retrieved online at http://library.cqpress.com/cqalmanac/cqal02-236-10378-664477

10. CQ Almanac. (2003). Homeland Security Provisions. *CQ Almanac 2002* 58th ed. Retrieved online at http://library.cqpress.com/cqalmanac/cqal02-236-10378-664477

11. Ridge, T. (2003). Homeland Security Secretary Swearing In. C-SPAN Video Library. Retrieved online at http://www.c-spanarchives.org/program/HomelandSecurityDepart

12. Napolitano, J. (2011). State of America's Homeland Security Address. Retrieved online at http://www.dhs.gov/ynews/speeches/sp_1296152572413.shtm

13. Napolitano, J. (2011). State of America's Homeland Security Address. Retrieved online at http://www.dhs.gov/ynews/speeches/sp_1296152572413.shtm

14. Napolitano, J. (2011). State of America's Homeland Security Address. Retrieved online at http://www.dhs.gov/ynews/speeches/sp_1296152572413.shtm

15. Public Intelligence. (2012). The Department of Homeland Security's New HQ is an Abandoned Insane Asylum. Retrieved online at http://publicintelligence.net/the-department-of-homeland-securitys-new-hq-is-an-abandoned-insand-asylum/

16. CQ Almanac. (2004). Quick Funds for Homeland Security. *CQ Almanac 2003*, 59th ed. Retrieved online at http://library.cqpress.com/cqalmanac/cqal03-835-24336-1084056

17. Napolitano, J. (2010). Remarks to Secretary Napolitano at the National Press Club. Retrieved online at http://www.dhs.gov/ynews/speeches/sp_1271433302831.shtm

18. Department of Homeland Security. (2012). *Federal Air Marshals.* Retrieved online at http://www.tsa.gov/lawenforcement/programs/fams/shtm

19. Department of Homeland Security. (2012). *Secure Flight Program.* Retrieved online at http://www.dhs.gov/files/programs/gc_1250693582433.shtm

20. Department of Homeland Security. (2012). *Security Screening.* Retrieved online at http://www.tsa.gov/what_we_do/screening/index.shtm

21. Department of Homeland Security. (2012). *Air Cargo Security Programs.* Retrieved online at http://www.tsa.gov/what_we_do/layers/aircargo/index.shtm

22. Department of Homeland Security. (2012). *Ammonium Nitrate Security Program.* Retrieved online at http://www.dhs.gov/files/programs/ammonium-nitrate-security-program.shtm

23. Department of Homeland Security. (2012). *Critical Infrastructure: Chemical Security.* Retrieved online at http://www.dhs.gov/files/programs/gc_1169501486179.shtm; See also Department of Homeland Security. (2012). *Chemical Sector: Critical Infrastructure and Key Resources.* Retrieved online at http://www.dhs.gov/files/programs/gc_1188567509125.shtm

24. Department of Homeland Security. (2012). *United States Secret Service, Criminal Investigations.* Retrieved online at http://www.secretservice.gov/criminal.shtml

25. Department of Homeland Security. (2012). *Automated Critical Asset Management System.* Retrieved online at http://www.dhs.gov/files/programs/gc_1190729724456.shtm

26. Department of Homeland Security. (2012). *CIKR Asset Protection Technical Assistance Program.* Retrieved online at http://www.dhs.gov/files/programs/gc_1195679577314.shtm

27. Department of Homeland Security. (2012). *Homeland Security Information Network.* Retrieved online at http://www.dhs.gov/files/programs/gc_1156888108137.shtm

28. Department of Homeland Security. (2012). *Critical Infrastructure Learning Series.* Retrieved online at http://www.dhs.gov/files/programs/gc_1231165582452.shtm

29. Department of Homeland Security. (2012). *Critical Infrastructure Sector Partnerships.* Retrieved online at http://www.dhs.gov/files/partnerships/editorial_0206.shtm

30. Department of Homeland Security. (2012). *Critical Infrastructure Protection.* Retrieved online at http://www.usfa.fema.gov/fireservice/subjects/emr-isac/index.shtm

31. Department of Homeland Security. (2012). *Delegation of Immigration Authority Section 287(g) Immigration and Nationality Act.* Retrieved online at http://www.ice.gov/287g/

32. Department of Homeland Security. (2012). *Anti-Human Trafficking Resources: Law Enforcement.* Retrieved online at http://www.dhs.gov/files/programs/gc_1298390940581.shtm

33. Department of Homeland Security. (2012). *Breakthrough Detection Technologies.* Retrieved online at http://www.dhs.gov/files/programs/dndo-breakthrough-detection-technologies.shtm

34. Department of Homeland Security. (2012). *Intelligent Radiation Sensing System.* Retrieved online at http://www.dhs.gov/files/programs/dndo-intelligent-radiation-sensing-system.shtm

35. Department of Homeland Security. (2012). *Shielded Nuclear Alarm Resolution.* Retrieved online at http://www.dhs.gov/files/programs/dndo-snar.shtm

36. Department of Homeland Security. (2012). *Container Security Initiative.* Retrieved online at http://www.cbp.gov/xp/cgov/trade/cargo_security/csi/

37. Department of Homeland Security. (2012). *Protecting Our Federal Networks Against Cyber Attacks.* Retrieved online at http://www.dhs.gov/files/programs/gc_1234200709381.shtm

38. Department of Homeland Security. (2012). *Stop. Think. Connect. Campaign.* Retrieved online at http://www.dhs.gov/files/events/stop-think-connect.shtm

39. Department of Homeland Security & the Federal Emergency Management Agency, Citizen Corps. (2012). *Community Preparedness Webinar Series.* Retrieved online at http://citizencorps.gov/resources/webinars/webinarlibrary.shtm

Homeland Security Community

Chapter Outline

Chapter Objectives

- Learn about the agencies responsible for homeland security in the U.S. including the intelligence, defense, and security communities

- Understand the role of coordination in the intelligence community as it relates to homeland security

- Learn how the intelligence and security communities interact with the criminal justice system

■ Introduction

When the report by the National Commission on Terrorist Attacks upon the United States (also known as *The 9/11 Commission Report*) came out, it was pointed in its critique of the intelligence community. In particular, the commission stated that, while the community was theoretically prepared to deal with threats such as 9-11 presented, in practice the community was separated by bureaucratic cultures that varied widely, had vastly different missions, and were facing a new and more complex threat from a more imaginative adversary than before.[1] This evaluation, by one of the most influential independent commissions ever appointed by the United States government, led to serious reevaluation of the structure and mission of the national intelligence apparatus.[2] Further, it led to significant changes in the way that the federal level of government cooperated with the state and local levels on matters of intelligence, particularly as it pertained to homeland security.[3]

This chapter introduces the reader to the homeland security community, consisting not only of the nation's intelligence agencies, but also the security and military communities that have important roles within a homeland security paradigm. Additionally, the chapter focuses on the relationship between these organizations and local and state agencies, which also play a part in the homeland security community. Finally, it examines the role the homeland security community plays within the justice system.

Courtesy of CIA.

■ Intelligence Community

The **intelligence community** in the U.S. is a complex one, with many organizations participating in specific capacities.[4] While most people have heard of the Central Intelligence Agency (CIA) and the National Security Agency (NSA), there are a large number of smaller agencies with more limited missions, such as the National Geospatial Intelligence Agency (NGA) that most have not heard of but that nevertheless play important roles in our national intelligence community.[5] In total, there are 17 agencies that make up the "intelligence community" of the United Sates, ranging across government departments as diverse as the Department of Energy and the Department of the Treasury (see **Box 6.1**).[6] While each of the agencies in the intelligence community has a specific mission to fulfill, the cooperation between agencies and how they cooperate with local and state authorities is essential to understanding homeland security operations within the United States.

▨ Office of the Director of National Intelligence

As provided for in the Intelligence Reform and Terrorism Prevention Act of 2004, the Director of National Intelligence (DNI) is responsible for coordinating the activities of the nation's other 16 intelligence agencies.[7] The 17th agency is the **Office of the Director of National Intelligence** (ODNI), which serves to support the DNI's mission. Additionally, the DNI is considered the nation's top official in relation to intelligence affairs and is responsible for advising the President's National Security Council (NSC) in regards to intelligence.[8] Perhaps most importantly, the DNI has budgetary responsibility for the majority of the nation's intelligence operations, and is responsible for making sure that the national intelligence program is implemented across all of these agencies (see FIGURE 6.1).[9]

The ODNI was developed as a direct response to the reforms proposed by the *9/11 Commission Report*, though the original proposal called for more comprehensive integration of the intelligence services under the DNI.[10] As the commission sug-

---

BOX 6.1   The 17 Agencies that Make Up the Intelligence Community

- Air Force Intelligence
- Army Intelligence
- Central Intelligence Agency
- Coast Guard Intelligence
- Defense Intelligence Agency
- Department of Energy
- Department of Homeland Security
- Department of State
- Department of the Treasury

- Drug Enforcement Administration
- Federal Bureau of Investigation
- Marine Corps Intelligence
- National Reconnaissance Office
- National Security Agency
- Navy Intelligence
- Office of the Director of National Intelligence
- National Geospatial-Intelligence Agency

Office of the Director of National Intelligence Organizational Chart

Leading Intelligence Integration

Leadership

Director (DNI)

Principal Deputy Director (PDDNI)

Chief Management Officer (CMO)

Core Mission

Intelligence Integration (DDNI/II)
Assistant Deputy DNI Intelligence Integration (ADDNI/II)

Integration Management Council (IMC)	National Counterterrorism Center (NCTC)*
• National Intelligence Managers (NIMs)	National Counterproliferation Center (NCPC)*
National Intelligence Council (NIC)	National Counterintelligence Executive (NCIX)*
Mission Integration Division (MID)	*Leaders of these organizations also serve as National Intelligence Managers.

Enablers

Policy & Strategy (P&S)	Chief Human Capital Officer (CHCO)
Partner Engagement (PE)	Chief Financial Officer (CFO)
Acquisition, Technology, & Facilities (AT&F)	Chief Information Officer (CIO)
Systems & Resource Analyses (SRA)	Information Sharing Environment (ISE)

Oversight

General Counsel (GC)	Inspector General (IG)
Civil Liberties and Privacy Office (CLPO)	IC Equal Employment Opportunity & Diversity (EEOD)
Public Affairs (PAO)	Legislative Affairs (OLA)

FIGURE 6.1   ODNI Organizational Chart

Modified from: Office of the Director of National Intelligence. (2012). Office of Director of National Intelligence: Organizational chart. Retrieved from http://odni.gov/files/documents/ODNI%20Org%20Chart.pdf on March 12, 2013.

gested, however, the DNI (originally called the National Intelligence Director [NID]) is responsible for being the cabinet-level official in charge of national intelligence, particularly regarding homeland security.[11]

Within the ODNI, there are several missions that directly support the intelligence community. Chief among these is the National Counterterrorism Center (NCTC), which is the primary government organization responsible for integration and analysis of all intelligence that relates to terrorism, outside of domestic terrorism.[12]

In addition to their focus on terrorism, the ODNI is also in charge of the Office of Intelligence and Analysis (I&A) within the Department of Homeland Security (DHS). This is the DHS intelligence component, responsible for developing intelligence products for policymakers in regards to homeland security threats. It has a particular focus on border security, and works extensively with state and local law enforcement.[13]

Central Intelligence Agency

The Central Intelligence Agency (CIA) is the only cabinet-level agency for which the primary mission is intelligence.[14] Developed originally at the end of World War II and in the early Cold War years, the agency represents the most important intelligence-gathering apparatus possessed by the U.S. government.[15] The agency is not limited to intelligence regarding homeland security issues, but rather produces an extremely varied catalogue of intelligence products to support missions across the government.[16] The agency is responsible for all-source intelligence analysis, which uses not only technological means of collection (such as satellites) but also human intelligence, developed from sources sometimes operating overseas retrieving information from enemies (see **Box 6.2**). Additionally, it has the capability of undertaking covert actions when directed to do so by the President.[17]

Despite its huge presence in the U.S. intelligence community, the CIA has a relatively small role to play in regard to homeland security because of the agency's limitations regarding American persons.[18] However, when foreign intelligence assets come to bear on domestic intelligence problems, such as terrorist organizations funded from overseas, the CIA has the ability to assist with disruption and other intelligence efforts.[19]

National Security Agency

The National Security Agency (NSA) is responsible for the nation's "signals intelligence." Signals intelligence, or SIGINT, refers to a variety of different collection methods including code-breaking, cryptanalysis, and foreign language analysis.[20] It further includes interception of messages on international telecommunications networks. Additionally, the agency is responsible for protecting the U.S. national security information systems.[21]

Military Intelligence

The intelligence apparatus of the military is one of the primary information-gathering tools of the U.S. intelligence community. The Department of Defense's (DOD's) worldwide reach, as well as their utilization of advanced intelligence-gathering

BOX 6.2   The "INTs"

While people tend to refer to "intelligence" as a single entity, finalized intelligence products usually consist of a variety of types of information put into a single context. The types of information used in these products can range from the popular view of 'secret' or 'covert' information to publicly accessible background information used by the public in other contexts every day. The different types of intelligence are referred to as intelligence collection disciplines and collectively are known as INTs. The different types are discussed here.

Human Intelligence (HUMINT)

Human intelligence is intelligence gathered from human sources. While this includes the popular versions of 'secret' intelligence gathering from covert sources, it also includes open collection, which may come from interrogation of suspects or witness interviews. HUMINT is generally handled domestically by the FBI and internationally by the CIA.

Signals Intelligence (SIGINT)

Signals intelligence refers to any intelligence gathered from electronic transmissions. These can be transmitted from a variety of locations including ground sites, ships, or satellites. Communications intelligence (COMINT) is a subset of SIGINT when communications between two parties is intercepted. SIGINT is generally the province of the National Security Agency, though other law enforcement agencies like the FBI collect some types of SIGINT through methods like wiretapping.

Imagery Intelligence (IMINT)

Usually consisting of photographs, IMINT is one of the oldest forms of intelligence. Beginning during the Civil War, it examines a wide variety of elements, from enemy movements to geographic issues. The National Reconnaissance Office is generally responsible for developing and building the satellites most frequently used for IMINT and the National Geospatial-Intelligence Agency is responsible for processing the images collected.

Open-Source Intelligence (OSINT)

Open-source includes any information that is publicly accessible. It can range from news broadcasts on radio and television to academic papers on specific research topics of interest to the intelligence community. OSINT, unlike other forms of intelligence, is not under the specific auspices of a single agency, but is instead collected by the entire intelligence community.

Data from: Federal Bureau of Investigation. (n.d.). Intelligence Collection Disciplines (INTs). Retrieved from http://www.fbi.gov/about-us/intelligence/disciplines on March 12, 2013.

technology, makes them one of the most indispensable tools for the intelligence mission of homeland security. However, much of the intelligence capacity of the military is used in support of their operations, especially in times of conflict, and the departmental independence in terms of budget and operations makes cooperation between the DOD and other intelligence agencies sometimes problematic.[22]

Defense Intelligence Agency

The primary intelligence agency within the DOD is the Defense Intelligence Agency (DIA). The DIA's major role is providing intelligence for the operations of the U.S. military around the world. As such, their function does not always overlap with the homeland security mission. However, within the context of homeland defense, the DIA is one of the primary intelligence agencies responsible for managing foreign military intelligence for the DOD. Additionally, given the agency's wide reach and extensive technical capacities, including drones, their role in the intelligence community's coordination is essential when dealing with the counter-terrorism mission of homeland security.[23]

☐ Other National-Level Intelligence Agencies

Other national-level intelligence agencies range in function and location within the government structure. For instance, the National Reconnaissance Office (NRO), which is in charge of the nation's satellites, is housed within the Department of Defense, but it not considered part of the DIA.[24] Similarly, the Department of State's Bureau of Intelligence and Research (INR) has the goal of analyzing information relevant to the Department of State's diplomatic mission.[25] The National Geospatial–Intelligence Agency (NGA) is, like the NRO, housed within the DOD and is in charge of developing map-based intelligence solutions and other issues surrounding intelligence imagery.[26]

KEY TERM

Intelligence cycle—a five step process for intelligence that consists of planning and direction, collecting, processing, analysis and production, and dissemination.

All of these agencies have missions that relate, some more directly than others, to the overall homeland security mission, and all of them participate in the **intelligence cycle** (See **Box 6.3**). Without the coordination of these agencies under the direction of the ODNI, the nation would be less secure both in terms of national defense and homeland security.[27] However, given the large spread of the agencies across the federal government and the highly specialized missions of some of the agencies, coordination is a difficult task.[28]

The intelligence community in the United States has the difficult but important job of making information accessible to policymakers and operators across the government.[29] In terms of homeland security, the community is responsible

---

BOX 6.3   The Intelligence Cycle

While generally thought of as a single step, intelligence is actually part of a process that begins with a question from lawmakers and ends with a final, finished intelligence product in those policymaker's hands. The process that different elements in the intelligence community go through to achieve a final product useful for answering the original question is called the "intelligence cycle." The **intelligence cycle** has five steps: planning, collecting, processing, analyzing, and disseminating intelligence information. Each one of the steps is essential to creating a useful, complete, and correct intelligence product.

Planning and Direction

The first step in the intelligence process is tasking from a policymaker, usually in order to answer a question. Identification of what information is already known and what information needs to be collected happens during this step. Additionally,

clarification is frequently required when tasking happens, and it is generally considered part of the planning and direction step in the intelligence cycle.

Collection

Once the information needed is identified, it must be collected. Collection can be overt or covert, and can consist of a variety of types of information (see Box 6.1 on "the INTs"). The collection of information, from whatever sources, is generally the step in the process most identified with "intelligence."

Processing

Once the information for answering the original query is found, it needs to be put into a usable format. This consists of putting the information into a report that can be used by an analyst to interpret the information. Much of the "raw data" collected would be unusable without this step in the intelligence cycle.

for coordinating both domestic and foreign intelligence, interfacing with law enforcement intelligence, and identifying threats to the homeland with enough lead time that policymakers have the ability to act.[30] Further still, given the number of agencies and their disparate responsibilities, the job of coordinating all-source intelligence for homeland security is difficult and has not always been carried out well. The 9/11 Commission pointed this out, saying:

> … no one [in the intelligence community] was firmly in charge of managing the case and able to draw relevant intelligence from anywhere in the government, assign responsibilities across the agencies (foreign and domestic), track progress, and quickly bring up obstacles to the level where they could be resolved.[31]

With the advent of ODNI and the increasing emphasis on coordination of effort across intelligence agencies, there has been definite improvement in our national intelligence capacity in regards to homeland security.[32] However, despite this increased ability, the system remains imperfect and is still changing to meet the needs of the new security environment (see FIGURE 6.2).[33]

FIGURE 6.2   The Intelligence Cycle

Modified from: Federal Bureau of Investigation. (n.d.). The intelligence cycle. Retrieved from http://www.fbi.gov/about-us/intelligence/image/intelligence-cycle-graphic on March 12, 2013.

Analysis and Production

After the information has been processed, it still lacks an interpretation that allows it to answer the policymaker's original question. The analysis and production stage of the intelligence cycle is the point at which the question is answered. There is an assessment of what is happening, why it is happening, and what impact the event(s) may have in the future—all in light of the original question.

Dissemination

The final step of the intelligence process is taking the finished intelligence product, developed in the analysis and production step, and getting it to the policymaker who originally provided the tasking. The policymaker can then use the information to inform policy development, or come back with additional tasking if more information is required.

Conclusion

While the intelligence cycle looks like a series of discrete steps taken to answer a policymaker's question, the way the process actually works is frequently more complicated. Often steps go in reverse, and there is collection happening to answer general, ongoing questions outside of a specific task requested. Several alternative models have been presented to this intelligence cycle, but generally, it remains the best overview of the process available.

Data from: Office of the Director of National Intelligence. (2009). National intelligence: A consumer's guide; Johnston, J.M., and Johnston, R. (n.d.). Testing the intelligence cycle through systems modeling and simulation.

■ Security Community

Along with the intelligence community responsible for actionable information in regards to homeland security, there is also the security community, consisting of federal agencies with specific homeland security-relevant missions.[34] Primary among these are the Department of Justice (DOJ) and DHS itself, though several other cabinet-level agencies, such as the Department of the Treasury, also have important roles.[35]

▦ Department of Justice

The DOJ is responsible for most federal law enforcement activities as well as containing the Office of the Attorney General.[36] Both of these elements are important to the homeland security goals of the United States. The DOJ is responsible for the prosecution of all federal terrorism cases, in addition to its large role in the investigation and apprehension of terrorists with domestic ties. After 9-11, DOJ came under fire for its lack of cooperation, along with other members of the U.S. intelligence community.[37] Most of this criticism was directed at the Federal Bureau of Investigation (FBI).

Federal Bureau of Investigation

In the context of homeland security, the FBI is the agency that bridges the intelligence world and the law enforcement community.[38] Though considered a full member of the intelligence community, the FBI is primarily geared towards law enforcement, with more emphasis on collecting evidence and prosecuting offenders than other agencies within the intelligence or security communities.[39] In addition to being the link between two federal-level functions, the FBI is responsible for the majority of coordination with state and local law enforcement agencies through both their participation in Joint Terrorism Task Forces (JTTFs) and normal law enforcement cooperation (see **TABLE 6.1**).[40]

Since 9-11, the FBI has taken on a much larger role in combating terrorism (see **Box 6.4**).[41] Though always responsible for investigating and deterring acts of domestic terrorism, the 9-11 attacks caused a significant shift in agency priorities that aligned it more with other members of the homeland security and intelligence communities.[42] As such, it is the primary organization in charge of domestic homeland security law enforcement functions, though with significant support from state and local agencies, particularly when responding to a specific incident. The FBI describes its mission this way:

> The FBI's top priorities are combating the threat of terrorism, counterintelligence, and cyber crime. As to counterterrorism, the FBI gives particular attention to terrorist efforts to acquire and use weapons of mass destruction ... The FBI must continuously adapt to trends in terrorist recruitment, financing and training, as well as terrorists' development of new explosive devices, biological and chemical agents.[43]

In addition to their homeland security functions, the FBI also is responsible for any domestic criminal activity that does not fall directly under the jurisdiction of other law enforcement

Courtesy of FBI.

TABLE 6.1 Anti-terrorism Task Force Participation of Local Police Departments

| | Local Police Departments with Officers Assigned to a Multi-agency Anti-terrorism Task Force | | | |
| | Officers assigned full time or part time | | Officers assigned full time | |
Population served	Percent of departments	Number of officers	Percent of agencies	Number of officers
All sizes	9%	2,693	4%	1,141
1,000,000 or more	100%	365	100%	364
500,000–999,999	90	121	84	105
250,000–499,999	80	105	80	101
100,000–249,999	54	196	43	146
50,000–99,999	29	200	16	97
25,000–49,999	16	262	7	65
10,000–24,999	10	663	3	145
2,500–9,999	5	347	2	87
Under 2,500	4	433	1	31

Data from: Reaves, Brian A. (2010). Local Police Departments, 2007. Washington, D.C.: U.S. Department of Justice.

agencies, as well as for crimes with which other law enforcement agencies request assistance.[44]

Department of Homeland Security

Unsurprisingly, given the primary goal of the agency, the Department of Homeland Security (DHS) has a large role to play in the security community as well as the intelligence community. After the government reorganization prompted by the 9-11 attacks, several security agencies found themselves newly housed within DHS.[45] Organizations like Customs and Border Protection and the Border Patrol were moved under the governance of the newly formed DHS, and new organizations were created for reasons of homeland security, such as the Transportation Security Administration (TSA).[46] Each of these agencies has an important role in homeland security.

Customs and Border Protection

Customs and Border Protection (CBP) is one of the largest security-oriented components of DHS. It is tasked with the protection of the borders from intrusion by terrorists and weapons smuggling, as well as enabling legal trade and travel.[47] It must do this at the same time while enforcing a large number of governmental regulations on border crossings, including immigration and drug trafficking. This, in turn, means that CBP is constantly working with agencies like the Drug Enforcement Agency (DEA) and Immigration and Customs Enforcement (discussed next), to fulfill their homeland security mission.[48]

BOX 6.4   The FBI's Intelligence Transformation

While the FBI has always used intelligence to assist in solving criminal cases, the September 11, 2001 attacks on the World Trade Center and Pentagon brought a new emphasis on intelligence operations at the Bureau. In fact, the change that has happened since 9-11 at the FBI has been described as transformative, and the development of the Bureau's Intelligence Directorate in 2005 has been heralded as a milestone on the way to a new, "intel-driven" FBI.

Increased Intelligence Analysis

While the FBI has had intelligence analysts for many years, the agency recently tripled the number of analysts from 1,000 to 3,000. This is in conjunction with its efforts not only in regards to terrorism, but also in its criminal cases. The increase also helps inculcate an "intelligence driven" philosophy across the Bureau, rather than confining it to its national security functions.

In conjunction with this reform, Senior Intelligence Manager Dina Corsi was quoted as saying, "IAs [intelligence analysts] could always do what was needed, but there was no system-wide program across the FBI as there is now, with formal training, standardized intelligence products, and clear-cut career paths for analysts."

Directorate of Intelligence

In 2005 the FBI created its intelligence directorate in order to assist with the transition to a more intelligence-centered FBI. The goal of the new directorate is to elevate the intelligence process in the FBI to a similar status as that of criminal investigation. The directorate, among other responsibilities, is in charge of intelligence policy within the Bureau, information technology for intelligence as well as training.

The development of the FBI's Directorate of Intelligence represents, in some ways, a major departure for the organization. There has been historical resistance to the idea of a domestic intelligence agency. However, the Directorate's development marks one of the signal achievements in recent years, especially in regards to the necessity for intelligence sharing among organizations participating in the intelligence community. Indeed, data sharing is one of the main outcomes of the DI, with over 7,500 finished intelligence products shared by 2006.

Conclusion

Though the FBI has undergone a transformation, it remains to be seen how well this transition will work in the long term. Organizational change is difficult, and there are institutional norms dealing with information-sharing and the role of law enforcement in the intelligence community that will be difficult to overcome. It is likely, however, that as homeland security remains a focus—particularly the issue of terrorism—the FBI will continue to evolve into a more efficient domestic intelligence agency.

Data from: Mueller III, R.S. (2006). Testimony before the House Appropriations Subcommittee on Science, the Departments of State, Justice and Commerce and Related Agencies; Federal Bureau of Investigation. (2011). Intelligence analysts: Central to the mission; Federal Bureau of Investigation. (n.d.). Intelligence overview; Mueller III, R.S.(2006). Testimony before the House Appropriations Subcommittee on Science, the Departments of State, Justice and Commerce and Related Agencies.

Immigration and Customs Enforcement

Immigration and Customs Enforcement (ICE) is the second largest investigative agency in the American government, employing over 50,000 people. It is tasked as the investigative arm of DHS and is the principal investigative unit housed within the department.[49] The agency focuses primarily on homeland security investigations, which are wide-ranging and include arms smuggling and immigration issues such as human trafficking as well as cybersecurity and other issues that affect customs.[50] It was established in 2003 through the merger of two previous agencies, the U.S. Customs Service and Immigration and Naturalization, and tasked with a primary role in the national homeland security plan.

Department of the Treasury

The Department of the Treasury is not usually considered to be an integral part of the homeland security community. However, when considering the importance of financial transactions in both funding terrorist operations, as well as tracking the terrorists themselves, it becomes clear that the role the department plays is essential. In particular, the department's Office of Intelligence and Analysis (OIA) was established to assist with tracking terrorist financing, insurgent financing, and the financing of rogue regimes around the world.

Military Community

While in most cases, the Department of Defense (DOD) is not the agency primarily responsible for homeland security, the agencies of the DOD play an important role in terms of protecting the homeland. Broadly speaking, these roles can be broken into two major components, aside from intelligence, as mentioned previously: homeland defense and civil support.[51]

Homeland defense is the primary mission of the DOD. It provides military security for the borders of the nation, as well as through applying force at the origin of the threat, in some cases to promote deterrence, as can be seen in the invasion of Afghanistan after the September 11th attacks. Not only were the Taliban, at the time leaders of Afghanistan, supporting Al Qaeda and Osama bin Laden, but they also provided a safe haven for the organization.[52] The invasion of Afghanistan, while a projection of military power to a foreign country, was also an extension of homeland security.

The homeland defense mission, aside from retaliation, also includes preemption and defense in a more traditional sense.[53] Further, it involves protection of what are considered "forward regions," which are areas outside the continental boundaries of the United States, including territories and bases, oceans and airspace surrounding the country. In each of these cases, the military is the only national organization with the capacity to defend against attacks and respond to the source of threats outside of the United States.[54]

Courtesy of Sgt. Brian E. Christiansen/DOD.

USNORTHCOM

The United States Northern Command (USNORTHCOM) has a particularly important role to play in regards to the homeland security of the United States.[55] It is the command of the U.S. military charged specifically with protection of the homeland. It was established as a combat command on October 2, 2002, partially in response to the attacks of September 11, 2001:

> USNORTHCOM's AOR includes air, land and sea approaches and encompasses the continental United States, Alaska, Canada, Mexico and the surrounding

water out to approximately 500 nautical miles. It also includes the Gulf of Mexico, the Straits of Florida, and portions of the Caribbean region to include The Bahamas, Puerto Rico, and the U.S. Virgin Islands. The commander of USNORTHCOM is responsible for theater security cooperation with Canada, Mexico, and The Bahamas.[56]

In addition to their defense mission, USNORTHCOM also has the lead military role in civil support during times of disaster. While the command does not have very many permanent troops assigned, they are able to request that troops be assigned for specific missions.[57] Because of this, in order for USNORTHCOM to become involved in a disaster, it must exceed the capabilities of local, state, and federal agencies to handle it before the command will mobilize, and they will only remain involved until the event is once again able to be handled by the other levels of government.[58]

■ State Level

Homeland security efforts at the state level are dictated by both national policy, such as the required adoption of the National Incident Management System (NIMS) and the National Response Framework (NRF) as well as state-level concerns.[59] As a direct response to 9-11, most states that did not already have the capacity immediately began developing a homeland security capability.[60] This new capability was, in many cases, merged with the states' existing emergency management offices to create state departments of homeland security. Additionally, as major partners in cooperative efforts for homeland security, like Joint Terrorism Task Forces (JTTFs), fusion centers, as well as in training and coordination within their respective territories, state-level governments and officials play a key role in homeland security. In short, as stated by Chenowith and Clarke in their article, *All Terrorism is Local*, "in a federal system, national responses are only as effective as their implementation through state and local governments."[61]

Because state-level agencies are independent from DHS, different states have adopted different methods of dealing with issues surrounding homeland security. Some states have taken existing agencies and rolled them into a single state-level homeland security department. Other states have developed an additional agency that deals specifically with homeland security, and still others have simply incorporated homeland security requirements into their existing agency structure.

■ Local Level

Homeland security on the local level is also unique. Just as "all politics is local," so are all terrorist attacks and other disasters.[62] This presents unique challenges at the local level as the resources to deal with these events are usually inadequate. However, since the advent of federal homeland security, local governments have been able to apply for funding for homeland security-related costs to help in their preparation. Additionally, there has been a concerted effort focus on training local officers for homeland security preparedness, as well as the advent of specific homeland security-related offices, such as JTTFs and fusion centers, mentioned previously.

Standardization

One of the problems highlighted by the 9-11 attacks was the interaction between local, state, and federal first-responding organizations, and in many cases, between different local agencies with differing jurisdictions. Noting this, the *9/11 Commission Report* stated:

> It is a fair inference, given the differing situations in New York City and Northern Virginia, that the problems in command, control, and communications that occurred at both sites will likely recur in any emergency of similar scale. The task looking forward is to enable first responders to respond in a coordinated manner with the greatest possible awareness of the situation.
>
> If New York and other major cities are to be prepared for future terrorist attacks, different first responder agencies within each city must be fully coordinated, just as different branches of the U.S. military are. Coordination entails a unified command that comprehensively deploys all dispatched police, fire, and other first responder resources. The attacks on 9-11 demonstrated that even the most robust emergency response capabilities can be overwhelmed if an attack is large enough. Teamwork, collaboration, and cooperation at an incident site are critical to a successful response.
> …
>
> Preparedness in the private sector and public sector for rescue, restart, and recovery of operations should include 1) a plan for evacuation, 2) adequate communications capabilities, and 3) a plan for continuity of operations.[63]

As a direct result, President George W. Bush issued Homeland Security Presidential Directive 5 (HSPD 5, 2003),[64] which standardized the response mechanism through the National Incident Management System (NIMS), and made its adoption effectively a requirement for all federal, state, and local response efforts. NIMS will be discussed elsewhere in this text.

Fusion Centers

In addition to the standardization of response, there has been an increasing emphasis on cooperation of all levels of government, not to the exclusion of cooperation between local agencies. One of the methods by which this cooperation has been enhanced is the **fusion center**.[65] These local (or sometimes regional) centers operate with multiple jurisdictions with the express purpose of combining intelligence information and crime data to help predict and deal with terrorist events.[66] Fusion centers arose in part out of the recognition of the difficulties of sharing classified information across levels of government, and most specifically from the federal level down to the local level. Fusion centers, with their integrated staff from all levels of government, theoretically allow for this diffusion of information across the various levels of government, and thus allow for a better coordinated response to any threat.

Fusion centers are not just responsible for relaying information, however. Many centers, especially those at the state level, engage in homeland security threat analysis, based on information from local and state agencies, which can then be shared across the government and with decision-makers at all levels. The National Security Strategy of 2009 states well the purpose of fusion centers:

> to prevent acts of terrorism on American soil, we must enlist all of our intelligence, law enforcement, and homeland security capabilities. We will continue to integrate

KEY TERM

Fusion centers—an information sharing center created by the U.S. Department of Homeland Security and the Department of Justice to assist state and local law enforcement.

Courtesy of Homeland Security & Governmental Affairs.

and leverage state and major urban area fusion centers that have the capability to share classified information; establish a nationwide framework for reporting suspicious activity; and implement an integrated approach to our counter-terrorism information systems to ensure that the analysts, agents, and officers who protect us have access to all relevant intelligence throughout the government.[67]

In short, fusion centers provide local law enforcement agencies ready access to federal and state level information and agencies, to better share information and coordinate response in the case of a terrorist threat or event.[68]

Fusion centers have come under fire recently (see **Box 6.5**). The Senate Permanent Subcommittee on Investigations under the Committee on Homeland Security and Governmental Affairs released a finding that fusion centers were largely overrated, and that little or no actionable intelligence had come from fusion centers since their inception after 2001.[69] While this finding has been disputed by some,[70] the effect of the report on fusion center use or funding has yet to be seen.

BOX 6.5   Fusion Center Criticism

In 2012, the U.S. Senate Permanent Subcommittee on Investigations for the Committee on Homeland Security and Governmental Affairs completed a 2-year investigation of the success of fusion centers. The findings of the committee, far from seeing utility in the centers, found that they had not provided any significant information useful for counterterrorism. This finding, while contested by DHS, was a significant blow. The major findings of the subcommittee investigation are detailed here.

Uneven Intelligence Quality

DHS officers who participated in state and local fusion centers were found to have produced shoddy intelligence reports whose contents may have endangered civil liberties of American citizens. There were also cases, cited by the subcommittee, of finished intelligence products containing information from already-published sources. Additionally, some of the material published in these reports was unrelated to terrorist activity.

No Unique Contribution to Counterterrorism

According to the subcommittee, there was no evidence provided that the fusion centers contributed to federal counter-terrorism efforts that contributed to the disruption of a terrorist plot. Additionally, nearly a third of all reports were never published for use by any organization within the intelligence community, perhaps because they contained no useful information. Some of the reports that were generated were not published because DHS officials did not make a decision on whether or not to publish them in a timely manner.

Funding Problems

The subcommittee also found that DHS did not effectively monitor how funds provided by the federal government were used to strengthen federal counter-terrorism efforts. Funds were used to purchase items like flat-screen TVs, sport utility vehicles, and surveillance equipment that were not directly related to the mission of the fusion centers. The subcommittee found that while these items were allowed under DHS policy, they did not help address deficiencies in the fusion centers' operations.

Conclusion

While the subcommittee investigation is troubling, DHS and other law enforcement agencies have defended the state and local fusion centers as important to the overall mission of counter-terrorism in the country. Additionally, while the fusion centers may not have provided information that directly led to the disruption of a terrorist plot, even the subcommittee noted that the fusion centers had identified criminal activity that may be related to terrorism. The long-term effects of the report have yet to be seen, but as DHS continues to argue for additional appropriations, the case against fusion centers is unlikely to help.

Data from: Permanent Subcommittee on Investigations. (2012). *Federal Support for and Involvement in State and Local Fusion Centers.* Retrieved from http://www.hsgac.senate.gov/download/report_federal-support-for-and-involvement-in-state-and-local-fusions-centers

One of the difficult transitions when moving to a homeland security paradigm is the fact that while national security is obviously a national problem, events such as terrorist attacks and natural disasters are, almost by definition, local. In an article examining the nature of a federal response to local phenomenon, Chenoweth and Clarke stated,

> City security is a core national security issue, but a local responsibility; in the United States, American cities and counties control and finance the police, fire, public health, and emergency services most needed in the face of a terrorist attack.[71]

In fact, law enforcement has borne the brunt of homeland security response, particularly in the case of terrorism, and while there is some suggestion that policing has changed and entered an era of homeland security,[72] the research on how prepared law enforcement is remains mixed (see TABLE 6.2).[73] Further, the preparation that has been done tends to have mirrored those steps taken at the state level, with increased emphasis on risk assessment and joint training exercises, rather than on emergency response plans or updated equipment.[74]

Homeland Security Policing

A more recent development has been the advent of homeland security policing. This form of policing focuses many of the aspects of problem oriented policing on the specific issue of homeland security and emphasizes that local law enforcement concentrate on homeland security, specifically terrorism prevention.[75] While it has not been adopted without controversy,[76] it has been considered by some to be the "fourth era" of policing, supplanting community-oriented policing.[77]

The focus of **homeland security policing** is similar, in many respects, to intelligence-led policing.[78] There is an emphasis on the SARA (Scanning, Analysis, Response and Assessment) technique, though the focus tends to be on terrorism rather than crime. Additionally, homeland security as a policing paradigm has been criticized in that it might create significant distance between

TABLE 6.2 Local Police Departments with a Written Terrorism Response Plan

Population Served	Percent of Departments
All sizes	54%
1,000,000 or more	100%
500,000–999,999	94
250,000–499,999	96
100,000–249,999	89
50,000–99,999	76
25,000–49,999	75
10,000–24,999	67
2,500–9,999	53
Under 2,500	42

Data from: Reaves, Brian A. (2010). *Local Police Departments, 2007*. Washington, D.C.: U.S. Department of Justice.

KEY TERM

Homeland security policing—the local
police role in protecting the homeland.

the communities that are being policed and the police themselves. This may be particularly true of minority communities that may be perceived by some as a potential source of terrorism.[79]

Regardless of whether or not homeland security becomes (or has become) the dominant paradigm of policing in the United States, there is little doubt that the change in emphasis on the national level has impacted local departments as well, in part due to potential funding opportunities via grants. The range of actions taken by local departments has varied, with some departments hiring more officers, some updating or writing their emergency action plans, and many increasing training.[80]

There has been a major change regarding the state and local levels of homeland security since 9-11.[81] While the scope of this change has yet to be fully understood, many state and local agencies have been reorganized and reoriented to focus on a homeland security mission (see **TABLE 6.3**),[82] which have in some cases supplanted

TABLE 6.3 Preparedness Activities of Local Police Departments

Population served	Percent of Departments That—					
	Participated in emergency preparedness exercises	Increased officer presence at critical areas	Disseminated information to increase citizen preparedness	Held community meetings on homeland security	Partnered with culturally diverse populations	Conducted a public anti-fear campaign
All sizes	62%	36%	33%	26%	13%	4%
1,000,000 or more	92%	77%	92%	85%	54%	46%
500,000–999,999	94	74	71	68	65	19
250,000–499,999	98	80	72	78	72	26
100,000–249,999	92	64	57	43	41	9
50,000–99,999	90	60	53	39	40	9
25,000–49,999	82	54	53	31	22	6
10,000–24,999	77	51	42	25	15	5
2,500–9,999	64	36	35	28	8	3
Under 2,500	47	23	20	21	11	2

Data from: Reaves, Brian A. (2010). *Local Police Departments, 2007*. Washington, D.C.: U.S. Department of Justice.

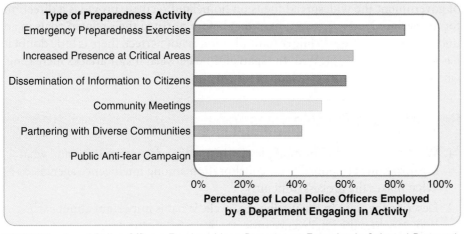

FIGURE 6.3 Local Police Officers Employed by a Department Engaging in Selected Preparedness Activities

Data from: Reaves, Brian A. (2010). *Local Police Departments, 2007*. Washington, D.C.: U.S. Department of Justice.

agencies at both the state and local level.[83] However, through the continued standardization across jurisdictions and the use of fusion centers, there seems to be significant improvement in our national ability to deal with the complex problem of homeland security—a national problem happening at a local level (see FIGURE 6.3).[84]

◼ Chapter Summary

There is little doubt that the homeland security community is a complex one, encompassing multiple levels of government and crossing over various areas of expertise.[85] With multiple agencies covering intelligence and security and involving all levels of government, the homeland security community has the difficult job of not only identifying and responding to threats to the homeland, but also coordinating activities among themselves to ensure our safety.[86]

With the advent of the ODNI, and the coordination it engenders, there is now more effective communications across lines than ever before. However, at the state and local levels the coordination remains more difficult, with mandates from higher levels of government somewhat assisting in the process, but likely insufficient by themselves. The research is inconclusive about preparation at the state and local levels for homeland security events, though there is promising improvement in several areas.

Additionally, at the local level, many jurisdictions have moved to a homeland security policing model.[87] While it remains to be seen whether this has supplanted community-oriented policing as the primary policing paradigm, there is little doubt that homeland security as an ongoing concern has impacted local police significantly. With increased emphasis on training and planning, officers are almost certainly better equipped to deal with an incident than in times past, but it is by no means clear that they are *well* prepared.[88]

In general, because homeland security is a complex and evolving concern, there is little that is known for sure. However, with the increased coordination at all levels of government the widespread focus on homeland security provides a direction for the various levels of government that before pursued their related goals in an uncoordinated fashion. While communication is not perfect, there is little doubt it has improved since 9-11. With the span of time between major attacks increasing, whether it remains a priority has yet to be seen.

■ Review/Discussion Questions

1. What role does collaboration play in the intelligence community, and what organization is responsible for collaboration among intelligence agencies? What makes the process difficult?
2. Describe the steps in the intelligence cycle. What is important about each step, and does the intelligence process always follow the cycle?
3. What role does the military play in the security community? Might they function as a bridge between the worlds of intelligence and law enforcement?
4. Fusion centers came under fire from the U.S. Senate. Why did they come under fire, and what might the fusion centers still be providing despite the problems identified?

■ Additional Readings

Lowenthal, M.M. (2005). *Intelligence: From Secrets to Policy*. Thousand Oaks, CA: CQ Press.

Sims, J.E. & Gerber, B. (Eds). (2005). *Transforming US Intelligence*. Washington, DC: Georgetown University Press.

■ Endnotes

1. National Commission on Terrorist Attacks Upon the United States. (2004). *The 9/11 Commission Report: Final Report of the National Commission on Terrorist Attacks Upon the United States (Authorized Ed.)*. New York: W.W. Norton & Company, Inc.
2. Best, R.A. (2011). *Intelligence Issues for Congress* (CRS Report No. RL33539). Retrieved from Congressional Research Service website: https://opencrs.com/document/RL33539/
3. Office of the Director of National Intelligence. (2012). *About the Intelligence Community*. Retrieved from Intelligence Community website: http://www.intelligence.gov/about-the-intelligence-community/
4. Office of the Director of National Intelligence. (2009). *Overview of the Intelligence Community for the 111th Congress of the United States of America*. Retrieved from http://cstsp.aaas.org/files/overview.pdf
5. Office of the Director of National Intelligence. (2009). *Overview of the Intelligence Community for the 111th Congress of the United States of America*. Retrieved from http://cstsp.aaas.org/files/overview.pdf
6. Office of the Director of National Intelligence. (2012). *About the Intelligence Community*. Retrieved from Intelligence Community website: http://www.intelligence.gov/about-the-intelligence-community/

7. Intelligence Reform and Terrorism Prevention Act of 2004. Pub.S.2845, 108th Cong. (2004).

8. Office of the Director of National Intelligence. (2012). *About the Intelligence Community*. Retrieved from Intelligence Community website: http://www.intelligence.gov/about-the-intelligence-community/

9. Best, R.A. (2011). *Intelligence Issues for Congress* (CRS Report No. RL33539). Retrieved from Congressional Research Service website: https://opencrs.com/document/RL33539/

10. Best, R.A. (2011). *Intelligence Issues for Congress* (CRS Report No. RL33539). Retrieved from Congressional Research Service website: https://opencrs.com/document/RL33539/; National Commission on Terrorist Attacks Upon the United States. (2004). *The 9/11 Commission Report: Final Report of the National Commission on Terrorist Attacks Upon the United States (Authorized Ed.)*. New York: W.W. Norton & Company, Inc.

11. Best, R.A. (2011). *Intelligence Issues for Congress* (CRS Report No. RL33539). Retrieved from Congressional Research Service website: https://opencrs.com/document/RL33539/; Office of the Director of National Intelligence. (2009). *Overview of the Intelligence Community for the 111th Congress of the United States of America*. Retrieved from http://cstsp.aaas.org/files/overview.pdf

12. Masse, T.M. (2005). *The National Counterterrorism Center: Implementation Challenges and Issues for Congress* (CRS Report No. RL32816). Retrieved from Congressional Research Service website: https://opencrs.com/document/RL32816/2005-03-16/; National Counterterrorism Center. (2012). *About the National Counterterrorism Center*. Retrieved from http://www.nctc.gov/about_us/about_nctc.html

13. Office of the Director of National Intelligence. (2009). *Overview of the Intelligence Community for the 111th Congress of the United States of America*. Retrieved from http://cstsp.aaas.org/files/overview.pdf

14. Office of the Director of National Intelligence. (2009). *Overview of the Intelligence Community for the 111th Congress of the United States of America*. Retrieved from http://cstsp.aaas.org/files/overview.pdf

15. Weiner, T. (2007). *Legacy of Ashes: The History of the CIA*. New York, NY: Doubleday.

16. Office of the Director of National Intelligence. (2009). *Overview of the Intelligence Community for the 111th Congress of the United States of America*. Retrieved from http://cstsp.aaas.org/files/overview.pdf

17. Central Intelligence Agency. (2012). *CIA Vision, Mission, and Values*. Retrieved from https://www.cia.gov/about-cia/cia-vision-mission-values/index.html; Office of the Director of National Intelligence. (2009). *Overview of the Intelligence Community for the 111th Congress of the United States of America*. Retrieved from http://cstsp.aaas.org/files/overview.pdf

18. Office of the Director of National Intelligence. (2009). *Overview of the Intelligence Community for the 111th Congress of the United States of America*. Retrieved from http://cstsp.aaas.org/files/overview.pdf

19. Office of the Director of National Intelligence. (2009). *Overview of the Intelligence Community for the 111th Congress of the United States of America*.

Retrieved from http://cstsp.aaas.org/files/overview.pdf; Weiner, T. (2007). *Legacy of Ashes: The History of the CIA*. New York, NY: Doubleday.

20. Aid, M. (2009). *The Secret Sentry: The Untold History of the National Security Agency*. London, UK: Bloomsbury Press; National Security Agency. (2012). *Vision*. Retrieved from http://www.nsa.gov/about/index.shtml; Office of the Director of National Intelligence. (2009). *Overview of the Intelligence Community for the 111th Congress of the United States of America*. Retrieved from http://cstsp.aaas.org/files/overview.pdf

21. Aid, M. (2009). *The Secret Sentry: The Untold History of the National Security Agency*. London, UK: Bloomsbury Press.

22. Best, R.A. (2011). *Intelligence Issues for Congress* (CRS Report No. RL33539). Retrieved from Congressional Research Service website: https://opencrs.com/document/RL33539/; Knight, W. (2008). *Homeland Security: Roles and Missions for United States Northern Command* (CRS report No. RL34342). Retrieved from Federation of American Scientists website: http://www.fas.org/sgp/crs/homesec/RL34342.pdf; Office of the Director of National Intelligence. (2009). *Overview of the Intelligence Community for the 111th Congress of the United States of America*. Retrieved from http://cstsp.aaas.org/files/overview.pdf

23. Office of the Director of National Intelligence. (2009). *Overview of the Intelligence Community for the 111th Congress of the United States of America*. Retrieved from http://cstsp.aaas.org/files/overview.pdf

24. Office of the Director of National Intelligence. (2009). *Overview of the Intelligence Community for the 111th Congress of the United States of America*. Retrieved from http://cstsp.aaas.org/files/overview.pdf

25. Office of the Director of National Intelligence. (2009). *Overview of the Intelligence Community for the 111th Congress of the United States of America*. Retrieved from http://cstsp.aaas.org/files/overview.pdf

26. Office of the Director of National Intelligence. (2009). *Overview of the Intelligence Community for the 111th Congress of the United States of America*. Retrieved from http://cstsp.aaas.org/files/overview.pdf

27. Office of the Director of National Intelligence. (2009). *Overview of the Intelligence Community for the 111th Congress of the United States of America*. Retrieved from http://cstsp.aaas.org/files/overview.pdf

28. Best, R.A. (2011). *Intelligence Issues for Congress* (CRS Report No. RL33539). Retrieved from Congressional Research Service website: https://opencrs.com/document/RL33539/

29. Best, R.A. (2011). *Intelligence Issues for Congress* (CRS Report No. RL33539). Retrieved from Congressional Research Service website: https://opencrs.com/document/RL33539/; Office of the Director of National Intelligence. (2012). *About the Intelligence Community*. Retrieved from Intelligence Community website: http://www.intelligence.gov/about-the-intelligence-community/

30. Office of the Director of National Intelligence. (2009). *Overview of the Intelligence Community for the 111th Congress of the United States of America*. Retrieved from http://cstsp.aaas.org/files/overview.pdf

31. National Commission on Terrorist Attacks Upon the United States. (2004). *The 9/11 Commission Report: Final Report of the National Commission on*

Terrorist Attacks Upon the United States (Authorized Ed.). New York: W.W. Norton & Company, Inc.

32. Best, R.A. (2011). *Intelligence Issues for Congress* (CRS Report No. RL33539). Retrieved from Congressional Research Service website: https://opencrs.com/document/RL33539/

33. Best, R.A. (2011). *Intelligence Issues for Congress* (CRS Report No. RL33539). Retrieved from Congressional Research Service website: https://opencrs.com/document/RL33539/

34. Best, R.A. (2011). *Intelligence issues for Congress* (CRS Report No. RL33539). Retrieved from Congressional Research Service website: https://opencrs.com/document/RL33539/; Office of the Director of National Intelligence. (2009). *Overview of the Intelligence Community for the 111th Congress of the United States of America*. Retrieved from http://cstsp.aaas.org/files/overview.pdf

35. Office of the Director of National Intelligence. (2009). *Overview of the Intelligence Community for the 111th Congress of the United States of America*. Retrieved from http://cstsp.aaas.org/files/overview.pdf

36. Cumming, A. (2005). *Intelligence Reform Implementation at the Federal Bureau of Investigation: Issues and Options for Congress* (CRS Report No. RL33033). Retrieved from Congressional Research Service Website: https://opencrs.com/document/RL33033/2005-08-16/; Office of the Director of National Intelligence. (2009). *Overview of the Intelligence Community for the 111th Congress of the United States of America*. Retrieved from http://cstsp.aaas.org/files/overview.pdf

37. National Commission on Terrorist Attacks Upon the United States. (2004). *The 9/11 Commission Report: Final Report of the National Commission on Terrorist Attacks Upon the United States (Authorized Ed.)*. New York: W.W. Norton & Company, Inc.

38. Best, R.A. (2011). *Intelligence Issues for Congress* (CRS Report No. RL33539). Retrieved from Congressional Research Service website: https://opencrs.com/document/RL33539/; Office of the Director of National Intelligence. (2009). *Overview of the Intelligence Community for the 111th Congress of the United States of America*. Retrieved from http://cstsp.aaas.org/files/overview.pdf

39. Federal Bureau of Investigation. (2012). *The Intel-driven FBI*. Retrieved from http://www.fbi.gov/about-us/intelligence/intel-driven; Office of the Director of National Intelligence. (2009). *Overview of the Intelligence Community for the 111th Congress of the United States of America*. Retrieved from http://cstsp.aaas.org/files/overview.pdf

40. Federal Bureau of Investigation. (2012). *The Intel-driven FBI*. Retrieved from http://www.fbi.gov/about-us/intelligence/intel-driven

41. Federal Bureau of Investigation. (2012). *The Intel-driven FBI*. Retrieved from http://www.fbi.gov/about-us/intelligence/intel-driven

42. Office of the Director of National Intelligence. (2009). *Overview of the Intelligence Community for the 111th Congress of the United States of America*. Retrieved from http://cstsp.aaas.org/files/overview.pdf

43. Federal Bureau of Investigation. (2012). *The Intel-driven FBI*. Retrieved from http://www.fbi.gov/about-us/intelligence/intel-driven

44. Federal Bureau of Investigation. (2012). *The Intel-driven FBI*. Retrieved from http://www.fbi.gov/about-us/intelligence/intel-driven

45. Office of the Director of National Intelligence. (2009). *Overview of the Intelligence Community for the 111th Congress of the United States of America*. Retrieved from http://cstsp.aaas.org/files/overview.pdf

46. Department of Homeland Security. (2012). *Border Security Overview*. Retrieved from http://www.dhs.gov/border-security-overview

47. Customs and Border Protection 2012.

48. Office of the Director of National Intelligence. (2009). *Overview of the Intelligence Community for the 111th Congress of the United States of America*. Retrieved from http://cstsp.aaas.org/files/overview.pdf

49. Sauter, M.A. and Carafano, J.J. (2011). *Homeland Security*. New York, NY: McGraw-Hill.

50. Sauter, M.A. and Carafano, J.J. (2011). *Homeland Security*. New York, NY: McGraw-Hill.

51. Joint Chiefs of Staff. (August 2, 2009). *Joint Publication 3–26: Homeland Security*.

52. National Commission on Terrorist Attacks Upon the United States. (2004). *The 9/11 Commission Report: Final Report of the National Commission on Terrorist Attacks Upon the United States (Authorized Ed.)*. New York: W.W. Norton & Company, Inc.

53. Joint Chiefs of Staff. (August 2, 2009). *Joint Publication 3–26: Homeland Security*; Knight, W. (2008). *Homeland Security: Roles and Missions for United States Northern Command* (CRS report No. RL34342). Retrieved from Federation of American Scientists website: http://www.fas.org/sgp/crs/homesec/RL34342.pdf

54. Joint Chiefs of Staff. (August 2, 2009). *Joint Publication 3–26: Homeland Security*.

55. Knight, W. (2008). *Homeland Security: Roles and Missions for United States Northern Command* (CRS report No. RL34342). Retrieved from Federation of American Scientists website: http://www.fas.org/sgp/crs/homesec/RL34342.pdf

56. Knight, W. (2008). *Homeland Security: Roles and Missions for United States Northern Command* (CRS report No. RL34342). Retrieved from Federation of American Scientists website: http://www.fas.org/sgp/crs/homesec/RL34342.pdf

57. Joint Chiefs of Staff. (August 2, 2009). *Joint Publication 3–26: Homeland Security*; Knight, W. (2008). *Homeland Security: Roles and Missions for United States Northern Command* (CRS report No. RL34342). Retrieved from Federation of American Scientists website: http://www.fas.org/sgp/crs/homesec/RL34342.pdf

58. Knight, W. (2008). *Homeland Security: Roles and Missions for United States Northern Command* (CRS report No. RL34342). Retrieved from Federation of American Scientists website: http://www.fas.org/sgp/crs/homesec/RL34342.pdf

59. Department of Homeland Security. (2008). *National Response Framework.* Retrieved from http://www.fema.gov/sites/default/files/orig/fema_pdfs/pdf/emergency/nrf/nrf-core.pdf

60. Chenoweth, E. & Clarke, S.E. (2010). "All Terrorism Is Local: Resources, Nested Institutions, and Governance for Urban Homeland Security in the American Federal System." *Political Research Quarterly, 63,* 495–507.

61. Chenoweth, E. & Clarke, S.E. (2010). "All Terrorism Is Local: Resources, Nested Institutions, and Governance for Urban Homeland Security in the American Federal System." *Political Research Quarterly, 63,* p. 495.

62. Chenoweth, E. & Clarke, S.E. (2010). "All Terrorism Is Local: Resources, Nested Institutions, and Governance for Urban Homeland Security in the American Federal System." *Political Research Quarterly, 63,* 495–507.

63. National Commission on Terrorist Attacks Upon the United States. (2004). *The 9/11 Commission Report: Final Report of the National Commission on Terrorist Attacks Upon the United States (Authorized Ed.).* New York: W.W. Norton & Company, Inc.

64. HSPD 5, 2003

65. Monahan, T. (2010). "Homeland Security Fusion Centers." *Social Justice, 37*(2–3), 84–98.

66. Monahan, T. (2010). "Homeland Security Fusion Centers." *Social Justice, 37*(2–3), 84–98.

67. Office of the Director of National Intelligence. (August 2009). *National Security Strategy of the United States of America 2009,* p. 20. Retrieved from Office of Director of National Intelligence website: http://www.dni.gov/files/documents/Newsroom/Reports%20and%20Pubs/2009_NIS.pdf

68. The White House 2010

69. Permanent Subcommittee on Investigations. (2012). *Federal Support for and Involvement in State and Local Fusion Centers.* Retrieved from http://www.hsgac.senate.gov/download/report_federal-support-for-and-involvement-in-state-and-local-fusions-centers

70. O'Harrow, R., Jr. (2012). "Homeland Security 'Fusion Centers' Defended in Response to Sharply Critical Senate Report." *Washington Post.* Retrieved from http://www.washingtonpost.com/world/national-security/fusion-centers-defendedin-response-to-senate-report/2012/10/03/58841b38-0da2-11e2-a310-2363842b7057_story.html

71. Chenoweth, E. & Clarke, S.E. (2010). "All Terrorism Is Local: Resources, Nested Institutions, and Governance for Urban Homeland Security in the American Federal System." *Political Research Quarterly, 63,* p. 496.

72. Oliver, W.M. (2006). "The Fourth Era of Policing: Homeland Security." *International Review of Law, Computers, and Technology, 20,* 49–62.

73. Giblin, M.J., Schafer, J.A., & Burruss, G.W. (2009). "Homeland Security in the Heartland: Risk, Preparedness, and Organizational Capacity." *Criminal Justice Policy Review, 20,* 274–289.

74. Giblin, M.J., Schafer, J.A., & Burruss, G.W. (2009). "Homeland Security in the Heartland: Risk, Preparedness, and Organizational Capacity." *Criminal Justice Policy Review, 20,* 274–289.

75. Chappell, A.T. & Gibson, S.A. (2009). "Community Policing and Homeland Security Policing: Friend or Foe?" *Criminal Justice Policy Review, 20,* 326–343.

76. Chappell, A.T. & Gibson, S.A. (2009). "Community Policing and Homeland Security Policing: Friend or Foe?" *Criminal Justice Policy Review, 20,* 326–343.

77. Oliver, W.M. (2006). "The Fourth Era of Policing: Homeland Security." *International Review of Law, Computers, and Technology, 20,* 49–62; Oliver, W.M. (2009). "Policing for Homeland Security: Policy and Research." *Criminal Justice Policy Review, 20,* 253–260.

78. Oliver, W.M. (2006). "The Fourth Era of Policing: Homeland Security." *International Review of Law, Computers, and Technology, 20,* 49–62.

79. Thatcher, D. (2005). "The Local Role in Homeland Security." *Law & Society Review, 39*(3), 635–676.

80. Burruss, G.W., Giblin, M.J., & Schafer, J.A. (2009). "Threatened Globally, Acting Locally: Modeling Law Enforcement Homeland Security Practices." *Justice Quarterly, 27,* 77–101.

81. Oliver, W.M. (2009). "Policing for Homeland Security: Policy and Research." *Criminal Justice Policy Review, 20,* 253–260.

82. Chenoweth, E. & Clarke, S.E. (2010). "All Terrorism Is Local: Resources, Nested Institutions, and Governance for Urban Homeland Security in the American Federal System." *Political Research Quarterly, 63,* 495–507.

83. Oliver, W.M. (2009). "Policing for Homeland Security: Policy and Research." *Criminal Justice Policy Review, 20,* 253–260.

84. Chenoweth, E. & Clarke, S.E. (2010). "All Terrorism Is Local: Resources, Nested Institutions, and Governance for Urban Homeland Security in the American Federal System." *Political Research Quarterly, 63,* 495–507.

85. Office of the Director of National Intelligence. (2009). *Overview of the Intelligence Community for the 111th Congress of the United States of America.* Retrieved from http://cstsp.aaas.org/files/overview.pdf

86. Office of the Director of National Intelligence. (2009). *Overview of the Intelligence Community for the 111th Congress of the United States of America.* Retrieved from http://cstsp.aaas.org/files/overview.pdf

87. Oliver, W.M. (2006). "The Fourth Era of Policing: Homeland Security." *International Review of Law, Computers, and Technology, 20,* 49–62.

88. Giblin, M.J., Schafer, J.A., & Burruss, G.W. (2009). "Homeland Security in the Heartland: Risk, Preparedness, and Organizational Capacity." *Criminal Justice Policy Review, 20,* 274–289.

Anti-terrorism and Counter-terrorism

Chapter Objectives

Chapter Outline

Introduction

They had trained for the mission hundreds of times, and each of them had been on deployments in areas as varied as the Philippines and Iraq.[1] While their packs were heavy on their backs in the helicopter on the way to the compound, they knew that every item in them was essential and could potentially save their lives. As the helicopter arrived at its destination, there was a minor malfunction, and they had to move to Plan B. Instead of a silent assault, sliding down ropes into the courtyard of the compound, they would have to disembark and assault from outside—giving any potential bad guys time to arm themselves and resist if they realized they were being attacked.[2]

After a controlled "hard landing" that involved striking the compound wall with the rotor of the helicopter, the members of Seal Team Six—a unit only recently recognized publicly by the government—flowed nearly silently from the downed helicopter, and another that had landed without incident, into the building owned by Arshad Khan, a Pashtun businessman from Afghanistan. Within Al Qaeda, however, Khan had another name—Abu Ahmed al-Kuwaiti.[3]

Upon entering the compound, Al-Kuwaiti was the first resistance the team encountered, opening fire from behind the guesthouse door before being shot himself. The second team of commandos attacked the main building, killing al-Kuwaiti's brother and killing one of Osama bin Laden's sons, Khalid, both of whom were unarmed. In the dark of the building, assisted by night-vision goggles, the team got their first glimpse of the target: Osama bin Laden. Retreating, it was unclear whether he was retrieving a weapon or a suicide vest, and though the first shot missed as he ducked into a room, the subsequent shots to the chest and above his eye effectively achieved the goal of mission.[4]

© Al-Jazeera/AP Images.

Osama bin Laden's death was the culmination of 10 years of activity ranging from an intense intelligence-gathering effort to the training of teams like Seal Team Six. It marked, in some ways, the close of an era of U.S. history based around the identity of a single man and his attack against the country. Despite this close, however, the threat he represented—terrorism against a vulnerable target—remains an important part of America's national psyche, and the defense against it is one of the primary goals of homeland security.

The killing of Osama bin Laden represents many things to different people. One thing that most agree on, however, is that it represents a triumph of U.S. counter-terrorism efforts. The ability to track down an elusive terrorist from across the globe and kill him shows not only the projection of power the U.S. is willing to undertake to achieve its counter-terrorism goals, but when combined with the lack of significant attacks against the homeland since 9-11, seems to represent a triumph of anti-terrorism as well.

■ Fighting Terrorism

Courtesy of the U.S. Immigration and Customs Enforcement/DHS.

Two of the primary requirements of the homeland security mission in the U.S. are counter-terrorism and anti-terrorism. While frequently used interchangeably, and in some ways very closely tied together, **counter-terrorism** and **anti-terrorism** are the two elements of homeland security dedicated to protecting the United States from violent extremism.[5] Counter-terrorism represents all offensive activities dedicated to tracking and eradicating terrorists both domestically and internationally. Anti-terrorism, on the other hand, refers to the defensive aspects of protection from terrorism and can range from academic study to "target-hardening."[6]

These two elements represent nearly the entire picture of the United States' efforts at combatting terrorism. Boaz Ganor, in his book, *The Counterterrorism Puzzle*, presents the scope of counter-terrorism (and anti-terrorism) efforts as including several goals:[7] eliminating terrorism, minimizing the damage cause by terrorism, and preventing the escalation of terrorism. These goals are clearly not relegated specifically to anti-terrorism or counter-terrorism, demonstrating the importance of understanding both topics.

In the sections following, the United States' approach to anti-terrorism and counter-terrorism are explored. The anti-terrorism section focuses primarily on the development of anti-terrorism policy post-9-11, with several important policies highlighted. It also examines closely the issue of critical infrastructure protection. The counter-terrorism section details the development of counter-terrorism strategy under both President George W. Bush and President Barack Obama. It details both domestic and international counter-terrorism and differentiates the approaches taken by the two administrations.

> **KEY TERM**
> **Anti-terrorism**—the defensive aspects of protection from terrorism and can range from academic study to "target-hardening."

> **KEY TERM**
> **Counter-terrorism**—all offensive activities dedicated to tracking and eradicating terrorists both domestically and internationally.

> **KEY TERM**
> *National Strategy for Counterterrorism*—the federal government's approach to dealing with the terrorist threat; it identifies the range of tools that are critical to the strategy's success.

◼ Anti-terrorism

In the American lexicon, anti-terrorism is an underutilized term. Most of the focus on combating terrorism, particularly in the media, has been focused on the often more "kinetic" counter-terrorism efforts. Even the recent ***National Strategy for Counterterrorism*** promulgated by the Obama administration eschews the use of the term anti-terrorism.[8] However, without anti-terrorism there would be little ability to actively engage in any kind of counter-terrorism effort, and if those efforts were unsuccessful, a lack of anti-terrorism planning would make any attack significantly worse. The U.S. Department of Defense defines anti-terrorism as "defensive measures used to reduce the vulnerability of individuals and property to terrorist acts, to include rapid containment by local military and civilian forces" (p. 19).[9] If this definition is broadly construed, anti-terrorism includes a variety of elements that people do not generally consider as combating terrorism, such as efforts undertaken to understand terrorists and their motivations as well as anti-terrorism policies such as the terrorism "watch list" that prevents terrorists from entering our country via air transportation. In general, anti-terrorism can be broken down into two broad areas: preventative measures and responsive measures, with preventative measures focusing on minimizing damage and responsive measures focusing on mitigation when an attack does happen.[10]

NATIONAL STRATEGY FOR COUNTERTERRORISM

June 2011

Courtesy of the White House.

Unsurprisingly, anti-terrorism legislation changed significantly between the pre- and post-9-11 era.[11] Much of this change was in reference to the prevention of terrorist attacks. For example, Homeland Security Presidential Directive 6 (HSPD6), which was signed by President George W. Bush in 2003, established the now-familiar security screening process that the U.S. uses to help ensure terrorists do not gain entry into the country by creating the Terrorism Threat Integration Center (which later became the National Counterterrorism Center) and requiring all appropriate bodies (Department of Defense, Department of State, etc.) to share all terrorist-related information with the center.[12] This was a significant adjustment to the previous screening process, which was limited to the Department of State's visa process and inspection (when appropriate) of a person by an immigration officer at the port of entry.[13]

In addition to the development of the Terrorist Screening Database (TSDB), other elements of anti-terrorism legislation went into effect under the auspices of the Uniting and Strengthening America by Providing Appropriate Tools Required to Intercept and Obstruct Terrorism Act, better known as the USA PATRIOT Act.[14] While certainly controversial when it was passed, the PATRIOT Act provides law enforcement additional anti-terrorism tools that were previously either limited or nonexistent.[15] Elements such as additional methods by which to gain and use a warrant against a suspected terrorist and additional surveillance options were included in the legislation to allow for enhanced ability to seek and apprehend suspected terrorists. The PATRIOT Act was seen as a turning point for the Department of Justice's handling of terrorism, particularly regarding investigations by the FBI, in that it focused on detecting and disrupting terrorism rather than simply prosecuting terrorists.[16] In the words of then Attorney General John Ashcroft, "[we] must prevent first, prosecute second" (n.p.).[17] This is in direct opposition to the traditional, reactive model of policing focused on prosecution.

The focus on anti-terrorism was by no means limited to the Department of Justice. The newly formed Department of Homeland Security (DHS) in 2002 had several well-known anti-terrorism initiatives, such as the much-maligned, color-coded Homeland Security Advisory System, and many less well known, like the anti-terrorism standards set for the chemical industry to protect dangerous chemicals and chemical manufacturing facilities from attack.[18] Other legislation is similarly meant to protect citizens from attack, either through strengthening potential targets or through deterring potential attackers. It is not just legislation that comprises anti-terrorism, however. DHS is the lead agency in many areas of anti-terrorism through its management of agencies like the U.S. Coast Guard and Immigration and Customs Enforcement, which seek to prevent illegal entry of not just immigrants, but also potential terrorists.

The most obvious examples of anti-terrorism activity take place on the federal level, though anti-terrorism is something that happens at all levels of government.[19] This is not only because many of the major agencies and departments that have a role are housed in the federal government, but also because of the necessity for coordination across all levels of government when it comes to anti-terrorism activities. In fact, the federal government's major role

© White House/Alamy Images.

in the context of anti-terrorism is coordination and legislation. These two areas represent the most wide-spread use of federal government authority in the context of anti-terrorism.

One of the things that makes anti-terrorism and counter-terrorism so difficult from an organizational perspective is the fact that there is no clear delineation between anti-terrorism and counter-terrorism responsibilities in practice. For instance, the National Counterterrorism Center (NCTC) has responsibilities in areas that could be termed both counter- and anti-terrorism (see **Box 7.1**).[20] Of course, in some ways this blurred line is by design, with the integration of information and establishment of joint responsibility being one of the major purposes of the NCTC.[21] One place where anti-terrorism is a clear focus across all levels of government is in the context of critical infrastructure protection, one of the most important aspects of anti-terrorism (see **Box 7.2**).

BOX 7.1 The NCTC's Role in Counterterrorism

The National Counterterrorism Center (NCTC) plays a unique role in the nation's counter-terrorism function. Developed as a direct response to the *9/11 Commission Report's* recommendation for a single entity that is responsible for joint operational planning and joint intelligence, staffed by personnel from different intelligence agencies, the NCTC's mission is to "Lead our nation's effort to combat terrorism at home and abroad by analyzing the threat, sharing that information with our partners, and integrating all instruments of our national power to ensure unity of effort."

The NCTC's Development

NCTC originated as the Terrorism Threat Integration Center (TTIC), which was enacted by Executive Order 13354, issued by President George W. Bush in 2003. The TTIC was developed on the recommendations of the 9/11 Commission, and was meant to deal with the primary issue the Commission saw as a problem in counterterrorism—information sharing. In 2004 the Intelligence Reform and Terrorism Prevention Act was signed, changing the TTIC's name to the NCTC. The scope of responsibility also grew to include the management of several databases.

NCTC's Operations

The operations of the NCTC can be broken down into three areas mentioned previously in the organization's mission statement. The first area, analyzing the threat, consists of NCTC's function of integrating *all* terrorist-related intelligence (save that of dealing solely with domestic terrorism) and producing finished analytic products for distribution among the intelligence community and with policymakers. The second area of responsibility, "sharing the information," is accomplished through literally collocating individuals and information. Over 30 networks are located at the NCTC, representing all of the major actors in regards to counterterrorism intelligence and activity. Finally, as part of its requirement to "integrate all instruments of national power," the NCTC conducts strategic and operational planning for counterterrorism operations across the government. This includes elements from diplomatic, financial, military, and homeland security to ensure that all parties are represented in the planning of these operations. While heavily involved in the planning process, NCTC does not participate in the execution of these operations, which remain under the auspices of the agency carrying them out.

Conclusion

The NCTC, through its unique role in the intelligence community, is one of the most tangible outcomes of the recommendations of the 9/11 Commission. The responsibilities that the agency carries out, integrating information, information sharing, and strategic and operational planning are essential to the counter-terrorism mission of homeland security. The NCTC operates under the authority of both the Homeland Security Council and the National Security Council under the direct operation of the ODNI, therefore making it one of the most powerful intelligence-sharing platforms within the U.S. government.

Data from: National Counterterrorism Center. (n.d.). About the National Counterterrorism Center. Retrieved from http://www.nctc.gov/about_us/about_nctc.html on March 12, 2013.

▪ Critical Infrastructure Protection

A large part of the anti-terrorism responsibility that falls under the rubric of the federal government is the area of **critical infrastructure and key resources** (CIKR) protection.[22] Critical infrastructure protection is comprised of the activities[23] meant to prevent, deter, neutralize, or mitigate the effects of a terrorist attack on the nation's critical infrastructure. Critical infrastructure itself is made up of areas considered essential to the country's continuing ability to function. Homeland Security Presidential Directive 7 identified 17 areas considered critical infrastructure[24] and DHS has identified an 18th:[25]

- Food and agriculture
- Banking and finance
- Chemical
- Commercial facilities
- Communications
- Critical manufacturing
- Dams
- Defense industrial base
- Emergency services
- Energy
- Government facilities
- Healthcare and public health
- Information technology
- National monuments and icons
- Nuclear reactors, materials, and waste
- Postal and shipping
- Transportation systems
- Water

These are the areas that have been deemed "vital to the United States that their incapacity or destruction would have a debilitating impact on our physical or economic security or public health or safety."[26] Because of this importance, ensuring the continuing operation of all these areas is a large part of anti-terrorism planning. The coordination of protection of capacities deemed to be part of critical infrastructure falls under the **National Infrastructure Protection Plan** (NIPP).[27] The NIPP lays out which government agencies are responsible for what areas of critical infrastructure protection as well as the risk-assessment methodology to be used in identifying risks and prioritizing protection.

Because critical infrastructure protection is so essential, there are a large number of agencies involved in its implementation from the Department of Agriculture to the Department of Defense. Each of these agencies, called Sector Specific Agencies (SSA), is assigned responsibility for a specific area of critical infrastructure protection. The Environmental Protection Agency, for instance, is responsible for protection of water resources, while the DHS Department of Infrastructure Protection (IP) is responsible for a variety of areas like dangerous chemicals, commercial facilities, critical manufacturing, dams and nuclear power facilities, materials, and waste.[28]

Because of the nature of critical infrastructure, many, if not all, of these areas of critical infrastructure are interdependent. This means coordination is essential in any critical infrastructure protection program, and the NIPP provides for this through several mechanisms focusing on coordination first within CIKR sectors and then across sectors and levels of government. The level of coordination defines these coordination mechanisms. At the national level, the IP facilitates the development of the NIPP itself as well as the Sector Specific Plans (SSPs), which focus on the risk-management strategy of the different areas of CIKR protection. At the sector partnership coordination level, there are several councils that work together to create partnerships between federal, state, local, and private stakeholders so they can work together across sectors to ensure protection of critical infrastructure. Finally, regional coordination is accomplished through organizations like the Great Lakes Hazard Coalition, which consists of critical infrastructure partners from all levels of government with a regional interest, which in this case are partners concerned about protecting the Great Lakes region. Together, these various levels, functioning within the context of the NIPP, allow for national coordination of CIKR protection.

One of the most interesting aspects of critical infrastructure protection is the fact that over 80% of the country's critical infrastructure is privately owned. This consists of many areas we rarely think about, from utilities in our communities to much of the cybersphere (which will be covered more in the text elsewhere). Additionally, as mentioned previously, there is no single area of government that is responsible for all of CIKR protection. The breakdown of roles is therefore somewhat complicated; the NIPP defines nine roles in CIKR protection:

1. **Department of Homeland Security:** DHS's primary area of responsibility is coordination. It is responsible for coordinating the overall CIKR protection efforts as well as the development of the NIPP. In addition, implementation of the NIPP and integration with other national preparedness efforts is the responsibility of DHS.

2. **Sector-specific agencies:** As mentioned previously, Sector Specific Agencies (SSAs) are responsible for implementation of the NIPP within their constituent areas. This means tailoring the overall goals of the NIPP to the sector that the agency is responsible for and making sure it fits within the overall NIPP.

3. **Other federal departments, agencies, and offices:** While some agencies or departments are responsible for a given sector of CIKR, some are not designated but still have an important role. These agencies, offices, and departments are responsible for making sure to implement their specific protection roles as designated in HSPD-7 or other relevant policy.

4. **State, local, tribal, and territorial governments:** All levels of government have an important role to play in the context of CIKR, and designing a protection program in accordance with the NIPP risk-management framework is essential to achieving overall CIKR protection as well as specific homeland security goals for these entities.

5. **Regional partners:** Regional partnerships, as mentioned previously, are designed to cross jurisdictional and sector boundaries and function within a specifically defined geographical area.

6. **Boards, commissions, authorities, councils, and other entities:** These groups perform regulatory, advisory, policy, or business oversight (depending on their specific missions) related to CIKR. They can be

either single-jurisdiction or multi-jurisdiction and tend to work across sectors.

7. **Private sector owners and operators:** As such a large part of critical infrastructure in the U.S. is owned by private entities, the cooperation of private sector actors is essential. Their function, in the context of CIKR, is to provide advice, recommendations, and subject matter expertise to those operating in a CIKR protection role.

8. **Homeland security advisory councils:** Homeland security advisory councils are designed to provide expertise to and recommendations for the government regarding any activities related to infrastructure protection, including any policy they are called on to evaluate.

9. **Academia and research centers:** Academia has a very important role in the context of CIKR protection. Academics and research centers provide independent analysis and evaluation of government programs, research and development, and educational programs developed to assist with CIKR protection.[29]

Anti-terrorism, though often overlooked or combined in people's minds with counter-terrorism, is a different and essential part of defending our country from terrorist acts. The legislation, activity, and research involved in all aspects of anti-terrorism, especially critical infrastructure and key resource protection, must be there to support the overall homeland security mission of the United States. Working across regions, sectors, and disciplines, anti-terrorism efforts

---

BOX 7.2   Critical Infrastructure Protection—The Illustrative Case of Food Security

Obviously, each element of critical infrastructure and key resource protection is essential to the nation's homeland security. Each also represents a challenge because of how intertwined the critical infrastructure is to the rest of the American economic and social system. Perhaps no element of critical infrastructure is as complex as food security. Because of this, it represents an illustrative case for the importance of CIKR protection, and a framework in which to view the other areas of CIKR protection.

Food and the Nation

The nation's food supply is complex, based on a large array of distinct business and operations that bring food not only to people in the U.S., but around the world. The post-harvest food industry accounts for at least 12% of the nation's economy and employs at least 10% of the country's workforce. In total, when including agriculture, the food industry is responsible for 20% of the U.S. economy. Within this, there are huge subsectors including processing, storage, transportation, retail, and food service.

Complexity

Because of the large number of private entities involved in the food industry, regulation of the industry is complex. Responsibility for food safety rests primarily with two federal agencies: the Food and Drug Administration (FDA), which oversees the processing of red meat, poultry, and eggs, and the Department of Health and Human Services (HHS), which regulates virtually all other food products. Additional regulation happens at both the state and local government level, with restaurants, institutional food service, and food retailers under local jurisdiction (primarily). However, with specific, intentional targeting of the food supply a significant threat, other agencies such as the FBI and DHS play an important role as well.

The Threat

The threat to food safety in the U.S. is significant. Tommy Thompson, former Secretary of Health and Human Services stated in 2004 that, "I, for the life of me, cannot understand why the terrorists have not attacked our food can only succeed with significant coordination, which is one of the primary responsibilities of DHS.

Counter-terrorism

Counter-terrorism, particularly international counter-terrorism, is one of the most visible aspects of the overall homeland security effort because of both the history of the development of modern homeland security as well as the media coverage it receives in the form of both news and entertainment. For instance, the recent Hollywood movie *Zero Dark Thirty* portrays the tracking and killing of Osama bin Laden. In its opening weekend, the movie grossed $24 million.[30] The news story of the killing of Osama bin Laden in 2011 was one of the most covered items over the course of that year. Similarly, *Homeland*—a series focused on domestic counter-terrorism—is one of the most popular shows on television.

Given this large amount of attention, it is perhaps surprising there are still significant questions the U.S. government is grappling with in terms of counter-terrorism. Questions about the legality of actions like drone strikes against terrorists in other countries, rendition, and lingering doubts about issues like 'enhanced interrogation' and indefinite detention make the topic controversial and the difficulty of measuring success makes policy decisions difficult. It is important to consider counter-terrorism from a variety of perspectives to gain an understanding of this complex function of homeland security.

supply because it is so easy to do." Indeed, the threat of direct, purposeful contamination of the food supply is the most significant concern in food safety and security. However, other types of threats also exist, both in terms of accidental foodborne illness outbreaks and contamination by elements such as heavy metals. Both intentional and unintentional contamination are significant dangers because of the large number of consumers products reach—with unintentional contamination reaching 300,000 people in past events.

Potential Impact

The potential impact, both in economic and human terms, of a successful attack against the nation's agriculture and food systems is massive. Not only can it directly affect people's health, but an attack could negatively affect both the nation's collective psychology as well how well the government operates. DHS specifically recognizes these areas—psychological impact, physical heath, government functioning, and the economy—as four areas that identify what qualifies as critical infrastructure. Additionally, should

an attack be successfully carried out, it would place huge burdens on those agencies responsible for mitigating the effects of such an attack, as those who fall victims may not be easily identifiable, and may also be geographically disparate.

Conclusion

Food safety is an issue that concerns every person in the U.S. The complexity of the problem, the potentially massive impacts of a successful attack—both psychological and physical—and the difficult nature of dealing with an attack if one does occur, demonstrates the problems faced in each of the areas of critical infrastructure. The 17 areas identified by DHS as CIKR all provide fundamentally necessary elements of American life, and therefore, like food safety, must be taken seriously in the context of homeland security.

Data from: Department of Homeland Security. (2007). The Department of Homeland Security's role in food defense and critical infrastructure protection. Retrieved from http://www.oig.dhs.gov/assets/Mgmt/OIG_07-33_Feb07.pdf

Pre-September 11th Counter-terrorism

As examined earlier, terrorism is not a new phenomenon and, by extension, neither is counter-terrorism. However, the scope and importance placed on counter-terrorism has undergone a sea change since the September 11th attacks. Prior to that event, terrorism was considered by policymakers a threat only in the case where it combined two other characteristics—a direct threat to the U.S. homeland and the use of weapons of mass destruction (WMDs). Scholars fared no better in predicting the threat that terrorism would become. As Martha Crenshaw suggested,

> The policy recommendations of scholars in the security studies and international relations fields typically did not cite terrorism as a major threat to American security … terrorism specialists tended to neglect the strategic dimensions of the issue … the study of terrorism was useful for a variety of things, such as understanding motivation, but it could not provide tactical warning, assess threats, or set priorities. (p. 447)[31]

However, despite the general unpreparedness of the United States for 9-11, there were those who suggested the threat terrorism posed was significant, even without the use of weapons of mass destruction. The U.S. Commission on National Security in the 21st Century released a report in 1999 that suggested that while conventional warfare was still a significant threat, the most significant threat would be subnational groups engaging in activities like bioterrorism or, eerily, an attack on the air-traffic control system on the East Coast. The Commission's report concluded that, "together, the evidence suggests that threats to American security will be more diffuse, harder to anticipate, and more difficult to neutralize than ever before."[32]

Considered overall, there was little clear direction in counter-terrorism before the 9-11 attacks. While it was on the country's security agenda, the station it occupied was low and there were few resources dedicated to terrorism outside of WMDs. This, of course, changed with the September 11th attacks, and a new focus on counter-terrorism, almost to the exclusion of all other threats, developed. The following section deals with counter-terrorism post-September 11th.

Counter-terrorism Post-9-11

Counter-terrorism is unique in that it is one of the few areas that the U.S. consistently operates outside of its own boundaries but still requires a domestic presence. This is functionally because the threat of terrorism, as it is popularly understood, is primarily an international phenomenon. Additionally, unlike warfare—which is handled almost solely by the Department of Defense—counter-terrorism is not focused on a single adversary. Even Al Qaeda, our primary target since September 11, 2001, is no longer considered a single operational unit, but rather a diffuse movement of similarly minded individuals and organizations.[33] Complicating matters still more is the fact that there is no single agency that has sole responsibility for the United States' counter-terrorism mission—roles change depending largely on the geography of the problem. Counter-terrorism overseas is usually the responsibility of the CIA and Department of Defense, while domestic counter-terrorism is a function primarily of the FBI and DHS.

These challenges, especially post-9-11, have led to significant changes in the way the United States handles counter-terrorism. Various aspects of foreign policy, the law, and warfare have all changed in an attempt to combat what is considered one of the most pressing problems the U.S. faces. However, despite these changes, there remains no grand and unified strategy in terms of combating terrorism, and developing a definitive one may not even be possible. Martha Crenshaw notes that, in fact, terrorism itself is not a single entity, but an aggregate of threats that we must be flexible enough to face in a variety of contexts—from international proxy wars to cyber-terrorism—and the rules for each of these may be different.[34]

Counter-terrorism Under President George W. Bush

Because of the widely differing threats under the one rubric of "terrorism," there have been a variety of approaches taken to combating it. The first approach post-9-11, undertaken by President George W. Bush, was the "War on Terror," which has been characterized as a "garbage pail" effort at counter-terrorism.[35] This, many argue, was ineffective and may have in fact been counterproductive,[36] especially with the increasing geopolitical complexity caused by the war in Iraq, beginning in 2003. Additionally, the original focus seemed to be on state sponsors of terrorism, though the changing phrases used to describe the war over time (e.g., "the long war") indicated a broader focus.[37]

The first detailed articulation of the country's post-9-11 counter-terrorism strategy came in 2002 with President George W. Bush's National Security Strategy. This, according to Bridget Nacos, had three primary elements that when combined formed what has been called the Bush Doctrine: Making the world safer and better, preemption in the face of imminent threat, and the unilateral use of force.[38]

The first of these elements, making the world better and safer, revolves around the United States' unique role as the sole remaining superpower and the belief in the superiority of a democratic system of government. The security strategy, therefore, focused on bringing elements important in American life to the rest of the world in the belief that it would assist those countries who adopted them. Democracy, free trade, and free markets were the watch-words of these efforts and the more global idea of "freedom" its banner.

The second element of the Bush Doctrine was preemption, the idea of stopping rogue states and terrorists before they became an imminent threat to the security of the United States. This is particularly relevant given the increasing number of countries with the ability to transfer knowledge of and materials for WMDs and, at the very least, provide support for terrorists. President Bush, in his commencement address to West Point in 2002, articulated this point well. The speech is significant enough to quote at length.

> For much of the last century, America's defense relied on the cold war doctrines of deterrence and containment. In some cases, those strategies still apply, but new threats also require new thinking. Deterrence—the promise of massive retaliation against nations—means nothing against shadowy terrorist networks with no nation or citizens to defend. Containment is not possible when unbalanced dictators with weapons of mass destruction can deliver those weapons on missiles or secretly provide them to terrorist allies. We cannot defend America and our friends by hoping for the best. We cannot put our faith in the word of tyrants who solemnly sign nonproliferation treaties and then systemically break them. If we wait for threats to fully materialize, we will have waited too long.
>
> Homeland defense and missile defense are part of stronger security; they're essential priorities for America. Yet, the war on terror will not be won on the defensive. We must take the battle to the enemy, disrupt his plans, and confront the worst threats before they emerge. In the world we have entered, the only path to safety is the path of action, and this Nation will act.[39]

Reproduced from: Bush, George W. (2002). "Commencement Address at the United States Military Academy in West Point, New York." Public Papers of the Presidents of the United States. Washington, D.C.: U.S. GPO.

The final element of the Bush Doctrine was the unilateral use of force, which was deemed by the administration as essential in order to adequately protect the United States. Unilateralism, in the context of the Bush administration, incorporated the notion that terrorists could be pursued wherever they went—even without the consent of the country in which they were hiding. It was, and remains, a controversial approach, in part because it may undermine multilateral efforts to stop terrorists.[40]

Counter-terrorism Under President Barack Obama

Though many elements of counter-terrorism remained the same from the Bush administration, the presidency of Barack Obama has introduced some significant change. In regards to the Bush Doctrine, President Obama has backed significantly away from the concepts of unilateralism and preemption, though in both cases there have been specific instances where they have been used. Interestingly, the most significant change seems to be the move away from terrorism as the single threat the United States faces in the international community. As stated by Michael Leiter, then the head of the National Counterterrorism Center, in 2009, "Counter-terrorism is part of larger U.S. policy … [it] rarely, if ever, should be the lead in that policy."[41]

Some of these shifts, however significant, are belied by some actions of the Obama administration, which suggest close ties between the current policy and past policy under President Bush. In fact, the seminal counter-terrorism act of the Obama presidency, killing Osama bin Laden, was carried out unilaterally in an (ostensibly) ally's territory.[42] Additionally, drone strikes in a variety of locations around the world, in both allied countries as well as countries more hostile to the U.S., would seem to indicate that while multilateralism is the preferred approach, the U.S. is willing to "go it alone" if necessary.

A second area in which the Obama administration has seemingly differed from the Bush administration is in which agencies it uses to address counter-terrorism. President Bush tended towards using the Department of Defense as his primary agency—prosecuting wars based on the Bush Doctrine in both Afghanistan and Iraq. The Obama administration, by contrast, has tended to view the CIA as its primary agency for counter-terrorism internationally, with DOD in a supporting role.

This shift is reflected in the *National Strategy for Counterterrorism* released by the Obama administration in 2011 (see **Box 7.3**). While there is mention of the military's role in counter-terrorism, the focus of the document is an approach that utilizes "every tool of American power," with an emphasis on the collective action required both within the United States' government and between our government and other nations, to succeed in countering the terrorism threat.[43]

Domestic Counter-terrorism

While international counter-terrorism is the purview of the federal government, domestic counter-terrorism touches on every level of government. Like its international counterpart, however, there is little strategy guiding overall domestic counter-terrorism in the United States, though the FBI is the lead agency. However, other federal agencies, such as the National Security Agency (which monitors signals intelligence) also play a role in domestic counter-terrorism. Interestingly, the

BOX 7.3   The National Strategy for Counter-terrorism

In June, 2011, President Obama released the *National Strategy for Counterterrorism*. This document represents the articulation of the national approach to the problem of terrorism, focusing specifically on what the administration views as the significant issues facing the country in terms of counter-terrorism and the best ways to combat those problems. It additionally identifies tools that are necessary for the strategy to succeed, building both on previous strategies as well as new information. As a whole, it represents the best individual source for examining the counter-terrorism efforts currently being undertaken by the government.

Structure of the Strategy

The strategy is broken down into two major parts. The first part, *Overarching Goals*, examines the desired end-states that the administration wishes to achieve. The second part, *Areas of Focus*, examines specific regions and groups relevant to the counter-terrorism strategy, particularly the threat that Al Qaeda and affiliated groups continue to represent. These two sections are examined in detail here.

Overarching Goals

The overarching goals of the National Strategy are relatively straightforward. They include:

- Protecting the American people, Homeland, and American Interests
- Disrupting, Degrading, Dismantling and Defeating Al Qaeda and its Affiliates and Adherents
- Preventing Terrorist Development, Acquisition, and Use of Weapons of Mass Destruction
- Eliminating Safe Havens
- Building Enduring Counter-terrorism Partnerships and Capabilities
- Degrading Links Between Al Qaeda and its Affiliates and Adherents
- Countering Al Qaeda Ideology and its Resonance and Diminishing the Specific Drivers of Violence that Al Qaeda Exploits
- Depriving Terrorists of their Enabling Means

These goals are the foundation for America's counter-terrorism activities. They represent the most important elements of counter-terrorism policymaking, and help to underline the important elements of any counter-terrorism operations.

Areas of Focus

The areas of focus within the *Strategy* are wide ranging. They examine issues as diverse as counter-terrorism to protect the homeland and combating terrorism in the Arabian Peninsula and East Africa. Perhaps most interesting is the focus on specific elements important to counter-terrorism, rather than regions. Areas such as terrorist financing and ideology figure prominently in the *Strategy* and, thus, represent significant threats in the perspective of the government. Additionally, though the strategy is overwhelmingly focused on Al Qaeda and its affiliate groups around the world, other organizations such as Hamas, Hizballah, and the FARC are mentioned as additional terrorist threats of which the country must remain cognizant.

Conclusion

In short, the *National Strategy for Counterterrorism* is an important document in terms of understanding the counter-terrorism goals for the United States. It examines both the goals the government hopes to achieve against terrorist activity, as well as some of the challenges that the country faces in achieving those goals. Perhaps the most important parts of the document, however, are outside of the direct areas pertaining to counter-terrorism. These areas focus on the adherence to core U.S. values, including respect for human rights, encouraging responsive governance, and instilling a respect for civil rights and liberties. Without these elements, the strategy would still stand as an important document, but it would be less uniquely American.

Data from: The White House. (2011). National Strategy for Counterterrorism. Retrieved from http://www.whitehouse.gov/sites/default/files/counterterrorism_strategy.pdf

two lead agencies for international counter-terrorism, the DOD and the CIA, have no role to play on the domestic front, as they are effectively barred from operating within the homeland.

Another significant difference between domestic and international counter-terrorism is the fact that local agencies have a large role to play on the domestic side. They engage in monitoring of groups, ranging from right-wing white supremacist organizations to left-wing anti-globalization groups. This activity is frequently in conjunction with agencies operating at the federal level.

Given this law enforcement focus within domestic counter-terrorism, much of the activity focuses on traditional law enforcement actions. Investigations into individuals and organizations attempting to engage in terrorism make up a significant part of today's domestic counter-terrorism operations. As an example of the importance of these domestic investigations, in the State of America's Homeland Security address in 2011, former Secretary of Homeland Security Janet Napolitano said,

> Historically, our domestic counter-terrorism efforts were based on the belief that we faced the greatest risk from attacks planned, and carried out, by individuals coming from abroad. But the arrests of an increasing number of U.S. persons on terror-related charges in the last 2 years mean that we must move beyond this paradigm. These include Najibullah Zazi, a legal permanent resident arrested in 2009 for plotting to attack the New York City subway system; Faisal Shahzad, a naturalized U.S. citizen, who attempted to explode a car bomb in Times Square last year (see **Box 7.4**); as well as more recent arrests in Portland, Oregon, Dallas, Texas, and here in the Washington area.
>
> Today, we operate under the premise that individuals prepared to carry out terrorist acts might already be in the country, and could carry out further acts of terrorist violence with little or no warning. We must all work to gain a better understanding of the behaviors, tactics, and other indicators that could point to terrorist activity.[44]

Reproduced from: Napolitano, J. (2011). State of America's homeland security address. Retrieved from http://www.dhs.gov/news/2011/01/27/state-americas-homeland-security-address

© U.S. Marshals Service/AP Images.

BOX 7.4 Faisal Shahzad and the 2010 Times Square Bombing

Introduction

In 2010 one of the most high-profile terrorist bombing attempts was stopped in New York City. The perpetrator, Faisal Shahzad, had attempted to detonate an explosive-filled SUV in Times Square, but the bomb failed to detonate. The response to the incident, and subsequent investigation and arrest of Shahzad, represents an excellent example of inter-agency cooperation in the pursuit of counter-terrorism goals.

The Bombing Incident

On May 1, 2010, a t-shirt vendor discovered an SUV parked in Times Square that was discharging smoke. The New York Police Department was notified, and one of the officers responding identified the smell of gunpowder. The bomb squad was subsequently dispatched and found an improvised explosive device in the vehicle, a Nissan Pathfinder. The bomb consisted of three propane tanks, two 5-gallon gasoline tanks, two clocks with batteries, fireworks, and a locked metal box filled with low-grade fertilizer. The bomb failed to detonate, but had it done so, it would have caused casualties, according to the NYPD investigators.

The Investigation

The investigation that led to the arrest of Faisal Shahzad unfolded very quickly. The Nissan Pathfinder used in the bombing had its VIN number vandalized, but forensic techs were able to recover the VIN. With this information, the Joint Terrorism Task Force (JTTF) traced the vehicle to Shahzad, who bought it with cash from a seller on April 24, 2010. Additionally, in the back of the SUV, the police recovered a set of keys for an Isuzu, which Shahzad drove as his normal vehicle. Also discovered early on in the investigation was Shahzad's use of a prepaid phone to call a fireworks store, as well as receive a number of calls from Pakistan. The phone stopped being used just 2 days before the bombing incident.

This increasing importance on the domestic side of counter-terrorism, and particularly the law enforcement function it contains, is essential to the long-term security of the nation. The efforts of both local- and state-level law enforcement have been considered the "first line" of the U.S.'s domestic counter-terrorism operations. Again, former Secretary Napolitano,

> But the homeland security enterprise extends far beyond DHS and the federal government. As I said, it requires not just a "whole of government," but a "whole of nation" approach. In some respects, local law enforcement, community groups, citizens, and the private sector play as much of a role in homeland security as the federal government. That is why I like to say that "homeland security starts with hometown security."[45]

Interestingly, the threat faced in the context of domestic terrorism is quite different from that which we face internationally, many of which have nothing to do with Islamist terrorism, which we generally associate with counter-terrorism.[46] The geography of terrorism within the United States is complex, with groups differing widely in ideology—ranging from anti-government to anti-corporate— many of which share the same tactical approach. This means that, in many cases, local law enforcement or local communities, are the first to notice actions or characteristics that lead to the identification of terrorism and its interdiction. Lest this just be considered idle talk, over 80% of the terrorist attacks stopped between 2001 and 2009 were originally identified by local law enforcement or community members.[47]

It is important to acknowledge that, while there is a difference between the efforts of domestic and international counter-terrorism, many of the laws have been changed since September 11, 2001 to try and bring these two activities closer together. The "freeing up" of surveillance activities for domestic law enforcement

> KEY TERM
> **Joint Terrorism Task Force**—a partnership between various American law enforcement agencies that is charged with taking action against terrorism.

On May 3rd, 2010, Shahzad was arrested at John F. Kennedy International Airport in New York City attempting to board a plane to Dubai. Upon his arrest, he admitted that he had received bomb-making training in Pakistan, and that $12,500 of the money for the plot was given to him by a co-conspirator from Pakistan affiliated with the Tehrik-e-Taliban, itself an affiliate of Al Qaeda. While much of the original investigation was done by the NYPD and FBI, the Department of Homeland Security's U.S. Customs and Border Protection (CBP) identified him as he was trying to leave the country. Additionally, the FBI's **Joint Terrorism Task Force (JTTF)** in New York City played a significant role in the investigation.

homeland security spectrum. From the local investigation by NYPD officials, to the participation of national-level agencies like the FBI and CBP, agencies quickly worked to identify and apprehend a suspect. While the bombing did not harm anyone, the threat it represented was very real, and the response of the law enforcement and intelligence agencies involved demonstrates the increased capacity of homeland security counter-terrorism operations post-9-11.

Data from: *United States of America vs. Faisal Shahzad.* 10 Cr. 541. (2010). United States Department of Justice. (2010). *Faisal Shahzad pleads guilty in Manhattan Federal Court to 10 federal crimes arising from attempted car bombing in Times Square.* Retrieved from http://www.justice.gov/opa/pr/2010/June/10-ag-721.html on March 12, 2013.

Conclusion

While counter-terrorism efforts in the U.S. are sometimes maligned, the Faisal Shahzad case represents an excellent example of cooperation among agencies across the

Table 7.1 Reporting Suspicious Activity

Report Suspicious Activity

Want to report suspicious persons or activity?	**Rewards for Justice** Website: *www.rewardsforjustice.net*, then click "Submit a Tip" E-mail: *rfj@state.gov* Phone: In the United States, call 1-800-US REWARDS (1-800-877-3927) **FBI** Website: *https://tips.fbi.gov* Phone: In the United States, call 202-324-3000 [FBI main switchboard] To find phone numbers of regional FBI offices in the United States, visit: *www.fbi.gov/contact-us/field* If outside the United States and want to reach the FBI, call the nearest US Embassy or Consulate office; for phone numbers, see *www.fbi.gov/contact-us/legat* **CIA** Website: *www.cia.gov*
Think you've seen a wanted person?	To view photographs of wanted terrorists, visit these sites: • *www.rewardsforjustice.net* • *www.fbi.gov/wanted/wanted_terrorists* • *www.fbi.gov/wanted/terrorinfo*

Wondering whether a business, charity, Nongovernmental Organization (NGO), or other entity has terrorist ties?	Do you want to make sure you can donate money to such an organization legally? View designated individuals and groups at these sites:
	• Designated Foreign Terrorist Organizations
	  www.state.gov/s/ct/rls/other/des/123085.htm
	• Individuals and entities designated under Executive Order 13224
	  www.state/gov/j/ct/rls/other/des/143210.htm
	• Specially Designated Nationals and Blocked Persons
	  www.treasury.gov/ofac/downloads/t11sdn.pdf
	  www.treasury.gov/ofac/downloads/sdnlist.txt

Other Resources	• US National Counterterrorism Center
	  www.nctc.gov
	• US State Department Office of the Coordinator for Counterterrorism
	  www.state.gov/s/ct
	• US State Department Country Reports on Terrorism
	  www.state.gov/j/ct/rls/crt/index.htm

Modified from: National Counterterrorism Center. (2013). Counterterrorism Calendar 2013, p. 148. Retrieved from http://www.nctc.gov/site/pdfs/ct_calendar_2013.pdf on March 12, 2013.

has proved to be important in domestic counter-terrorism, but also has provided a source of controversy. The FBI has reoriented itself into a so-called "intelligence driven" organization—with a focus on stopping terrorism rather than prosecuting those who are responsible for it.[48]

While the federal government maintains its overall leadership role in the counter-terrorism mission of homeland security, there is an increasing significance to state and local law enforcement regarding domestic counter-terrorism. This is largely obscured by the greater focus on international counter-terrorism—particularly the pursuit of Al Qaeda and the focus of the mass media on these events.

■ Chapter Summary

Anti-terrorism and counter-terrorism are the two chief elements of the homeland security mission that are often thought to be the same but, in fact, are distinctly different. Anti-terrorism legislation and programs aim to keep Americans safe and to promote resiliency through reactive measures for when terrorism happens and proactive measures that attempt to stop terrorism by identifying those involved. Counter-terrorism, on the other hand, seeks to not only identify and apprehend terrorists, but to counter the threat before it occurs, usually through kinetic or offensive means. Since 9-11, both anti-terrorism and counter-terrorism have become essential parts of the homeland security mission. They have, especially during the first George W. Bush administration, been the centerpiece of homeland security strategy, to the limited extent that an overall strategy existed. More recently, under President Barack Obama, they have played a more limited, though still important, policy role.

While it is uncertain what changes the second Obama presidency will bring in terms of anti-terrorism and counter-terrorism, it is unlikely there will be a dramatic shift from the policies enacted over the past 12 years. These have provided, thus far, a high level of safety for the American homeland and are thus considered successful by most. Nearly all sources agree, however, that it is not a question of whether the U.S. will be attacked again, but when, and the question remains of what impact that will have on existing anti-terrorism and counter-terrorism policies.

■ Review/Discussion Questions

1. What is the difference between anti-terrorism and counter-terrorism, and why does the difference matter?
2. What is the NIPP, and what role does it play in anti-terrorism policy in the United States?
3. What makes critical infrastructure and key resources so important? What are the areas of critical infrastructure?
4. Explain the U.S. Senate's criticism of state and local fusion centers. Is the criticism deserved?
5. What are the major elements of the *National Strategy for Counterterrorism* and how do they match up with the Obama Administration's counter-terrorism actions? Do they compare with previous administration's actions?

◼ Additional Readings

Howard, R.D., Sawyer, R.L., & Bajema, N.E. (2009). *Terrorism and Counterterrorism: Understanding the New Security Environment* (3rd ed.). New York, NY: McGraw Hill.

The White House. (2011). *National Strategy for Counterterrorism.* Retrieved from http://www.whitehouse.gov/sites/default/files/counterterrorism_strategy.pdf

◼ Endnotes

1. Ownen, M. & Maurer, K. (2012). *No Easy Day: The Firsthand Account of the Mission that Killed Osama bin Laden.* New York, NY: Dutton Adult.

2. Ownen, M. & Maurer, K. (2012). *No Easy Day: The Firsthand Account of the Mission that Killed Osama bin Laden.* New York, NY: Dutton Adult.

3. Sherwell, P. (May 7, 2011). "Osama bin Laden Killed: Behind the Scenes of the Deadly Raid." *The Telegraph.* Retrieved from http://www.telegraph.co.uk/news/worldnews/al-qaeda/8500431/Osama-bin-Laden-killed-Behind-the-scenes-of-the-deadly-raid.html

4. Sherwell, P. (May 7, 2011). "Osama bin Laden Killed: Behind the Scenes of the Deadly Raid." *The Telegraph.* Retrieved from http://www.telegraph.co.uk/news/worldnews/al-qaeda/8500431/Osama-bin-Laden-killed-Behind-the-scenes-of-the-deadly-raid.html

5. Department of Defense. (2010). *Dictionary of Military and Associated Terms.* Retrieved from http://www.dtic.mil/doctrine/new_pubs/jp1_02.pdf

6. Department of Defense. (2010). *Dictionary of Military and Associated Terms.* Retrieved from http://www.dtic.mil/doctrine/new_pubs/jp1_02.pdf

7. Ganor, B. (2007). *The Counter-terrorism Puzzle.* New York, NY: Transaction Publishers.

8. The White House. (2011). *National Strategy for Counter-terrorism.* Retrieved from http://www.whitehouse.gov/sites/default/files/Counterterrorism_strategy.pdf

9. Department of Defense. (2010). *Dictionary of Military and Associated Terms.* Retrieved from http://www.dtic.mil/doctrine/new_pubs/jp1_02.pdf

10. Schneider, R.H. (2003). "American Anti-terrorism Planning and Design Strategies: Application for Florida Growth Management, Comprehensive Planning and Urban Design." *University of Florida Journal of Law & Public Policy, 15,* 129–154.

11. Conway, M. (2002). "Terrorism, the Law, and Politics as Usual: A Comparison of Anti-terrorism Legislation Before and After 9/11." *Touro Law Review, 18,* 735–781.

12. Homeland Security Presidential Directive 6. (2003). Retrieved from http://www.fas.org/irp/offdocs/nspd/hspd-6.html

13. Written testimony of Office of Policy Senior Director for Screening Coordination Kelli Ann Walther for a House Committee on Homeland Security, Subcommittee on Border and Maritime Security hearing titled "Eleven Years Later: Preventing Terrorists from Coming to America." 113th Cong. (2012).

14. Uniting and Strengthening America by Providing Appropriate Tools Required to Intercept and Obstruct Terrorism Act of 2001, Pub. L. No. 107–56, 115 Stat. 272 (2001).

15. United States Department of Justice. (n.d.). *The USA PATRIOT Act: Preserving Life and Liberty*. Retrieved from http://www.justice.gov/archive/ll/what_is_the_patriot_act.pdf

16. Whitehead, J.W. & Aden, S.H. (2002). "Forfeiting 'Enduring Freedom' for 'Homeland Security': A Constitutional Analysis of the USA Patriot Act and the Justice Department's Anti-terrorism Initiatives." *American University Law Review, 51*(6), 1081–1133.

17. Homeland Defense Before the Senate Committee on the Judiciary, 107th Cong. (2001). Retrieved from http://www.justice.gov/archive/ag/testimony/2001/0925AttorneyGeneralJohnAshcroftTestimonybeforetheSenateCommitteeontheJudiciary.htm

18. Department of Homeland Security. (2007). *Chemical Facility Anti-terrorism Standards*. Retrieved from http://www.dhs.gov/chemical-facility-anti-terrorism-standards

19. Schneider, R.H. (2003). "American Anti-terrorism Planning and Design Strategies: Application for Florida Growth Management, Comprehensive Planning and Urban Design." *University of Florida Journal of Law & Public Policy, 15*, 129–1554.

20. National Counter-terrorism Center. (2009). *Strategic Intent 2009-2013*. Retrieved from http://www.nctc.gov/docs/nctc_strategic_intent.pdf

21. National Counter-terrorism Center. (2009). *Strategic Intent 2009-2013*. Retrieved from http://www.nctc.gov/docs/nctc_strategic_intent.pdf

22. Department of Homeland Security. (2009). *National Infrastructure Protection Plan: Partnering to Enhance Protection and Resiliency*. Retrieved from http://www.dhs.gov/xlibrary/assets/NIPP_Plan.pdf

23. Department of Homeland Security. (2009). *National Infrastructure Protection Plan: Partnering to Enhance Protection and Resiliency*. Retrieved from http://www.dhs.gov/xlibrary/assets/NIPP_Plan.pdf

24. Homeland Security Presidential Directive 7. Retrieved from http://www.dhs.gov/homeland-security-presidential-directive-7#1

25. Department of Homeland Security. (n.d.). *Critical Infrastructure Protection*. Retrieved from http://www.dhs.gov/topic/critical-infrastructure-protection

26. Department of Homeland Security. (n.d.). *Critical Infrastructure Protection*. Retrieved from http://www.dhs.gov/topic/critical-infrastructure-protection

27. Department of Homeland Security. (2009). *National Infrastructure Protection Plan: Partnering to Enhance Protection and Resiliency*. Retrieved from http://www.dhs.gov/xlibrary/assets/NIPP_Plan.pdf

28. Department of Homeland Security. (2009). *National Infrastructure Protection Plan: Partnering to Enhance Protection and Resiliency*. Retrieved from http://www.dhs.gov/xlibrary/assets/NIPP_Plan.pdf

29. Department of Homeland Security. (2009). *National Infrastructure Protection Plan: Partnering to Enhance Protection and Resiliency*. Retrieved from http://www.dhs.gov/xlibrary/assets/NIPP_Plan.pdf

30. Fritz, B. (14 January 2013). "'Zero Dark Thirty' Wins Weekend Box Office Battle." *The Los Angeles Times*. Retrieved from http://www.latimes.com/entertainment/envelope/cotown/la-et-mn-zero-dark-thirty-boxoffice-20130114,0,7161365.story

31. Crenshaw, M. (2004). Terrorism, Strategies, and Grand Strategies. In: Howard, R.D., Sawyer, R.L., & Bajema, N.E. (2009). *Terrorism and Counter-terrorism: Understanding the New Security Environment* (3rd ed.). New York, NY: McGraw Hill.

32. U.S. Commission on National Security/21st Century. (1999). The Phase I Report on the Emerging Global Security Environment for the First Quarter of the 21st Century. Retrieved from http://www.au.af.mil/au/awc/awcgate/nssg/nwc.pdf

33. Jenkins, B.M. (2012). *New Challenges to U.S. Counter-terrorism Efforts: An Assessment of the Current Terrorist Threat*. Testimony presented before the Senate Homeland Security and Governmental Affairs Committee on July 11, 2012. Retrieved from http://www.rand.org/content/dam/rand/pubs/testimonies/2012/RAND_CT377.pdf

34. Crenshaw, M. (2004). Terrorism, Strategies, and Grand Strategies. In: Howard, R.D., Sawyer, R.L., & Bajema, N.E. (2009). *Terrorism and Counter-terrorism: Understanding the New Security Environment* (3rd ed.). New York, NY: McGraw Hill.

35. Howard, R.D., Sawyer, R.L., & Bajema, N.E. (2009). *Terrorism and Counter-terrorism: Understanding the New Security Environment* (3rd ed.). New York, NY: McGraw Hill.

36. Scheuer, M. (2004). *Imperial Hubris: Why the West Is Losing the War on Terror*. Dulles, VA: Potomac Books.

37. Nacos, B.M. (2012). *Terrorism and Counter-terrorism* (4th ed.). New York, NY: Pearson.

38. Nacos, B.M. (2012). *Terrorism and Counter-terrorism* (4th ed.). New York, NY: Pearson.

39. Bush, G.W. "Commencement Address at the United States Military Academy in West Point, New York." The United States Military Academy, West Point, NY. 1 June 2003. Commencement Address. Retrieved from http://www.presidency.ucsb.edu/ws/index.php?pid=62730&st=America%5C%27s+defense+relied+on+the+cold+war+doctrines&st1=

40. Nacos, B.M. (2012). *Terrorism and Counter-terrorism* (4th ed.). New York, NY: Pearson.

41. Leiter, M. (2009). *Roundtable with Michael Leiter, Director of the National Counter-terrorism Center*. Retrieved from http://www.aspeninstitute.org/events/2009/04/09/director-national-counterterrorism-center-michael-leiter-speaks-aspen-institute

42. Roggio, B. (2011). Pakistan Critical of 'Unilateral' Raid that Killed Osama bin Laden. Retrieved from http://www.longwarjournal.org/archives/2011/05/pakistan_expresses_d.php

43. The White House. (2011). *National Strategy for Counter-terrorism.* Retrieved from http://www.whitehouse.gov/sites/default/files/Counterterrorism_strategy.pdf

44. Napolitano, J. (2011). *State of America's Homeland Security Address.* Retrieved from http://www.dhs.gov/news/2011/01/27/state-americas-homeland-security-address

45. Napolitano, J. (2011). *State of America's Homeland Security Address.* Retrieved from http://www.dhs.gov/news/2011/01/27/state-americas-homeland-security-address

46. Jenkins, B.M. (2012). *New Challenges to U.S. Counter-terrorism Efforts: An Assessment of the Current Terrorist Threat.* Testimony Presented before the Senate Homeland Security and Governmental Affairs Committee on July 11, 2012. Retrieved from http://www.rand.org/content/dam/rand/pubs/testimonies/2012/RAND_CT377.pdf

47. Napolitano, J. (2011). *State of America's Homeland Security Address.* Retrieved from http://www.dhs.gov/news/2011/01/27/state-americas-homeland-security-address

48. Federal Bureau of Investigation. (2011). *Talking Strategy: The New Intelligence-driven FBI.* Retrieved from int http://www.fbi.gov/news/stories/2010/april/sps_040210

The National Strategy for Homeland Security

Courtesy of Patsy Lynch/FEMA.

Chapter Objectives

■ Understand the documents that define the government's responses to emergencies that occur in the U.S.

■ Know the difference between the National Strategy for Homeland Security and the National Response Plan

■ Comprehend the evolution of the National Strategy for Homeland Security

■ Understand the roles of the federal, state, local, and tribal governments when an emergency occurs

Chapter Outline

- Introduction
- Homeland Security: A National Strategy
  - National Strategy (2002)
  - National Response Plan (2004)
  - National Strategy (2007)
  - National Response Framework (2008)
  - Strategic Plan (2012)
- Chapter Summary

■ Introduction

Toward the end of 2002, President Bush and the Congress established a commission to investigate the attacks of September 11th. The bipartisan committee, formally named the National Commission on Terrorist Attacks Upon the United States, or the **9/11 Commission**, was given the task of examining the circumstances surrounding the attacks, providing an assessment of the government's response to the attacks, and making recommendations for establishing improved security policies for the future. To do this, the Commission members interviewed government officials, members of law enforcement, intelligence officers, and many others who provided their perspective of events.

KEY TERM

9/11 Commission—formally named the National Commission on Terrorist Attacks Upon the United States, it was formed after the terrorist attacks on September 11, 2001 to investigate the attacks and to make recommendations for future preparations.

© Charles Dharapak/AP Images.

The Commission completed its report in August of 2004. The details provided an account of the events leading up to the attacks and a review of why the national security apparatus failed to detect and prevent the incident. The Commission reported that several intelligence agencies had prior information about the attacks, as well as the identities of those involved, but detailed that no agency, even those at the highest level, was able to put all the information together. They concluded that the intelligence agencies were not prepared for such a large-scale attack and that there were serious gaps between the different intelligence groups in terms of information sharing.

The report included 41 recommendations organized into three broad areas: (1) homeland security and emergency response; (2) intelligence and congressional reform; and (3) foreign policy and nonproliferation. They proposed that Congress should establish a committee to oversee homeland security, that funding to states and local governments should be based on potential targets, and that the TSA should screen all passengers, cargo, and luggage for explosives at borders and at sites of critical infrastructure. Additionally, the report noted that the government's intelligence agencies should be reorganized with one person who would oversee all national intelligence operations, and to ensure that all of the intelligence agencies shared information with each other.

■ Homeland Security: A National Strategy

> **KEY TERM**
> **National Strategy for Homeland Security**—a strategic document which guides, organizes, and unifies our Nation's homeland security efforts.

> **KEY TERM**
> **National Response Plan**—was the original national plan to respond to emergencies such as natural disasters or terrorist attacks. It was replaced with the National Response Framework.

> **KEY TERM**
> **National Response Framework**—part of the National Strategy for Homeland Security which provides the guiding principles enabling all levels of domestic response partners to prepare for and provide a unified national response to disasters and emergencies.

The *9/11 Report* formed the basis of further governmental action to increase the homeland's security. Immediately after the report was issued, President Bush asked his administration to create new policies that would help guide the national effort to ensure a more coordinated response should another terrorist attack occur. The plans would help to not only prevent an attack but also help minimize any damage done by an attack, and then help the country recover quickly. In 2002, the White House created the **National Strategy for Homeland Security**. Two years later, the Department of Homeland Security published the **National Response Plan**. This was followed in 2007 with an update to the National Strategy, and then in 2008 with the **National Response Framework** (from DHS), a document that replaced the National Response Plan. Finally, in 2012, a new Strategic Plan was put forth by the Department of Homeland Security. Understanding the evolution of America's strategy for Homeland Security is the focus of this chapter.

National Strategy (2002)

The 2002 National Strategy was the plan developed by the White House Office of Homeland Security to set a broad agenda for protecting America's safety.[1] The plan was intended to provide guidance to, and organize the efforts of, those agencies within the federal government that play some role in homeland security. The Strategy stated goals that needed to be met, particular programs that should be implemented, and responsibilities that needed to be fulfilled in order to keep Americans safe. As President Bush wrote, the Strategy was a "comprehensive plan for using America's talents and resources to enhance our protection and reduce our vulnerability to terrorist attacks." More of his introductory letter describing the Strategy is listed in **Box 8.1**.

There were three primary objectives to the Strategy: (1) to prevent terrorist attacks within the U.S.; (2) reduce America's vulnerability to terrorism, and (3) minimize the damage and recovery from attacks that do occur. In addition, there were eight principles outlined in the National Strategy:

1. To require responsibility and accountability: The report designated, to the extent possible, the executive departments or agencies that would be responsible for federal homeland security initiatives.
2. To mobilize our entire society: state and local governments, private institutions, and the American people must all be involved in protecting the country.
3. To manage risk and allocate resources judiciously: There are a finite amount of resources for homeland security, and the Strategy must identify priority programs that will receive funding.
4. To seek opportunity out of adversity: It is possible to improve security while at the same time advance other important public goals or principles.
5. To foster flexibility: A flexible response to terrorism is needed because terrorists will adapt their tactics to exploit any perceived weaknesses in our defenses.

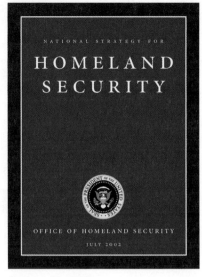

Courtesy of the DHS.

BOX 8.1 President Bush's Letter of Introduction for the 2002 National Strategy

"The National Strategy for Homeland Security is the product of more than 8 months of intense consultation across the U.S. My administration has talked to literally thousands of people—governors and mayors, state legislators, and members of Congress, concerned citizens and foreign leaders, professors and soldiers, firefighters and police officers, doctors and scientists, airline pilots and farmers, business leaders and civic activists, journalists and veterans, and the victims and their families. We have listened carefully. This is the national strategy, not a federal strategy. We must rally our entire society to overcome a new and very complex challenge. Homeland security is a shared responsibility. In addition to a national strategy, we need compatible, mutually supporting state, local, and private-sector strategies. Individual volunteers must channel their energy and commitment in support of the national and local strategies. My intent in publishing the National Strategy for Homeland Security is to help Americans achieve a shared cooperation in the area of homeland security for years to come. The Strategy seeks to do so by answering four basic questions:

- What is "homeland security" and what missions does it entail?
- What do we seek to accomplish, and what are the most important goals of homeland security?

- What is the federal executive branch doing now to accomplish these goals and what should it do in the future?
- What should nonfederal governments, the private sector, and citizens do to help secure the homeland?

The National Strategy for Homeland Security is a beginning. It calls for bold and necessary steps. It creates a comprehensive plan for using America's talents and resources to enhance our protection and reduce our vulnerability to terrorist attacks. We have produced a comprehensive national strategy that is based on the principles of cooperation and partnership. As a result of this Strategy, firefighters will be better equipped to fight fires, police officers better armed to fight crime, businesses better able to protect their data and information systems, and scientists better able to fight Mother Nature's deadliest diseases. ..."

Reproduced from: Bush, George W. (2002). "Letter on the National Strategy for Homeland Security." Public Papers of the Presidents of the United States. Washington, D.C.: U.S. GPO.

6. Measure preparedness: Every person responsible for homeland security must be accountable and their behaviors should be measured against a standard developed by the department.

7. Sustain efforts over the long term: Keeping the country safe is an ongoing, permanent task.

8. Constrain government spending: It is necessary to limit spending if possible through programs like cost-sharing arrangements with state and local governments or the private sector.[2]

The National Strategy separated homeland security functions into six mission areas, which are described in **TABLE 8.1**. The first three of the mission areas are

TABLE 8.1 Missions

Mission Area	Initiatives
Intelligence and Warning: "We must have an intelligence and warning system that can detect terrorist activity before it manifests itself in an attack so that proper preemptive, preventive, and protective action can be taken. The United States will take every necessary action to avoid being surprised by another terrorist attack."	1. Enhance the analytic capabilities of the FBI 2. Build new capabilities through the Information Analysis and Infrastructure Protection Division of the proposed Department of Homeland Security 3. Implement the Homeland Security Advisory System 4. Utilize dual-use analysis to prevent attacks 5. Employ "red team" techniques
Border and Transportation Security: "We must therefore promote the efficient and reliable flow of people, goods and services across borders, while preventing terrorists from using transportation conveyances or systems to deliver implements of destruction."	1. Ensure accountability in border and transportation security 2. Create "smart borders" 3. Increase the security of international shipping containers 4. Implement the Aviation and Transportation Security Act of 2001 5. Recapitalize the U.S. Coast Guard 6. Reform immigration services
Domestic Counterterrorism: "While law enforcement agencies will continue to investigate and prosecute criminal activity, they should assign priority to preventing and interdicting terrorist activity within the U.S."	1. Improve intergovernmental law enforcement coordination 2. Facilitate apprehension of potential terrorists 3. Continue ongoing investigations and prosecutions 4. Complete FBI restructuring to emphasize prevention of terrorist attacks 5. Target and attack terrorist financing 6. Track foreign terrorists and bring them to justice
Protecting Critical Infrastructure and Key Assets: "We must … improve protection of the individual pieces and interconnecting systems that make up our critical infrastructure."	1. Unify America's infrastructure protection effort in the Department of Homeland Security 2. Build and maintain a complete and accurate assessment of America's critical infrastructure and key assets

Mission Area	Initiatives
	3. Enable effective partnership with state and local governments and the private sector
	4. Develop a national infrastructure protection plan
	5. Secure cyberspace
	6. Harness the best analytic and modeling tools to develop effective protective solutions
	7. Guard America's critical infrastructure and key assets against "inside" threats
	8. Partner with the international community to protect our transnational infrastructure
Defending Against Catastrophic Threats: "…the threat of terrorist attacks using chemical, biological, radiological, and nuclear weapons requires new approaches, a focused strategy, and a new organization."	1. Prevent terrorist use of nuclear weapons through better sensors and procedures
	2. Detect chemical and biological materials and attacks
	3. Improve chemical sensors and decontamination techniques
	4. Develop broad spectrum vaccines, antimicrobials, and antidotes
	5. Harness the scientific knowledge and tools to counter terrorism
	6. Implement the Select Agent Program
Emergency Preparedness and Response: "An effective response to a … natural disaster … depends on being prepared. Therefore, we need a comprehensive national system to bring together and coordinate all necessary response assets quickly and effectively …"	1. Integrate separate federal response plans into a single all-discipline incident management plan
	2. Create a national incident management system
	3. Improve tactical counterterrorist capabilities
	4. Enable seamless communication among all responders
	5. Prepare healthcare providers for catastrophic terrorism
	6. Augment America's pharmaceutical and vaccine stockpiles
	7. Prepare for chemical, biological, radiological, and nuclear decontamination
	8. Plan for military support to civil authorities
	9. Build the Citizen Corps
	10. Implement the First Responder Initiative of the Fiscal Year 2003 Budget
	11. Build a national training and evaluation system
	12. Enhance the victim support system

Modified from: Office of Homeland Security. (2002). National Strategy for Homeland Security. Retrieved online at http://www.ncs.gov/library/policy_docs/nat_strat_hls.pdf

intended to prevent terrorist attacks, and the next two are related to reducing vulnerabilities. The last mission deals with minimizing damage and recovering quickly from any attacks that do occur.

The National Strategy recognizes four foundations for developing a safer homeland, which refer to four strengths that America has that cut across all of the mission areas, across all levels of government, and across all sectors of our society. They include law, science and technology, information sharing and systems, and international cooperation.

The first foundation is law, which suggested new federal laws to help in the war against terror, such as the USA PATRIOT Act or the Aviation and Transportation Security Act, among others, which will enable the country to respond more quickly to terrorist activities. In the second foundation, science and technology, the need for new processes and technologies to expand the analysis of information to detect and counter potential attacks was acknowledged. Initiatives in this area include developing countermeasures for chemical, biological, radiological, and nuclear weapons, and improving the technical capabilities of first responders. New technologies will help prevent and minimize the damage from future terrorist attacks.

The third foundation was information sharing and systems. Information is vital for protecting the nation, and it was acknowledged that while information technology in the U.S. is the most advanced in the world, it has not adequately supported the homeland security mission. The Strategy indicated the existence of gaps in databases of federal law enforcement, immigration, and other agencies, as well as the need for all interested parties to share information. Further, the majority of first responders in state and local agencies do not have compatible communications equipment.

The fourth foundation was international cooperation, something a successful homeland security initiative clearly requires. This could include creating "smart borders," identifying fraudulent travel documents, increasing the security of international shipping containers, intensifying international law enforcement cooperation, and helping foreign nations fight terrorism.[3]

In the end, many of the recommendations made in the National Strategy were based on the findings of the 9/11 Commission. The recommendations covered five broad areas: (1) cooperation, (2) information, (3) border and transportation security, (4) critical infrastructure, and (5) response (see **TABLE 8.2**).

1. *Cooperation*: The Strategy made it clear that it was not only federal agencies that are an essential for homeland security, but that it was necessary to have a coordinated effort throughout society, including state and local governments, private companies and organizations, and individual citizens. They stressed that state and local agencies play a critical role in protecting the nation because they have the primary responsibility for funding, preparing, and operating emergency services that respond first to a terrorist attack. There is a need for states to create services that reinforce those in the federal government but not duplicate them. Instead, federal and local agencies must act as partners and work cooperatively with each other.

   The private sector (private companies) is a key partner in providing for homeland security according to the Strategy, because it has a

TABLE 8.2 Implementing the National Strategy for Homeland Security

- The National Strategy for Combating Terrorism will define the U.S. war plan against international terrorism
- The National Strategy to Combat Weapons of Mass Destruction coordinates America's many efforts to deny terrorists and states the materials, technology, and expertise to make and deliver weapons of mass destruction.
- The National Strategy to Secure Cyberspace will describe our initiatives to secure our information systems against deliberate, malicious disruption.
- The National Money Laundering Strategy aims to undercut the illegal flows of money that support terrorism and international criminal activity.
- The National Defense Strategy sets priorities for our most powerful national security instrument.
- The National Drug Control Strategy lays out a comprehensive U.S. effort to combat drug smuggling and consumption.

Modified from: Office of Homeland Security. (2002). National Strategy for Homeland Security. Retrieved online at http://www.ncs.gov/library/policy_docs/nat_strat_hls.pdf

wealth of information, new ideas, and technology that can be used to help protect the United States from terrorism. For example, pharmaceutical companies can produce vaccines to protect citizens against dangerous biological agents. It was recognized that the government must create partnerships with the private sector to increase homeland security.

The Strategy also recognized the important role citizens play in protecting the nation. It notes that every person has a key role to play, and that every person must be willing to do their part to protect our homeland. One example is the Citizen Corps' (FEMA) Community Emergency Response Team (CERT), which trains volunteers to support first responders to help victims of an attack or natural disaster. Volunteers are also used to assist law enforcement and the Medical Reserve Corps, which can help healthcare professionals during an emergency.

The Strategy emphasized the importance of cooperation between federal, state, and local government, both horizontally and vertically, by creating complementary systems that provide essential services while at the same time avoiding duplication of services. The Strategy promised to increase collaborative efforts and coordinate services between all levels of government.

2. *Information*: The U.S. must be able to gather information and analyze it to successfully detect terrorist activity before enemies are able to carry out attacks. At this point in time, the government had not developed a unified, coherent method to analyze and share information that would reliably be able to predict a terrorist attack within the U.S. The Strategy recognized that the U.S. needed to develop the means for quick and accurate threat analysis in order to disrupt and prevent future terrorist

acts. It also recognized the need to continuously collect and analyze data on terrorist organizations to better them and predict their future actions. In part, this included understanding their identities, their sources of support, their motivation, goals, current and future capabilities, and vulnerabilities.

3. *Border and Transportation Security*: The security of the borders and transportation systems is vital for keeping the homeland safe. The U.S. shares a land border with Canada and Mexico, as well as a maritime border. Every day, people and goods enter the U.S. The U.S. therefore must create a system for the safe and efficient flow of people, goods, and services across all our borders, while at the same time preventing terrorists from entering the country.

4. *Critical Infrastructure*: The critical infrastructure of the U.S. provides the essential services to its citizen, and it is vital these are protected. They include agriculture, food, water, emergency services, the defense industrial base, information and telecommunications, energy, transportation, banking and finance, the chemical industry, and postal and shipping industry. Moreover, the nation must also protect other key assets, such as historic monuments, that, if destroyed, would not endanger any vital systems, but could affect our nation's morale. In addition, some high-profile events are also part of our national identity and require special protection. The effects of a terrorist attack on our critical infrastructure could be devastating, having both immediate and long-term consequences. Protecting our critical infrastructure and other key assets from terrorist activity will require the cooperation of all levels of government.

5. *Response*: The country must be prepared to minimize the damage of any possible attack and be able to recover quickly. To do this, we need to develop a comprehensive system that ensures that all necessary response assets can be brought together quickly and effectively. That means that many different organizations must be equipped and trained and prepared to respond to any emergency. America's first line of defense for a terrorist attack is its first responders, including police officers, firefighters, and emergency medical providers, among others. In the case of a serious emergency, the federal government can assist state and local responders. It is imperative that any gaps in the current response plans are filled.

National Response Plan (2004)

In Homeland Security Presidential Directive (HSPD) 5, President Bush ordered the Department of Homeland Security to create a National Response Plan (NRP) to align federal resources into a single, unified, all-discipline, and all-hazards approach to managing domestic emergency incidents.[4] The intent of the Plan was to reduce the "patchwork" of existing federal and local plans and replace them with a national framework that established a single, comprehensive approach for managing responses to emergencies while improving the management of these critical incidents. The objective was to create a clear and coordinated system of communication from the local level all the way to the national level in time of an emergency.

The NRP was published in 2004. It provides a range of incident management activities covering the prevention of, preparedness for, response to, and recovery from terrorism, natural disasters, and other major emergencies. It creates an overall structure that coordinates the actions of federal, state, local, and tribal organizations (NGOs), nongovernmental organizations, and private-sector groups in emergency situations so that the coordinated response can be quicker and more efficient. The plan applies to fire, rescue, emergency management, law enforcement, public works, and emergency medical services.

Courtesy of the DHS.

The NRP assumes that all levels of government, the private sector, and NGOs will take part in preventing, preparing for, responding to, and recovering from incidents of national significance. However, the NRP assumes that emergency incidents should be managed at the lowest possible jurisdictional level. This means that state or local government personnel, particularly police, fire, public health, and medical personnel are the first to arrive and often the last to leave an incident site. Under this approach, the local executive, such as a mayor or city manager, is responsible for coordinating local resources that will be used in an emergency situation. The local executive can communicate to the public, and help people, businesses, and organizations recover from local disasters. In some cases, they may have powers to suspend local laws to establish curfews, direct evacuations, and even under some circumstances, order a quarantine, if needed. Local incident command structures (Area Command) are responsible for directing on-scene emergency management and maintaining command and control of on-scene incident operations. If the situation is serious enough, or if issues cannot be resolved at the local level, the local executive can request state or federal assistance.

A state governor is responsible for the coordination of state resources that are needed to prevent, prepare for, respond to, and recover from incidents. For example, a state governor, as the commander-in-chief of state military forces, has the ability to use, under certain conditions, police power to establish order. He or she can encourage participation in mutual aid programs and can request federal assistance if the state is unable to respond effectively.

At the regional level, the coordination is provided by a Regional Response Coordination Center (RRCC), which will oversee regional response efforts until a Joint Field Office (JFO) is established. A JFO is a temporary federal facility established locally to coordinate operational federal assistance activities to the affected jurisdiction(s) during incidents of national significance. They are multi-agency centers established locally to provide a central location for the coordination of federal, state, and local organizations that have the responsibility for responding to threats and incidents. There are various sections or departments within JFOs, including operations, planning, logistics, and finance/administration.

If needed, federal authorities will assist in coordinating the response to an attack. In that situation, the Secretary of Homeland Security will be responsible for coordinating federal operations and/or resources through the Homeland Security Operations Center. This can occur if states have requested federal assistance, if more than one federal department is substantially involved in responding to the incident, or if the Secretary has been directed by the President to take over the management responsibilities of the incident.

The Homeland Security Operations Center is the primary national center for coordinating domestic incident management operations. It combines representatives from law enforcement, national intelligence, emergency response, and the private-sector to facilitate sharing of information and coordinate operations with other federal, state, local, tribal, and nongovernmental emergency operations centers (EOCs). The Homeland Security Operations Center includes officials from various federal departments, including the Departments of Agriculture, Commerce, Defense, Energy, Health and Human Services, Transportation, Veterans Affairs, the U.S. Postal Service, the Nuclear Regulatory Commission, and others.

In some cases, the Department of Justice will provide assistance. The U.S. Attorney General has the responsibility for coordinating any investigations concerning terrorist acts or terrorist threats made within U.S. boundaries or made against U.S. citizens and or institutions overseas. After a terrorist threat or incident, the Attorney General's office will seek to identify the perpetrators and bring them to justice. During a terrorist attack, the local FBI Special Agent-in-charge will be responsible for coordinating activities with other members of the law enforcement community.

The Secretary of Defense authorizes Defense Support of Civil Authorities (DSCA) for domestic incidents as directed by the President. The Department of State coordinates response activities on the international scene. Other federal agencies may play roles as well, including the Secretary of Agriculture, the administrator of the small business administration, Secretary of Commerce, Secretary of Health and Human Services, and the U.S. Army Corps of Engineers.

Many other federal agencies may play a role in coordinating response to terrorist acts. For example, the Department of Homeland Security Council/National Security Council are responsible for interagency policy coordination for incident management, and work together to ensure that incident management efforts are united. Moreover, the Interagency Incident Management Group (IIMG) is a federal headquarters-level multi-agency group that oversees incident management. The Group is activated by the Secretary of Homeland Security when needed, depending upon the nature, severity, magnitude, and complexity of the incident. The Group is comprised of senior representatives from DHS, other federal departments and agencies, and NGOs, but the exact membership is flexible and depends on the specific incident.

The FBI's Strategic Information and Operations Center (SIOC) is the control center for all federal intelligence and law enforcement activities concerning terrorist incidents or threats. They will serve as an information clearinghouse to collect, process, and disseminate any relevant information that may be of assistance to those investigating the incident or threat. Found within the SIOC is the National Joint Terrorism Task Force whose mission is to increase the communication and cooperation among federal, state, local, and tribal agencies representing the intelligence, law enforcement, defense, diplomatic, public safety, and homeland security communities.

The role of NGOs and volunteer organizations is part of the NRP. Agencies such as the American Red Cross work with first responders, governments at all levels, and various agencies. Additionally, the role of the private sector is important and will vary based on the organization itself as well as the type of incident. The private organization may provide specialized teams or equipment. Citizen groups such as the U.S. Citizen Corps help to educate and train community volunteers to assist in emergencies. These groups include Community Emergency Response Teams (CERTS), Medical Reserve Corps, Neighborhood Watch, and Volunteers in Police Service.

The many elements of the NRP can either be partially or fully implemented, depending upon the context and level of threat. The NRP supersedes the Initial National Response Plan (INRP), the Federal Response Plan (FRP), the U.S. Government Interagency Domestic Terrorism Concept of Operations Plan (CONPLAN), and the Federal Radiological Emergency Response Plan (FRERP).

Under the NRP, specific actions used to prevent incidents are essential. These include collecting, analyzing, and applying intelligence and other information; conducting investigations to determine the full nature and source of a threat; implement countermeasures, conducting activities to prevent terrorists, terrorist weapons, and associated materials from entering into the U.S.

If an incident occurs, federal, state, local, tribal, private-sector, and NGOs organizations must report details of the incident using established communications channels. When the Homeland Security Operations Center (HSOC) receives the information, they will make a determination about the most appropriate response. If necessary, resources such as special teams or emergency facilities will be activated. The HSOC will also report incidents to the Secretary of Homeland Security, who then determines the need to activate components of the NRP. If the Secretary declares the activity to be an incident of national significance, federal departments and agencies will be notified. At that point, state governors or other federal agencies can request assistance from DHS.

Recovery actions need to be implemented immediately after all life-saving and property stabilization efforts are finalized and the scene of the incident is secure. Recovery actions include developing, coordinating, and implementing site-restoration plans and the reconstitution of government operations and services.

National Strategy (2007)

In 2007, The Homeland Security Council published an updated version of the 2002 National Strategy as a way to "guide, organize, and unify our nation's homeland security effort."[5] Described as a national, as opposed to a federal, strategy, the updated National Strategy combines homeland security with natural disaster preparedness. This new Strategy reflects a better understanding of the current terrorist threats that confront the U.S., while at the same time acknowledging that natural disasters can be catastrophic, and thus, have significant implications for homeland security. The aftermath of these natural disasters might result in situations that could be exploited by terrorists and other seeking to do harm.

In the introduction to the Strategy, President Bush acknowledged that the country continued to face the challenges related to preventing terrorist attacks and preparing for natural disasters.

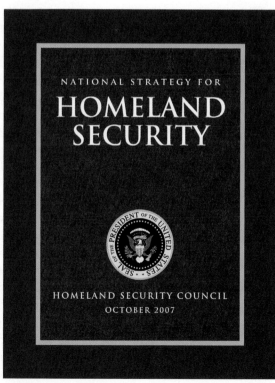

Courtesy of the DHS.

Bush also expressed that the country learned from the events of Hurricane Katrina, and indicated that the new Homeland Security Strategy applies the lessons learned from Katrina to make sure that America is safer, stronger, and better prepared for the future.

The 2007 National Strategy provides a framework for a national approach to protecting homeland security, as did the 2002 version. The report outlining the new strategy presents updated procedures for guiding, organizing, and unifying the country's efforts for a safe homeland. It provides four goals for the nation: preventing and disrupting terrorist attacks; protecting the American people, our critical infrastructure, and key resources; responding to and recovering from incidents that do occur; and continuing to strengthen the basic response mechanism in order to ensure our long-term success. The report noted that terrorists can be deterred from conducting attacks if they fear potential consequences for their actions.

At the same time, the 2007 National Strategy states that the country needs to focus on natural disasters in a similar way to terrorist attacks. Events such as naturally occurring infectious diseases can pose a significant hazard to the country. Natural events such as hurricanes, earthquakes, and tornadoes, or even catastrophic accidents such as chemical spills can pose potential threats to our nation's critical infrastructure. Therefore, these events need to have the same kinds of government responses to protect the victims, provide services when needed, and rebuild the affected communities as quickly and efficiently as possible.

The new Strategy again reiterates that protecting the country is a shared responsibility between federal, state, local, and tribal governments, the private and nonprofit sectors, communities, and individual citizens. State and local governments will provide the first response to most incidents. The revised Strategy acknowledges that when an incident occurs, first responders will be local personnel. They will assess the situation and must determine the possible causes, the extent of the affected population and geographic area, and the degree of damage. After that, they must take action. Those responding must prioritize and coordinate their actions in an attempt to mitigate the consequences of the incident. They must have a consistent approach and work together effectively to deploy people, resources, and capabilities to where they are most needed. They must also anticipate any additional support that may be needed and consider requesting additional assistance if necessary. It is important that the partnerships between the federal government and state, local, and tribal governments be strengthened.

However, while most incidents can be handled at the local level, more serious events may require additional support. In those cases where state and local governments are overwhelmed, the federal government will provide additional support.

According to the updated Strategy, even as an initial response to an attack is under way, the need to begin recovery operations quickly will be necessary. This can include restoration of interrupted utility services, reestablishment of transportation routes, or the provision of food and shelter. This can come from local officials but can also be from federal officials. Long-term rebuilding efforts may take months. Community services must be restored, which will require planning and coordination from key local officials. Long-term assistance for displaced victims might be necessary. Critical infrastructures will be rebuilt.

The U.S. Congress must also take steps to protect the country. Congress should create laws to ensure that governments have the tools needed to address changing threats while protecting privacy and civil liberties, according to the new report.

National Response Framework (2008)

In 2008, a new document was generated by the federal government concerning homeland security.[6] The National Response Framework (NRF) replaced the original National Response Plan and reflected improvements in the country's ability to respond to national emergencies. The new Framework is based on the previous NRP and retains much of the same content. The title was changed after some claimed the original document was not a plan but a framework for coordinated incident management. The National Response Plan was renamed to more accurately reflect the intent of the document and to encourage the continued refinement of emergency operations plans.

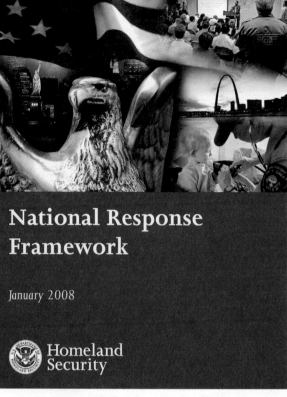

National Response Framework

January 2008

Homeland Security

Courtesy of the DHS.

Like the NRP, the Framework provides local, tribal, state, and federal officials with guidelines as to how they should respond to critical incidents. It presents a plan so that all responders are prepared for an emergency and know how to respond effectively should an event occur. This document attempts to create a comprehensive, national, all-hazards approach to responding to a terrorist attack or natural disaster, providing guidelines for how tribes, local government, states, the federal government, private-sector, and nongovernmental officials should respond. It is understood that the most effective response will require a unified approach in which the different levels of government provide support for the others. The Framework also incorporates appropriate responses for private-sector agencies, NGOs, individuals, and households.

The Framework is supported by a NRF Resource Center, which has a website with documents to provide all emergency responders access to the information and tools they might need to carry out their roles under the Framework.[7] Any updates or changes to the Framework will also be available on the website.

The NRF is built on five principles, which help to define the response actions. Taken together, these five principles of operation make up the national response doctrine. They are: engaged partnerships (leaders at all levels must communicate and support partnerships by developing shared goals and aligning capabilities so that no one is overwhelmed in times of crisis); tiered responses (incidents must be managed at the lowest possible jurisdictional level and supported by additional capabilities when needed); scalable, flexible, and adaptable operational capabilities (as incidents change in size, scope, and complexity, the response must adapt to meet requirements); unity of effort through unified command (effective unified command is indispensable to response activities and requires a clear understanding of the roles and responsibilities of each participating organization); readiness to act (effective response requires readiness to act balanced with a clear understanding of risk). From individuals and communities to local, state, and federal governments, national response depends on the instinct and ability to act.

If needed, the federal government can provide assistance to state and local governments when responding to events. For example, the federal government can provide extra resources to an area affected by an emergency. In situations where there may be holes in the needed services, the federal government could offer assistance. The federal government could provide an incident command structure if local and state jurisdictions are unable to do so on their own. If state or local authorities were able to reestablish their own incident command structure, the federal government could withdraw and return to its normal support role.

Private-sector organizations play a key role before, during, and after an incident. In many facets of incident response, the government works directly with private-sector groups as partners in emergency management.

One change in the new Framework revolves around the term "Incident of National Significance." Previously, some people assumed that the Secretary of Homeland Security needed to declare an incident to be one of national significance before the NRP would be implemented and assistance provided. Although this was not the case, many officials continued to be confused about the term. Thus, the term was not included in the new Framework.

The new Framework states that the federal government provides support and resources to state and local governments when there are significant special events such as the United States hosting the Olympics. Events such as these are designated as National Special Security Events (NSSEs) by the Secretary of Homeland Security. Such events are those that may be attractive targets for terrorists because of their political, economic, symbolic, or religious significance. If an event is designated a NSSE, then the lead agency responsible for coordinating the security is the U.S. Secret Service

Another change revolves around the term "Joint Coordination Group." Instead, the new report uses the term "Unified Coordination Group." The JFO is led by the Unified Coordination Group, which is comprised of specified senior leaders representing state and federal interests, and in certain circumstances tribal governments, local jurisdictions, the private sector, or NGOs.

Department of Homeland Security Strategic Plan

Fiscal Years 2012-2016

February 2012

Courtesy of the DHS.

Strategic Plan (2012)

In February 2012, the Department of Homeland Security announced a new Strategic Plan for Fiscal Years 2012–2016.[8] Each chapter of the report identifies missions, goals, and objectives for the department as it moves into the future (see FIGURE 8.1).

The first mission identified in the Plan is to prevent terrorism and enhance security in the United States. The primary goal is to prevent terrorist attacks and other threats on citizens. This will be accomplished through understanding

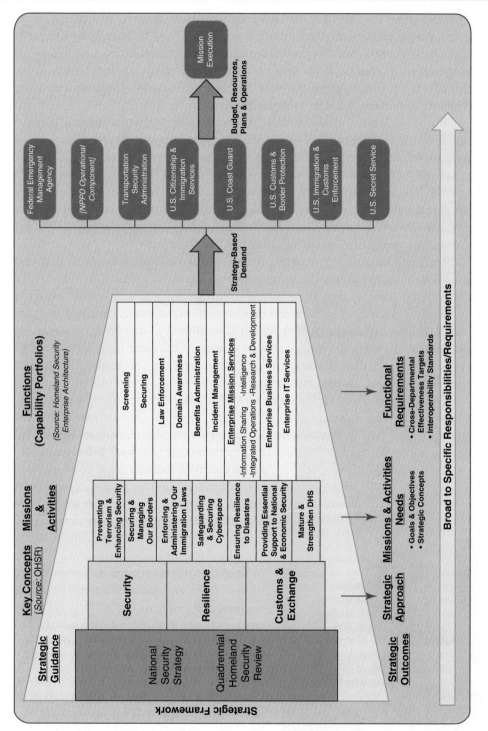

FIGURE 8.1 Department of Homeland Security Integrated Strategic Framework, 2012

Reproduced from: Department of Homeland Security. (2012). Department of Homeland Security Strategic Plan, Fiscal Years 2012–2016. Courtesy of the DHS.

the threat, detecting and deterring terrorist operations, and stopping the spread of violent extremism. Another goal to prevent attacks is to stop the unauthorized use of chemical, biological, radiological, and nuclear (CBRN) materials.

The objectives for DHS in this area are to control access to CBRN materials, control their movement, and protect against their use by hostile agents. DHS identified the importance of protecting critical infrastructure, leaders, and events as their third goal in the mission to prevent terrorism. Their plans to accomplish this include protecting critical infrastructure and making that infrastructure resilient to damage and adaptable to change.

The second mission identified by DHS in the 2012 plan is to secure and manage our air, land, and sea borders as a way to safeguard trade and travel. Three goals were identified to accomplish this mission. One is to prevent the illegal flow of people and goods across the borders while at the same time allowing for the safe and efficient flow of legal trade and travel. Another goal is to build partnerships in the global market to help ensure legal global trade and transportation. The third goal is to disrupt and dismantle transnational criminal organizations and terrorist groups that traffic in illegal drugs, humans, and weapons.

The third mission in the 2012 plan is the enforce immigration laws as a way to remove criminal aliens who pose a threat to the safety of the United States. To do this, DHS plans to strengthen immigration laws and see they are administered effectively. This means that any gaps in immigration policy are identified and corrected, and that the immigration system is simplified so that lawful immigrants can more easily integrate into American society. At the same time, DHS plans to reduce conditions that encourage unlawful immigration. Those who are found in the country illegally or who violate laws will be identified and removed.

The fourth mission identified by DHS is to safeguard and secure cyberspace. This involves federal executive branch agencies as well as privately owned infrastructure. One goal in this mission is to create a safe, secure, and resilient global cyberspace environment. By understanding the nature of cyber threats and managing the risks, malicious use of cyberspace can be limited. Another goal is to promote a general knowledge of cybersecurity and support innovative steps to increase awareness of threats and means to prevent them.

The fifth mission in the 2012 Plan is to prepare for, protect against, respond to, recover from, and mitigate a terrorist attack or natural disaster or any other large-scale emergency situation. Because it is essential to strengthen the ability of all levels of government to withstand such hazards, this was identified as the first goal. This includes reducing the vulnerabilities of families and individuals while also mitigating the risks to communities. DHS will work to enhance the preparedness of the country to respond to emergencies

Courtesy of Pete Souza/White House.

of all types. This involves strengthening the ability of agencies to respond quickly and effectively, and to recover quickly.

Along with protecting the homeland, two other elements make up national security, according to the 2012 Plan, and these are national defense and economic security. In order to provide for these, DHS is involved with collecting customs revenue, maintaining the safety of maritime transportation, and conducting law enforcement activities, particularly related to preventing the exploitation of children. They also support national defense missions and support post-conflict reconstruction through the Department of State.

The final section of the 2012 report looks to the future and strengthening the Department of Homeland Security, with the goal of making it more effective in the future. The report indicates that, in order to reach this goal, DHS will, among other things, enhance the management functions, increase the department's analytic capabilities, and strengthening their counterintelligence capabilities, enhance information sharing, and develop more international agreements. Other plans include strengthening the workforce with training, programs for employee health, and increased workforce diversity.

■ Chapter Summary

Since 9-11 four plans have been developed by the federal government to coordinate the country's preparedness for, and responses to, future terrorist threats and natural disasters. They each recognize the important role that local first-responders play in controlling the harm resulting from these incidents. The coordination of activities and the sharing of information, across agencies at all levels, is key to preventing and mitigating future events. These four plans address these issues in different ways.

■ Review/Discussion Questions

1. What is the National Strategy, and why is it important to homeland security?
2. What is the National Response Plan, and why is it important to homeland security?
3. Why was a new National Strategy for Homeland Security written in 2007, and how does it differ from the original report?
4. What is the National Response Framework, and how does it relate to the National Response Plan?
5. What are the key missions and goals identified in the 2012 Department of Homeland Security Strategic Plan?

■ Additional Readings

Department of Homeland Security. (2004). *National Response Plan.* Available online at http://www.it.ojp.gov/fusioncenterguidelines/NRPbaseplan.pdf

Department of Homeland Security. (2007). *National Strategy for Homeland Security.* Available online at http://www.dhs.gov/national-strategy-homeland-security-october-2007

Department of Homeland Security. (2008). *National Response Framework.* Available online at http://www.fema.gov/pdf/emergency/nrf/nrf-core.pdf

Department of Homeland Security. (2012). *Department of Homeland Security Strategic Plan, Fiscal Years 2012–2016.* Available online at http://www.dhs.gov/xlibrary/assets/dhs-strategic-plan-fy-2012-2016.pdf

Office of Homeland Security. (2002). *National Strategy For Homeland Security.* Available online at http://www.ncs.gov/library/policy_docs/nat_strat_hls.pdf

■ Endnotes

1. This section is based on the Office of Homeland Security. (2002). *National Strategy for Homeland Security.* Retrieved online at http://www.ncs.gov/library/policy_docs/nat_strat_hls.pdf

2. Office of Homeland Security. (2002). *National Strategy for Homeland Security.* Available online at http://www.ncs.gov/library/policy_docs/nat_strat_hls.pdf, pg. 3–4.

3. Office of Homeland Security. (2002). *National Strategy for Homeland Security.* Available online at http://www.ncs.gov/library/policy_docs/nat_strat_hls.pdf

4. This section is based on Department of Homeland Security. (2004). *National Response Plan.* Retrieved online at http://www.it.ojp.gov/fusioncenterguidelines/NRPbaseplan.pdf

5. This section is based on Department of Homeland Security. (2007). *National Strategy for Homeland Security.* Retrieved online at http://www.dhs.gov/national-strategy-homeland-security-october-2007

6. This section is based on Department of Homeland Security. (2008). *National Response Framework.* Retrieved online at http://www.fema.gov/pdf/emergency/nrf/nrf-core.pdf

7. The National Response Framework Resource Center can be found at www.fema.gov/NRF

8. This section is based on Department of Homeland Security. (2012). *Department of Homeland Security Strategic Plan, Fiscal Years 2012-2016.* Retrieved online at http://www.dhs.gov/xlibrary/assets/dhs-strategic-plan-fy-2012-2016.pdf

Homeland Security Threats

Chapter Objectives

- Understand the different types of threats (chemical, biological, radiological, nuclear, and explosives) facing the U.S.

- Understand the effects of these types of weapons on humans

Chapter Outline

- Introduction
- CBRNE
  - Chemical
  - Biological
  - Radiological/Nuclear
  - Explosives
- Natural Threats
- Chapter Summary

Introduction

During the peak of the morning rush hour on March 20, 1995 in Tokyo, Japan, five members of the Aum Shinrikyo cult carried plastic bags wrapped in newspapers into the subway system. Inside each bag was liquid sarin, a nerve agent that can cause temporary blindness, neurological damage, or even death. Once on the subway train, the cult members punctured the packets with sharpened umbrellas and then immediately left the subway. The liquid sarin leaked onto the floor, evaporated, and was inhaled by passengers. Thirteen commuters were killed, and thousands of others sickened by the attack.

One reason why the cult's actions did not kill more victims was because of the poor quality of the sarin they used. But the attack clearly demonstrated the potential dangers posed by chemical weapons that could easily be used by terrorists to injure or kill innocent people.

■ CBRNE

Chemical weapons like sarin, along with biological, radiological, nuclear, and explosive weapons, are referred to as **CBRNE**. These are weapons that, if used by terrorists, have the potential to cause widespread death and injury, and in some cases, mass destruction of physical facilities. The primary reason terrorist groups would use these weapons is to maximize death and destruction in an effort to bring attention to their political, ideological, or religious agenda.

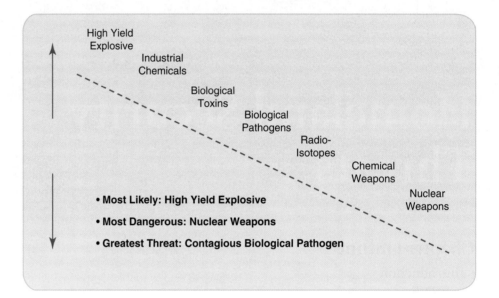

The use of a CBRNE can result in both short-term and long-terms effects. In the short term, there can be mass death and injury to victims and destruction to buildings, infrastructure, and the environment. First responders may be overwhelmed after such an event, as could hospitals, medical facilities, and other personnel. The long-term effects may be even more harmful. A city attacked by a CBRNE may experience significant negative consequences to its economy, which could then reverberate across the country and even the world. Those who suffered injuries may have to deal with both physical and psychological effects for many years, if not a lifetime. There may also be long-term psychological effects for some who did not suffer direct harm. The effects on the environment may be long-lasting, including a community's agricultural resources, food, and water supplies. Moreover, the impact of such an event may reach farther than the immediate site. Someone may be contaminated with a biological agent then return to their home, spreading the germ to others. This can occur with little or no warning.

It has become one goal of homeland security officials to reduce the opportunities that terrorists have for obtaining these weapons, and to reduce the likelihood that they will use them against the U.S. Nonetheless, communities must prepare for a potential attack and be prepared to mitigate the potential impact on critical infrastructure, the economy, and daily life.

Unfortunately, our knowledge of CBRNEs that may be used by terrorists is limited. Many of the characteristics and destructive qualities of large amounts of chemicals and biological threats are still relatively unknown by experts. To date, Americans have had little or no experience in dealing with CBRNEs or their consequences.

Following is a description of CBRNE.

Chemical

A **chemical weapon** is a device that uses poisonous liquids, solids, gases, and vapor agents to cause death or injury to humans, animals, and plants. The exposure to the chemical can occur through inhalation, exposure of the skin or eyes, or even ingestion. Depending on the chemical, the concentration, and the dose received, these weapons can inflict a variety of ailments, ranging from simple discomfort to permanent injuries and death. The effects of a chemical can be immediate or may be delayed.

Chemicals can be spread in liquid, solid (generally powdered), or gas forms. They can be released into the air by bombs (explosives) or sprayed from a vehicle. The optimal method for mass dispersal of a chemical is a sprayer such as a crop duster. A chemical attack could also occur through product tampering or using the chemical to poison food or water supplies for a community. Another way to disperse chemicals is by using containers to hold the chemicals, then breaching those containers in some way, thereby exposing the chemical to the air.

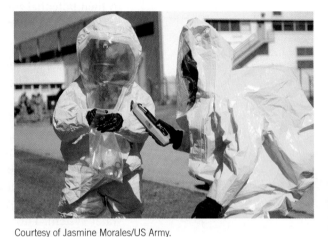
Courtesy of Jasmine Morales/US Army.

KEY TERM
Chemical weapon—a device that uses poisonous liquids, solids, gases, and vapor agents to cause death or injury to humans, animals, and plants.

A large-scale lethal attack would have to take place in a large, open area, which is not easy to accomplish. However, smuggling small quantities of chemical agents into a small, confined space and releasing them with a simple method would be relatively easy. Trucks, trains, and ships could easily carry large amounts of chemical materials into an area. In this case, hundreds, if not thousands, of people could be exposed.

It is thought that many potential terrorist groups have the technology and expertise needed to produce chemical weapons. Those terrorist groups with access to even modest resources could potentially produce small amounts of an effective chemical weapon. Clandestine labs in which the chemicals are made can be easily hidden and used to make enough chemicals to cause significant deaths. There is an ongoing concern that there are still stockpiles of chemicals in arsenals left over from the Cold War that could easily be sold, stolen, or sabotaged by terrorist groups. However, any major chemical attack would require a large volume of chemical, making it very unlikely.

In some cases, a chemical attack is quickly and easily recognized because the effects on victims are readily evident. However, in other cases, it can be unclear to victims and responders that there has been a chemical (or even biological) attack, until further testing has occurred. Identifying the chemical used can be difficult sometimes because some evaporate quickly. Other chemical weapons may remain in the affected area long after the attack.

First responders need proper training and equipment so they are able to respond to possible chemical attacks safely and efficiently. If not, they face potential injury or death from their exposure. They need to be trained to identify the symptoms of chemical interactions, anticipate the consequences, and be able to treat victims appropriately.

There are many chemicals that are potentially toxic to humans, animals, and plants, but not all of these chemicals can be easily made into and used as weapons. Still, there are many different chemicals that have been developed and can be used as weapons. There are seven different categories of chemicals, which are organized by their potential effects on victims. They include nerve agents, blister agents, choking/pulmonary agents, irritants, and incapacitating agents.

Nerve Agents

Nerve agents are the most dangerous chemical agents as they affect the body's nervous system. These chemicals will sometimes cause the nervous system of those exposed to become inactive, causing death within minutes. Nerve agents can be inhaled or absorbed by the skin or ingested through food, water, or the air.[1] The most widely known nerve agents are sarin and VX.

Sarin is a man-made nerve agent. It is a clear, colorless, and tasteless liquid with no odor in its pure form, but it can be made into a vapor to spread into the environment. Victims can be exposed by breathing air that contains sarin, but because the drug can be easily mixed with water, it can also be used to poison a community's water system. Those exposed to sarin may experience runny nose, watery eyes, eye pain, blurred vision, drooling, excessive sweating, cough, chest pains, rapid breathing, diarrhea, increased urination, confusion, drowsiness, weakness, headache, nausea, vomiting, low or high blood pressure, or even death. A person who inhaled just a small amount of sarin (.05 grams) for 1 minute would have a 50% chance of dying within 15 minutes.[2]

VX has the texture of motor oil, making it especially dangerous as it can remain in the environment for long periods. It is odorless and tasteless and can be distributed as a liquid or an aerosol. Early symptoms of contact with the chemical include muscular twitching, sweating, nausea, vomiting, blurred vision, or headache. A victim may also experience a shortness of breath, runny nose, chest pains, or death.[3]

It is unlikely that terrorist groups will use chemical weapons. In order to produce large quantities of chemical weapons, an industrial facility would be needed. To do this, new facilities could be built or existing plants could be converted into a facility in which chemical agents could be produced. Another obstacle to a terrorist group using a chemical is the delivery of the chemical. Transporting and dispensing a large amount of chemicals is a difficult challenge, made more so in this country in recent years with our heightened security measures.

Blister Agents

Blister agents attack the skin of those exposed, resulting in blisters and skin burns. They are chemicals that contain acid-forming compounds that must come into contact with the victims' skin in order to have an effect. If a victim comes into contact with a blister agent, it is unlikely they will die, but they will probably suffer from burns and blisters to the skin. However, if these agents are inhaled by a victim, they can be deadly. In most cases, blister agents primarily cause irritation to the lungs, eyes, and airway. The most common blister agent is mustard gas.[4]

Mustard gas (sulfur mustard) has an odor of garlic, onions, or mustard, but sometimes has no odor at all. The chemical can take the form of a gas, an oily liquid, or a solid. Mustard gas is not found naturally in the environment but must be manufactured. The chemical can be delivered through the air as a vapor. Victims can also drink it if it is in the water. The effects of mustard gas depend on how much of the agent the victim is exposed to; exposure can lead to blistering of the skin, damage to eyes and respiratory tract, redness and itching of the skin, swelling and tearing of the eyes, runny or bloody nose, sneezing, abdominal pain, diarrhea, fever, and nausea. Exposure to mustard gas typically is not fatal.[5]

Lewisite is another blister agent. It is a colorless liquid with an odor similar to geraniums.[6] People exposed to lewisite (or mustard-lewisite) may experience serious burns to the skin, burning sensations in the nasal passages, cough, shortness of breath, nausea, or vomiting. Long-term effects may include respiratory damage, damage to bone marrow and blood vessels. Those exposed to high levels may die.[7]

Blood Agents

Blood agents are chemical weapons that prevent the victim's body from using oxygen in the blood. These chemicals must come into contact with a victim's skin in order to cause a reaction. An example is hydrogen cyanide.

Hydrogen cyanide is a potentially deadly chemical that can take the form of a colorless gas; it can also be found in a crystal form. The gas may have an odor like bitter almonds, but not always. Victims of cyanide poisoning may be exposed by inhaling the drug, drinking contaminated water, eating contaminated food, or touching soil that contains cyanide. This chemical prevents the cells of the body from using oxygen, which then affects the heart and brain. Symptoms of cyanide poisoning include rapid breathing and heart rate, restlessness, dizziness, weakness, headache, nausea, and vomiting. Victims can be confused and may experience low blood pressure, slow heart rate, loss of consciousness, lung injury, respiratory failure, and death.[8]

Choking/Pulmonary Agents

Choking agents affect the respiratory system of victims by attacking the lungs and causing them to fill with fluid, which can result in suffocation. The victim can either have skin contact with the chemical or inhale it. Depending on the amount of the agent to which a victim is exposed, choking agents can be deadly. The most common choking agents are chlorine and phosgene.

Chlorine is a yellow-green gas with a strong, irritating odor. It can be converted to a liquid under pressure or under cold temperatures. A person who comes into contact with chlorine can experience irritation to the nose, throat, and eyes, and in high doses, coughing, changes in the breathing rate, and damage to the lungs.[9]

Phosgene is a colorless gas that smells similar to new-mown hay. It can be inhaled or ingested through skin contact. The effects may be mild and delayed, causing victims to unwittingly inhale more gas over time. Effects include irritation to the skin, eyes, or respiratory tract. Victims may also experience coughing, choking, tightness in the chest, nausea, vomiting, and headache. Phosgene poisoning may cause respiratory and cardiovascular failure.[10]

Irritants

Irritants are chemicals that produce an immune response that causes irritation. In some cases a victim's skin may never fully recover. The skin may become red, itchy, scaly, chapped, or sensitive to the touch. Respiratory irritants need to be inhaled to be most effective, but skin irritants need only be exposed to the skin. The extent of injury to victims varies depending upon on the type of chemical and the dose received. The symptoms include pain and swelling of skin or mucous membranes, irritation to the eyes, swelling, pain and temporary blindness, difficulty breathing, runny nose, coughing, and in some situations, even death.

One type of irritant is pepper spray that includes the active ingredient capsaicin, a chemical derived from the chili pepper. As the name implies, this chemical is usually sprayed but can also be put into projectiles and fired from a paintball gun. Another common irritant is tear gas, which can affect a victim through inhalation, ingestion, or contact with the skin or eyes. It can cause irritation to the skin, eyes, or respiratory system, or pulmonary edema.[11]

Incapacitating Agents

Incapacitating agents are chemicals that produce temporary physiological or mental effects or an altered state of mind. They make people unable to think clearly or cause an altered state of consciousness or even unconsciousness.[12] Two types of incapacitating agents are BZ and Agent 15.

BZ, or 3-quinuclidinyl benzilate, is an odorless chemical that is dispersed as an aerosol so the victim may inhale it, or it can be absorbed through the skin. It can remain for weeks if dispersed in moist air, and can remain in soil and water and other surfaces for long periods. BZ is highly soluble in water. While the symptoms of exposure to BZ may be immediate, in others they may not appear for several hours after contact. The effects can include blurry vision, dry mouth, rapid heartbeat, unconsciousness, delusions, hallucinations, short attention span, slurred speech, disorientation, dizziness, and/or confusion.[13]

Biological

Biological weapons are those that use a biologically derived or living microorganism, bacteria, virus, rickettsia, or fungi to deliberately harm people, animals, or crops through infections that can incapacitate or kill. A biological attack occurs when someone deliberately releases germs or other biological material for the purpose of making people sick or killing them.[14] Even a gram or less of many biological weapons can be highly lethal.

There are two types of biological weapons. The first is pathogens, which are disease-causing organisms that often spread long after they are first released. When used, there is a potential for hundreds, if not thousands, of fatalities. However, it is difficult to deliver these agents to large numbers of people. Examples of pathogens include anthrax and smallpox. The second kind of biological weapon is a toxin, which is a poisonous substance produced by living things. Many of these weapons are lethal even in small quantities, and examples include ricin and botulinum.

Biological weapons are easier to use than nuclear material and are more dangerous than chemical weapons because they are relatively easy to produce or obtain. Biological weapons can be delivered in many ways. The most lethal method for delivering biological agents is in an aerosol form, such as a sprayer. They can also be delivered through an explosive device such as self-dispensing cluster bombs, which can destroy the biological agent when detonated. Food and water can also be contaminated with a biological weapon. Another way

KEY TERM

Biological weapon—weapons that use a biologically derived or living microorganism, bacteria, virus, rickettsia, or fungi to deliberately harm people, animals, or crops through infections that can incapacitate or kill.

© Haryadi CH/ShutterStock, Inc.

terrorists could use biological weapons is to spread an infectious disease through humans or animals that is not common in the U.S., such as cholera, dengue, dengue hemorrhagic fever, and dengue shock syndrome. The release of biological agents could initially cause disease in one country that could easily be spread to other countries.

Infecting a municipal water supply is difficult because they are designed to filter out or kill impurities and pathogens. Most water utilities employ a combination of filtration and disinfection technologies when treating the water supply. These protections eliminate most risks to contaminated water.

Signs that a biological weapon has been used include an unusually high number of dead or dying animals, a high number of human casualties, an unusual illness for a specific region or area, a pattern of illness that is inconsistent with natural disease progression, the presence of an unusual or suspect liquid, spray, vapor, or powder, spraying devices and unusual packages or letters.

The use of biological weapons can be difficult to recognize quickly because their consequences can take hours, days, or even weeks to emerge. With some biological agents, the incubation period may be weeks. In such a case, most people would have no idea that they had been exposed until much later because they would not exhibit symptoms. In the meantime, they could be infecting others with whom they come into contact. This means that terrorists could deploy the biological agent over a large geographic area and then disappear before it is clear that an attack took place. In attacks focused on food crops, significant destruction of crops could result that could be devastating to an entire industry, community, or region. Terrorists could use biological weapons to infect cattle and poultry, thus harming the food supply.

It is important to train first responders about the potential use of biological weapons. That way, biological attacks can be detected more quickly, helping to prevent any potential diseases from spreading too widely and creating a major public health emergency.

Victims can be treated during an attack with vaccines, but some vaccines are costly, and others may take time to develop and may require significant investment in research and testing. Sometimes there is even a risk of fatalities by administering a particular vaccine.

KEY TERM
Category A biological weapon—agents that can easily be disseminated over a large area and infect many people and could cause a public health catastrophe.

Biological agents are grouped into three categories, designated A, B, and C. **Category A** are agents that can easily be disseminated over a large area and infect many people and could cause a public health catastrophe. Examples of diseases caused by such agents are anthrax, smallpox, plague, botulism, tularemia, and viral hemorrhagic fevers. **Category B agents** are also easily disseminated over a large area but have a lower mortality rate. Examples include salmonella, ricin, Q fever, typhus, and glanders. Finally, those in **Category C** are more common pathogens that could potentially be used as terrorist weapons and include hantavirus and tuberculosis.

KEY TERM
Category B biological weapon—agents that are easily disseminated over a large area but have a lower mortality rate.

KEY TERM
Category C biological weapon—common pathogens that could potentially be used as terrorist weapons.

Category A Agents

One Category A agent is anthrax, which most commonly occurs in hoofed mammals but can also infect humans. This is a serious disease that can easily be used by terrorists in a biological weapon. The U.S. experienced several anthrax attacks in the days after 9-11, forcing many Americans to learn about the disease and its effects for the first time. A description of these attacks, sometimes referred to as "Amerithrax," is described in **Box 9.1**.

There are several types of anthrax, depending on how the agent is introduced into the body: skin anthrax (cutaneous) is ingested through contact with the skin; lung anthrax is ingested through inhalation; and digestive or gastrointestinal anthrax is ingested through swallowing. Cutaneous anthrax and inhalation anthrax may occur after people have handled products from infected animals or by breathing in anthrax spores from infected animal products, such as wool.[15] Gastrointestinal anthrax occurs when people eat undercooked meat from infected animals. Person-to-person spread of anthrax is rare.

The most obvious symptom of cutaneous anthrax is a small sore that develops into a blister, which then turns into a skin ulcer with a black area in the center. The symptoms of gastrointestinal anthrax include nausea, loss of appetite, bloody diarrhea, fever, and severe stomach pain, which may appear after consumption of contaminated food.[16] Symptoms of inhalation anthrax include cold or flu symptoms such as sore throat, mild fever, and muscle aches, as well as cough, chest discomfort, shortness of breath, tiredness, and muscle aches. The symptoms of each type of anthrax typically appear within 7 days of contact.[17]

In most cases, early treatment with antibiotics can cure cutaneous anthrax. Even if untreated, 80% of people who become infected with cutaneous anthrax do not die. However gastrointestinal anthrax is more serious; about 25–60% of cases results in death. Inhalation anthrax is much more severe. In 2001, about half the cases of inhalation anthrax ended in death.[18]

Another Category A biological agent is smallpox, a serious, contagious, and sometimes fatal disease that has, at this time, no specific treatment. About 7–17 days after a person is infected with smallpox, they may suffer from fever, malaise, head and body aches, and vomiting. A rash may appear on the tongue and inside the mouth that develops into sores that break open. Later a rash appears on the face and body that looks like small raised bumps. In recent years, the disease has become largely eradicated due to a successful worldwide vaccination program.[19]

BOX 9.1   Anthrax Attacks: Ameri-thrax

After 9-11, letters containing anthrax were mailed to various offices across the United States, killing five people and infecting 22 others. Letters containing anthrax spores were mailed to the offices of several news media and the offices of two Democratic U.S. Senators, Tom Daschle and Patrick Leahy. In Boca Raton, Florida, letters with anthrax were mailed to the American Media, Inc. building, which housed the offices of the *National Enquirer*, the *Sun* and other tabloid magazines. One photo editor, 63-year-old Robert Stevens, died after inhaling anthrax spores, the first to die in the attacks. A letter mailed from New Jersey was sent to news anchor Tom Brokaw at Rockefeller Studios in New York City. Days later, an employee at the *The New York Post* was diagnosed with anthrax poisoning, as was a son of an employee at *ABC News*. It is assumed that letters were sent to other media offices but may have been thrown away. Prosecutors later announced that Bruce Edwards Ivins sent the letters. Ivins was a scientist who worked at the federal government's biodefense labs. In 2008, Ivins committed suicide. Prosecutors announced that he was guilty, and on February 19, 2010, the FBI closed the investigation.

The pneumonic plague is one more example of a Category A biological agent. This is an infectious disease caused by bacteria typically found in rodents and their fleas in many parts of the world. Infection in humans occurs when the bacteria enters the lungs. The first symptoms of infection are fever, headache, weakness, and cough. The pneumonia typically progresses between 2 and 4 days and may cause septic shock and death. Early treatment is essential.[20]

Category B Agents

Category B agents are less fatal than those categorized in the A group. One Category B biological agent is ricin. This agent is found in the form of a powder mist, or pellet, and can be dissolved in water or in a weak acid. Those coming into contact with ricin may inhale the mist or powder and be poisoned or can swallow the agent through contaminated water or food. The symptoms displayed by a victim will depend on the delivery system. If inhaled, the symptoms include coughing, tightness in the chest, difficulty breathing, nausea, and aching muscles as the victim's airways become inflamed. If ingested, the victim will suffer from internal bleeding in the stomach and intestines as well as possible vomiting and bloody diarrhea. If injected, the liver and kidneys may stop working, and the person could die from multiple organ failure.[21]

Category C Agent

One Category C Agent is hantavirus, which, if it progresses far enough, can be fatal. It is usually found in rural areas where rodents live in forests, fields, and farms. Early symptoms of hantavirus include fatigue, fever, and muscle aches. There may also be headaches, dizziness, chills, nausea, vomiting, and diarrhea. Later symptoms include coughing, shortness of breath, and fluid in the lungs.[22]

Radiological/Nuclear

Nuclear weapons are the most devastating of the various CBRNEs and therefore raise the most concern. Even a small nuclear weapon detonated in a major city could result in significant destruction and a high number of deaths, as well as long-term environmental damage. There are three mechanisms by which terrorists can carry out a radiological attack: detonation of a nuclear bomb, dispersal of radiological material, or an attack on a facility housing nuclear material (power plant, research laboratory, storage site).

During a nuclear explosion, there is intense light and damaging heat. Radioactive material can contaminate the air, water, and ground for many miles. The damage will depend on the size of the weapon, which can range in size from one carried by a missile to a small portable device.

If a nuclear weapon were used by terrorists, it would cause death and damage to property in two ways. First, when the bomb detonates, there is a violent blast where a large amount of energy is released. The initial shock wave will destroy all structures within a range of up to several miles and send debris through the air. This is followed

KEY TERM
Nuclear weapon—an explosive device that derives its destructive force from nuclear reactions, either fission or a combination of fission and fusion.

Courtesy of National Nuclear Security Administration/Nevada Site Office.

by a heat wave close to the point of detonation. There will be high winds that accompany the shock and heat waves. An exploded nuclear device could result in a considerable amount of property damage and many people killed or injured from the blast itself.

The second means by which nuclear weapons inflict harm is through harmful radiation, which is most dangerous close to the area of detonation and can cause rapid death. However, radiation can also exist for years after the explosion.

Radiation is a form of energy that exists everywhere, and people are exposed to it every day. We are exposed through microwave ovens and x-rays. Some types of radiation have more energy than others. The radiation from these sources is so small that any adverse health effects may not be apparent for many years. Effects can be as simple as reddening of the skin or as serious as cancer and even death. However, large amounts of radiation could cause extensive death and casualties. It can also result in long-term conditions such as cancer.

Terrorists could also use these weapons against Americans by introducing radioactive material into the food or water supply. This would cause great concern and fear, but would not cause much contamination or increase the danger of adverse health effects by a significant amount.

KEY TERM
Dirty bomb—a device that involves the use of conventional explosive material that also contains radioactive material.

Terrorists could use explosives (such as dynamite) to scatter radioactive materials over a large area. This is called a "dirty bomb." **Dirty bombs** involve the use of a conventional explosive material that also contains radioactive material. When the explosives are detonated, the radioactive materials are dispersed into the environment. Dirty bombs are sometimes called radiological dispersion devices (RDDs), which can spread radioactive material without use of a nuclear explosion. An attack with a dirty bomb would most likely kill, injure, or sicken a great number of people. However, it is not likely a terrorist dirty bomb would contain enough radioactive material to cause serious radiation sickness among large numbers of people.

Another way terrorists could spread nuclear material is by bombing or destroying a nuclear facility. An aircraft could be crashed into a nuclear power plant or a large amount of explosives could be set to detonate around the facility. There are many facilities around the country that store nuclear materials, including nuclear power plants, hazardous material storage sites, medical facilities, military facilities, and industrial facilities. If these facilities were damaged, radiological materials could be released into the atmosphere. This type of attack would have essentially the same effects as a dirty bomb except the effects would, in all likelihood, be much greater. An explosion at a nuclear plant could cause the reactor core to melt down or spent fuel waste to be released into the environment, which could then spread across a large geographical area. People at the facility would probably be contaminated with radioactive material and possibly injured as well, as would residents in the surrounding area. An attack on a nuclear power plant could result in a major release of radiation and kill tens of thousands of citizens.

© vasakkohaline/ShutterStock, Inc.

Radiological weapons are also the most difficult for terrorist groups to develop. Getting highly enriched uranium or constructing the explosive lens used to construct the core of a plutonium implosion device is difficult and expensive to master. Acquiring highly enriched uranium or plutonium would require considerable technical, industrial, and financial resources.

Because of that, radiological weapons are considered the lowest threat when compared to other types of weapons. However, terrorists could acquire a nuclear weapon by stealing or purchasing an existing one. Or they could gather the materials needed and construct a weapon. Some of the technologies required for production are well-known and not even state-of-the-art. Terrorists can obtain low-level radioactive materials from hospitals, construction sites, and food irradiation plants. That means that some terrorists groups could explode a small nuclear device, causing great harm. If a terrorist succeeded at making a nuclear weapon, it would more than likely be a very crude weapon; it would be large, weighing a ton or more, and would require a large amount of highly enriched uranium or plutonium. Smuggling that amount of material would be difficult.

In order to reduce the chance that nuclear material will be collected by terrorists, the Domestic Nuclear Detection Office within the Department of Homeland Security attempts to monitor the movement and smuggling of nuclear material within the U.S. and around the world. Many officials are concerned that the former Soviet Union could be a source of nuclear materials because many of their nuclear sites have low levels of security. After the Soviet Union collapsed, it was difficult to account for all the nuclear weapons in that country, leading to the fear that some of these weapons could end up in the hands of terrorists. In addition, a substantial amount of radiological materials remain unaccounted for in the U.S. and around the world.

Explosives

Bombs kill by the effect of the blast, by flying debris, and fires and other damage resulting from the explosion. Virtually any size terrorist group could undertake a large-bomb attack. The supplies to make bombs are readily available or can be easily bought illicitly or stolen. Specific instructions for making various **explosive weapons** are readily available on the Internet.

KEY TERM
Explosive weapon—conventional weapons that have explosive properties.

In the case of a bomb explosion, first responders must be able to treat multiple injuries. More than likely, there will also be considerable structural damage to buildings and facilities. First responders must also be alert to subsequent explosives that may be set to go off a short period after the first series of explosions, not an uncommon practice. In some cases, while it may initially appear that an explosion caused little harm, there may be biological or radioactive agents involved, which are unseen and unfelt by victims and first responders alike.

In 1995, the U.S. experienced a bomb explosion as the result of an act of domestic terrorism when Timothy McVeigh succeeded in blowing up much of the Alfred P. Murrah Building in Oklahoma City, Oklahoma. This is described in **Box 9.2.**

© Aaron Favila/AP Images.

BOX 9.2   The Oklahoma City Bombing

The bombing of the Alfred P. Murrah Building in Oklahoma City was a terrorist bomb attack that occurred on April 19, 1995. It was the most serious terrorist act on U.S. soil until the terrorist attacks of September 11, 2001. One hundred sixty-eight people were killed that day, including 19 children, and over 680 people were injured. Hundreds of buildings in the surrounding area were damaged.

The person responsible for the bombing was Timothy McVeigh. He was assisted by Michael Fortier and Terry Nichols, both of whom helped McVeigh prepare the bomb. McVeigh was a member of the American militia movement and hated the federal government for its mishandling of the attack on the Waco complex of the Branch Davidians and the events at Ruby Ridge between militia member Randy Weaver and the federal government.

McVeigh drove an explosive-filled rental truck to a drop-off zone near a daycare center located in the building, covered up the car's Vehicle Identification Number (VIN) and returned to his home state of Kansas. As he was driving to Kansas, about 90 minutes after the explosion, McVeigh was stopped and arrested for driving without a license plate and having a concealed weapon.

McVeigh was tried in 1997 in federal court and found guilty of 11 counts of murder and conspiracy. He was executed by lethal injection on June 11, 2001. Nichols was found guilty of conspiring to build a weapon of mass destruction and of eight counts of involuntary manslaughter of federal officers. He was also found guilty on 161 counts of first-degree murder and sentenced to 161 consecutive life terms without the possibility of parole.

■ Natural Threats

Threats to homeland security not only come from man-made sources but also from natural events. Many natural disasters may strike at any moment, such as earthquakes.

Courtesy of NESDIS/NOAA.

Other natural disasters may occur with some warning, or at least we will know that the conditions are there for these to occur, such as hurricanes, floods, landslides, volcanic eruptions, tornadoes, thunderstorms, and wildfires. Other events may occur over long periods of time with worsening effects, such as droughts and prolonged bouts of extreme cold, as well as winter storms that continued to accumulate snow and ice. We know how to track hurricanes and how to build structures to minimize earthquake damage, but it is virtually impossible to prevent these events from occurring. However, the loss of life from these events can often be minimized through efforts such as better preparation, earlier warnings, and mandatory evacuations. The steps for emergency preparedness for natural disasters are often the same as preparing for other threats; steps such as having a family plan, especially a communication plan, as well as an emergency kit, all help people prepare for any hazardous event. It is equally true that the response to these disasters are also similar to other events such as terrorist attacks, but like each terrorist attack, each natural disaster brings its own complexities and the types of resources needed may very well be different. A drought may not cause the physical destruction of buildings like an earthquake or a hurricane may, but it can bring serious threats to human and animal life, and can have compounding effects. Therefore, while nature may bring on these particular events, not man, the potential destruction that can occur should not be overlooked.

Chapter Summary

Threats to American homeland security come from man-made sources, such as chemical, biological, radiological, and nuclear weapons, as well as natural events. Terrorists will use the weapons that best meet their budget, expertise, target, and the resources they have available. However, the odds of a terrorist attack with a CBRNE is fairly unlikely (see **Box 9.3**). An attack with a nuclear or radiological weapon has the potential to be the most dangerous, but they are difficult to obtain and/or manufacture. Biological and chemical weapons can be produced more easily

---

BOX 9.3 A National Strategy for CBRNE Standards

A committee formed from the Office of the President, the Department of Homeland Security, and the Department of Commerce came together in 2011 to develop a national strategy specifically oriented toward CBRNE standards. The committee noted the following:

Emergency response teams across the nation require reliable and interoperable chemical, biological, radiological, nuclear, and explosives (CBRNE) equipment that can be used with confidence for the protection of life, health, property, and commerce. The United States Government will, together with commercial and end-user communities, facilitate the development and implementation of national consensus CBRNE standards and establish an enduring capability to coordinate, prioritize, and implement those standards.

It is the vision of the National Science and Technology Council (NSTC) to establish and coordinate implementation of an integrated standards development approach that spans the full spectrum of standards, including performance, interoperability, testing and evaluation, conformity assessment, operating procedures, training, and certification. This will ensure that equipment is reliable and interoperable, and provides consistent and accurate results.

This strategy describes the elements of a standards and testing infrastructure needed to counter CBRNE threats. The subcommittee has consulted across the federal government to identify research efforts and current practices with respect to performance specifications and test methods, as well as standards development needs. The subcommittee recognizes that the CBRNE mission may be only one component of what users do each and every day. Therefore, the goals reflect not just the technical performance of the technology, but the interoperability with their suite of equipment, as well as concepts of operations involved in their deployment and the training of the users.

The following goals outline how to help achieve the vision:

GOAL 1: Establish an interagency group for CBRNE standards to promote the coordination of these standards among federal, state, local, and tribal communities.

GOAL 2: Coordinate and facilitate the development of CBRNE equipment performance standards and promote the use of standards for federal, state, local, and tribal communities.

GOAL 3: Coordinate and facilitate the development and adoption of interoperability standards for CBRNE equipment.

GOAL 4: Promote enduring CBRNE standard operating procedures for federal, state, local, and tribal use to improve national preparedness and response.

GOAL 5: Establish voluntary CBRNE training and certification standards for the federal, state, local, and tribal communities and promote policies that foster their adoption.

GOAL 6: Establish a comprehensive CBRNE equipment testing and evaluation (T&E) infrastructure and capability to support conformity assessment standards.

Reproduced from: Subcommittee on Standards. (2011). A National Strategy for CBRNE Standards. Retrieved online at http://www .whitehouse.gov/sites/default/files/microsites/ostp/chns_cbrne_ standards_final_24_aug_11.pdf but delivering them in such a way as to cause significant casualties is difficult. Few groups have access to these weapons or the logistical support necessary to carry out a successful attack. Nonetheless, many people are fearful that a terrorist group will use CBRNEs against U.S. citizens. It is widely accepted that most terrorists have a desire to use CBRNEs against Americans.

■ Review/Discussion Questions

1. What are CBRNEs?
2. What are the effects of chemical, biological, radiological/nuclear, and explosive weapons?
3. What are the dispersal methods for CBRNEs?
4. How likely is it that terrorists could use these weapons against the U.S.?

■ Additional Readings

Breen, C. (2012). *CBRNe, Terrorism, Medical and Major Incident Management.* New York, NY: CreateSpace.

Subcommittee on Standards. (2011). *A National Strategy for CBRNE Standards.* Retrieved online at http://www.whitehouse.gov/sites/default/files/microsites/ostp/chns_cbrne_standards_final_24_aug_11.pdf

■ Endnotes

1. Centers for Disease Control and Prevention. (2012). *Toxic Substances Portal: Nerve Agents.* Retrieved online at http://www.atsdr.cdc.gov/toxfaqs/tf.asp?id=524&tid=93
2. Centers for Disease Control and Prevention. (2012). *Toxic Substances Portal: Nerve Agents.* Retrieved online at http://www.atsdr.cdc.gov/mmg/mmg.asp?id=523&tid=93
3. Centers for Disease Control and Prevention. (2012). *Facts about VX.* Retrieved online at http://www.bt.cdc.gov/agent/vx/basics/facts.asp
4. Centers for Disease Control and Prevention. (2012). *Toxic Substances Portal: Blister Agents HN-1, HN-2, HN-3, Nitrogen Mustard.* Retrieved online at http://www.atsdr.cdc.gov/substances/toxsubstance.asp?toxid=189
5. Centers for Disease Control and Prevention. (2012). *Toxic Substances Portal: Blister Agents HN-1, HN-2, HN-3, Nitrogen Mustard.* Retrieved online at http://www.atsdr.cdc.gov/substances/toxsubstance.asp?toxid=189; Centers for Disease Control and Prevention. (2012). *ToxFAQs for Blister Agents: HN-1, HN-2, HN-3 (Nitrogen Mustards).* Retrieved online at http://www.atsdr.cdc.gov/toxfaqs/tf.asp?id=921&tid=189
6. Centers for Disease Control and Prevention. (2012). *Blister Agents: Lewisite (L), Mustard-Lewisite Mixture (HL).* Retrieved online at http://www.atsdr.cdc.gov/substances/toxsubstance.asp?toxid=190

7. Centers for Disease Control and Prevention. (2012). *Toxic Substances Portal—Blister Agents Lewisite (L), Mustard-Lewisite Mixture (HL)*. Retrieved online at http://www.atsdr.cdc.gov/toxfaqs/tf.asp?id=923&tid=190

8. Centers for Disease Control and Prevention. (2012). *Cyanide*. Retrieved online at http://www.atsdr.cdc.gov/substances/toxsubstance.asp?toxid=19; Centers for Disease Control and Prevention. (2012). *ToxFAQs for Cyanide*. Retrieved online at http://www.atsdr.cdc.gov/toxfaqs/tf.asp?id=71&tid=19

9. Centers for Disease Control and Prevention. (2012). *Toxic Substances Portal: Chlorine*. Retrieved online at http://www.atsdr.cdc.gov/substances/toxsubstance.asp?toxid=36; Centers for Disease Control and Prevention. (2012). *ToxFAQs for Chlorine*. Retrieved online at http://www.atsdr.cdc.gov/toxfaqs/tf.asp?id=200&tid=36

10. Centers for Disease Control and Prevention. (2012). *Toxic Substances Portal: Phosgene*. Retrieved online at http://www.atsdr.cdc.gov/MMG/MMG.asp?id=1201&tid=182

11. Centers for Disease Control and Prevention. (2012). *NIOSH Pocket Guide to Chemical Hazards*. Retrieved online at http://www.cdc.gov/niosh/npg/npgd0119.html

12. Centers for Disease Control and Prevention. (2012). *Incapacitating Agents*. Retrieved online at http://emergency.cdc.gov/agent/incapacitating/

13. Centers for Disease Control and Prevention. (2012). *Case Definition: 3-Quinuclidinyl Benzilate (BZ)*. Retrieved online at http://www.bt.cdc.gov/agent/bz/casedef.asp

14. Federal Emergency Management Agency. (2012). *Biological Threats*. Retrieved online at http://www.ready.gov/biological-threats

15. Centers for Disease Control and Prevention. (2012). *Q&A: Anthrax and Animal Hide Drums*. Retrieved online at http://emergency.cdc.gov/agent/anthrax/faq/pelt.asp

16. Centers for Disease Control and Prevention. (2012). *Q&A: Gastrointestinal (GI) Anthrax*. Retrieved online at http://emergency.cdc.gov/agent/anthrax/gi/

17. Centers for Disease Control and Prevention. (2012). *Anthrax: What You Need to Know*. Retrieved online at http://emergency.cdc.gov/agent/anthrax/needtoknow.asp

18. Centers for Disease Control and Prevention. (2012). *Questions and Answers about Anthrax*. Retrieved online at http://emergency.cdc.gov/agent/anthrax/faq/

19. Centers for Disease Control and Prevention. (2012). *Smallpox Basics*. Retrieved online at http://emergency.cdc.gov/agent/smallpox/disease/

20. Centers for Disease Control and Prevention. (2012). *Pneumonic Plague*. Retrieved online at http://emergency.cdc.gov/firsthours/plague/index.asp

21. Centers for Disease Control and Prevention. (2012). *Facts about Ricin*. Retrieved online at http://emergency.cdc.gov/agent/ricin/facts.asp

22. Centers for Disease Control and Prevention. (2012). *Hantavirus*. Retrieved online at http://www.cdc.gov/hantavirus/

The Homeland Security Cycle

Chapter Objectives

- To understand the elements of the homeland security cycle and why they are important to homeland security

- To understand the role of federal, state, local, and tribal governments in the homeland security cycle

Introduction

In May 2012, FBI agents foiled a plan by five suspected terrorists (and self-proclaimed anarchists) to destroy a bridge near Cleveland, Ohio. The plan was thwarted after an FBI informant infiltrated the group and recorded conversations in which the plot was discussed in the months before the attempted bombing. The five men were arrested by members of a Joint Terrorism Task Force who claimed that the public was never in any danger because the explosives they tried to use were provided by an undercover FBI agent and were not operable explosives.[1] Four of the men eventually pleaded guilty. Three men received sentences of 8–11 years in prison, and the fourth received a sentence of 6 years in prison. The last of the five men received a psychiatric evaluation, which was ruled inconclusive.

The FBI's use of a paid informant to gather intelligence on the anarchists represents the first stage in the homeland security cycle. In this stage, information is collected and analyzed as a way to prevent terrorist attacks, as was done in this case.

KEY TERM

Mitigation—the effort to reduce loss of life and property by lessening the impact of disasters.

KEY TERM

Preparedness—a continuous cycle of planning, organizing, training, equipping, exercising, evaluating, and taking corrective action in an effort to ensure effective coordination during incident response.

KEY TERM

FEMA—the Federal Emergency Management Agency is the agency within the Department of Homeland Security responsible for responding to catastrophes and issuing a disaster and/or emergency declaration, thereby allowing them to provide monetary assistance.

Other actions taken by the FBI or local law enforcement and first responders could be taken to prepare for events, should they take place. These would constitute the second stage of the homeland security cycle and could include, for example, carrying out mock drills that allow responders to "practice" their actions. The third stage of the cycle is response, which would take place right after an event. If the five suspects had been able to carry out their plot, first responders would need to react quickly and provide necessary services for any victims. The final stage, had the suspects carried out their plot, would be recovery from the event, which might include rebuilding the bridge or other actions to restore the local community.

The Homeland Security Cycle

The homeland security cycle refers to the four stages necessary to prepare for an event and to respond to it. The first two stages, **mitigation** and **preparedness**, occur before an emergency happens, whereas the final two, response and recovery, are the actions taken in the aftermath. Mitigation means to lessen the effects of an emergency, and preparedness is simply being ready for it. The third stage, response, refers to the activities that take place immediately after the event. The final stage, recovery, occurs after immediate needs are met and any dangers subside.

On the federal level, the **Federal Emergency Management Agency (FEMA)** is largely responsible for helping America with the different stages of the cycle. This is in line with their mission, which is "to lead America to prepare for, prevent, respond to, and recover from disasters." There are also state and local agencies that assist with all four stages of the cycle.

Mitigation

The term mitigation refers to the process through which attempts are made to prevent a possible emergency or to reduce the potential impact of that emergency (be it terrorist attacks, natural disasters, or human-made disasters) before it occurs. In other words, mitigation refers to those steps taken to reduce the risk of an attack or emergency. These steps can also be thought of as any actions taken with the intent of avoiding an incident or intervening in an effort to limit the effects if an incident should occur. Mitigation also includes a level of risk management. For instance, more attention will be given to protecting the country's critical infrastructure.

The activities considered to be part of the mitigation stage are varied, but they all have the common goal of reducing the risks associated with potential hazards. They are the policies and actions that can be implemented as a way to reduce risk to people and property from hazardous events. These can include a range of activities such as restrictive building codes, improved surveillance of critical sites, immunizations to prevent diseases, and increased security operations.

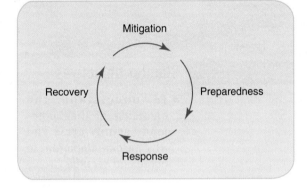

Mitigation

Recovery

Preparedness

Response

Courtesy of Rosanna Arias/FEMA.

Mitigation efforts usually address two components: the probability of an event occurring (likelihood) and the consequences of an event. When it comes to reducing the probability, it is relatively easy to implement policies that minimize the risk of a man-made attack. These can include such activities as gathering "actionable" information about terrorist activity, analyzing that intelligence, oversight of a group's communications, and various surveillance techniques. All of these activities are focused on preventing a threat from being carried out. Much of this is done by the Department of Homeland Security along with certain state and local agencies.

State and local fusion centers also collect intelligence from various agencies and organizations and analyze it in an effort to prevent terrorist actions. These centers collect and "fuse" sensitive information from many sources, including law enforcement, task forces, the National Counterterrorism Center, other fusion centers, and first responders. Today, over 70 state and local intelligence fusion centers exist, with "satellite" offices that focus on intelligence gathering and dissemination in different parts of the state.[2]

The National Strategy for Homeland Security notes that intelligence and information analysis is an integral part of the nation's effort to reduce America's vulnerabilities. They note four categories of intelligence analysis, including: (1) tactical threat analysis (analysis of a group's current and potential activities); (2) strategic analysis of the enemy (knowing the group's identities, financial and political sources of support, motivation, goals, current and future capabilities); (3) vulnerability assessments (the consequences of a terrorist attack against specific sites or facilities); and (4) threat-vulnerability integration (mapping terrorist threats and the vulnerabilities of their potential targets).

There are numerous agencies that assist with mitigation. Within the Department of Homeland Security, a Mitigation Directorate was created as part of FEMA; its mission is to protect lives and prevent loss of property resulting from natural and man-made events. This group is responsible for implementing any risk-reduction programs for the nation that have been authorized by Congress.

FEMA has developed different courses of action for mitigation policy. One of those is the Reference Manual to Mitigate Potential Terrorist Attacks Against Buildings. This document, written for architects, engineers, and builders, provides guidelines on ways to reduce the effects of potential terrorist attacks by reducing the physical damage to buildings that can occur during an attack. Such changes will also reduce human casualties.

While it is impossible to implement policies that prevent a natural hazard such as a hurricane or earthquake from occurring, it is possible to reduce the impact of a natural disaster with actions taken before the event occurs. Some activities include stricter building codes, evacuation plans, building levees, and other structures. In some cases, it can simply involve educating citizens on measures they can take to reduce injury and death (e.g., first-aid techniques).

As a way to mitigate the effects of hurricanes, FEMA has created the National Hurricane Program that conducts assessments of, and provides assistance to, state and local agencies with their own hurricane education plans. Through FEMA, experts also conduct analyses of storms to help predict the most likely effects of storm surges and high winds, help to assess shelter availability and capacity for those residents affected by the storm, and calculate evacuation times required, if needed.

Additionally, FEMA has created the National Earthquake Hazards Reduction Program. Along with the U.S. Geological Survey, FEMA conducts and supports ongoing earth science research to better understand the nature, the effects, and the likelihood of earthquakes.

FEMA also supports the Mitigation Grant programs to provide financial assistance to states. These grant programs include the Hazards Mitigation Grant Program, Pre-Disaster Mitigation Program, Flood Mitigation Assistance Program, the Severe Repetitive Loss Grant Program, and the Repetitive Flood Claims Grant Program. They also oversee the National Flood Insurance Program (NFIP), which was created by Congress as a way to mitigate future losses due to flooding. This program supports building and zoning ordinances and access to affordable, federally backed flood insurance for property owners.

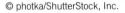

Preparedness

The second stage of the homeland security cycle is preparedness, which refers to those activities that help officials be prepared in the case of an emergency. It is

© photka/ShutterStock, Inc.

the "state of readiness" that local, state, and federal officials must develop so they are prepared to respond to a variety of emergencies. These plans include a range of activities, programs, and systems so that officials may respond quickly and effectively in time of a disaster. Being prepared and responding quickly to a disaster is critical for minimizing deaths, injuries, financial losses, property damage, and interruption of business activities.

Activities related to preparedness are very closely tied to activities taken in the mitigation stage, and the distinction between them is often not clear. However, preparedness refers to actions taken to plan for the best response to an event, whereas mitigation includes all the actions taken to minimize the scope of the event before it happens.

Many activities can be considered to be part of the preparedness stage, but they generally include developing plans and procedures to ensure that first responders are properly trained and equipped to provide assistance should an event occur. In many areas, mock exercises or drills are developed and carried out as a way to establish processes and procedures that will be used during an actual emergency. Preparedness also includes establishing (and testing or practicing, when possible) evacuation procedures from buildings, first-response training to employees (such as first aid), public education, and emergency operations centers. These are the kinds of actions that can help people survive disasters by teaching them specific procedures so that they are comfortable should they ever be needed. Whenever possible, this includes testing of all procedures before an event to ensure their effectiveness.

Preparedness also includes developing plans to coordinate all resources in a community that may be needed in an actual emergency. Every relevant agency or organization should be ready to provide a specific level of service, depending on the nature and seriousness of the incident. All organizations should ensure that they are prepared to respond to an incident and know what their specific role will be. It is crucial that all organizations and personnel who could be part of a response team are completely cognizant of their roles and responsibilities. Moreover, a comprehensive system for communication between these organizations must be established.

Some of the nation's actions to prepare for emergencies can be found in the **National Response Framework**. In this document, it is noted that a "unified national effort" is needed to prepare for a response. In the report it is noted that all levels of government have a responsibility to develop detailed all-hazards contingency plans that clearly articulate procedures that are tailored to each jurisdiction, and should be integrated, operational, and incorporate the private-sector. The report also indicates that well-qualified teams should be assembled and provided with the equipment necessary to respond to a variety of incidents. Finally, these teams must be trained through a series of exercises that not only train individuals but also contain a mechanism for corrective action. This is particularly important for states, as they will often be the first responders to most emergencies. Every state has established a homeland security or emergency management system, some of which are listed in **Box 10.1**.

> **KEY TERM**
> **National Response Framework**—the NRF is a guide to how the nation responds to all types of disasters and emergencies.

BOX 10.1 State-level Agencies Preparing for Attacks

Louisiana Governor's Office for Homeland Security and Emergency Preparedness: encourages families and businesses to make plans so people know what to do if an emergency strikes; informs the public when serious weather is approaching; provides guidance on how to receive help; helps families and businesses mitigate damages by providing advice on ways to prevent flood damages, food safety rules, and how to build safe homes.

Pennsylvania Emergency Management Agency (PEMA): provides disaster assistance to families, businesses, and communities after a disaster to help them recover and move forward. They also have a Division of Exercise and Evaluation that oversees training programs for responders. The director of this agency also serves as the homeland security adviser to the governor.

Tennessee Office of Homeland Security: top priority is to protect the lives and livelihood of the citizens of the state. They seek to educate, train, organize, and utilize citizens during an emergency to maintain a Citizen Corps program that includes five programs: CERT Training, Neighborhood Watch, Volunteers in Police Service, Medical Reserve Corps, and Fire Corps. They have instituted a Citizen Outreach program to help citizens be prepared for an emergency, a program to protect the infrastructure in the state, and a grant program for first responders, among others.

Oklahoma Office of Homeland Security: has identified their objectives to include preventing a terrorist attack in Oklahoma, reducing Oklahoma's vulnerability to terrorist attack, and minimizing the damage from and respond to a terrorist attack should one occur. The duties of their office are to develop and implement a comprehensive statewide homeland security strategy, to plan and implement a statewide response system, to administer the homeland security advisory system, to coordinate, apply for, and distribute federal homeland security grant funds, and to implement national homeland security plans.

New York Division of Homeland Security and Emergency Services: has four key offices, including Intelligence and Analysis, Public Safety, Critical Infrastructure Protection, and Federal Grant Program Administration. They also have programs to prepare citizens for future attacks, and an Office of Cybersecurity.

Data from: Louisiana Governor's Office of homeland Security and Emergency Preparedness. (2012). Retrieved online at http://gohsep.la.gov/; Pennsylvania Emergency Management Agency. (2012). Retrieved online at http://www.pema.state.pa.us/portal/server.pt/community/training_and_exercises/4684; Tennessee Office of Homeland Security. (2012). Retrieved online at http://www.tn.gov/homelandsecurity/index.shtml; Oklahoma Office of Homeland Security. (2012). Retrieved online at http://www.ok.gov/homeland/About_Us/index.html; New York Division of Homeland Security and Emergency Services. (2012). Retrieved online http://www.dhses.ny.gov/

Preparedness also takes place on the community level. In preparation, the communities need to identify possible shelter locations for those affected by an emergency, along with food, clothing, and evacuation routes.[3] Once the potential hazards in a community are identified, officials can proceed to develop a comprehensive preparedness plan. Many communities have developed different warning systems and signals that alert citizens of dangerous weather systems. Many communities broadcast warnings through emergency radio and television broadcasts. In other areas, there are reverse 911 calls, or special sirens, or emergency workers may go door-to-door to warn people. The Emergency Alert System (EAS) is a way to warn the entire nation of a national threat or emergency on very short notice.[4]

In order to oversee the coordinated response approach developed in the **National Response Plan**, the federal government created the **National Incident Management System (NIMS)** as a way to provide a nationwide method for federal, state, and local governments to work effectively and efficiently together to prepare for, respond to, and recover from incidents. According to NIMS, all agencies should have at least a minimal level of preparedness for communications between agencies, resource management, and command structure.

On the national level, FEMA helps states and local governments develop preparedness plans and to be ready for an event. FEMA oversees the Homeland Security Grant Program, that helps state and local governments develop their strategic plans.[5] For example, FEMA suggests preparing for a biological threat by ensuring that all citizens are current with required immunizations. They also suggest having extra water, a battery-powered or hand-cranked radio, and extra flashlights and batteries available in the house. A plan for contacting other family members nearby during an emergency is essential.[6]

FIGURE 10.1   Preparing for a Zombie Apocalypse: The CDC is encouraging people to prepare for a zombie invasion! In case flesh-eating zombies invade, people need to have water, food, medications, tools and supplies, sanitation and hygiene, clothing and bedding, important documents, and first aid supplies to protect themselves. They will also need a plan that outlines to meet other family members, a list of emergency contacts, and an evacuation route.

U.S. Centers for Disease Control. (2011). Preparedness 101: Zombie Apocalypse. Retrieved online at http://blogs.cdc.gov/publichealthmatters/2011/05/preparedness-101-zombie-apocalypse/

Similar suggestions are made by FEMA in order to prepare for a chemical threat. However, in the case of a chemical attack, FEMA suggests using plastic to seal doors, windows, and vents as a way to prevent chemicals from entering the home.[7] FEMA's suggestions for preparing for a nuclear attack include having an evacuation plan, especially if you live near a potential target, which, generally speaking, includes strategic missile sites, military bases, government centers (Washington, D.C. or a state capital), key transportation or communication centers, manufacturing or industrial centers, petroleum refineries, financial centers, and major ports. In order to protect from radioactive fallout, it would be necessary to take shelter in an underground area or in the middle of a large building.[8] Adequately preparing for a radioactive event, according the FEMA, will require a 2-week emergency kit with water, food, and other supplies. It would be helpful to have duct tape, scissors, and plastic for covering vents, windows, and doors to block radioactive material from entering the building.[9]

In addition to FEMA other federal agencies help in the planning process, such as the Centers for Disease Control (CDC). As a way to encourage people to be prepared for an emergency, the CDC has developed a tongue-in-cheek educational program that encourages people to be prepared for a zombie apocalypse (see **FIGURE 10.1**). It is a way to reach out to new audiences and encourage them to be prepared for most any emergency. If you are prepared for a zombie attack, you will be prepared for other emergencies. It is a way to teach the importance of emergency preparedness in an entertaining way.

State and local governments also take part in strategic planning. The plans will vary depending on the jurisdiction, but most state and local governments focus on an "all-hazards" approach that includes terrorism as one hazard.[10]

Response

The third stage of the homeland security cycle is **response**, which refers to any measures taken at the onset of an emergency to save lives and protect property. These measures often require coordination between different levels of government.

There are many types of response efforts, and they will vary depending on the type and severity of the emergency. They can include issuing warnings to notify the public to take action, notifying emergency response personnel of the event, providing immediate medical assistance to victims, rescuing victims, providing traffic control, evacuating residents, or providing shelter for those affected. These actions all have the goal of restoring order in the affected area in a quick and safe manner.

Courtesy of Walt Jennings/FEMA.

KEY TERM

Response—any measures taken at the onset of an emergence to save lives and protect property.

Response actions are generally carried out by first responders such as local police, fire, and emergency medical personnel. These officials take immediate action in order to secure the scene, maintain order, assist victims, contain any fires that have started, contain the spread of any biological or nuclear material, identify the type of chemical or biological agent used, or retrieving any bodies. Their role may be complicated because the site may be contaminated with chemical, biological, or radioactive substances. At the same time, first responders often need to collect evidence to aid in the subsequent investigation.

One critical step to responding to an event is to ensure that all response tasks are carried out, while at the same time ensuring there is limited overlap. In these situations, clear Command and Control (C^2) is essential, which allows all agencies to perform their designated roles to reduce the effects of the emergency while avoiding redundant actions and the wasting of resources.[11]

In addition to fire, police, and emergency personnel, volunteer groups often respond to emergencies and assist on the front lines. This could include groups such as the American Red Cross, the National Volunteer Organization Against Disasters, Feeding America, American Radio Relay League, or the Salvation Army. These volunteers have usually been trained to provide specific emergency response services in support of the first responders. They often work alongside local, state, and federal authorities to address the immediate needs of disaster victims by providing food, shelter, and clothing. Many of these volunteer groups are listed in more detail in **Box 10.2**.

Other volunteer opportunities for responding to emergencies were established by the White House and The Department of Homeland Security. When announcing these groups in 2002, Bush called for 2 years of volunteer service from every American citizen. One of the groups is the Citizen Corps that provides

Volunteer Groups

American Red Cross: trains volunteers in their Disaster Action Team to assist victims in emergencies.

National Volunteer Organization Against Disasters: founded in 1970, this group is made up of nonprofit organizations who are involved in providing assistance to communities and survivors. They provide training for their volunteers so they are acquainted with the proper procedures before the actual disaster occurs. There are national members in the organization who are responsible for coordinating volunteer efforts at the national level, while state/territory members ensure coordination efforts among organizations at the state and local level.

Feeding America (formerly America's Second Harvest): works to provide food to survivors of disaster-affected communities.

American Radio Relay League: trains volunteers who wish to provide emergency communications in times of emergency. They also provide public service announcements as needed.

Salvation Army: has the Salvation Army Team Emergency Radio Network (SATERN) that is made up of volunteers who provide emergency communications during disasters. The organization also provides disaster relief services such as basic services, financial assistance, food and shelter, assistance with clean-up and reconstruction efforts.

Data from: National Voluntary Organizations Active in Disaster. (2012). Retrieved online at http://www.nvoadd.org/index/php?option=com_context&view=article&id; Feeding America. (2012). Retrieved online at http://feedingamerica.org/how-we-fight-hunger/mission-and-values.aspx; American Radio Relay League. (2012). Retrieved online at http://www.arrl.org/emergency-communications; Salvation Army. (2012). Retrieved online at http://disaster.salvationarmeyusa.org/aboutus/

opportunities for any citizens who have a desire to make their communities safer. Many groups are part of Citizen Corps, including Citizen Corps Councils, Community Emergency Response Teams (CERTs), Volunteers in Police Service (VIPS), Medical Reserve, Neighborhood Watch, and Fire Corps. These groups are detailed in **Box 10.3**.

The National Response Plan outlines the federal government's plan for responding to an emergency. The report focused on a unified approach to managing incidents that involves many participants from all levels of government. The report notes that once an incident occurs, priorities must shift to employing resources to save lives, protect property and the environment, and preserve the social, economic, and political structure of the jurisdiction. It is essential that affected governments quickly gain and maintain situational awareness and then activate and deploy resources. After that, response actions must be coordinated, as should any requests for additional support.

The federal government has many options for responding to emergencies, and there are many federal agencies that play some role in the response stage of the homeland security cycle, some of which are listed in **Box 10.4**.

FEMA has suggested ways to respond to various attacks. For example, they suggest that during a chemical threat, people should move quickly away from the impacted area without passing through the contaminated area. If it is not possible to leave a building, they suggest closing all doors and windows and turning off the ventilation. They suggest the room/s be sealed with plastic sheeting and duct tape.[12]

During a nuclear blast, FEMA suggests listening for officials to make statements about what to do: take shelter, go to a specific place, or evacuate. If it is not pos-

BOX 10.3 Citizen Corps

USA Freedom Corps: within the Executive Office of the President, it is the fifth policy council (along with Domestic, Economic, National Security, and Homeland Security) in the White House. The Corps promotes volunteerism across the nation and seeks to connect Americans to various volunteer opportunities in other federal agencies such as AmeriCorps, Peace Corps, and Senior Corps, while also encouraging citizens to find local opportunities for volunteering.

Citizen Corps: within the DHS Office of Domestic Preparedness. Volunteers in this agency assist in the recovery process after an attack or natural disaster. As a component of USA Freedom Corps, the Citizen Corps encourages people to prepare for emergencies.

Community Emergency Response Team (CERT): CERTs are sponsored by local fire departments or emergency management groups. Volunteers are trained to help in emergencies or to provide medical assistance, crowd control, or conduct training for others. They also help to raise funds to purchase equipment. Sometimes CERT teams go by other names, including Neighborhood Emergency Response Teams (NERT)

or in the case where most of the team consists of teenagers: Teen Community Emergency Response Teams (TEEN CERT).

Fire Corps: volunteers help local fire/EMS departments in nonemergency situations. As part of Citizens Corps, these men and women help to increase the ability of fire departments to assist and protect the community.

Medical Reserve Corps: as part of Citizen Corps, these volunteers make up a network of public health members in a community who volunteer to provide medical assistance during emergencies.

Volunteers in Police Service (VIPs): part of Citizen Corps, this group provides support to law enforcement agencies by performing clerical tasks, assisting with search and rescue operations, or crowd control.

Data from: Citizen Corps. (2012). Retrieved online at http://citizencorps.gov/citizencorps/index.html; FEMA. (2012). Retrieved online at http://www.fema.gov/about/regions/regioniii/citizen_corps.shtm; Community Emergency Response Teams (CERT). (2012). Retrieved online at http://www.citizencorps.gov/cert/; Volunteers in Police Service. 2012). Retrieved online at http://www.policevolunteers.org/

sible to evacuate, they suggest finding a building made of brick or concrete to limit exposure to radioactive material. Once in the building, you should go as far below ground as possible or into the center of the structure. If possible, stay there at least 24 hours, until radiation levels decrease. If outside, FEMA suggests taking cover behind anything that may offer protection, and lie flat on the ground, covering your head. It is important to get clean as quickly as possible, removing the outer layer of clothing, placing it in a plastic bag and moving it far away from any people or animals.[13]

Another type of plan for responding to incidents on the federal level is NIMS. This was created after President George W. Bush called on the Secretary of Homeland Security, through Homeland Security Presidential Directive No. 5, to develop a nationally based **incident command system**. The purpose was to provide a consistent, nationwide approach for federal, state, local, and tribal governments to work together to prepare for, prevent, respond to, and recover from domestic incidents. It is a set of principles, terminology, and organizational processes that together serves as a comprehensive, standardized approach to the management of domestic incidents at all government levels. The procedures in NIMS are designed to be used to coordinate the different response actions. It is presumed that all responders will be able to share a common understanding and will be able to work together to respond effectively to an emergency.

KEY TERM

Incident command system—the Incident Command System (ICS) is a standardized, on-scene, all-hazards incident management approach.

BOX 10.4   Federal Response Agencies

Integrated Hazard Information Services: works with emergency managers, the media, private sector, and weather forecasters to inform the public about hazardous weather conditions.

Center for Domestic Preparedness Consortium: A part of FEMA, this is a partnership of several organizations that work to further counter-terrorism preparedness needs for the nation's first responders. They help enhance preparedness of federal, state, local, and tribal emergency responders as a way to reduce the nation's vulnerabilities. The members include:

- Center for Domestic Preparedness: the only federally chartered training center for weapons of mass destruction.
- The Energetic Materials Research and Testing Center: a research-oriented public university that specializes in training for explosives, live explosives, and incendiary devices.
- National Center for Biomedical Research and Training: training for weapons of mass destruction, counter-terrorism, and high-consequence events for

emergency management personnel, law enforcement, HazMat, public health, EMS, and agricultural.

- National Emergency Response and Rescue Training Center: designs, develops, and delivers training and technical assistance for first responders.
- Nevada Test Site's Counter-Terrorism Operations Support Program: provides training for radiological/nuclear weapons; teaches first responders to detect, prepare for, prevent, respond to, and recover from acts of terrorism with WMDs.
- Transportation Technology Center, Inc: provides training for first responders as well as surface transportation security, such as railroads and heavy freight transport systems.
- National Disaster Preparedness Training Center at the University of Hawaii: provides training to island communities throughout the Pacific so they are able to respond, recover, and reconstruct their communities after a catastrophe.

Domestic Preparedness Office: was originally established by the FBI in 1998 as a way to coordinate all

On the local level, each township has the responsibility to provide qualified first responders who can handle a variety of emergencies. This usually includes police, firefighters, and emergency medical staff. If the emergency covers a wide region beyond their capabilities, the local leaders will rely on the state for assistance.[14] More than likely, the state and local agencies will be the first responders to an emergency. If needed, they can ask for assistance from neighboring communities or states. If the emergency is complex or requires more resources than are available, or if the costs are too high for local governments, the mayor or governor can request assistance from the federal government. The specific procedures by which a state can make an appeal to the federal government are outlined in the NRF.

If a state governor wishes, he or she can formally request that the president declare a major disaster or make an **emergency declaration**. Such a request will first be analyzed by the regional FEMA administrator, who will then make a recommendation to the national FEMA administrator. This administrator will then make a recommendation to the president, who will decide whether to declare a disaster based partly on the FEMA recommendation. If a declaration is made, the FEMA administrator will then determine which components of the NRF to activate.

KEY TERM

Emergency declaration—declarations to trigger aid that protects property, public health, and safety and lessens or averts the threat of an incident becoming a catastrophic event.

▪ Recovery

The last stage of the homeland security cycle is **recovery**, or the efforts taken to restore the infrastructure and the social and economic underpinnings of a community to a state of normalcy. This stage begins in the period immediately

KEY TERM

Recovery—the efforts taken to restore the infrastructure and the social and economic underpinnings of a community to a state of normalcy.

federal efforts surrounding WMDs. The office works with other federal agencies to assist state and local first responders to respond to a WMD attack. The office was moved to the DHS in 2003.

Domestic Emergency Support Team: was created by the Presidential Decision Directive 39 by President Clinton in June 1995; made up of many teams who can be deployed quickly from the FBI, FEMA, Department of Defense, Department of Energy, and others who respond to attacks made with WMDs. President Bush transferred it to DHS from the Justice Department in 2003.

National Disaster Medical System: combines federal and nonfederal medical resources to establish an integrated national medical response capability that can assist first responders in times of emergency. The agency is part of the Department of Health and Human Services.

Strategic National Stockpile: has large quantities of medicine and supplies that could be used if local supplies are exhausted as a result of an emergency.

Medicine could be delivered to any state and would be free. There are enough supplies to protect people in several large cities.

Other Response Agencies: The FBI has many offices that help with response efforts. These include the Domestic Terrorism/Counterterrorism Planning Section, the Laboratory Division, and the Critical Incident Response Group. Other federal agencies play a role in response, such as the Department of Defense, Department of Energy, Department of Health and Human Services, the EPA, the Department of Agriculture, and the Nuclear Regulatory Commission.

Data from: Integrated Hazard Information Services. (2012). Retrieved online at http://fxa.noas.gov/NGWT; Consortium" Center for Domestic Preparedness, FEMA. (2012). Retrieved online at http://cdp.dhs.gov/consortium.html; Domestic Preparedness Office, (2012). Retrieved online at http://www.faqs.org/espionage/De-Eb/Domestic-Preparedness-Office-NDPO-United-States; National Disaster Medical System. (2012) Retrieved online at http://www.phe.gov/Preparedness/responders/ndms/Pages/default.aspx; Strategic National Stockpile. (2012). Retrieved online at http://www.cdc.gov/phpr/stockpile/stockpile.htm

following a disaster and can continue for months and, in some cases, years. Recovery is a gradual process, and the health and safety of the residents must be the first concern.

With most incidents, there are both short-term recovery needs as well as long-term recovery needs. In the short term, people will need functioning transportation systems (i.e., roads), utilities, schools, medical facilities, and government buildings. Some victims will need food, shelter, and other government assistance programs. The essential infrastructure will need to be repaired or maintained, such as power, communication systems, and water and sewage.

Long-term recovery may take months or even years. This will involve any actions taken to return the commu-

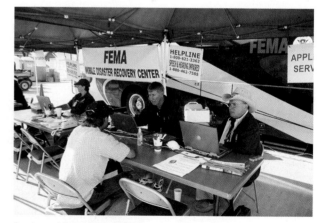

Courtesy of Greg Henshall/FEMA.

nity to one that functions well for its citizens. Any areas that were directly affected by the incident may need to have homes or commercial buildings permanently repaired or rebuilt. Economic activity will need to be restored by resuming regular business and employment. Long-term recovery may also require emergency economic aid, accessible business loans, environmental monitoring, and long-term mental health services.

The National Response Framework addresses the need for specific policies for helping individuals and communities to recover from an emergency and return to self-sufficiency. Recovery efforts will, of course, be unique to each community, but should be overseen by a **Joint Field Office**. The JFO will do things such as coordinate assistance programs that will help individuals, households, and businesses return to normal, establish Disaster Recovery Centers, and coordinate public assistance grant programs.

The federal government plays the largest role in providing the technical and financial support for recovery. For the most part, recovery is the responsibility of FEMA. The assistance they provide to each community after a disaster will vary depending on the community and the type and severity of the emergency. The response to a hurricane, for instance, will be very different from that required from an attack that involved chemical agents.

FEMA also suggests ways to recover from different types of emergencies. For example, they recommend that after a chemical attack, it is necessary to decontaminate the area as quickly as possible in order to minimize potential health consequences. They suggest citizens stay in a shelter until officials announce it is safe to leave. Plus, anyone who has had any contact with a chemical agent should receive medical treatment.[15]

Effective recovery efforts may require contributions from all sectors of society. The Joint Field Office serves as the central coordination point for all levels of government, as well as private-sector and nongovernmental entities.

■ Chapter Summary

There are four stages to the homeland security cycle. They include mitigation, preparedness, response, and recovery. The first two stages revolve around activities that can be taken to lessen the chance that an event may occur, or to lessen the impact of an event. The second two stages occur after an attack or natural disaster to help citizens and communities respond and recover from the event. Activities during all four stages of the cycle may involve all levels of government, from local up to federal.

■ Review/Discussion Questions

1. What are the four stages to the homeland security cycle? Why are they important to homeland security?
2. What are the roles of the federal, state, local, and tribal governments in each of the stages of the homeland security cycle?
3. What role do volunteers play in the homeland security cycle?

■ Additional Readings

Bush, G.W. (2001). Presidential Policy Direction/PPD-8: National Preparedness. Retrieved online at http://www.dhs.gov/presidential-policy-directive-8-national-preparedness

Logan, K.G. & Ramsay, J.D. (2012). *Introduction to Homeland Security*. Boulder, CO: Westview.

Pelfrey, W.V. (2004). *Homeland Security Disciplines and the Cycle of Preparedness.* Retrieved online at http://homelandsecurityroundtable.com/wp-content/uploads/2012/07/Homeland-Security-Disciplines-and-the-Cycle-of-Preparedness.pdf

Endnotes

1. Barrett, D. (2012). "Five Charged in Plan to Bomb Ohio Bridge." *The Wall Street Journal.* Retrieved online at http://online.wsj.com/article/SB10001424052702304050304577377851612024974.html

2. Lahneman, W.J. (2012). Homeland Security Intelligence. In Logan, K.G. & Ramsay, J.D. *Introduction to Homeland Security.* Boulder, CO: Westview, pp. 97–124.

3. Federal Emergency Management Agency. (2012). *Shelter.* Retrieved online at http://www.ready.gov/shelter; Federal Emergency Management Agency. (2012). *Evacuating Yourself and Your Family.* Retrieved online at http://www.ready.gov/evacuating-yourself-and-your-family

4. Federal Emergency Management Agency. (2012). *Warning Systems and Signals.* Retrieved online at http://www.ready.gov/warning-systems-signals

5. Clovis, S.H., Jr. (2012). Strategic Planning. In Logan, K.G. & Ramsay, J.D. *Introduction to Homeland Security.* Boulder, CO: Westview, pp. 285-311.

6. Federal Emergency Management Agency. (2012). *Biological Threats.* Retrieved online at http://www.ready.gov/biological-threats

7. Federal Emergency Management Agency. (2012). *Chemical Threats.* Retrieved online at http://www.ready.gov/chemical-threats

8. Federal Emergency Management Agency. (2012). *Nuclear Blast.* Retrieved online at http://www.ready.gov/nuclear-blast

9. Federal Emergency Management Agency. (2012). *Radiological Dispersion Device.* Retrieved online at http://www.ready.gov/radioactive-dispersion-device.rdd

10. Clovis, S.H., Jr. (2012) Strategic Planning. In Logan, K.G. & Ramsay, J.D. *Introduction to Homeland Security.* Boulder, CO: Westview, pp. 285-311.

11. Chumar, M. (2012). Public- and Private-Sector Partnerships in Homeland Security. In Logan, K.G. & Ramsay, J.D. *Introduction to Homeland Security.* Boulder, CO: Westview, pp. 47-68.

12. Federal Emergency Management Agency. (2012). *Chemical Threats.* Retrieved online at http://www.ready.gov/chemical-threats

13. Federal Emergency Management Agency. (2012). *Nuclear Blast.* Retrieved online at http://www.ready.gov/nuclear-blast

14. Logan, K.G. (2012). A First Look at the Department of Homeland Security. In Logan, K.G. & Ramsay, J.D. *Introduction to Homeland Security.* Boulder, CO: Westview, pp. 5-18.

15. Federal Emergency Management Agency. (2012). *Chemical Threats.* Retrieved online at http://www.ready.gov/chemical-threats

National Incident Management System and Incident Command System

Chapter Objectives

- Understand the overall concept of NIMS

- Know the five components of NIMS and their purpose

- Understand the overall concept of ICS

- Recognize the 14 proven management characteristics of ICS

- Know the members of the command and general staffs in ICS

■ Introduction

On August 23, 2005, Hurricane Katrina formed as a tropical storm off the coast of the Bahamas.[1] Over the next 7 days, the tropical storm grew into a catastrophic hurricane

that made landfall first in Florida and then along the Gulf Coast in Mississippi, Louisiana, and Alabama, leaving a trail of heartbreaking devastation and human suffering. Katrina caused staggering physical destruction along its path, flooded the historic city of New Orleans, ultimately killed over 1,300 people, and became the most destructive natural disaster in American history.

Awakening to reports of Katrina's landfall on the Gulf Coast the morning of Monday, August 29, American citizens watched events unfold with an initial curiosity that soon turned to concern and sorrow. The awe that viewers held for the sheer ferocity of nature was soon matched with disappointment and frustration at the seeming inability of the "government"—local, state, and federal—to respond effectively to the crisis. Hurricane Katrina and the subsequent sustained flooding of New Orleans exposed significant flaws in federal, state, and local preparedness for catastrophic events and the capacity to respond to them. Emergency plans at all levels of government, from small town plans to the 600-page National Response Plan—the federal government's plan to coordinate all its departments and agencies and integrate them with state, local, and private-sector partners—were put to the ultimate test, and came up short.

© RON EDMONDS/AP Images.

In the aftermath of Hurricane Katrina, President Bush commissioned a group to study the federal response to Hurricane Katrina and to identify what went wrong. A report was issued in 2006 that noted, among many of the lessons learned, that the National Incident Management System and the use of Incident (and Area) Command Systems was not widely developed, and therefore, because of the lack of training and exposure to these systems, the federal response (and to some degree the state and local responses, although not the subject of the report) was inadequately prepared for the natural disaster. The recommendation was that efforts needed to be redoubled to more widely educate all responders at all levels through training and exercises in the National Incident Management System (NIMS) and the Incident Command System (ICS), the primary topics to which this chapter now turns.

■ National Incident Management System (NIMS)

The September 11, 2001 terrorist attacks and the 2004 and 2005 hurricane seasons highlighted the need to focus on improving emergency management, incident response capabilities, and coordination processes across the country.[2] A comprehensive, national approach, applicable to all jurisdictional levels and across functional disciplines, improves the effectiveness of emergency management/response personnel across the full spectrum of potential incidents and hazard scenarios (including, but not limited to, natural hazards, terrorist activities, and other man-made disasters). Such an approach improves coordination and cooperation between public and private agencies in a variety of emergency management and incident response activities. The National Incident Management System (NIMS) framework sets forth this comprehensive, national approach (see **TABLE 11.1**).

Incidents typically begin and end locally, and are managed on a daily basis at the lowest possible geographical, organizational, and jurisdictional level. However, there are instances in which successful incident management operations depend on the involvement of multiple jurisdictions, levels of government, functional agencies, and/or emergency responder disciplines. These instances require effective and efficient coordination across this broad spectrum of organizations and activities.

NIMS uses a systematic approach to integrate the best existing processes and methods into a unified, national framework for incident management. Incident management refers to how incidents are managed across all homeland security activities, including prevention, protection, response, mitigation, and recovery.

This framework forms the basis for interoperability and compatibility that will, in turn, enable a diverse set of public and private organizations to conduct well-integrated and streamlined emergency management and incident response operations. Emergency management is the coordination and integration of all activities necessary to build, sustain, and

NATIONAL INCIDENT MANAGEMENT SYSTEM

December 2008

Homeland Security

Courtesy of the DHS.

TABLE 11.1 Overview of the National Incident Management Framework

What NIMS Is:

- A comprehensive, nationwide, systematic approach to incident management, including the Incident Command System, Multiagency Coordination Systems, and Public Information
- A set of preparedness concepts and principles for all hazards
- Essential principles for a common operating picture and interoperability of communications and information management
- Standardized resource management procedures that enable coordination among different jurisdictions or organizations
- Scalable, so it may be used for all incidents (from day-to-day to large-scale)
- A dynamic system that promotes ongoing management and maintenance

What NIMS Is NOT:

- A response plan
- Only used during large-scale incidents
- A communications plan
- Only applicable to certain emergency management/incident response personnel
- Only the Incident Command System or an organization chart
- A static system

Data from: Department of Homeland Security. (2008). National Incident Management System. Washington, D.C.: Department of Homeland Security. Courtesy of the DHS.

improve the capability to prepare for, protect against, respond to, recover from, or mitigate against threatened or actual natural disasters, acts of terrorism, or other man-made disasters. It does this through a core set of concepts, principles, procedures, organizational processes, terminology, and standard requirements applicable to a broad community of NIMS users.

NIMS is based on the premise that utilization of a common incident management framework will give emergency management/response personnel a flexible but standardized system for emergency management and incident response activities. NIMS is flexible because the system components can be utilized to develop plans, processes, procedures, agreements, and roles for all types of incidents; it is applicable to any incident regardless of cause, size, location, or complexity. Additionally, NIMS provides an organized set of standardized operational structures, which is critical in allowing disparate organizations and agencies to work together in a predictable, coordinated manner.

The components of NIMS are adaptable to any situation, from routine, local incidents to incidents requiring the activation of interstate mutual aid to those requiring a coordinated, federal response, whether planned (e.g., major sporting or community event), predicted (e.g., hurricane) or no-notice (e.g., earthquake). This flexibility is essential for NIMS to be applicable across the full spectrum of potential incidents, including those that require multiagency, multijurisdictional (such as incidents that occur along state or international borders), and/or multi-disciplinary coordination. Flexibility in the NIMS framework facilitates scalability of emergency management and incident response activities, and it also provides for unique implementation in specific areas around the nation.

Flexibility to manage incidents of any size requires coordination, standardization, and a common understanding among emergency management/response personnel and their affiliated organizations. NIMS provides a set of standardized organizational structures that improve integration and connectivity among jurisdictions and disciplines, starting with a common foundation of comprehensive preparedness and planning. Organizations that have adopted the common NIMS framework are able to work together, thereby fostering cohesion among the various organizations involved in all aspects of an incident. NIMS also provides and promotes common terminology, which fosters more effective communication among agencies and organizations responding to an incident.

NIMS integrates existing best practices into a consistent, nationwide, systematic approach to incident management that is applicable at all levels of government, **nongovernmental organizations (NGOs)**, and the private sector, and across functional disciplines in an all-hazards context. Five major components make up this systems approach: (1) preparedness, (2) communications and information management, (3) resource management, (4) command and management, and (5) ongoing management and maintenance.

Preparedness

NIMS provides the mechanisms for emergency management/response personnel and their affiliated organizations to work collectively by offering the necessary tools to enhance preparedness. Preparedness is achieved and maintained through a continuous cycle of planning, organizing, training, equipping, exercising, evaluating, and taking corrective action. Ongoing preparedness efforts among all those involved in emergency management and incident response activities ensure coordination during times of crisis. Moreover, preparedness facilitates efficient and effective emergency management and incident response activities.

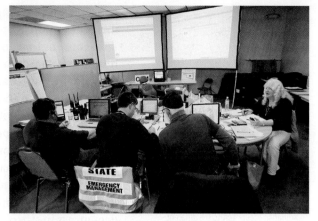

Courtesy of Bob McMillan/FEMA.

This NIMS component describes specific measures and capabilities that emergency management/response personnel and their affiliated organizations should develop and incorporate into their overall preparedness programs to enhance the operational preparedness necessary for all-hazards emergency management and incident response activities. In developing, refining, and expanding preparedness programs and activities within their jurisdictions and/or organizations, emergency management/response personnel should leverage existing preparedness efforts and collaborative relationships to the greatest extent possible.

Communications and Information Management

Effective emergency management and incident response activities rely on flexible communications and information systems that provide a common operating picture to emergency management/response personnel and their affiliated organizations. Establishing and maintaining a common operating picture and ensuring accessibility and interoperability are the principal goals of the communications and information management component of NIMS. Properly planned, established, and applied communications enable the predictable dissemination and sharing of information with all command and support elements and, as appropriate, cooperating agencies and organizations.

Incident communications are facilitated through the development and use of a common communications plans and interoperable communications equipment, processes, standards, and architectures. During an incident, this integrated approach allows operational and support units of the various organizations to maintain communications connectivity and situational awareness. Communications and information management planning should address the incident-related policies, equipment, systems, standards, and training necessary to achieve integrated communications.

Resource Management

Emergency management and incident response activities require carefully managed resources (i.e., personnel, teams, facilities, equipment, and supplies) to meet incident needs. Utilization of the standardized resource management concepts such as typing, inventorying, organizing, and tracking will facilitate the dispatch, deployment, and recovery of resources before, during, and after an incident. Resource management should be flexible and scalable in order to support any incident and be adaptable to changes that may occur during an incident. Efficient and effective deployment of resources requires that the established resource management concepts and principles be used in all phases of emergency management and incident response.

From routine, local incidents to incidents that require a coordinated, federal response, resource management involves the coordination, oversight, and processes that provide timely and appropriate resources during an incident. Resources may support on-scene and command operations through the **Incident Command Post (ICP)** or function within the **Multiagency Coordination System (MACS)** serving at an **Emergency Operations Center (EOC)** or similar site.

As incident priorities are established, needs are identified, and resources are ordered, resource management systems are used to process the resource requests. In the initial stages of an incident, most of the resources requested are addressed locally or through mutual aid agreements and/or assistance agreements. As an incident grows in size or complexity, or if it starts on a large scale, resource needs may have to be met by other sources. In a case of competition for critical resources, MACS may be used to prioritize and coordinate resource allocation and distribution according to resource availability, needs of other incidents, and other constraints and considerations.

Command and Management

The NIMS components discussed previously—preparedness, communications and information management, and resource management—provide a framework to facilitate clear response authority, resource acquisition, and effective management during incident response. The Incident Command System (ICS), MACS, and public information are the fundamental elements of incident management. These elements provide standardization through consistent terminology and established organizational structures. Emergency management and incident response refer to the broad spectrum of activities and organizations providing effective and efficient operations, coordination, and support. Incident management, by contrast, includes directing specific incident operations; acquiring, coordinating, and delivering resources to incident sites; and sharing information about the incident with the public. Taken together, these elements of command and management are the most visible aspects of incident management, typically executed with a sense of urgency. ICS, MACS, and public information will all be described later in more detail.

Ongoing Management and Maintenance

The ongoing management and maintenance component of NIMS contains two parts or "sections": the National Integration Center (NIC) and Supporting Technologies. The NIC section of the NIMS document sets forth the responsibilities of the NIC. The Supporting Technologies section discusses principles necessary to leverage science and technology to improve capabilities and lower costs.

National Integration Center

Homeland Security Presidential Directive 5 required the Secretary of Homeland Security to establish a mechanism for ensuring the ongoing management and maintenance of NIMS, including regular consultation with other federal departments and agencies; state, tribal, and local stakeholders; NGOs; and the private sector. To this end, the Secretary established the NIC to serve as an informational assistance resource for government agencies at all levels, NGOs, and groups in the private sector that are implementing NIMS. The NIC provides strategic direction for and oversight of NIMS, supporting routine maintenance and continuous refinement of the system and its components over the long term. The NIC solicits ongoing feedback from all of its stakeholders, and revisions to NIMS and other issues can be proposed by all NIMS users (including federal, state, local, and tribal governments, as well as the private sector, NGOs, voluntary organizations, academia, nonprofit organizations, and other NIMS-related professional associations).

Additionally, the NIC administers NIMS compliance requirements, facilitates the development of guidance standards for typing and credentialing, supports NIMS training and exercises, and manages the publication of various NIMS-related materials.

Supporting Technologies

Ongoing development in the area of science and technology is integral to the continual improvement and refinement of NIMS. Strategic research and development helps to ensure that NIMS continues to be enhanced. NIMS also relies on scientifically based technical standards that support incident management. Maintaining a focus on appropriate science and technology solutions necessitate a long-term collaborative effort among NIMS partners.

To ensure the effective development of incident-management science and technology solutions, the NIC works in coordination with the DHS's Under Secretary for Science and Technology to continually assess the needs of emergency management/response personnel and their affiliated organizations.[3]

■ Incident Command System (ICS)

Most incidents are managed locally and are typically handled by local communications/dispatch centers and emergency management/response personnel within a single jurisdiction.[4] The majority of responses need go no further. In other instances, incidents that begin with a single response within a single jurisdiction rapidly expand to multidisciplinary, multijurisdictional levels requiring significant additional resources and operational support. The Incident Command System (ICS) provides a flexible core mechanism for coordinated and collaborative incident management, whether for incidents where additional resources are required or are provided from different organizations within a single jurisdiction or outside the jurisdiction, or for complex incidents with national implications (such as an emerging infectious disease or a bioterrorism attack). When a single incident covers a large geographical area, multiple local emergency management and incident response agencies may be required. The responding "agencies" are defined as the governmental agencies, though in certain circumstances NGOs and private-sector organizations may be included. Effective cross-jurisdictional coordination and communication is absolutely critical in this situation.

ICS is a widely applicable management system designed to enable effective, efficient incident management by integrating a combination of facilities, equipment, personnel, procedures, and communications operating within a

Courtesy of NOAA.

common organizational structure. ICS is a fundamental form of management established in a standard format, with the purpose of enabling incident managers to identify the key concerns associated with the incident—often under urgent conditions—without sacrificing attention to any component of the command system.

ICS is used to organize on-scene operations for a broad spectrum of emergencies from small to complex incidents, both natural and man-made. The field response level is where emergency management/response personnel, under the command of an appropriate authority, carry out tactical decisions and activities in direct response to an incident or threat. Resources from federal, state, tribal, or local levels, when appropriately deployed, typically come under the command of the Incident Commander who, through the Incident Command System, determines how they will be deployed.

As a system, ICS is extremely useful: not only does it provide an organizational structure for incident management, but it also guides the process for planning, building, and adapting that structure. Using ICS for every incident or planned event helps hone and maintain skills needed for the more demanding large-scale incidents.

ICS is used by all levels of government—federal, state, tribal, and local—as well as by many NGOs and the private sector. ICS is also applicable across disciplines. It is normally structured to facilitate activities in five major functional areas: command, operations, planning, logistics, and finance/administration. Intelligence/investigations is an optional sixth functional area, which is activated on a case-by-case basis.

Acts of biological, chemical, radiological, and nuclear terrorism may present unique challenges for the traditional ICS structure. Incidents that are not site-specific, are geographically dispersed, or evolve over longer periods of time will require extraordinary coordination among all participants—something the ICS system, if properly utilized, can provide.

Management Characteristics

When the ICS was created, it was based on 14 field-tested management characteristics, each of which applies to the current system. They are as follows:

1. *Common Terminology*

   ICS establishes common terminology that allows diverse incident management and support organizations to work together across a wide variety of incident management functions and hazard scenarios. This common terminology covers the following:
   - Organizational functions: Major functions and functional units with incident management responsibilities are named and defined. Terminology for the organizational elements is standard and consistent.

- Resource descriptions: Major resources—including personnel, facilities, and major equipment and supply items—that support incident management activities are given common names and are "typed" with respect to their capabilities to help avoid confusion and to enhance interoperability.
- Incident facilities: Common terminology is used to designate the various facilities in the vicinity of the incident area that will be used during the course of the incident.

2. *Modular Organization*

The ICS organizational structure develops in a predictable and modular fashion based on the size and complexity of the incident, as well as the specifics of the hazard environment created by the incident. When needed, separate functional elements can be established, each of which may be further subdivided to enhance internal organizational management and external coordination. Responsibility for the establishment and expansion of the ICS modular organization ultimately rests with Incident Command, which bases the evolving ICS structure on the requirements of the situation. As incident complexity increases, the organization expands from the top down as additional functional responsibilities are delegated. Concurrently with structural expansion, the number of management and supervisory positions expands to address the requirements of the incident adequately.

3. *Management by Objectives*

Management by objectives is communicated throughout the entire ICS organization and includes:
- Establishing incident objectives
- Developing strategies based on incident objectives
- Developing and issuing assignments, plans, procedures, and protocols
- Establishing specific, measurable tactics or tasks for various incident management functional activities, and directing efforts to accomplish them, in support of defined strategies
- Documenting results to measure performance and facilitate corrective actions

4. *Incident Action Planning*

Centralized, coordinated incident action planning should guide all response activities. An Incident Action Plan (IAP) provides a concise, coherent means of capturing and communicating the overall incident priorities, objectives, strategies, and tactics in the context of both operational and support activities.

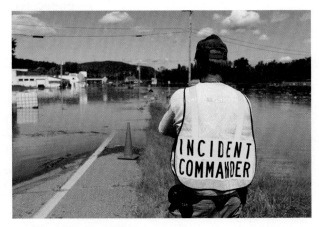

Every incident must have an action plan. However, not all incidents require written plans. The need for written plans and attachments is based on the requirements of the incident and the decision of the Incident Commander (IC) or Unified Command (UC). Most initial response operations are not captured with a formal IAP. However, if an incident is

Courtesy of Robert Rose/FEMA.

likely to extend beyond one operational period, become more complex, or involve multiple jurisdictions and/or agencies, preparing a written IAP will become increasingly important to maintain effective, efficient, and safe operations. (See **Box 11.1**.)

5. *Manageable Span of Control*

Manageable span of control is key for effective and efficient incident management. Supervisors must be able to adequately supervise and control their subordinates, as well as communicate with and manage all resources under their supervision. The type of incident, nature of the task, hazards and safety factors, and distances between personnel and resources all influence span-of-control considerations.

6. *Incident Facilities and Locations*

Various types of operational support facilities are established in the vicinity of an incident, depending on its size and complexity, to accomplish a variety of activities. The Incident Commander will direct the identification and location of facilities based on the requirements of the situation. Typically, designated facilities include incident command posts, bases, camps, staging areas, mass casualty triage areas, point-of-distribution sites, and others as required.

7. *Comprehensive Resource Management*

Maintaining an accurate and up-to-date picture of resource utilization is a critical component of incident management and emergency response. Resources to be identified in this way include personnel, teams, equipment, supplies, and facilities available or potentially available for assignment or allocation. Effective resource management is a major component of NIMS.

8. *Integrated Communications*

Incident communications are facilitated through the development and use of a common communications plan and interoperable communications processes and systems. The ICS has a form (Form 205) that is available to assist in developing a common communications plan. This integrated approach links the operational and support units of the various agencies involved, which is necessary to maintain communications connectivity and discipline and to enable common situational awareness and interaction. Preparedness planning should address the equipment, systems, and protocols necessary to achieve integrated voice and data communications.

BOX 11.1   Advantages of Using Unified Command

- A single set of objectives is developed for the entire incident.
- A collective approach is used to develop strategies to achieve incident objectives.
- Information flow and coordination are improved between all jurisdictions and agencies involved in the incident.

- All agencies with responsibility for the incident have an understanding of joint priorities and restrictions.
- No agency's legal authorities will be compromised or neglected.
- The combined efforts of all agencies are optimized as they perform their respective assignments under a single IAP.

9. *Establishment and Transfer of Command*

The command function must be clearly established from the beginning of incident operations. The agency with primary jurisdictional authority over the incident designates the individual at the scene responsible for establishing command. If and when command is transferred, the process must include a briefing that captures all essential information for continuing safe and effective operations.

10. *Chain of Command and Unity of Command*

Chain of command refers to the orderly line of authority within the ranks of the incident management organization. Unity of command means that all individuals have a designated supervisor to whom they report to at the scene of the incident. These principles clarify reporting relationships and eliminate the confusion caused by multiple, conflicting directives. Incident managers at all levels must be able to direct the actions of all personnel under their supervision.

11. *Unified Command*

In incidents involving multiple jurisdictions—a single jurisdiction with multiagency involvement, or multiple jurisdictions with multiagency involvement—**unified command** allows agencies with different legal, geographic, and functional authorities and responsibilities to work together effectively without affecting individual agency authority, responsibility, or accountability. (See **Box 11.2**.)

12. *Accountability*

Effective accountability of resources at all jurisdictional levels and within individual functional areas during incident operations is essential. To that end, check-in/check-out, incident action planning, unity of command, personal responsibility, span of control, and resource tracking are the principles of accountability, which must be adhered to.

13. *Dispatch/Deployment*

Resources should respond only when requested or when dispatched by an appropriate authority through established resource management systems. Resources not requested must refrain from spontaneous deployment to avoid overburdening the recipient and compounding accountability challenges.

KEY TERM

Unified command (UC)—a structure that brings together the "Incident Commanders" of all major organizations involved in the incident in order to coordinate an effective response while at the same time carrying out their own jurisdictional responsibilities.

BOX 11.2	Comparison of Single IC and UC

Single Incident Commander: The IC is solely responsible (within the confines of his or her authority) for establishing incident objectives and strategies. The IC is directly responsible for ensuring that all functional area activities are directed toward accomplishment of the overall strategy.

Unified Command: The individuals designated by their jurisdictional or organizational authorities (or by departments within a single jurisdiction) must jointly determine objectives, strategies, plans, resource allocations, and priorities, and work together to execute integrated incident operations and maximize the use of assigned resources.

14. *Information and Intelligence Management*

The incident management organization must establish a process for gathering, analyzing, assessing, sharing, and managing incident-related information and intelligence. This is usually done by the operations section (see following text) or it can become its own section if ordered by the Incident Commander. (See **Box 11.3**.)

Incident Command and Command Staff

Incident Command (IC) is responsible for overall management of the incident. Overall management includes command staff assignments required to support the command function. The command and general staffs are typically located at the Incident Command Post (ICP).

The incident command function may be conducted in two general ways. The first is through a single incident commander. When an incident occurs within a single jurisdiction and there is no jurisdictional or functional agency overlap, a single IC should be designated with overall incident management responsibility by the appropriate jurisdictional authority. In some cases where incident management crosses jurisdictional and/or functional agency boundaries, a single IC may be designated, if agreed upon. The designated IC will develop the incident objectives on which subsequent incident action planning will be based.

The second way that incident command may function is through a Unified Command (UC). UC is an important element in multijurisdictional or multiagency incident management. It provides guidelines to enable agencies with different legal, geographic, and functional responsibilities to coordinate, plan, and interact effectively. As a team effort, UC allows all agencies with jurisdictional authority or functional responsibility for the incident to jointly provide management direction through a common set of incident objectives and strategies and a single IAP. Each participating agency maintains its authority, responsibility, and accountability.

Command Staff

KEY TERM
Command staff—Incident Command's staff that provides information, liaison, and safety services for the entire Incident Command and reports directly to the Incident Commander.

In an incident command organization, the **command staff** typically includes a public information officer, a safety officer, and a liaison officer, who all report directly to the IC/UC and may have assistants as necessary (see FIGURE 11.1). Additional positions may be required, depending on the nature, scope, complexity, and location(s)

BOX 11.3   Primary Functions of the Incident Commander (or Unified Commander)

- Have clear authority and know agency policy
- Ensure incident safety
- Establish the ICP
- Set priorities and determine incident objectives and strategies to be followed
- Establish ICS organization needed to manage the incident

- Approve the IAP
- Coordinate command and general staff activities
- Approve resource requests and use of volunteers and auxiliary personnel
- Order demobilization as needed
- Ensure after-action reports are completed
- Authorize information release to the media

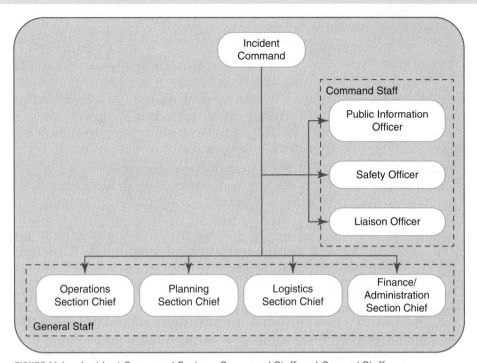

FIGURE 11.1   Incident Command System: Command Staff and General Staff

Reproduced from: Department of Homeland Security. (2008). National Incident Management System. Washington, D.C.: Department of Homeland Security. Courtesy of the DHS.

of the incident(s), or according to specific requirements established by the IC/UC. The following are the duties and functions of the various command staff members:

1. *Public Information Officer*

   The public information officer is responsible for interfacing with the public and media and/or with other agencies with incident-related information requirements. The public information officer gathers, verifies, coordinates, and disseminates accurate, accessible, and timely information on the incident's cause, size, and current situation; resources committed; and other matters of general interest for both internal and external audiences. The public information officer may also perform a key public information-monitoring role. (See **Box 11.4.**) Whether the command structure is single or unified, only one public information officer should be designated per incident. Assistants may be assigned from other involved agencies, departments, or organizations. The IC/UC must approve the release of all incident-related information.

   © wellphoto/ShutterStock, Inc.

2. *Safety Officer*

   The safety officer monitors incident operations and advises the IC/UC on all matters relating to operational safety, including the health and safety of emergency responder personnel. The ultimate responsibility for the safe

> **BOX 11.4**   Primary Functions of the Public Information Officer
>
> - Determine, according to direction from IC, any limits on information release
> - Develop accurate, accessible, and timely information for use in press/media briefings
> - Obtain the IC's approval of news releases
> - Conduct periodic media briefings
> - Arrange for tours and other interviews or briefings that may be required
> - Monitor and forward media information that may be useful to incident planning
> - Maintain current information summaries and/or displays on the incident
> - Make information about the incident available to incident personnel
> - Participate in planning meetings
> - Implement methods to monitor rumor control

conduct of incident management operations rests with the IC/UC and supervisors at all levels of incident management. The safety officer is, in turn, responsible to the IC/UC for the systems and procedures necessary to ensure ongoing assessment of hazardous environments, including the incident safety plan, coordination of multiagency safety efforts, and implementation of measures to promote emergency responder safety, as well as the general safety of incident operations. The safety officer has immediate authority to stop and/or prevent unsafe acts during incident operations. It is important to note that the agencies, organizations, or jurisdictions that contribute to joint safety management efforts do not lose their individual identities or responsibility for their own programs, policies, and personnel. Rather, each contributes to the overall effort to protect all responder personnel involved in incident operations. (See **Box 11.5**.)

3. *Liaison Officer*

   The liaison officer is Incident Command's point of contact for representatives of other governmental agencies, NGOs, and the private sector (with no jurisdiction or legal authority) to provide input on their agency's policies, resource availability, and other incident-related matters. Under either a single IC or a UC structure, representatives from assisting agencies and organizations coordinate through the liaison officer. Agency and organizational representatives assigned to an incident must have the authority to speak for their parent agencies or organizations on all matters, following appropriate consultations with their agency leadership. Assistants and personnel from other agencies or organizations, public or private, involved in incident management activities may be assigned to the liaison officer to facilitate coordination. (See **Box 11.6**.)

4. *Additional Command Staff*

   Additional command staff positions may also be necessary, depending on the nature and location(s) of the incident(s) or specific requirements established by Incident Command. For example, a legal counsel might be assigned to the planning section as a technical specialist or directly to the command staff to advise incident command on legal matters, such as emergency proclamations, the legality of evacuation and quarantine orders, and legal rights and restrictions pertaining to media access. Similarly, a medical

BOX 11.5   Primary Functions of the Safety Officer

- Identify and mitigate hazardous situations
- Create a safety plan
- Ensure safety messages and briefings are made
- Exercise emergency authority to stop and prevent unsafe acts
- Review the IAP for safety implications

- Assign assistants qualified to evaluate special hazards
- Initiate preliminary investigation of accidents within the incident area
- Review and approve the medical plan
- Participate in planning meetings to address anticipated hazards associated with future operations

BOX 11.6   Primary Functions of the Liaison Officer

- Act as a point of contact for agency representatives
- Maintain a list of assisting and cooperating agencies and agency representatives
- Assist in setting up and coordinating interagency contacts
- Monitor incident operations to identify current or potential interorganizational problems

- Participate in planning peetings, provide current resource status, including limitations and capabilities of agency resources
- Provide agency-specific demobilization information and requirements

advisor might be designated to provide advice and recommendations to incident command about medical and mental health services, mass casualty, acute care, vector control, epidemiology, or mass prophylaxis considerations, particularly in response to a bioterrorism incident. In addition, a special needs advisor might be designated to provide expertise regarding communication, transportation, supervision, and essential services for diverse populations in the affected area.

General Staff

The **general staff** is responsible for the functional aspects of the incident command structure. The general staff typically consists of the operations, planning, logistics, and finance/administration section chiefs. The section chiefs may have one or more deputies assigned, with the assignment of deputies from other agencies encouraged in the case of multijurisdictional incidents (see FIGURE 11.2 as an example of how an Incident Command General Staff may be created). The functional sections are discussed more fully next.

1. *Operations Section*

   This section is responsible for all tactical activities focused on reducing the immediate hazard, saving lives and property, establishing situational control, and restoring normal operations. Lifesaving and responder safety will always be the highest priorities and the first objectives in the IAP. (See **Box 11.7** and FIGURE 11.3.)

KEY TERM

General staff—this staff focuses the key functions of incident command, operations, planning, logistics, and finance/administration and reports directly to the Incident Commander.

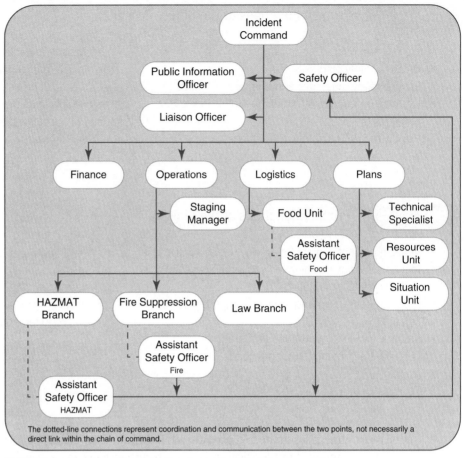

FIGURE 11.2   Example of a More Developed Incident Command Staff

Reproduced from: Department of Homeland Security. (2008). National Incident Management System. Washington, D.C.: Department of Homeland Security. Courtesy of the DHS.

BOX 11.7   Primary Functions of the Operations Section Chief

- Ensure safety of tactical operations
- Manage tactical operations
- Develop operations portions of the IAP
- Supervise execution of operations portions of the IAP
- Request additional resources to support tactical operations
- Approve release of resources from active operational assignments
- Make or approve expedient changes to the IAP
- Maintain close contact with the IC, subordinate operations personnel, and other agencies involved in the incident

2. *Planning Section*

The planning section collects, evaluates, and disseminates incident situation information and intelligence to the IC/UC and incident management personnel. This section then prepares status reports, displays situation information, maintains the status of resources assigned to the incident, and prepares and documents the IAP, based on operations section input and guidance from the IC/UC. (See **Box 11.8**.)

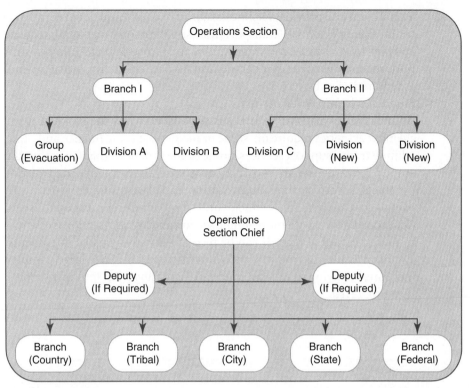

FIGURE 11.3   Operations Section Organized by Geography or Multiple Jurisdictions

Reproduced from: Department of Homeland Security. (2008). National Incident Management System. Washington, D.C.: Department of Homeland Security. Courtesy of the DHS.

BOX 11.8   Primary Functions of the Planning Section Chief

- Collect and manage all incident-relevant operational data
- Supervise preparation of the IAP
- Provide input to the IC and operations in preparing the IAP
- Incorporate traffic, medical, and communications plans and other supporting material into the IAP
- Conduct/facilitate planning meetings
- Reassign out-of-service personnel within the ICS organization already on scene, as appropriate
- Compile and display incident status information
- Establish information requirements and reporting schedules for units (e.g., Resources Unit, Situation Unit)

- Determine need for specialized resources
- Assemble and disassemble task forces and strike teams not assigned to operations
- Establish specialized data collection systems as necessary (e.g., weather)
- Assemble information on alternative strategies
- Provide periodic predictions on incident potential
- Report significant changes in incident status
- Oversee preparation of the demobilization plan

---

3. *Logistics Section*

The logistics section is responsible for all service support requirements needed to facilitate effective and efficient incident management, including ordering resources from off-incident locations (see FIGURE 11.4 as an example).

This section also provides facilities, security (e.g., of the incident command facilities and personnel), transportation, supplies, equipment maintenance and fuel, food services, communications and information technology support, and emergency responder medical services (including inoculations), as required. (See **Box 11.9.**)

4. *Finance/Administration Section*

A finance/administration section is established when the incident management activities require on-scene or incident-specific finance and other administrative support services. Some of the functions that fall within the scope of this section are recording personnel time, maintaining vendor contracts, administering compensation and claims, and conducting an overall cost analysis for the incident. If a separate section is established, close coordination with the planning section and logistics section is essential so that operational records can be reconciled with financial documents. The finance/administration section is a critical part of ICS in large, complex incidents involving significant funding originating from multiple sources. (See **Box 11.10.**)

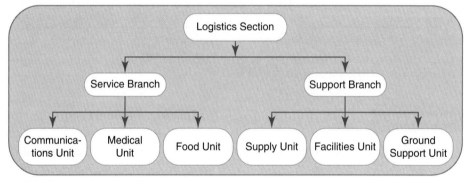

FIGURE 11.4   Logistics Section

Reproduced from: Department of Homeland Security. (2008). National Incident Management System. Washington, D.C.: Department of Homeland Security. Courtesy of the DHS.

BOX 11.9   Primary Functions of the Logistics Section Chief

- Provide all facilities, transportation, communications, supplies, equipment maintenance and fueling, food, and medical services for incident personnel, as well as all off-incident resources.
- Manage all incident logistics
- Provide logistics input to the IAP
- Brief logistics staff as needed

- Identify anticipated and known incident service and support requirements
- Request additional resources as needed
- Ensure and oversee development of traffic, medical, and communications plans as required
- Oversee demobilization of logistics section and associated resources

BOX 11.10   Primary Functions of the Finance/Administration Section Chief

- Manage all financial aspects of an incident
- Provide financial and cost analysis information as requested
- Ensure compensation and claims functions are being addressed relative to the incident
- Gather pertinent information from briefings with responsible agencies
- Develop an operational plan for the finance/administration section and fill section supply and support needs
- Determine the need to set up and operate an incident commissary

- Meet with assisting and cooperating agency representatives as needed
- Maintain daily contact with agency(s) headquarters on financial matters
- Ensure that personnel time records are completed accurately and transmitted to home agencies
- Ensure that all obligation documents initiated at the incident are properly prepared and completed
- Brief agency administrative personnel on all incident-related financial issues needing attention or follow-up
- Provide input to the IAP

Additional Management Structures

The incident command structure also allows for the system to continue working when the incident becomes complex: for instance, if there are multiple incidents handled by a single incident command (incident complex) or if there are multiple incident commands handling one incident (area command). There are also those events requiring the resources of not only multiple local agencies, but also state and federal resources as well (multiagency coordination system). Descriptions of these additional structures or processes (as in the multiagency coordination system) follow:

1. *Incident Complex*

   An incident complex refers to two or more individual incidents located in the same general area assigned to a single IC or UC. When an incident complex is established over several individual incidents, the general guideline is that the previously identified incidents become branches within the operations section of the Incident Management Team (IMT). This provides greater potential for future expansion if required. Each branch thus has the increased flexibility to establish divisions or groups. Additionally, because divisions and groups may already have been established at each of the incidents, the same basic structure can be propagated. If any of the incidents within a complex has the potential to become a large-scale incident, it is best to establish it as a separate incident with its own ICS organization.

2. *Area Command*

   Area command is an organization to oversee the management of multiple incidents handled individually by separate ICS organizations or to oversee the management of a very large or evolving incident engaging multiple incident management teams. An agency administrator/executive or other public official with jurisdictional responsibility for the incident usually makes the decision to establish an area command. An area command is activated only if necessary, depending on the complexity of the incident and incident management span-of-control considerations. Area commands are particularly relevant to incidents that are typically not site-specific, are not immediately identifiable, are geographically dispersed, and evolve over longer periods of time (e.g., public health emergencies, earthquakes, tornadoes, civil disturbances, etc.).

3. *Multiagency Coordination Systems*

Multiagency coordination is a *process* that allows all levels of government and all disciplines to work together more efficiently and effectively. Multiagency coordination occurs across the different disciplines involved in incident management, across jurisdictional lines, or across levels of government.

Multiagency coordination can and does occur on a regular basis whenever personnel from different agencies interact in such activities as preparedness, prevention, response, recovery, and mitigation. Often, cooperating agencies develop a MACS to better define how they will work together in order to work more efficiently; however, multiagency coordination can take place without established protocols. MACS may be put in motion regardless of the location, personnel titles, or organizational structure. MACS include planning and coordinating resources and other support for planned, notice, or no-notice events. MACS define business practices, standard operating procedures, processes, and protocols by which participating agencies will coordinate their interactions. Integral elements of MACS are dispatch procedures and protocols, the incident command structure, and the coordination and support activities taking place within an activated emergency operation center. Fundamentally, MACS provide support, coordination, and assistance with policy-level decisions to the ICS structure managing an incident.

Written agreements allow agencies within the system to conduct activities using established rules, which are often self-defined by the participating organizations. A fully implemented MACS is critical for seamless multiagency coordination activities and essential to the success and safety of the response whenever more than one jurisdictional agency responds. Moreover, the use of MACS is one of the fundamental components of command and management within NIMS, as it promotes scalability and flexibility necessary for a coordinated response.[5]

Chapter Summary

In the aftermath of the September 11, 2001 attacks, the federal government created a National Response Plan that set into motion the National Incident Management System (NIMS) and the Incident Command System (ICS). When Hurricane Katrina struck New Orleans, the National Response Plan was tested and found to be highly deficient, in part because it was not widely implemented and many of those at various levels of government had not been trained on either system. In the aftermath of Hurricane Katrina, NIMS has become the method by which the nation at all levels coordinates the preparations and response throughout the homeland security cycle, and ICS is the means by which local first responders react to all incidents and are then supported by other agencies at all levels of government.

Review/Discussion Questions

1. Explain how the National Incident Management System fits into the homeland security apparatus.

2. What are the five components of NIMS? Explain each in detail.

3. The ICS is said to be based on 14 previously time-tested management characteristics. Name five of these and describe each in detail.

4. Describe the makeup of the ICS, paying special attention to the command staff and the general staff.

Additional Readings

Department of Homeland Security. (2013). *National Incident Management System*. Retrieved online at http://www.fema.gov/national-incident-management-system

Department of Homeland Security. (2013). *Incident Command System*. Retrieved online at http://www.fema.gov/incident-command-system

Walsh, D.W., Hank, T.C., Miller, G.T., Callsen, C.E., Jr., Cilluffo F.J., & Maniscalco, P.M. (2005). *National Incident Management System: Principles and Practice*. Sudbury, MA: Jones and Bartlett Publishers.

Endnotes

1. This section is based on Department of Homeland Security. (2006). *The Federal Response to Hurricane Katrina: Lessons Learned*. Washington, D.C.: U.S. Department of Homeland Security.

2. This section is based on Department of Homeland Security. (2008). *National Incident Management System*. Washington, D.C.: U.S. Department of Homeland Security.

3. See also Department of Homeland Security. (2013). *National Incident Management System*. Retrieved online at http://www.fema.gov/national-incident-management-system

4. This section is based on Department of Homeland Security. (2008). *National Incident Management System*. Washington, DC: U.S. Department of Homeland Security.

5. See also Department of Homeland Security. (2013). *Incident Command System*. Retrieved online at http://www.fema.gov/incident-command-system

Political Responses to Homeland Security

Chapter Outline

- Introduction
- Political Responses
  - Presidential Action
  - Congressional Action
  - State Action
- Chapter Summary

Chapter Objectives

- To help the reader have a better knowledge of presidential responses to terrorism

- To help the reader become more informed about the legislation passed by Congress to deter terrorism or help the country respond to an emergency event such as terrorism or a natural disaster

Introduction

Najibullah Zazi was a legal U.S. resident from Afghanistan living in Denver, Colorado. On September 9, 2009, Zazi drove from his home in Denver, Colorado to New York City with plans to detonate explosives on the New York City subway during rush hour. After being told by a local imam that he was being watched by law enforcement, Zazi aborted his plans and flew back to Denver, where he was arrested days later by the FBI. He was charged on September 24, 2009, with one count of conspiring with others to use weapons of mass destruction, including bombs or other explosives. On February 22, 2010, Zazi pled guilty to conspiring to use weapons of mass destruction, conspiring to commit murder in a foreign country, and providing material support to a terrorist organization. Zazi faces a possible life sentence without possibility of parole for the first two counts, and an additional sentence of 15 years for the third count.

U.S. officials point to the Zazi case as evidence that the expanded surveillance powers given to law enforcement after 9-11 allowed officials to disrupted a possible terrorism plot against the U.S. Authorities first noticed Zazi's suspicious behavior when he traveled to Pakistan, where they caught him talking on his cell phone about chemicals. After that, the FBI agents from the Denver field office were on his trail. The ability of law enforcement to search business records and use roving wiretaps allowed officials to connect Zazi with Al Qaeda and the plot to use explosives in the subway, potentially causing death and injuries to citizens and destruction of property.[1]

Political Responses

Immediately after the attacks of September 2001, there was great public outcry for the president and Congress to pass new laws that would allow law enforcement to investigate the terrorists and to take action against them as a way to deter future acts. The president responded by issuing 24 Homeland Security Presidential Directives (HSPDs) and announced National Security Presidential Directives (NSPDs) on homeland security. Congress also reacted. Between the time of the attacks and January 11th of 2002, 98% of the official business in the House of Representatives and 97% of that in the Senate was related to preventing and investigating terrorism. During that time, over 450 counter-terrorist resolutions were passed, compared with 1,300 in the entire U.S. legislative history.[2] It is clear that as a result of public concern about terrorism, there have been many presidential actions and new laws passed by Congress designed to help keep U.S. citizens safe from future terrorist activity.

KEY TERM
Executive order—a presidential order that directs the executive branch or a specific agency within the executive branch to take some form of action.

KEY TERM
Homeland Security Presidential Directives—similar to an executive order, these directives are focused on directing the various agencies in the executive branch focused on homeland security.

KEY TERM
National Security Presidential Directives—similar to an executive order, these directives are focused on directing the various agencies in the executive branch focused on matters concerning national security.

Presidential Action

Within days of the attacks, President Bush took action by issuing numerous **executive orders**, presidential directives on homeland security (**Homeland Security Presidential Directives,** or **HSPDs**), and **National Security Presidential Directives (NSPDs)** on homeland security. Executive orders are regulations or instructions from the executive office geared toward governing policy. One type of executive order is a Presidential Directive, which is given by a President with the advice and consent of an executive-level agency or department. All executive orders are checked by Congress through their budget authority.[3] NSPDs are directives used to transmit decisions on national security matters. Many of them govern homeland security policy (see **TABLE 12.1**). Although none of these actions create new legislation, per se, they still have the force of law.

One example of presidential activity in homeland security is HSPD-20 / NSPD 51, which deals with the continuity of the federal government in the event of a catastrophic emergency. It describes

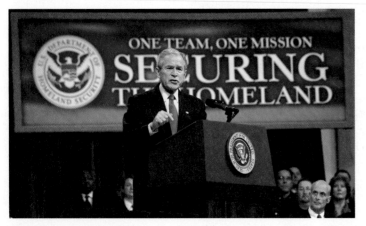

© Mannie Garcia/UPI/Landov.

TABLE 12.1 Examples of President Bush's NSPDs on Homeland Security

National Security Presidential Directive No.	Title	Year of Issue
NSPD 9	Defeating the Terrorist Threat to the U.S.	2001
NSPD 21	Support for Inspections in Iraq	2002
NSPD 26	Intelligence Priorities	2003
NSPD 33	Biodefense for the 21st Century	2004
NSPD 36	U.S. Government Operations in Iraq	2004
NSPD 37	Relating to Support of Iraqi Government	2004
NSPD 38	National Strategy to Secure Cyberspace	2004
NSPD 46	U.S. Strategy and Policy in the War on Terror	2006
NSPD 47	National Strategy for Aviation Security	2006
NSPD 51	National Continuity Policy	2007
NSPD 59	Biometrics for Identification and Screening to Enhance National Security	2008

the need for a cooperative effort among the executive, legislative, and judicial branches of the federal government, coordinated by the president, which will take the place of the nation's regular government if terrorists attack government structures.

In Homeland Security Presidential Directive 3 (HSPD-3), a Homeland Security Advisory System was established as a way to provide information about the risk of a possible terrorist act. In this directive, the president announced a color-coded warning system to indicate the nation's alert level. For example, yellow meant an "elevated or significant" risk of an attack and orange indicated a "high" risk of a terrorist attack.

Homeland Security Presidential Directive 5 (HSPD-5) was announced by President Bush on February 28, 2003. The goal of the directive was to increase the ability of the U.S. to manage emergencies more effectively. The president ordered that there be a single, comprehensive national incident management system, and that all levels of government be involved in it. To do this, the president asked the Secretary of Homeland Security to establish the National Incident Management System (NIMS) as a means to organize the response for possible attacks.[4]

President Bush called for federal initiatives to protect critical infrastructure and described the role of the private sector in that process in HSPD-7.[5] He established a national policy for federal departments and agencies to identify and prioritize critical infrastructure and key resources and to protect these from terrorist attacks.

Courtesy of Jocelyn Augustino/FEMA.

In HSPD-8, President Bush gave the DHS the task of creating a national preparedness system and policies to strengthen all-hazards preparedness capabilities for domestic terrorist attacks, major disasters, and other emergencies. This was modified and updated by President Obama in 2011.

In the National Security Presidential Directive 47 (NSPD 47), along with the Homeland Security Presidential Directive-16 (HSPD-16), President Bush requested that a National Strategy for Aviation Security be created to protect the airlines from terrorist activity.

Executive Order 13340 was an interpretation of the Geneva Conventions concerning detention and interrogation. Through this executive order, prohibitions against abuse and torture could be removed for certain members of Al Qaeda, the Taliban, and other groups the CIA considered to be "unlawful enemy combatants" or who were thought to have information that could be used to detect or prevent terrorist attacks. Because of this action, the CIA was then allowed to detain and interrogate prisoners.

Homeland Security Information Sharing was the focus of Executive Order 13311, along with Executive Order 13356, entitled Strengthening the Sharing of Terrorism Information to Protect Americans. Together, these presidential actions allowed federal agencies to share information concerning potential terrorists and terrorist activities.

President Bush's Homeland Security Advisory Council and Senior Advisory Committee for Homeland Security were established with Executive Order 13260. These groups served as advisors to the president before the Department of Homeland Security was created. Executive Order 13407, the Public Alert and Warning System (along with Homeland Security Presidential Directive #3), established the color-coded warning system used to advise the public of terrorist threat levels.

President Obama has also addressed issues surrounding homeland security. His executive orders relating to homeland security are listed in TABLE 12.2.

TABLE 12.2 President Obama's Executive Orders Relating to Homeland Security

Executive Order 13491: Ensuring Lawful Interrogations—January 22, 2009: Revoked an earlier Executive Order (13440) from the Bush Administration. Specifies that detainees should be treated humanely and not subjected to violence or torture.

Executive Order 13492: Review and Disposition of Individuals Detained at the Guantanamo Bay Naval Base and Closure of Detention Facilities—January 22, 2009: Requires review and disposition of all pending cases against prisoners held by the Department of Defense at Guantanamo Bay Naval Base. Required closure of that detention facility.

Executive Order 13493: Review of Detention Policy Options—January 22, 2009: Created a Special Interagency Task Force on detainee disposition to identify options for detaining individuals captured or detained in connection with counter-terrorism operations.

Executive Order 13526: Classified National Security Information—December 29, 2009: Defines what information may be considered "classified" and under what circumstances.

Executive Order 13527: Establishing Federal Capability for the Timely Provision of Medical Countermeasures Following a Biological Attack—December 30, 2009: Made it a policy to plan and prepare for provision of medical countermeasures in the event of a biological attack.

Executive Order 13539: President's Council of Advisors on Science and Technology—April 21, 2010: Created the President's Council of Advisors on Science and Technology to, among other things, advise the president on policy concerning national and homeland security.

Executive Order 13456: Optimizing the Security of Biological Select Agents and Toxins in the United States—July 2, 2010: To ensure that biological agents shall be secured in a manner appropriate to minimize the risk of misuse, theft, loss, and accidental release.

Executive Order 13549: Classified National Security Information Program for State, Local, Tribal, and Private Sector Entities—August 18, 2010: Created a Classified National Security Information program to safeguard and govern access to classified national security information shared by the federal government with state, local, tribal, and private sector entities.

Executive Order 13553: Blocking Property of Certain Persons with Respect to Serious Human Rights Abuses by the Government of Iran and Taking Certain Other Actions—September 28, 2010: Prevented property in the U.S. from being transferred to an official of Iran's government, or a person who ordered or directed the commission of serious human rights abuses against people in Iran.

Executive Order 13558: Export Enforcement Coordination Center—November 9, 2010: Ordered the creation of an interagency Federal Export Enforcement Coordination Center that would share information about detection, prevention, disruption, investigation, and prosecution of activities that may threaten national security.

Executive Order 13567: Periodic Review of Individuals Detained at Guantanamo Bay Naval Station Pursuant to the Authorization for Use of Military Force—March 7, 2010: Ordered a review of certain detainees being held at the Guantanamo Bay facility.

Executive Order 13584: Developing an Integrated Strategic Counterterrorism Communications Initiative and Establishing a Temporary Organization to Support Certain Government-Wide Communications Activities Directed Abroad—September 9, 2011: To reinforce communications efforts about counter-terrorism efforts directed to audiences outside the U.S. and targeted against violent and terrorist organizations.

Executive Order 13587: Structural Reforms to Improve the Security of Classified Networks and the Responsible Sharing and Safeguarding of Classified Information—October 7, 2011: Ordered reforms to ensure sharing of information on computer networks are protected for privacy and civil liberties.

Executive Order 13597: Establishing a Visa and Foreign Visitor Processing Goals and the Task Force on Travel and Competitiveness—January 19, 2012: Ordered the Department of Homeland Security to maintain a process for coordinating and implementing proposals to enhance and expedite travel to, and arrival into, the U.S. by foreign nationals.

Congressional Action

Congress has passed many new laws related to terrorism since September 2011. The most recognized was entitled the Uniting and Strengthening America by Providing

KEY TERM

USA PATRIOT Act—an act of Congress passed in 2001, six weeks after the 9-11 terrorist attacks, that gave new tools to investigate potential terroristic threats in the United States.

Appropriate Tools Required to Intercept and Obstruct Terrorism, more commonly known as the **USA PATRIOT Act.**

Immediately following the terrorist attacks of 9-11, President Bush and Attorney General John Ashcroft asked Congress for new laws that would increase the ability of law enforcement to gather intelligence related to terrorism. They requested that Congress pass a bill that gave law enforcement the ability to use roving wiretaps, nation-wide search warrants, wider electronic access, Internet disclosure, immigrant detention, consolidated appeals, foreign wiretap evidence, define the term "terrorist," and tougher penalties for convicted terrorists.[6] The proposed bill that emerged was the USA PATRIOT Act. The intent of the Patriot Act was to grant law enforcement officials more authority to investigate and prosecute those who were responsible for the terrorist attacks on America and to protect the country from future attacks.

Courtesy of Barry Bahler/DHS.

At first, both Republican and Democratic members of Congress were hesitant to support the bill because of concerns related to privacy and civil liberties. They were apprehensive about proposals allowing government officials to track emails and other electronic communications, and if law enforcement should be permitted to "watch over the shoulders" of computer users. They claimed that some provisions were too vague and sweeping, and therefore could be abused by law enforcement.

But other members supported the proposal. The FBI and other law enforcement groups argued it was necessary that they had more advanced technology to help infiltrate terrorist cells and prevent future attacks.[7] The Bush administration pushed hard for their proposal, and eventually both the House and Senate agreed to the bill.[8] President Bush signed the anti-terrorism legislation into law (HR 3162 / PL 107-56) on October 26, 2001.

The final bill contained 10 titles and over 1,000 sections. It addressed issues such as intelligence, investigations, controlled substances, and financial transactions (see **TABLE 12.3**). It contained much of what Attorney General Ashcroft and President Bush requested, including authority for the government to obtain nationwide search warrants and roving wiretaps to conduct secret searches of suspects' property, and to detain immigrants indefinitely if they were viewed as national security threats. It also strengthened money-laundering laws and removed the statute of limitations on some terrorism crimes. It modified or amended over a dozen existing federal statutes and greatly expanded the powers of the executive branch of government and law enforcement officials. Some of the most controversial provisions (i.e., wiretaps) were set to expire on December 31, 2005.

In 2003, only 18 months after the Patriot Act was passed, the President and some members of Congress sought to give law enforcement more tools for investigating suspected terrorists. However, some members preferred to take back some provisions of the original law that they believed could infringe on civil liberties. Because of the controversy, Congress could not agree to revise the act. But they did expand the

TABLE 12.3 Intelligence Law Provisions

Focal Area	What the Law Changed
Director of National Intelligence	Created a Director of National Intelligence (DNI) to be the head of the U.S. intelligence community who would serve as the principal adviser to the president, the National Security Council, and the Homeland Security Council.
Information Sharing	The DNI would establish a system to share information between agencies, which included purchasing necessary technology to allow for easy communication.
Improving Analysis and Coordination	Created the National Intelligence Council and the National Counterterrorism Center as part of the DNI Office to analyze intelligence on international terrorism and counter-terrorism. Also created the National Counter-Proliferation Center to analyze intelligence on the proliferation of weapons of mass destruction.
Civil Liberties	Established the Civil Liberties Protection Office to ensure that the civil liberties of U.S. citizens were protected.
Other Intelligence Changes	The DNI would develop educational materials and linguistic training for the intelligence community to improve their ability to gather information on terrorists and interpret intercepted communications. The law required the DNI to ensure that the intelligence community would monitor unclassified information on national security threats, establish a National Intelligence Reserve Corps comprised of former intelligence employees who could be called to work during a national emergency; and mandated the CIA to develop a more effective foreign language program and to hire agents with more diverse backgrounds, including Arab or Middle-Eastern.
Transportation Security	The Secretary of DHS would create a national strategy to improve transportation security and create a recovery plan in the case of an attack. The Secretary would also begin biometric screening systems at airports that would include methods such as retinal or iris scanning, fingerprints, or face recognition. The TSA would test a "no fly" list. Employees of airports, airlines, and security services would also have to undergo screening. The TSA was required to create a plan for screening all passengers and their luggage for explosives. The TSA would have to make it easier for air marshals to protect their anonymity. New screening of passengers and crew members on cruise ships would be created.
Border Security and Immigration	DHS would add 2,000 border patrol agents every year from 2006 to 2010 and 800 new immigration investigators; it would provide 40,000 new beds in detention facilities to house illegal aliens; it was authorized to use unmanned planes and other technologies to patrol the border; expanded the number of U.S. immigration officers in foreign airports; created a new visa and passport security program; created a Human Smuggling and Trafficking Center; barred any foreign national from entering the U.S. who had committed torture or other atrocities abroad.

Continued

TABLE 12.3 Intelligence Law Provisions (Continued)

Focal Area	What the Law Changed
Terrorism Prevention	The law amended the Foreign Intelligence Surveillance Act (FISA) to allow the FBI to conduct surveillance on a single terrorist, otherwise known as a "lone wolf"; terrorist suspects would be denied bail and held in jail until trial, unless they could prove they were not flight risks or a danger to society; made it a crime to provide support (money, lodging, advice, training) to anyone involved in a potential terrorist act; made it a crime to use the mail to carry out an attack with a weapon of mass destruction; expanded criminal penalties for production, possession, and use of radiological explosive devices, or "dirty bombs."
Financial Provisions	Authorized $35.5 million to support the Financial Crimes Enforcement Network to fund a program designed to analyze data from financial institutions; required the Treasury Department to create a national strategy for combating money laundering; authorized the Bureau of Engraving and Printing to print foreign currency and other sensitive documents of foreign governments as a way to test anti-counterfeiting measures.
Foreign Policy Provisions	Declared that the U.S. should help Pakistan control its territorial borders and waived restrictions on foreign assistance to Pakistan through fiscal 2006; authorized funds for assisting Afghanistan in fiscal 2005 and 2006; reiterated U.S. support of the U.N. Human Rights Commission; declared that the U.S. would work toward creating a "Middle East Free Trade Area."
Homeland Security	Authorized mutual aid between local governments and regional authorities in the Washington area that could be used by regional or local authorities to share emergency services or resources in responding to a terrorist attack, which included provisions aimed at improving emergency communications systems; called for a greater emphasis on providing grants to high-threat areas while guaranteeing a minimum to all states; authorized a study to determine if DHS could develop a homeland security warning system to disseminate information; expanded the duties of the counter-narcotics office to allow the director to serve on the Joint Terrorism Task Force; created an Office of Geospatial Management in DHS to coordinate mapping, satellite analysis, and other geographic technologies.

Data from: "Details of the Intelligence Overhaul Law." In *CQ Almanac 2004*, 60th ed., 11-9-11-13. Washington, DC: *Congressional Quarterly*, 2005. Retrieved from http://library.cqpress.com/cqalmanac/cqal04-836-24353-1084612

FBI's ability to access financial records when investigating suspected terrorists with another new bill (under a law reauthorizing intelligence programs for fiscal 2004).[9]

Many of the controversial provisions in the original Patriot Act were to be phased out in December 2005. At that time, President Bush and the Republicans in Congress sought to make the surveillance provisions of the original law permanent and give law enforcement additional powers. But other members of Congress sought increased protections for civil liberties as well as establishment of additional time limits on some of the more contentious parts of the act. Congress compromised by supporting a bill (HR 3199 / PL 109-177) that gave the FBI power to seek "roving wiretaps" and get access to business records. The bill also included a 4-year extension of a provision in the intelligence law (PL 108-458) that allowed law enforcement to seek warrants against "lone-wolf" terrorists who were acting alone and not associated with a foreign power.[10]

The law made 14 provisions of the original Patriot Act permanent. The law:

- Allowed law enforcement to use wiretaps and other surveillance techniques to investigate suspected acts of terrorism such as computer fraud.
- Allowed law enforcement to share information on matters of national security.
- Made it easier to issue orders for *pen register* and *trap-and-trace devices* that could be used to track telephone calls and Internet communications.
- Extended the length of time for the use of wiretaps and search warrants from 90 days to 120 days, with possible extensions of up to 1 year.
- Allowed officials to use search warrants to get access to voice mail.
- Permitted Internet providers to disclose customer records to law enforcement in emergency situations.
- Allowed law enforcement to intercept electronic communications if the owner of a computer system believed someone was hacking into his system from the outside.
- Allowed federal judges with jurisdiction over a particular investigation to issue search warrants for electronic evidence stored anywhere in the country.
- Provided for civil suits against unlawful disclosure of information obtained through the law's wiretapping authority, while giving immunity to those who assist in the carrying out of investigations under the law.

The new law also added some additional safeguards to the legislation, including provisions to:

- Require the FBI director or deputy to sign off on applications for court orders for library, bookstore, firearm sales, tax return, and educational and medical records.
- Allow those ordered to turn over business records, credit reports, or telephone records under a National Security Letter (a letter from a U.S. government agency that demands information without a search warrant because it is related to national security) to contact an attorney and challenge the order in court.
- Require the government to notify the subject of a "sneak and peek" search (conducted secretly without notifying the subject of the search) within 30 days, with a possible extension.
- Require that investigators seeking a roving wiretap order identify the specific target or evidence they seek, and that they notify the court within 10 days after beginning surveillance of any new phone.[11]

In 2009, the USA PATRIOT Act was scheduled for reauthorization again. This time, Congress extended the three expiring sections of the Patriot Act. The first of the three provisions, for "business records," gave the FBI the authority to get a court order for "any tangible thing," such as a list of books someone was reading, or even blood or DNA. This could happen when officials claimed they would need such evidence as part of an investigation. The second provision, for "roving wiretaps," provided investigators the authority to obtain court orders to track terrorism suspects who used various types of communication methods such as multiple telephones, cellular phones, or Internet connections. The third was the "lone wolf" provision, which allowed investigators to seek warrants from the Foreign Intelligence Surveillance Court to spy on suspected terrorists who were not connected with a foreign power or other recognized organization. [12]

President Obama supported the reauthorization with as few changes as possible. The American Civil Liberties Union and some members of Congress argued that the laws gave the FBI powers that directly contravened the Fourth Amendment's protections against unreasonable search and seizure. [13]

In 2011, the USA PATRIOT Act faced renewal again. In S 990 (PL 112-14), the PATRIOT Sunsets Extension Act of 2011, the original law was once again extended, this time until 2015. Provisions concerning roving electronic surveillance orders and requests for business records and other tangible things were extended. The "lone wolf" provision was extended until June 1, 2015.

107th Congress (2001–02)

In addition to the Patriot Act, Congress passed other terrorist-related bills in the 107th Congress. One law was the Aviation Security Act (S 1447 / HR 2951 / PL 107-71). This act created the TSA and defined its responsibilities. Additionally, the new law made passenger screening at airports a responsibility of the federal government; prior to this, passenger security was the responsibility of the airlines.

After the anthrax attacks on members of Congress, a proposal was made that would direct the Secretary of Health and Human Services to further develop and implement a coordinated and comprehensive strategy to prepare and respond to a possible bioterrorism attack or other public health emergency. This was called the Public Health Security and Bioterrorism Preparedness and Response Act of 2002 (HR 3448 / PL 107-188). The act called for close coordination with the states. Moreover, Congress passed an appropriations bill that provided $2.5 billion for the purchase of vaccines and antibiotics to be used during a bioterrorism attack. [14]

The Enhanced Border Security and Visa Entry Reform Act (HR 3525 / PL 107-173) was a bill to increase the number of Immigration and Naturalization Service (INS) investigators and inspectors by 200 full-time employees above the number authorized by the Patriot Act. It also directed U.S. law enforcement groups to share alien admissibility- and deportation-related information with the INS.

Two bills dealt with ports and port security during this session. One of those was S 1214 (PL 107-777), the Maritime Transportation Security Act of 2002. This bill directed the Secretary of Transportation to identify those vessel types and U.S. port facilities that pose a high risk of being involved in a transportation security incident. The Secretary would then need to prepare a national Maritime Transportation Security Plan for deterring and responding to a possible security incident at U.S. ports.

The second bill that dealt with port security was S 1215 (PL 107-295), which was passed to increase security at U.S. ports. For the first time, a comprehensive anti-terrorism plan would be developed for the nation's 361 commercial seaports. It also expanded the role played by the Coast Guard in port security following any attacks (see **Box 12.1**).

| BOX 12.1 | Provisions of the Port Security Act |

- Required the Coast Guard to conduct assessments of U.S. ports, vessels, and other facilities such as nuclear power plants or chemical facilities that could be vulnerable to terrorist attack. These reports will be used to develop local and national security plans, as well as customized plans for specific facilities and vessels identified as vulnerable.
- Created local security advisory committees at every port to coordinate planning between law enforcement, intelligence agencies, the Customs Service, Coast Guard, immigration, port authorities, shipping companies, and port workers.
- Directed the Coast Guard to establish teams that could be deployed quickly in the event of a terrorist threat or criminal action.
- Authorized armed Coast Guard personnel to act as "sea marshals" to board incoming vessels to prevent or respond to acts of terrorism.
- Created a new grant program to assist ports in upgrading port security.
- Authorized $15 million a year for research and development of technologies to assist the Customs Service in targeting suspicious cargo and detecting explosives, chemical and biological agents, and nuclear materials.

- Asked the Transportation Department to develop and issue a new national transportation security card that would allow eligible port workers, merchant mariners, and truck drivers to work in "secure" areas of ports and other transportation facilities.
- Required the Coast Guard to assess security measures at foreign ports and authorized them to stop vessels from entering U.S. ports if they came from a foreign port that failed to meet security standards.
- Required the Transportation Department to develop and maintain an anti-terrorism cargo identification, tracking, and screening system for containerized cargo shipped through U.S. ports. It also required the department to develop standards for container seals and locks as well as a system to detect tampering.
- Required the Transportation Department to establish a program to collect and analyze information concerning any vessel operating in U.S. waters.

Reproduced from: "Law Calls for Tighter Port Security" In *CQ Almanac 2002*, 58th ed., 19-5-19-7. Washington, DC: *Congressional Quarterly*, 2003. Retrieved from http://library.cqpress.com/cqalmanac/cqal02-236-10372-664261.

The Terrorism Risk Insurance Act (TRIA) of 2002 (PL 107-297) was intended to help stabilize the commercial property and casualty insurance markets after the attacks in September 2001. In the time after the attacks, the insurance industry was in disorder because of the extreme number of claims made by those who lost loved ones, were injured, or who suffered property damage. Insurers claimed they would no longer offer terrorism insurance unless the federal government agreed to share the risk. Without terrorism insurance coverage, mortgages for big projects would have been too costly for builders. Congress agreed to provide help to the industry and passed legislation that mandated that insurers must provide coverage against terrorist acts, but made the federal government responsible for 90% of claims above $15 billion. The government's responsibility topped out at $100 billion.[15] The law provided for a 3-year program that would give private insurance companies a transition period in which they could develop pricing and risk models.

President Bush supported the legislation, saying, "The Terrorism Risk Insurance Act will provide coverage for catastrophic losses from potential terrorist attacks. Should terrorists strike America again, we have a system in place to address financial losses and get our economy back on its feet as quickly as possible. With this new law, builders and investors can begin construction in real estate projects that have been stalled for too long and get our hardhats back to work."[16]

108th Congress (2003–04)

After the 9/11 Commission reported on the failure of U.S. intelligence to detect and deter the terrorist attacks, it was clear that the government needed to improve the cooperation between intelligence agencies so that intelligence would be more effectively shared. Congress sent President Bush a bill to overhaul and reorganize the U.S. intelligence community. The new law (PL 108-458) created the position of Director of National Intelligence (DNI) who would serve as head of the U.S. intelligence community, as well as the principal adviser to the president, the National Security Council, and the Homeland Security Council. The director would be appointed by the president and require confirmation by the Senate. The director would ensure that all federal agencies, the Joint Chiefs, and relevant committees of Congress had access to all necessary information. The DNI would have access to all national intelligence that had been acquired by any federal department. The bill also authorized additional Border Patrol agents, created uniform security clearance procedures, and included provisions related to transportation security and efforts to combat money laundering and terrorist financing.

In addition to changes in the intelligence agencies, Congress also passed the Identity Theft Penalty Enhancement Act (HR 1731 / PL 108-275) that established new penalties for stealing someone's identity. It also altered the existing identity theft prohibition to include acts of domestic terrorism.

Another effort by Congress in this session was Project Bioshield (S 15 / PL 108-276). This refers to the Bush administration's initiative to permit the government to develop and stockpile vaccines and medications to be used in the case of a bioterrorism attack. The bill authorized the Secretary of Health and Human Services to conduct research regarding countermeasures such as a drug, biological product, or other device that could be used to treat, identify, or prevent harm from any biological, chemical, radiological, or nuclear weapon.[17]

The Terrorism Insurance bill passed in the earlier session (PL 107-297) was set to expire in 2005. Insurers and the real estate industry won a 2-year extension through December 31, 2007 (PL 109-144), which also raised the insurers' threshold to $50 million in 2006 and $100 million in 2007.[18]

109th Congress (2005–06)

In the 109th Congress, the members worked on changes to immigration and illegal entry of aliens and terrorists. One bill they passed was the Secure Fence Act (HR 6061 / PL 109-367). This new law directed the Secretary of DHS to take actions to achieve more effective border surveillance through better use of personnel and technology, including physical infrastructure enhancements as a way to prevent unlawful border entry. The bill also facilitated border protection by U.S. Customs and Border Protection by adding additional checkpoints.

In another bill (HR 5441 / PL 109-295), Congress passed a $34.8 billion fiscal spending bill that included $1.8 billion in funds for border security. Most of the emergency funding—$1.2 billion—was intended for the construction of fencing along the U.S.–Mexico border. This was described as a physical and "virtual" barrier, using sensors and cameras in remote areas.

The Secretary of Energy was instructed to increase the safety and security of nuclear facilities from deliberate attacks in the Energy Policy Act (HR6 / PL 109-190). In this new law, Congress mandated the Secretary to analyze the security of existing nuclear power plants and to consider the viability of a private security force for defending nuclear plants from possible threats. Another provision in this bill established the Task Force on Radiation Source Protection and Security that would evaluate the security of radiation sources from potential terrorist threats. It would also require that anyone given unescorted access to facilities must have a criminal history and fingerprint check.

The Coast Guard and Maritime Transportation Act (HR 889 / PL 109-204) authorized the Secretary of Transportation, during an act of terrorism, to order the Coast Guard Ready Reserve members to active duty. The Act also directed the Coast Guard Commandant to report on the potential costs and effectiveness of developing technology that could identify inbound vessels and their cargo for any possible threats to national security before they reach U.S. ports.

Congress passed a bill aimed at security in U.S. ports, and President Bush signed it on October 13 (HR 4954 / PL 109-347). In it, Congress authorized over $2 billion over 5 years for port and container security programs. It required the 22 largest U.S. ports to scan all incoming containers for radiation, established protocols to resume trade in the event of a catastrophic incident that suspended trade, and offered new benefits for trusted shipping companies. The effectiveness of each port's security plans would be verified at least twice a year, including at least one unannounced inspection. Other provisions established a network of Interagency Operational Centers at appropriate seaports, and created a program to train port security officers, law enforcement, and the private sector to prepare for and respond to port security incidents.[19]

110th Congress (2007–08)

During the 110th Congress, the members passed the Court Security Improvement Act of 2007 (HR 660 / PL 110-177). The law required the U.S. Marshals Service to consult with the Judicial Conference regarding security requirements for the courts. It also provided additional funds to hire new deputy U.S. Marshals to provide security for the courts, and prohibited possession of dangerous weapons in federal courts.

The Terrorism Risk Insurance Program Reauthorization Act of 2007 (HR 2761 / PL 110-160) passed Congress in this session. The law reauthorized the Terrorism Risk Insurance Act for 7 years. It redefined an act of terrorism to eliminate the requirement that the individual or individuals committing a terrorist act be acting on behalf of any foreign person or foreign interest. The new program required insurance firms that sold commercial property and casualty insurance to offer clients insurance coverage for damages caused by foreign terrorist attacks. The government would pay 90% of claims arising from a terrorist attack once insurers' aggregate losses exceeded a certain threshold, beginning at $15 billion and rising annually after that. The government's responsibility was capped at $100 billion per year. President Bush signed it into law on December 26, 2007.[20]

The safety of transportation was the focus of one bill during this session, called The Railroad Safety Enhancement Act of 2008 (HR 2095 / PL 110-432). The bill authorized appropriations for railroad safety by requiring the Federal Railroad Administration to make safety in railroad transportation the highest priority and to develop a long-term strategy for improving railroad safety.

Congress passed legislation (HR 556 / PL 110-49) to revise the process for reviewing foreign investments that might affect U.S. national security. The law made the Committee on Foreign Investment in the U.S. (CFIUS) permanent. The committee would review investments to determine if there were any national security implications of any transaction that might result in foreign control of a company engaged in interstate commerce. CFIUS was also required to complete an investigation if a review found that the transaction threatened to impair national security, if the transaction involved a company owned by a foreign government, or if it involved critical infrastructure and national security concerns. The committee would notify Congress on any investigation, as well as submit an annual report.[21]

After the 9/11 Commission released its report in 2004, Congress passed an overhaul of the U.S. intelligence community (PL 108-458). It created a new director of national intelligence to oversee intelligence agencies, authorized additional Border Patrol agents, created uniform security clearance procedures, and included provisions related to transportation security, efforts to combat money laundering, and terrorist financing. But this law did not include all of the commission's recommendations. During the 110th Session, Congress passed a bill (HR 1) that made the remaining recommendations law. The bill required that federal grants for first responders be distributed based on risk, expanded the scrutiny of cargo for nuclear devices, and created a new grant program to improve emergency communications between agencies.[22] President Bush signed the bill on August 5, 2007 (PL 110-53). More details of the bill are listed in **Box 12.2**.

After Bush's policy of surveillance on Americans without a court order became public, there was public outcry for legislation to ban such activity. However, the administration submitted a proposal for a new law, arguing that it was necessary for the government to conduct counter-terrorism-related electronic surveillance and have the ability to spy without warrants on foreign-to-foreign communications

---

BOX 12.2   Provisions of the Homeland Security Bill

- **Grant distribution:** changed the distribution of the homeland security grant programs by reducing the minimum amounts guaranteed for each state and requiring that the rest of the money be distributed on the basis of risk.
- **Intelligence budget:** required the government to disclose the total amount appropriated each year for intelligence programs.
- **Cargo screening:** required all U.S.-bound seaborne cargo containers loaded in foreign ports to be scanned.
- **Aviation security:** required that, within 3 years of enactment, all air cargo placed on passenger aircraft be screened.
- **Surface transportation:** authorized $4 billion over 4 years for rail, transit, and bus security grant programs; also required the development of risk assessments and security plans, set training requirements for workers, and extended whistleblower protections to transit employees.

- **Emergency communications:** established a grant program to improve the interoperability of state and local emergency communications.
- **Civil liberties:** the Privacy and Civil Liberties Oversight Board was made an independent agency in the executive branch.
- **Liability shield:** provided immunity from civil lawsuits in federal, state, and local courts for individuals who in good faith reported suspicious activities relating to passenger safety. Officials who responded to their warning also received immunity.
- **Visa waivers:** expanded the visa-waiver program, under which nationals of certain allied countries could enter the country for short periods without visas.
- **Nonproliferation:** repealed limits on the aid that could be given to former Soviet states for nuclear nonproliferation and anti-terrorism activities.

that passed through the United States. In response, Congress passed a bill to loosen rules for electronic surveillance (S 1927 / PL 110-56).

111th Congress (2009–10)

In the 111th Session, Congress passed a bill to permit the Commissioner of U.S. Customs and Border Protection to convert an employee serving overseas on a limited appointment a permanent appointment if they prove successful in that capacity. The bill was called the U.S. Customs and Border Protection Agents Employment Act (HR 1517/ PL 111-252).

In the Pre-disaster Hazard Mitigation Act of 2010, Congress agreed to increase the amount of money guaranteed to each state under the pre-disaster hazard mitigation program (HR 1746 / PL 111-351). This would allow states to help prevent and prepare for possible terrorist attacks in their local jurisdictions.

Congress also agreed to expand the food safety activities of the Secretary of Health and Human Services. Under the new law, records related to food would be inspected more often; there would be improvements to guarantee the safety of imported food; and there would be more capacity to detect and respond to food safety problems. The name of this bill was the FDA Food Safety Modernization Act (HR 2751 / PL 111-353).

Another example of action taken by Congress to keep the public safe was HR 3360 / PL 111-207, entitled the Cruise Vessel Security and Safety Act. In this law, minimum training standards were set and new certification required for passenger vessel security personnel and law enforcement officials focused on the prevention, detection, evidence preservation, and reporting of criminal activities in the international maritime environment.

State Action

After the 9-11 terrorist attacks on New York and Washington, the federal government launched new agencies and policies to help the government prepare for, and respond to, future terrorist activities and natural disasters. State governments did the same. State officials realized their agencies were most likely to be the first to respond to an emergency and therefore had to be prepared to manage the immediate response. In the time since the 9-11 attacks, every state has reviewed their existing emergency response plans and either developed new agencies and policies, or updated and modified existing ones, to prepare officials and citizens for what may lie ahead.

It is fundamental that cities prepare for emergencies because they are most at risk to be targeted in an attack. To date, terrorist attacks have been an urban phenomenon and they have been highly localized events. Local governments are likely to be the first on the scene of an emergency and therefore in charge of managing the essential services such as police, fire, medical, and other emergency service personnel.[23] Additionally, cities have the fiscal duty to pay for these services. This all means they must be ready for all types of urgent situations.

© LM Otero/AP Images.

Knowing this, state and local governments have developed and implemented their own security plans. They assigned police to protect any critical infrastructure that may be the target of an attack, bought new equipment, and trained their fire, police, and medical communities. However, Congress provided only limited funds for these activities, putting this burden primarily on the states. Many states found it difficult to fund such programs. To make matters worse, while Bush created the Homeland Security Council in the Executive Office, there were no representatives from state or local governments on it.[24] The lack of cooperation between the state and federal government when it came to homeland security quickly became readily apparent.

Consequently, it became evident that it was essential to establish a new approach to intergovernmental cooperation in homeland security, and that existing gaps in the provision of services by federal, state, and local agencies had to be filled in a more coordinated fashion. The tasks related to emergency response now had to be interconnected between the federal, state, and local governments in order to provide a comprehensive response in a way that had not been done before. It was now essential that all states coordinate their activities with other agencies within the state, in other states, and the federal government. This required that changes be made in the way governments were organized, how agencies communicated with others, and the funding structure.

Many changes were made and since then, there have been improvements to intergovernmental relations (IGR) surrounding homeland security activities. The federal government is now providing more grant money to states allowing them to develop response plans, purchase equipment, and provide necessary training. In the Patriot Act, the Office of Domestic Preparedness was given the duty to oversee grants to state and local governments that would help fund training for, and plan responses to, terrorist acts. Two of those grants were the State Homeland Security Grant Program (SHSGP) and the Urban Area Security Initiative (UASI).[25] In the beginning, there were problems in getting the money to the state and local governments, but issues were addressed and the funds found their way to the states.[26]

With the additional funds, states continue to develop new ways to respond to emergencies. The particular response plans developed by each state will vary, depending upon the characteristics of the state. In the state of Florida, for example, Governor Jeb Bush took only 1 month after the 9-11 attacks to prepare an Executive Order that created seven Regional Domestic Security Task Forces that were placed under the Florida Department of Law Enforcement. It is now their responsibility to "coordinate responses to terrorist incidents, endure proper training for state and local personnel, and collect and disseminate terrorist intelligence."[27] The task forces are comprised of police chiefs, health officials, state and local government officials, and executives from private agencies. The task forces answer to the State Emergency Response Team.[28]

In New York, officials created the New York State Division of Homeland Security and Emergency Services in 2010. Comprised of five offices, it is geared toward improving the state's response to a terrorist

© Matt Rourke/AP Images.

attack or natural disaster. They provide training and disseminate information as a way to improve readiness, response, and recovery capabilities of state officials, and provide assistance with federal grants. They also provide direct assistance to the public though weather, travel, fire, and safety alerts, as well as safety information. It also makes it easy for citizens to report suspected terrorist activities through their website.

Other states have developed various agency structures, a few of which are outlined in **Box 12.3.**

BOX 12.3   Examples of State Homeland Security Agencies

New York State Division of Homeland Security and Emergency Services

The responsibilities for this agency were divided into five offices:

1. Office of Counter Terrorism (OCT): created as part of a merger that resulted in the Division of Homeland Security and Emergency Services; OCT supports initiatives by federal, state, local, tribal, and private sector agencies to prevent, protect against, and prepare for acts of terrorism. While OCT is not a law enforcement agency itself, the agents work closely with law enforcement to help mitigate and respond to threats. Units within the OCT include:
   a. Intelligence and Analysis Unit: analyzes and disseminates information concerning terrorist threats.
   b. Public Safety Unit: works with first responders regarding preparedness and response activities; coordinates actions toward security on the northern border.
   c. Critical Infrastructure Protection Unit: oversees actions geared toward protecting critical infrastructure between agencies in the public and private sectors; includes the Automated Critical Asset Management System that collects data on the use of infrastructures, assesses vulnerabilities, and develops plans for recovery in the event of an attack.
   d. Federal Grant Program Administration Unit: the administrative agency for federal grants; manages grants process and requirements.
2. Office of Cyber Security: oversees development of cyber security and GIS training for state and local government employees.
3. Office of Emergency Management: provides training and exercises to first responders so they are ready for an event.
4. Fire Prevention and Control: Provides training for firefighters, first responders, and emergency responders.
5. Office of Interoperable and Emergency Communications: responsible for the effective communications training in the case of an event.

Nebraska Emergency Management Agency

This office was given the task of "reducing the vulnerabilities of the people in Nebraska from the damage, injury, and loss of life and property resulting from natural, technological, or man-made disasters and emergencies." They have four units:

1. Preparedness: this includes planning, the continuity of government plan, grants, State Emergency Operations Plan, NIMS, training, and Citizen Corps.
2. Response and Recovery: offices here include response and recovery plans, the governor's emergency plan, and an emergency fund.
3. Technical Hazards: this office is prepared to respond to technical hazards, radiological preparedness, and the state Emergency Response Commission.

Maine Emergency Management Agency

In Maine, the Emergency Management Agency (MEMA) is tasked with homeland security and terrorism-related incidents and natural disasters. The agency is housed within the Department of Defense, Veterans and Emergency Management. The Commissioner of the Agency is also the Adjutant General of the Maine National Guard and the Governor's official Homeland Security Advisor. MEMA coordinates activities in the state such as training, equipment, and planning; provides technical assistance and grant funding to state and local agencies; and coordinates with the Maine Intelligence Analysis Center or the fusion center to provide information to interested parties. The Homeland Security Advisory Council, established in 2005, advises the governor on all matters related to homeland security. Additionally, it coordinates homeland security planning and citizen preparedness.

◼ Chapter Summary

Since 9-11, the president and Congress have taken action to keep Americans safe. Both President Bush and President Obama have issued multiple executive orders and presidential directives that have impacted the U.S. policy toward terrorism and homeland security in some way. Members of Congress have also passed numerous pieces of legislation geared toward limiting terrorist acts and/or helping communities respond quickly to an emergency event. In the end, all of these political actions are responses to the 9-11 attack and are attempts to prevent another similar attack.

◼ Review/Discussion Questions

1. What have President Bush and President Obama done in response to the threat of terrorism?
2. Since 9-11, what laws have been passed by Congress to deter terrorism or help the country respond to an emergency event such as terrorism or a natural disaster?
3. What are some elements of the USA PATRIOT Act?

◼ Additional Readings

Kettle, D.F. (2007). *System Under Stress: Homeland Security and American Politics.* 2nd ed. Washington, D.C.: CQ Press.

Logan, G. & Ramsay, J.D. (2012). *Introduction to Homeland Security.* Boulder, CO: Westview.

Sylves, R. (2008). *Disaster Policy and Politics: Emergency Management and Homeland Security.* Washington, D.C.: CQ Press.

◼ Endnotes

1. Austin, J. (2010). "'Patriot Act' Gets Short-Term Renewal." *CQ Almanac 2009,* 65th ed. Retrieved online at http://library.cqpress.com/cqalmanac/cqal09-1183-59545-2251457; *The New York Times.* (2010). "Najibullah Zazi." Retrieved online at http://topics.nytimes.com/topics/reference/timestopics/people/z/najibullah_zazi/index.html; Baker, A. (2009). "An Enemy Within: The Making of Najibullah Zazi." *Time.* Retrieved online at www.time.com/time/magazine/article/0,9171,1927280,00.html
2. Christie, K. (2008). *America's War on Terrorism.* Lewiston, NY: Edwin Mellen Press, p. 109.
3. Bentley, E. (2012). "Homeland Security Law and Policy." In Logan, K.G. & Ramsay, J.D. *Introduction to Homeland Security.* Boulder, CO: Westview, pp. 19–45.
4. Chumar, M. (2012). "Public- and Private-Sector Partnerships in Homeland Security." In Logan, K.G. & Ramsay, J.D. *Introduction to Homeland Security.* Boulder, CO: Westview, pp. 47–68.

5. Chumar, M. (2012). "Public- and Private-Sector Partnerships in Homeland Security." In Logan, K.G. & Ramsay, J.D. *Introduction to Homeland Security*. Boulder, CO: Westview, pp. 47–68.

6. CQ Almanac. (2002). "Anti-Terror Bill Zooms Into Law." *CQ Almanac* 2001, 57th ed. Retrieved online at http://library.cqpress.com/cqalmanac/cqal01-106-6376-328229

7. CQ Almanac. (2002). "Anti-Terror Bill Zooms Into Law." *CQ Almanac* 2001, 57th ed. Retrieved online at http://library.cqpress.com/cqalmanac/cqal01-106-6376-328229

8. CQ Almanac. (2002). "Anti-Terror Bill Zooms Into Law." *CQ Almanac* 2001, 57th ed. Retrieved online at http://library.cqpress.com/cqalmanac/cqal01-106-6376-328229

9. CQ Almanac. (2003). "Congress Re-Examines Patriot Act." *CQ Almanac* 2003, 59th ed. Retrieved online at http://library.cqpress.com/cqalmanac/cqal03-835-24329-1083713

10. CQ Almanac. (2006). "Disputes Delay Reauthorization of Anti-Terrorism Act Provisions." *CQ Almanac 2005*, 61st ed. Retrieved online at http://library.cqpress.com/cqalmanac/cqal05-766-20097-1042102

11. CQ Almanac. (2006). "Disputes Delay Reauthorization of Anti-Terrorism Act Provisions." *CQ Almanac 2005*, 61st ed. Retrieved online at http://library.cqpress.com/cqalmanac/cqal05-766-20097-1042102

12. CQ Almanac. (2010). "'Patriot Act' Gets Short-term Renewal." *CQ Almanac 2009*, 65th ed. Retrieved online at http://library.cqpress.com/cqalmanac/cqal09-1183-59545-2251457

13. CQ Almanac. (2010). "'Patriot Act' Gets Short-term Renewal." *CQ Almanac 2009*, 65th ed. Retrieved online at http://library.cqpress.com/cqalmanac/cqal09-1183-59545-2251457

14. CQ Almanac. (2001). "Bio-Terrorism Bill Founders." *CQ Almanac 2001*, 57th ed. Retrieved online at http://library.cqpress.com/cqalmanac/cqal01-106-6374-328201

15. CQ Almanac. (2001). "Bio-Terrorism Bill Founders." *CQ Almanac 2001*, 57th ed. Retrieved online at http://library.cqpress.com/cqalmanac/cqal01-106-6374-328201

16. Bush, G.W. (2002). "Remarks on Signing the Terrorism Risk Insurance Act of 2002." Retrieved online at www.presidency,ucsb.edu/ws/?pid=73349

17. CQ Almanac. (2004). "Bioshield Funding Decision Delayed." *CQ Almanac 2003*, 59th ed. Retrieved online at http://library.cqpress.com/cqalmanac/cqal03-835-24327-1083669

18. CQ Almanac. (2005). "Terrorism Insurance Extension Dies." *CQ Almanac 2004*, 60th ed. Retrieved online at http://library.cqpress.com/cqalmanac/cqal04-836-24362-1085047

19. CQ Almanac. (2007). "Ports Debate Focuses on Screening." *CQ Almanac 2006*, 62nd ed. Retrieved online at http://library.cqpress.com/cqalmanac/cqal06-1421202

20. CQ Almanac. (2008). "TRIA Extension Backs Up Insurers." *CQ Almanac 2007*, 63rd ed. Retrieved online at http://library.cqpress.com/cqalmanac/cqal07-1006-44908-2047783

21. CQ Almanac. (2008). "Bipartisan CFIUS Overhaul Calls for Tighter Review of Foreign Investment." *CQ Almanac 2007*, 63rd ed. Retrieved online at http://library.cqpress.com/cqalmanac/cqal07-1006-44916-2048037

22. CQ Almanac. (2008). "Sept. 11 Recommendations Enacted, Making Good on Democrats' Pledge." *CQ Almanac 2007*, 63rd ed. Retrieved online at http://library.cqpress.com/cqalmanac/cqal07-1006-44905-2047715

23. Chenoweth, E. & Clarke, S.E. (2010). "All Terrorism is Local: Resources, Nested Institutions and Governance for Urban Homeland Security in the American Federal System." *Political Research Quarterly*, *64*, 495–507.

24. Krane, D. (2002). "The State of American Federalism, 2001-2002: Resilience in Response to Crisis." *Publius: The Journal of Federalism*, *32*, 1–21.

25. Eisinger, P. (2006). "Imperfect Federalism: The Intergovernmental Partnership for Homeland Security." *Public Administration Review*, *66*, 537–545; Chenoweth, E. & Clarke, S.E. (2010). "All Terrorism is Local: Resources, Nested Institutions and Governance for Urban Homeland Security in the American Federal System." *Political Research Quarterly*, *64*, 495–507.

26. Eisinger, P. (2006). "Imperfect Federalism: The Intergovernmental Partnership for Homeland Security." *Public Administration Review*, *66*, 537–545.

27. Caruson, K. & MacManus, S.A. (2006). "Mandates and Management Challenges in the Trenches: An Intergovernmental Perspective on Homeland Security." *Public Administration Review*, *66*, 522–536.

28. Caruson, K. & MacManus, S.A. (2006). "Mandates and Management Challenges in the Trenches: An Intergovernmental Perspective on Homeland Security." *Public Administration Review*, *66*, 522–536.

Legal Responses to Homeland Security

Chapter Outline

- Introduction
- USA PATRIOT Act
  - Objections
  - Support
  - Other Concerns
- Executive Power
  - Guantanamo Bay
- Civil Liberties
  - Police
  - Courts
- Chapter Summary

Chapter Objectives

- Understand the balance between civil rights and the need to collect intelligence

- Understand the objections civil rights advocates have about the USA PATRIOT Act

- Understand the Supreme Court's reactions to U.S. policies toward detainees

Introduction

Jose Padilla was born in Brooklyn, New York. As a young adult, he adopted the practice of Islam and traveled extensively in the Middle East. Upon returning to the U.S. after one trip from Pakistan, Padilla was arrested at Chicago's O'Hare airport as he exited the plane. Law enforcement suspected him of being involved in a terrorist plot, alleging that Padilla conspired with senior Al Qaeda members to build and detonate a radioactive "dirty bomb." Padilla claimed that his actions were simply a ploy to escape from Pakistan and return to the U.S.

Although Padilla was not engaged in any threatening activity at the time of his arrest, the government held him as an unlawful **enemy combatant** without

KEY TERM

Enemy combatant—historically, it meant someone fighting against the United States military, but the Bush Administration used the term to mean someone who was fighting the United States unlawfully and therefore did not have the protections of the Geneva Convention as a soldier fighting for a country.

© J. Pat Carter/AP Images.

providing him the opportunity to defend himself against the charges. He was detained in Chicago, where he appeared before a district court and had a public defender appointed to represent him. After, he was transferred to a naval brig in Charleston, South Carolina. The only evidence against him was a short written statement by a U.S. government agent. Padilla was not allowed to have contact with an attorney, his family, or any nonmilitary personnel for 18 months.

Padilla's legal treatment was questioned by some civil rights leaders. They argued Padilla was denied his due process rights granted to U.S. citizens in the Constitution, which were designed to protect American citizens from unlawful arrest and jailing. These rights include the right to representation in court, the right of accused persons to know the evidence against them, and the right to confront their accusers. Civil rights leaders questioned if American citizens could be held indefinitely without a trial simply because the government believed them to be dangerous.

The case was appealed to the Supreme Court, and in November 2005 the justices decided that, as an American citizen, Padilla was entitled to due process. Padilla either had to be formally charged or released. In essence, the justices declared that American citizens accused of any crime, including terrorism, are entitled to due process, including the right to defend themselves in court and to be given a timely trial.[1]

Padilla's legal rights as a U.S. citizen against improper treatment by the government are granted to him through the Constitution. Immediately after 9-11, many people were detained for offenses related to terrorism, some allegedly unfairly. There are estimates that nearly 15,000 people were detained worldwide since 9-11, the majority of whom were held without being charged or tried.[2]

When U.S. citizens are charged or tried illegally, it is said that their civil and human rights have been violated. The term "civil liberties" refers to the individual freedoms people have under a system of law. They are the rights granted by law to citizens that protect them from unfair treatment by the government. A related term is "human rights." which are the basic rights that all people should have, but are not necessarily guaranteed by law. They are the rights that most people agree should be given to all people, regardless of their citizenship. These rights include such things as safe food, water, and shelter, along with the right not to be physically abused or punished cruelly.

In the U.S., the civil rights granted to all citizens are outlined in the Constitution, specifically in the Bill of Rights, or the first 10 amendments to the Constitution. The amendments most often used to challenge government anti-terrorist activities are the First, Fourth, Fifth, Sixth, Seventh, and Eighth Amendments, which relate to free speech, illegal search and seizure, and the

© JMiks/ShutterStock, Inc.

conduct of criminal trials. These limit the power of government while protecting the rights and freedoms of citizens, which are listed in TABLE 13.1.

While the Constitution and Bill of Rights provide legal limits on government actions against citizens, it is limited in the sense that the Constitution also allows the government to act in certain ways during times of emergency. In other words, the government is constitutionally granted the power to carry out actions that would be prohibited during times when no emergency exists. Unfortunately, there is no clear understanding of what constitutes an "emergency." After 9-11, the Bush Administration used this clause to carry out certain actions that some regarded as unconstitutional, arguing that terrorism is not a continuing emergency.

The problem of how to balance national security objectives (and providing for safety and security from terrorism) while at the same time protecting civil liberties remains a significant problem for U.S. officials in the time after 9-11.[3] The United States and other liberal democracies often point out that the rights of citizens and minorities in their societies are protected. After 9-11, some would argue that the U.S. created an imbalance in this area.[4] This concern—of the erosion of civil liberties—was highlighted with the USA PATRIOT Act.

TABLE 13.1 Rights Guaranteed Under Bill of Rights

First Amendment: Freedom of Speech, Press, Religion, Assembly, and Petition. The government cannot interfere with a person's right to practice any religion they choose. Citizens have the right to speak freely, assemble in groups, and make their voices heard.

Fourth Amendment: Protection against Search and Seizure. Citizens' bodies, houses, papers, and property cannot be searched or seized by the government without evidence of wrongdoing. A court must issue a warrant to conduct a search, which then must include the specific place to be searched and the evidence being collected.

Fifth Amendment: Protection against Illegal Prosecutions. A person can be tried for a crime after a grand jury determines that there is evidence that the person may have committed that offense. However, during times of war or public danger, there are exceptions. The Amendment also allows those accused of crimes to refuse to make statements that could incriminate themselves in a court of law. Moreover, no one's life, liberty, or property can be taken without a proper trial. The Fifth Amendment also prevents a person from being put on trial twice for the same offense and guarantees due process of law.

Sixth Amendment: Right to a Speedy and Public Trial. The Sixth Amendment states that in all criminal cases, those accused of a crime have the right to a speedy and public trial by an impartial jury. Additionally, a person accused of a crime has the right to be informed of the charges against him or her. The accused person also has the right to see the witnesses who are providing evidence against them, to have witnesses speak in his or her favor, and to have the assistance of competent legal representation.

Seventh Amendment: Right to a Trial by Jury. This amendment guarantees that someone accused of a crime can be tried by a jury in a court of law.

Eighth Amendment: Excessive Bail, Cruel and Unusual Punishment. Under the Eighth Amendment, judges cannot impose unusually large bail on a defendant, and cruel and unusual punishments cannot be applied to those convicted of crimes.

Fourteenth Amendment: Addresses rights of citizenship and equal protection under the law. Suspects cannot lose their rights except by due process of law.

■ USA PATRIOT Act

▥ Objections

The Patriot Act was passed immediately after 9-11 as a way to provide law enforcement with added powers to track down and punish those responsible for the attacks and to protect the U.S. against any similar act from occurring in the future. The act gave the Department of Justice and law enforcement agencies such as the FBI new and significantly broader investigatory authority. These new powers were very controversial, and opponents argued they violated Americans' civil rights and allowed law enforcement to encroach upon the civil liberties of citizens.[5] Objectors say the law violates the First, Fourth, Fifth, Sixth, and Eighth Amendments. Opponents claim that the powers granted to law enforcement are simply too wide-ranging and will erase the protections granted by the Constitution and may affect the freedom of its citizens. They also argue that U.S. citizens are given the right to be free from having their government infringe on those freedoms guaranteed in the Constitution and Bill of Rights.

One simple objection concerned the new definition of "domestic terrorism," which was expanded to include nonviolent crimes such as computer fraud and leaks of intelligence agents' identities. This revised definition allowed law enforcement to use surveillance against a greater number of citizens, and some argue that this new definition discourages political dissent because it includes activities of unpopular political organizations within the U.S.[6] They argue that enforcement agencies should not be allowed to interfere with citizens who choose to engage in political associations, even if they are unpopular.

To make matters worse, the ability of law enforcement to use surveillance against citizens (i.e., watching and listening to people, usually without their knowledge) was made easier by passage of the Patriot Act. Now, law enforcement can carry out electronic surveillance on more forms of communications. Restrictions on placing wiretaps on telephones were lessened so that police could monitor the private conversations of individuals who are suspected of criminal activity, even without probable cause. Law enforcement was also given the right to track and intercept other types of communication such as email for both law enforcement and intelligence purposes. Police could pursue suspected computer hackers without warrants.

Surveillance tactics by police were further expanded by changes to the Foreign Intelligence Surveillance Act (FISA), a law that lowered standards for courts to approve surveillance of foreign intelligence gathering. Under this law, the standards for approval of a criminal wiretap are far less strict than in a criminal case. The Patriot Act amended FISA so that surveillance requests do not have to establish that surveillance is for intelligence-gathering for national security reasons, Instead, all that is now required is that surveillance is needed for a "significant" purpose. This makes it easier for officials to get around limits on permissible domestic surveillance. The concern, obviously, is that the government might use its newly expanded powers without sufficient discretion.[7]

Some of the wiretaps police could now use are called "roving wiretaps." This means that a wiretap targeted to a particular person would not be confined to a single computer or telephone. Instead, the wiretap could "rove" wherever the target goes.

The roving wiretaps are of great concern to some. Before the Act, a pen register/trap order was only valid in the district in which it was obtained. A pen register is an electronic device that records all of the numbers being called from a specific phone and the trap order allows the government to capture this information. That meant if a suspect moved to a different district, law enforcement would have to obtain another pen/trap order from this second district. Under the Patriot Act, once a pen/trap order is obtained, it is valid throughout the U.S. This violates the Fourth Amendment's requirement that a warrant specify the place to be searched and evidence to be seized.[8]

In addition to phone conversations, law enforcement was given easier access to an individual's personal financial, credit, educational, medical, and other records. Federal agents can now browse those records, or even library records, without first showing evidence of a crime.[9]

If law enforcement believes that national security is jeopardized, the law allows federal agents to secretly enter people's homes and offices and search and remove people's possessions, read and photograph letters and documents, and read and copy files on computers without a warrant or prior notification. If the search is conducted, it is legal for the government to keep that search secret (called a gag order). This is called a "sneak and peek" search.

Objectors point to the Fourth Amendment, which forbids searches of homes and property (including personal records) without a warrant based on evidence that a person is involved in a specific crime. "Sneak and peak" searches allow the FBI to evade the requirement that probable cause be shown before a warrant is issued to search a home or place of business. Instead, if the FBI believes that information might provide some intelligence and help an investigation, it can search for evidence and seize it. In short, the FBI can spy on Americans whom no court has determined have done anything wrong. Opponents argue that law enforcement should only gather intelligence when there is a clear reason to suspect criminal activity.

Another concern with the Patriot Act stemmed from provisions requiring phone companies and Internet service providers to turn over customer records to law enforcement. If required to do so, the companies would be forbidden from telling their customers of their actions. While the government argued that such secrecy is necessary so as not to alert potential terrorists, opponents argued that the gag orders related to searches violate the First Amendment, which guarantees people's right to free speech. In addition, objectors point out that in "typical" criminal cases, a court gives law enforcement agents a warrant that gives them permission to monitor the activities of a specific person for a limited time period, and when the investigation is over the person must be told that the surveillance occurred.

The Patriot Act has provisions that allow the government to oversee bank records with more ease, making some people uncomfortable. The government argued this was necessary in order to curtail financing of terrorism, because if terrorists do not have access to financial resources they are unable to carry out future attacks. The Patriot Act imposes new bookkeeping requirements on financial institutions. It gives the Secretary of Treasury increased regulatory powers to combat corruption of U.S. financial institutions involved in foreign money-laundering activities. Federal law enforcement can now interact with banking regulators, and have the power to arrest suspects outside U.S. borders if an individual is suspected of financing terrorism and conducting money laundering.

The law also has new provisions concerning immigration, seeking to tighten security at the borders, closing them off to terrorists. Other provisions serve to detain and expel terrorists who may already be in the country. Authorities can detain and even prosecute non-U.S. citizens suspected of being involved in hostile activities against the U.S. The law revised immigration laws to expand the categories of who could be deported based on possible connection with terrorist activity, and reduced the procedural protections surrounding their deportation.[10] Any immigrants who were "certified" as posing a threat to national security would be detained without bond pending deportation proceedings. In those cases where the country would not accept the alien, detention could become indefinite.[11] To protect the border, the new law increased border patrols and monitoring of foreigners within the U.S.

The law makes it easier for law enforcement to share sensitive intelligence on Americans with other law enforcement, immigration officers, and intelligence agencies such as the CIA. Any government law enforcement officer or attorney can share the contents of intercepted communications or from a "sneak and peak" operation to other federal officers, including the CIA.[12] The Regional Information Sharing System (RISS) could now be used to share intelligence with ease, whereas prior to the Patriot Act, RISS was only used in criminal investigations.

Traditionally, law enforcement agents investigate and collect evidence on a specific crime that has already been committed. But under the Patriot Act, the government's surveillance activities are not necessarily intended to catch specific terrorists. They are scanning huge amounts of computerized records and other information as a way to look for patterns that may indicate terrorist activity. This is called data mining.

Support

Supporters of the Patriot Act claimed these provisions were necessary to allow law enforcement to find evidence that a person is engaged in terrorist activity against the U.S. Police agents argued that the new provisions for increasing intelligence would allow them to track terrorists who use modern technology to plan and carry out their crimes. In the end, supporters argued that the Patriot Act would increase the federal law enforcement's ability to respond to terrorism.

Critics understand the need to keep some information secret, such as the identity of agents who are working undercover within terrorist organization. However, there is a big concern when the press's access to government officials and information is restricted. This makes it very hard for the public to know if the government's activities are legal.

While there are certain instances when the intelligence community should share info with the criminal justice community, Congress give these agencies and others too much power to share intelligence without judicial review.

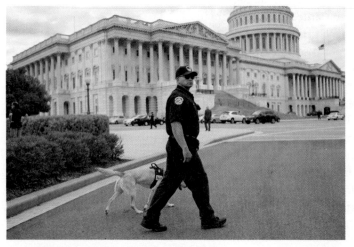
© Chris Maddaloni/CQ-Roll Call Group/Getty Images.

Other Concerns

There are other concerns about government policies passed after 9-11. One of those is the "No-Fly Watch List" and the "Automatic Selectee" list that are maintained by the U.S. government. These lists can restrict a person's ability to travel by air. Any person whose name appears on the No-Fly list is not permitted to board airplanes at all, whereas those on the Automatic Selectee list are identified for closer scrutiny when passing through airport security.

The reason for having these lists is clear: to stop any terrorists who may be attempting to board an airplane with the intent to harm others. These lists also make it more difficult for terrorists' to travel to another location to carry out an act of terrorism.

However, the data supplied by U.S. intelligence agencies is often incomplete and/or inaccurate. Many travelers have the same name as a terrorist on the list and have been incorrectly identified as being potential terrorists. In September 2006, the Congressional Research Service (CRS) issued a report that the data supplied by the intelligence agencies included numerous incorrect entries and a lot of outdated information. In May 2012, an 18-month-old girl was "flagged" as being on the No Fly List and her parents taken off a flight.[13]

The No-Fly list has about 20,000 names on it, including the names of about 500 Americans. It is maintained by the FBI's Terrorist Screening Center. In 2010, the ACLU filed a suit with the U.S. District Court in Portland, Oregon for 15 plaintiffs who were all U.S. citizens and Muslims. The plaintiffs claim the government refuses to explain why their names are on the list.[14]

In the past, the No-Fly Watch List has been challenged in the courts. The ACLU has questioned the legality of the No-Fly Watch List and has gone to court to try to stop the use of such lists, claiming that the collection and sharing of information on citizens who are not under investigation for a specific crime is forbidden by the Bill of Rights.

Another concern revolves around a proposed national DNA database. The Department of Justice is considering a plan to add a DNA database to the FBI's existing crime-related database. When this database is operational, DNA would be collected from those people arrested as being a suspect in the War on Terror, anyone arrested and accused of committing a federal crime (even if they are not found guilty), and people accused of entering the country illegally or those who stay longer in the country than their visas allow.

While supporters of the database argue that it will make it easier for law enforcement to track potential terrorists, to stop illegal aliens from entering the U.S., and help solve crimes committed by illegal aliens, opponents argue that collecting DNA from people who are not convicted of offenses violates their civil liberties. They argue that the database will not prevent crimes because DNA is collected after the crime has been committed and cannot be used to stop crimes from occurring. They also argue that a database like this would be ineffective because it is simply too difficult to analyze the DNA of such a large number of people.

Yet another proposal is the National Identity System, which would be used to identify potential terrorists and follow their movements. This would involve issuing some type of an identity card that includes a photo and information about each person. In general, such an ID would help a person accurately identify him or herself. Those opposed to the law argue that the ID system would simply be a way for the government to collect information on all citizens, even if they have not been accused of a crime. It could be used to force people to produce identification without reasonable suspicion that they had done anything wrong.

■ Executive Power

After 9-11, President Bush and Vice President Cheney felt that the president and the executive branch had the power to designate certain terrorists as enemy combatants, allowing for their trial in special military courts. Along those same lines, they also argued that the president has the authority to ask federal law enforcement and other national security intelligence agencies to listen to telephone calls that originate in the U.S. but are directed to suspected terrorists in foreign countries. President Bush and the U.S. Attorney General developed new policies that allowed law enforcement to rely only on reasonable suspicion as a standard for launching an investigation. The FBI was able to search for indicators of illegal activity by monitoring chat rooms and attending political rallies or religious events as a way to identify possible threats. Local FBI offices were permitted to begin inquiries based on their own information. In doing these things, Bush and Cheney were making decisions without congressional oversight—in essence, expanding the power of the executive office.

Critics of this approach argue that increasing executive power to counter terrorism is abuse of executive power. As presidential and police power increase, citizen protections have been decreasing. During times of emergency, police are allowed more intrusions into people's behavior, but were the events of September 11th a time of an emergency?

■ Guantanamo Bay

Anyone suspected of carrying out, or engaging in, terrorist actions have been labeled by the U.S. government as an "unlawful enemy combatant." Since 9-11 the U.S. would often place those individuals in custody in Iraq or Afghanistan. They are interrogated with the hope that any intelligence gathered will help prevent new terrorist attacks.

Some detainees are held at a detention camp and naval base in **Guantanamo Bay**, Cuba. Because Guantanamo Bay (GB) is not a part of the U.S. mainland, it is more difficult for the press and other Americans to follow events or hold protests there. The majority of those being detained at Guantanamo Bay were captured abroad. Some of the detainees are members of Al Qaeda and were involved in active plots against Americans. But not all of the detainees are members of a terrorist group. Instead, they may be loose associates of terrorists, such as friends or family members of supporters of terrorist groups.

Many human rights issues have come to the forefront because of the actions taken by the government against suspected terrorists held at Guantanamo Bay. Detainees can be held at Guantanamo Bay for years

© Shane T. McCoy/US Navy/AP Images.

without access to legal protection. Conditions for detainees at the GB camp are reportedly harsh. Those prisoners who have been released later reported that detainees were tortured and abused. Another controversial question surrounded the right of detainees to file a writ of habeas corpus. The president is allowed to suspend habeas corpus in times of national emergency—but, again, what exactly constitutes an emergency?

President Bush declared that his administration had the right to detain those individuals who were suspected of terrorist acts. He argued that the detainees at Guantanamo are enemy combatants, not prisoners of war, so they are not entitled to certain rights under the Geneva Conventions. The definition, then, was trying to separate out the difference between lawful combatants (prisoners of war) versus unlawful combatants (dubbed enemy combatants). Bush declared that the detainees are not entitled to protections described in the Geneva Conventions because they are not members of any specific entity that abides by the agreement, and thus the protections are not relevant. Bush also said that if the prisoners were to be tried for their actions, it would be in military courts that provide fewer human rights and civil liberty protections than criminal courts in the U.S.

One argument that has been made to justify suspending civil rights of detainees is that terrorism is a crime unlike any other, and one terrorist can do enormous harm; therefore, different standards and a different legal approach should apply.

Human rights advocates seek to change policy so that detainees are treated humanely, including given the right to be tried in court within a reasonable time after their arrest. Some human rights advocates question if the Geneva Conventions should apply to those detainees being held at Guantanamo Bay. The term "Geneva Conventions" refers to four international treaties signed in Geneva, Switzerland, and that detail, among other things, the way enemy soldiers and prisoners of war must be treated by those holding them. The documents outlaw the use of torture, require that prisoners be fed and treated humanely, and that prisoners be tried and sentenced by a court.

Moreover, because Guantanamo is on foreign soil (although leased from Cuba since 1903), the detainees are beyond the reach of U.S. law.[15]

There are many possible violations of civil rights in military courts as opposed to criminal courts in the U.S. In a civilian criminal case, defendants are entitled to review all the evidence against him or her. In military courts, officers acting as judges can consider evidence that is not released to the accused individual. This affects the ability of the accused to build a defense. Second, in typical criminal court hearings, any evidence obtained by use of torture is not admissible. In military courts, this rule does not apply; instead, that evidence would be admitted. Third, in a civilian proceeding, if a prisoner is found not guilty, he or she must be released. In military hearings, the government may choose to detain a prisoner after a hearing, even if the court does not find the defendant guilty.

In June 2006, the U.S. Supreme Court ruled against President Bush when they decided that trying detainees in military courts would be a violation of both U.S. law and the Geneva Conventions.

© J. Scott Applewhite/AP Images.

This meant that the detainees had to be tried in U.S. courts. In response, Bush convinced Congress to pass the Military Commissions Act of 2006. The law allowed detainees to be tried by a special military commission called military tribunals. These tribunals allow secret or classified information to be used against the detainees. In essence, the act returned power to the President to decide the fate of the detainees.

Many U.S. citizens favor detention without arrest and military tribunals for suspected terrorists, even if it includes denying the civil rights to accused terrorists. On the other hand, civil libertarians tend to support providing constitutional protections to suspected terrorists, including trials in civilian courts and dismantling detention facilities like Guantanamo Bay. For more on legal issues surrounding homeland security, see **Box 13.1**.

When he became president Barack Obama vowed to reverse many of the Bush administration policies. Just after taking office, Obama worked to close the facility at Guantanamo Bay and tried to have five suspects involved in the September 11th attacks moved to New York City for a civilian trial. The president also asked the Department of Justice to look for a new detention facility within the U.S. Opposition immediately arose on the grounds that the terrorists would use the publicity surrounding the trials as a stage. In the end, the Obama administration reversed its decision. It also continued many of the security measures originally started in the Bush administration, such as monitoring communications.

Civil Liberties

Police

Police are at the forefront of the battle against terrorism. Their behavior determines whether civil liberties are protected or whether they are abused. Police are responsible for collecting information, which can be personal information that may have no relation to a criminal offense. Their attempts to gather intelligence may alter the expectations citizens have about law enforcement. This new role changes the focus of police work, which can interfere with the traditional role of fighting crime.

After 9-11, local, state, and federal government began to share information like never before. State and local law enforcement agencies and the FBI created Joint

---

BOX 13.1   Homeland Security Watch—Legal Issues Surrounding Homeland Security

Christian Beckner, a former senior homeland security analyst, is the founder of the blog *Homeland Security Watch* (http://www.hlswatch.com/). Started in December of 2005, it has become a primary website for keeping current with news, legal aspects, and critical issues related to homeland security. According to the blog, the website "features breaking news, rigorous analysis, and informed commentary on the critical issues in homeland security today." The blog takes a very cross-disciplinary approach and the material is archived by categories such as biosecurity, Congress, and

investigations and enforcement, among other categories. Among its many contributors, it includes Christopher Bellavita, an instructor at the Naval Postgraduate School in Monterey, California, and a leading expert on homeland security. The blog also serves as a starting point for other homeland security-related links, blogs, and websites dedicated to national security. It is a good starting place for researching homeland security topics, obtaining current news, and understanding many of the legal issues surrounding homeland security.

Terrorism Task Forces. There were also Anti-Terrorism Task Forces created within the nation's U.S. Attorneys' offices; this name changed to Anti-Terrorist Assistance Coordinators in 2003.

Under the Fourth Amendment, law enforcement cannot collect information without reasonable suspicion. Citizens' civil liberties may be at risk if law enforcement collects that information illegally.

Courts

In January 2003, The American Library Association issued a resolution stating that some sections of the Patriot Act violated the constitutional and privacy rights of library patrons. They announced that they were opposed to any use of governmental power to suppress the free and open exchange of knowledge and information, and encouraged U.S. librarians to support free and open access to information. They considered sections of the act to be a danger to the constitutional and privacy rights of library users.[16]

Some Supreme Court decisions have reversed White House policies that have served to expand executive authority since 2001. In June 2004, the Court made two decisions that allowed enemy combatants the right to contest their arrests. In April 2006, the Court decided that U.S. citizens who were arrested in the U.S. could not be tried outside the U.S. criminal court system. Then, in June 2006, the Court declared the military tribunal system that had been established at Guantanamo Bay was illegal because it did not have the approval of Congress and did not follow the Geneva Conventions. As a result, charges against two enemy combatants were dropped based on the June 2006 Supreme Court decision.

In *Hamdi v. Rumsfeld* (542 US 507, 2004), the Supreme Court justices clarified the status of 21-year-old American citizen Yaser Hamdi. Hamdi was captured by American forces while fighting for the Taliban in Afghanistan in the fall of 2001. He was held for over 2 years without access to the courts. He was initially detained at Guantanamo Bay where administration officials labeled him as an "enemy combatant" even though they could not provide any evidence that Hamdi had any links to terrorists. Because he was an American, he was moved to the naval brig in Norfolk, Virginia. Because he was deemed an "enemy combatant," he was not entitled to legal representation. Further, he could be held for an indefinite period of time without charges being filed. If a lawyer was present, all conversations had to be recorded, a violation of the Fourth Amendment. The Court held that Hamdi's detention was proper, and the U.S. could continue to detain him. But it also held that Hamdi, as a U.S. citizen, had the due process right to challenge the government's justification for his detention (to challenge his status as an enemy combatant) before a neutral decision-maker.[17]

In *Rasul v. Bush* (542 US 466, 2004), a majority of the justices on the Supreme Court held that the detainees at Guantanamo Bay who are not U.S. citizens have the right to file habeas corpus petitions in federal court to challenge the legality of their detention. They held that the foreign nationals (non-U.S. citizens) were wrongfully imprisoned. This had to do with four British and Australian citizens who were captured by the American military in Pakistan and Afghanistan. The men were held in Guantanamo Bay. Their families filed for a writ of habeas corpus to have their detention declared unconstitutional. The government claimed that since the men were not U.S. citizens, the federal courts did not have jurisdiction to hear the case.

Together, the *Rasul* and *Hamdi* cases determined that detainees on American soil or being held in American facilities must be given the chance to contest the legality of their detention.

The Supreme Court addressed the legality of military commissions set up by the Bush administration in *Hamdan v. Rumsfeld* (548 US 557, 2006). Salim Ahmed Hamdan, a citizen of Yemen, served as a bodyguard and chauffeur for Osama bin Laden and was captured by Afghani forces. He was turned over to the U.S. and sent to Guantanamo Bay, where he was charged with conspiracy to commit terrorism and tried before a military tribunal. Hamdan then filed a petition for a writ of habeas corpus in a federal district court, arguing that the military commission that had been convened to try him was illegal because it did not provide him with the civil rights protections required under the Geneva Conventions. Supreme Court justices decided that the military commissions that the Bush Administration set up to try detainees being held at Guantanamo could not proceed because they did not follow the Geneva Conventions. Further, the President did not have the authority to set up the special military commissions without oversight by Congress. Because of this, the commissions were deemed illegal.[18]

In another ruling the same day as *Hamdan v. Rumsfeld*, the Court decided in a 5-4 ruling that the Jose Padilla case was filed in the wrong jurisdiction and against the wrong defendant. They sidestepped the constitutional issues of the Padilla case. In *Rumsfeld v. Padilla* (542 US 426, 2004), the court addressed the Padilla case (described previously). Padilla was a U.S. citizen who had been labeled an "enemy combatant" in the war on terror. Unlike Hamdi or Hamdan, Padilla was arrested on U.S. soil rather than overseas. In the case, attorneys for Padilla asked whether the defendant had the right to contest the legality of his detention in a federal court.

All three of these cases illustrated the question of individual rights versus government power. The decisions in these cases dealt the Bush administration a major blow in its belief that the executive branch wielded enough power to bypass constitutional rights and liberties. The Court decided the executive branch could not hold foreign-born prisoners at Guantanamo Bay indefinitely without access to the American judicial system and the rights of due process.

Boumediene v. Bush (553 US 723, 2008) involved Lakhdar Boumediene, a naturalized citizen of Bosnia and Herzegovenia, who was being held in Guantanamo Bay. He was accused of being involved in a plot to attack the U.S. embassy. While in Guantanamo Bay, Boumediene filed a petition for a writ of habeas corpus. The Supreme Court found in favor of the detainees. They declared that those detained in Guantanamo Bay had a right to habeas corpus and that the Military Commissions Act was an unconstitutional suspension of that right.[19]

In January 2010, The Supreme Court gave its first ruling against the provision in the Patriot Act that prohibits providing material support to any group labeled a terrorist organization, and attached a possible 15-year sentence. In other words, the Patriot Act made it a crime to provide support, including humanitarian aid, literature, and political advocacy, to a "terrorist group." In *Holder v. Humanitarian Law Project* (561 US _____, 2010), the justices decided that the provisions prohibiting material support were not vague and did not violate freedom of speech.[20]

In *Ashcroft v. Al-Kidd* (563 US _____, 2011), the Supreme Court ruled against a former star college football player from the University of Idaho who, while in college, converted to Islam. As he was boarding a flight to Saudi Arabia, he was arrested and held as a material witness in a terrorism probe for 16 days. He was never charged with a crime and ultimately released from custody. Al-Kidd claimed that he was mistreated while in custody. He claimed he was strip-searched, shackled, interrogated like a terrorist, and held with hardened criminals. He brought a suit against Attorney General John Ashcroft because he was detained on suspicion of supporting terrorists even though there was no evidence to charge him with a crime.

The justices found in an 8-0 decision that the Attorney General could not be personally sued in the case. They said there was no violation of the Constitution. Additionally, Justice Scalia concluded that Ashcroft was entitled to qualified immunity because he did not violate clearly established law. For more on the legal complexities involving many homeland security activities, see **TABLE 13.2**.

TABLE 13.2 The Legal Complexity of Cybersecurity

In order to understand the legal complexity of homeland security, the topic of cybersecurity was selected as an example of how previous laws may impact current day issues. The following list is based on a congressional report that assessed all of the federal laws that may be related to the issue of cybersecurity in the United States.

- Posse Comitatus Act of 1879
- Antitrust Laws and Section 5 of the Federal Trade Commission Act
- National Institute of Standards and Technology Act
- Federal Power Act
- Communications Act of 1934
- National Security Act of 1947
- U.S. Information and Educational Exchange Act of 1948 (Smith–Mundt Act)
- State Department Basic Authorities Act of 1956
- Freedom of Information Act (FOIA)
- Omnibus Crime Control and Safe Streets Act of 1968
- Racketeer Influenced and Corrupt Organizations Act (RICO)
- Federal Advisory Committee Act (FACA)
- Privacy Act of 1974
- Counterfeit Access Device and Computer Fraud and Abuse Act of 1984
- Electronic Communications Privacy Act of 1986 (ECPA)
- Department of Defense Appropriations Act, 1987
- High Performance Computing Act of 1991
- Communications Assistance for Law Enforcement Act of 1994 (CALEA)
- Communications Decency Act of 1996
- Clinger-Cohen Act (Information Technology Management Reform Act) of 1996
- Identity Theft and Assumption Deterrence Act of 1998
- Homeland Security Act of 2002 (HSA)
- Federal Information Security Management Act of 2002 (FISMA)
- Terrorism Risk Insurance Act of 2002
- Cyber Security Research and Development Act, 2002
- E-Government Act of 2002
- Identity Theft Penalty Enhancement Act
- Intelligence Reform and Terrorism Prevention Act of 2004 (IRTPA)

Data from: Fischer, E.A. (2012). *Federal Law Relating to Cybersecurity: Discussion of Proposed Revisions.* Washington, DC: Congressional Research Service.

◼ Chapter Summary

After 9-11, the government had to figure out how to balance the need to obtain information and intelligence with the need to protect law-abiding citizens from being treated unfairly. They had to find a balance in policies that preserve citizens' civil liberties and allows people to feel secure from unjustified attacks by the government while at the same time being protected from terrorists.[21]

◼ Review/Discussion Questions

1. What are the rights guaranteed to U.S. citizens by the Bill of Rights?
2. What are some objections held by civil rights advocates against the Patriot Act?
3. What has the Supreme Court decided concerning U.S. government's actions toward detainees?

◼ Additional Readings

Alperen, M.J. (2011). *Foundations of Homeland Security: Law and Policy.* Hoboken, NJ: John Wiley & Sons, Inc.

Brasch, W. (2005). *America's Unpatriotic Acts.* New York, NY: Peter Lang.

Christie, K. (2008). *America's War on Terrorism.* Lewiston, NY: Edwin Mellen Press.

Whitley, J.D. & Zusman, L.K. (2009). *Homeland Security: Legal and Policy Issues.* Washington, DC: American Bar Association.

◼ Endnotes

1. Brasch, W. (2005). *America's Unpatriotic Acts.* New York, NY: Peter Lang.
2. Christie, K. (2008). *America's War on Terrorism.* Lewiston, NY: Edwin Mellen Press, p. 121.
3. Davis, D.W. & Silver B.D. (2004). "Civil Liberties vs. Security: Public Opinion in the Context of the Terrorist Attacks on America." *American Journal of Political Science, 48,* 28–46.
4. Christie, K. (2008). *America's War on Terrorism.* Lewiston, NY: Edwin Mellen Press.
5. McAdams, A.J. (2005). "Internet Surveillance after September 11: Is the United States Becoming Great Britain?" *Comparative Politics, 37,* 479–498.
6. Rackow, S.H. (2002). "How the USA Patriot Act will Permit Governmental Infringement Upon the Privacy of Americans in the Name of 'Intelligence' Investigations." *University of Pennsylvania Law Review, 150,* 1651–1696.
7. Henderson, N.C. (2002). "The Patriot Act's Impact on the Government's Ability to Conduct Electronic Surveillance of Ongoing Domestic Communications." *Duke Law Journal, 52,* 179–209.

8. Henderson, N.C. (2002). "The Patriot Act's Impact on the Government's Ability to Conduct Electronic Surveillance of Ongoing Domestic Communications." *Duke Law Journal, 52*, 179–209.

9. McAdams, A.J. (2005). "Internet Surveillance after September 11: Is the United States Becoming Great Britain?" *Comparative Politics*, *37*, 479–498; Rubel, A. (2007). "Privacy and the USA Patriot Act: Rights, the Value of Rights, and Autonomy." *Law and Philosophy*, *26*, 119–159.

10. Sinnar, S. (2003). "Patriotic or Unconstitutional? The Mandatory Detention of Aliens Under the USA Patriot Act." *Stanford Law Review, 55*, 1419–1456.

11. Sinnar, S. (2003). "Patriotic or Unconstitutional? The Mandatory Detention of Aliens Under the USA Patriot Act." *Stanford Law Review, 55*, 1419–1456.

12. Henderson, N.C. (2002). "The Patriot Act's Impact on the Government's Ability to Conduct Electronic Surveillance of Ongoing Domestic Communications." *Duke Law Journal, 52*, 179–209; Van Bergen, J. (2002). Repeal the USA Patriot Act. *Truthout*. Retrieved online at http://www.truthout.org/docs_02/04.02A.JVB.Patriot.htm

13. Pfeiffer, E. (2012). 18-month-old Baby Pulled from Flight, Parents Interviewed by TSA. *Yahoo! News*. Retrieved online at http://news.yahoo.com/blogs/sideshow/18-month-old-baby-pulled-flight-parents-interviewed

14. Springer, D. (2012). Muslims, ACLU Challenge the Government's No-fly List. *Foxnews.com*. Retrieved online at http://www.foxnews.com/politics/2012/05/09/muslims-aclu-challenge-government-no-fly-list/

15. Christie, K. (2008). *America's War on Terrorism*. Lewiston, NY: Edwin Mellen Press, p. 122.

16. American Library Association. (2003). Resolution on the USA Patriot Act and Related Measures That Infringe on the Rights of Library Users. Retrieved online at http://www.ala.org/Template.cfm?Section=ifresolutions&Template=/ContentManagement/ContentDisplay.cfm&ContentID=11891

17. Hamilton, M. (2004). "The Supreme Court's Terrorism Cases: What They Held, and Why They Are Important." *FindLaw/Legal Commentary*. Retrieved online at http://writ.news.findlaw.com/hamilton/20040701.html; Brasch, W. (2005). *America's Unpatriotic Acts*. New York, NY: Peter Lang.

18. The Oyez Project. (2012). *Hamdan v. Rumsfeld*. The Oyez Project. Retrieved online at http://www.oyez.org/cases/2000-2009/2005/2005_05_184

19. The Oyez Project. (2012). *Boumediene v. Bush*. The Oyez Project. Retrieved online at http://www.oyez.org/cases/2000-2009/2007/2007_06_1195

20. Humanitarian Law Project. (2012). Supreme Court Ruling Criminalizes Speech in Material Support Law Case. Retrieved online at http://hlp.home.igc.org/

21. Christie, K. (2008). *America's War on Terrorism*. Lewiston, NY: Edwin Mellen Press.

Homeland Security Communication and Technology Issues

Chapter Outline

Chapter Objectives

- To understand the role of communications and communications technology in homeland security and identify some of the major programs dealing with homeland security communications

- To identify different types of cyber threats and attacks, and understand the importance of cyber-terrorism in homeland security

- To understand the role of technology in the context of homeland security, both as a benefit to homeland security professionals as well as a potential threat to homeland security

Introduction

One of the identifiable elements of modern society is technology.[1] No matter the field or in what area of the country, computers, tablets, and cell phones have become virtually ubiquitous. As of mid-2012, there were more cell phones than people in the United States.[2] Along with providing convenience, however, these technologies, and especially those linked to (and sometimes running) our infrastructure, also provide targets for potential enemies.[3] Further exacerbating the threat is the fact that many of the systems have developed independently from one another, with agencies adopting communications platforms that work well for them, but not across jurisdictions or agencies.[4] This fact was perhaps made most clear on September 11th, when the communication systems at the World Trade Center were overwhelmed and miscommunication between agencies was a significant problem.[5] At the same time, technology is providing homeland security professionals with additional tools to protect the homeland in both the "cyber world" as well as the physical world. The double-edged sword of technology is something that is essential for understanding the modern elements of homeland security.

Courtesy of Adam DuBrowa/FEMA.

This chapter examines these pressing problems of technology and vulnerability—as well as addressing what the homeland security apparatus is doing to prevent technology-based problems in the future. The chapter is divided into three parts, the first examining communication issues in homeland security and the policies and organizations that have arisen to address these issues. The second section deals with cyber threats in the context of homeland security and how these threats are being combatted. Finally, in the third section, general issues of technology and homeland security are addressed, focusing on the state and local levels.

Homeland Security and Communications

One of the most significant problems facing homeland security post 9-11 was the issue of operational communications between and among agencies. According to the *9/11 Commission Report*,

> The inability to communicate was a critical element at the World Trade Center, Pentagon, and Somerset County, Pennsylvania crash sites, where multiple agencies and multiple jurisdictions responded. The occurrence of this problem at three very different sites is strong evidence that compatible and adequate communications among public safety organizations at the local, state, and federal levels remains an important problem.[6]

While the original identification of the problem is now well over 10 years old, and some progress has been made, there is still no comprehensive solution to the issue of communications within a homeland security context.[7] Elements of a communications plan have been included in significant legislation like the Intelligence Reform and Terrorism Prevention Act of 2004 (IRTPA), but with the requirements for a comprehensive broadband solution to communications issues costing tens of billions of dollars over the next several decades,[8] political will for a solution has been somewhat lacking.[9] Provisions included in the IRTPA include the mandate that communications systems be interoperable and that there be a system in place that allows for emergency communications across all levels of government, but there was little in terms of specific guidance for how these goals should be accomplished.[10]

In response to the requirements for emergency communications during a homeland security incident, as well as problems experienced during 9-11 and Hurricane Katrina, the Department of Homeland Security in 2007 created the Office of Emergency Communications (OEC), which is responsible for partnering with communications stakeholders at all levels of government to improve emergency capabilities. In order to successfully carry out this mission, the OEC has six branches responsible for various elements of emergency communications coordination:

- *Policy and Planning Branch*: Responsible for the coordination of strategy and policy for the OEC, including development of communications protocols in line with the requirements of the IRTPA. Additionally, they provide research and position papers on policy issues affecting communications and direct special projects focusing on elements of emergency communications.[11]
- *Public Safety and National Security and Emergency Preparedness Partnership Branch (NS/EP)*: Responsible for partnerships across all levels of government and internationally as well as with the private sector, focusing on issues of national security and public safety from an emergency communications perspective.[12]
- *Technical Assistance Branch*: Responsible for handling requests for technical assistance from the states (and other levels of government) as well as national-priority technical assistance.[13]
- *Regional Coordination Branch*: Responsible for building collaboration among partners at the regional level, through the coordination by regional coordinators, to achieve operability and interoperability in emergency communications.[14]
- *Architecture and Advanced Technology Branch*: Responsible for technical analyses and assessments of new technology in homeland security-related functions.[15]
- *Communications Portfolio Management Branch (CPM)*: Responsible for managing priority telecommunications services including several specific programs (mentioned next).[16]

As part of the 2010 National Security Strategy, the president mandated that the United States must, as part of its national security response, prevent disruptions to critical communications.[17] Pursuant to that strategy, President Obama issued Executive Order 13618, which changed the way the federal government operated in terms of emergency communications. Among the ways it changed these operations was by abolishing the National Communications System and establishing a National Security/Emergency Preparedness Communications Executive Committee (CEC), responsible for program management through the Communications Portfolio

Branch, mentioned previously. This branch is specifically responsible for managing several programs fundamental to communications during times of national crisis.[18]

Specifically, programs were developed to assist the government in times of national security, like **the Government Emergency Telecommunications Service (GETS) program** (see **Box 14.1**), which keeps call completion rates high on land lines for national security and emergency planning officials during emergencies,[19] and the TSP program, which allows NS/EP organizations to get priority for telecommunications services during national emergencies—even on private networks.[20] This has caused some controversy, with some critics complaining that the new executive order allows for a government takeover of private communications during a national emergency.[21]

Recent activity has focused on the necessity for the government to secure bandwidth for use by officials during times of emergency. This is a difficult and expensive proposition because, along with the important interoperability issues the OEC currently faces, there is the additional challenge of having to manage change into

---

BOX 14.1   The Government Emergency Telecommunications Service (GETS)

With an increasing reliance on telecommunications technology comes an increased risk during times of emergency if the system goes down or becomes otherwise unusable. One of the primary dangers is that phone lines get overloaded and calls do not connect. This is particularly problematic when the individuals trying to use the phone system are national security or emergency planning personnel. The Government Emergency Telecommunications Service (GETS) is designed to circumvent this problem by providing priority access to those individuals with appropriate designations. The program is directed by the White House, but administered as part of the National Communications System in the Office of Cybersecurity and Communications Division, National Protection and Programs Directorate in the Department of Homeland Security.

The Need for GETS

New technology like broadband communications, fiber optic networks, and high-speed digital switching has changed the way we communicate. This increase in technology also leads to increased vulnerabilities in the system. Major events, such as natural disasters and terrorist attacks, and even minor events like power outages and cables being cut, have demonstrated that entire regions of the telecommunications system can be disrupted. Back-up systems, though present, cannot always cope with the increased traffic during disasters. The necessity for uninterrupted communications among homeland security professionals during these times of increased traffic is obvious, and GETS provides a system to provide that.

How GETS Works

During an emergency, phone lines are sometimes overwhelmed by the number of calls being placed. This, in turn, makes communications difficult for emergency management professionals. The GETS program is activated by the White House in these emergencies to accommodate those individuals with a particular need to communicate. These personnel are given an access number and pin, which they use to gain priority routing through the telephone system, leading to a much lower number of dropped or incomplete calls. The system works by providing priority processing through the Public Switched Telephone Network (PSTN), which gives access to approved individuals using either land lines or cell phones.

Conclusion

GETS is one of several programs in place to enhance the communications capability of emergency management and homeland security professionals during a crisis. By utilizing a private system to prioritize relevant calls, GETS ensures that telecommunications among those who need it most will not be interrupted. The program has met with success thus far, however, given the increase in technology, new systems will likely need to be developed or the current systems will need to continue to evolve.

Data from: Department of Homeland Security. (n.d.). *GETS Program Information*. Retrieved from http://gets.ncs.gov/program_info.html on March 13, 2013.

the future. This requires anticipating new technological developments and making sound policy that allows for emergency access when necessary.[22]

In addition to coordinating at the federal level, the OEC has also mandated states and territories to develop and submit Statewide Communication Interoperability Plans (SCIPs), which both examine current interoperability issues as well as plan for future development of better emergency communications across jurisdictions.[23] These plans have helped jurisdictions progress in their interoperability goals, but there still remain significant hurdles to overcome at all levels of government.

Communications is one of many important elements that affect homeland security and it is an area we have made significant strides in over the past decade. From the policy recommendations of the *9/11 Commission Report* to the recent executive order from the president, the communications strategy of DHS has changed in important ways designed to help ensure that emergency communications are interoperable and secure, today and well into the future. While there has been controversy over some of the policies implemented, the changes represent an important step in addressing an issue essential to both homeland security and emergency management.

Cybersecurity

Many areas of homeland security are influenced by technology, either through methods of detection and threat elimination as in the case of counter-terrorism, or through new threats from adversaries wanting to damage the United States. **Cyber attack**s, and more specifically, **cyber-terrorism**, are one of the most technology-reliant threats—and potentially one of the most damaging if carried out on a large scale successfully. Cyber attacks are, however, not a *new* threat, with the link between computer technology and national security dating from at least 1991, when it was mentioned in a report by the National Academy of Sciences.[24]

Cybersecurity involves a broad set of issues, dealing with national security threats from other nations, sub-national actors (like terrorist organizations), and even private organizations and individuals.[25] This makes defining it a difficult proposition, and attempts have used both the effects of the attack (how much and the type of damage done) as well as the motivation for the attack (e.g., economic versus political). There is some agreement on the fact that three somewhat different cyber threats exist: cyber attacks (which is the broadest category, in which the others fit), **cyber crime** (which is criminal activity carried out through computing) and cyber-terrorism, discussed next. A fourth category, cyber warfare, relies on the identity of those carrying out the attack—specifically a nation-state—in order to meet its definitional criteria. In general, all cyber attacks are uses of malicious computer code meant to disrupt the normal processing or logic of the target system or to steal information from the target system.[26] Of these types of attacks, cyber-terrorism gets the most media attention.

Cyber-terrorism

Given the general definitional problems arising around terrorism and cybersecurity, cyber-terrorism is even more difficult to define.[27, 28] Take, for instance, the case of a country that hires a terrorist organization to carry out an attack against a privately held critical infrastructure. The line between warfare, crime, and terrorism is difficult

KEY TERM
Cyber attack—any type of attack on America carried out through computing.

KEY TERM
Cyber-terrorism—an attack that is conducted for terroristic purposes against the United States and is carried out through computing.

KEY TERM
Cybersecurity—measures taken to protect computers against criminal or unauthorized use of electronic data.

KEY TERM
Cyber crime—criminal activity carried out through computing.

to draw in such a circumstance, and the scenario is not unlikely.[29] Definitions of cyber-terrorism therefore are contentious among academics and practitioners. In fact, the government does not officially define cyber-terrorism at all, though definitions erroneously assigned to the FBI exist. Dorothy Denning, in the influential book *Networks and Netwars*, defines the term as "… politically motivated hacking operations intended to cause grave harm such as loss of life or severe economic damage."[30]

Though the threat was identified over 20 years ago, the threat of cyber-terrorism has still not been realized in any broad sense; however, concern is growing.[31] Former FBI Director Robert Mueller stated, "terrorists increasingly use the Internet to communicate, conduct operational planning, proselytize, recruit, train, and to obtain logistical and financial support. That is a growing and increasing concern for us."[32] In fact, some use of cyber crime to support ongoing terrorist activity seems to an important element in the definition of cyber-terrorism. For example, in at least one case, through an email, an Internet user was directed to a fake eBay site in which she entered her financial information, which helped finance a terrorist cell planning physical attacks in both Europe and the Middle East (see **Box 14.2**).[33]

Though it has not yet happened, physical damage through malicious computer use is a possibility. A 2007 test conducted by researchers in conjunction with DHS and the Department of Energy demonstrated the ability of hackers to get into an energy plant's information systems and cause a generator to self-destruct.[34] Similar threats have been popularized by the mass media,[35] though there is disagreement

---

BOX 14.2   2009 Cyberspace Policy Review—The Need for Change

In 2009, under the direction of the White House, a comprehensive policy review was undertaken to examine the effectiveness of the nation's cybersecurity policies. The review of these policies was not positive. The final document pointed out several issues with the nation's cybersecurity, including its vulnerability to attack and the government's current inability to secure the digital infrastructure of the United States. The review specifically states,

> The architecture of the nation's digital infrastructure, based largely upon the Internet, is not secure or resilient. Without major advances in the security of these systems or significant change in how they are constructed or operated, it is doubtful that the United States can protect itself from the growing threat of cybercrime and state-sponsored intrusions and operations.

However, in pointing out these deficiencies, the review also suggests a way forward—government working with the private sector to enhance the security of cyberspace and America's digital interests.

Problem with Cybersecurity in America

The Internet and associated technologies represent the nation's "nervous system," and without these technologies the government and economy could not function. As such, the digital infrastructure has been designated by DHS as one of the areas of critical infrastructure (see chapter on "Anti-terrorism and Counter-terrorism"). One of the problems with defending the nation's cyber interests is the fact that most of the country's digital infrastructure is privately owned by both American and international companies. Further, the security management of cyberspace is distributed over a wide array of federal departments and agencies, making coordination of cyber defense difficult.

Exacerbating the problem is the fact that digital threats have already manifested as actual attacks. Digital criminals have stolen hundreds of millions of dollars, and nation-states have captured sensitive military data and intellectual property. The increase in these digital intrusions may only be precursors to even more damaging cyber attacks, including the potential for crippling the communications systems of on how close terrorists are to being able to conduct these types of attacks successfully.[36, 37]

The general consensus, insofar as one has developed, suggests that while terrorists likely lack the capability to conduct these attacks, there is the possibility that they will contract with countries or organizations that do.[38] Indeed, as with terrorists using cyber crime to raise funds, they may also be working with hackers to exploit vulnerabilities in software that the government relies on to either maintain critical infrastructure or communications. In the latter case, it is believed that, should there be a large physical attack, communications could be disrupted to amplify the effects of the attack.[39]

Cyber Defense

In the context of homeland security, then, it is important the threat of cyber attacks is dealt with, despite the scant agreement on the definitions involved. Increasing the complexity of the problem of defense is the fact that cyber-terrorism is not limited to the realms of homeland security or national security specifically. So, as with other areas of homeland security (counter-terrorism specifically), there are several agencies involved in the activities surround cyber defense. Chief among these are DHS, the Department of Defense, the FBI, and the NSA.

CYBERSPACE POLICY REVIEW

Assuring a Trusted and Resilient Information and Communications Infrastructure

Courtesy of the White House.

the country or damaging the ability of the military to defend the nation.

The Way Forward

Despite the problems identified in the review, there are significant things the government can do to improve cybersecurity. Understanding the position of the government vis-à-vis the technology curve—in short, the government is behind—is the first step in addressing the problems presented by cyber threats. The review puts the matter succinctly: "The status quo is no longer acceptable." It offers significant ways to enhance the current approach to digital infrastructure in the U.S.:

- Begin a national dialogue on cybersecurity to help people understand the importance of the topic.
- Enhance partnerships with the private sector, without which the goals of cybersecurity are impossible.
- Develop a comprehensive framework that will allow the government to plan for, and respond to, significant cybersecurity incidents.

- Define security objectives for next-generation technologies being developed and deployed that allow for government to engage in cybersecurity operations.

Conclusion

While the nation's current ability to defend against cyber-attack is low, the defense of our digital infrastructure is improving. The review establishes significant steps that can be undertaken to enhance the government's ability to engage in cyber defense. These steps are only an outline for comprehensive cybersecurity, and many of the details are significant. The way these details are addressed will determine how secure our nation's digital infrastructure is in the future, and given the growing importance of the Internet and related technologies, may be some of the most important security policies developed.

Data from: The White House. (2009). *Cyberspace Policy Review.* Retrieved from http://www.dhs.gov/sites/default/files/publications/Cyberspace_Policy_Review_final_0.pdf on March 13, 2013.

Department of Homeland Security

DHS's role in the realm of cyber defense is largely focused on preparation and mitigation in the event of a cyber attack. The National Cyber Security Division (NCSD), housed under the of Office of Cybersecurity and Communications (CS&C), is responsible for the coordination of relevant agencies in the wake of cyber-terrorism and has several programs in place to assess the vulnerabilities of the nation's critical infrastructure. They describe their mission as:

> The National Cyber Security Division seeks to protect the critical cyber infrastructure 24 hours a day, 7 days a week. The National Cyberspace Response System coordinates the cyber leadership, processes, and protocols that will determine when and what action(s) need to be taken as cyber incidents arise.[40]

Two programs falling under the purview of DHS in the realm of cybersecurity are worth highlighting. The first is the National Cyber Response Coordination Group, which is made up of 13 federal agencies and is the principal entity responsible for coordination and recovery in the event of a cyber attack. The second, and perhaps the most important program falling under DHS's cyber portfolio, is the Federal National Security (FNS) branch of the NCSD, which is responsible for securing government networks in the case of a cyber emergency.

Another component of DHS's role in the context of cybersecurity is the Computer Emergency Response Team (US-CERT), the operational arm for the NCSD, tasked specifically with the security of government cyber operations and collaboration among state and local partners as well as those operating in the private sector. Under the auspices of this program, security alerts are distributed to relevant partners and responses are developed to assist with defense and resiliency. Additionally, US-CERT is tasked with the management of information-sharing across all partners.

Department of Defense

In addition to the DHS coordination efforts, the Department of Defense (DOD) is also responsible for cybersecurity issues, though its role tends to be more offensive than DHS's role.[41] While much of what the DOD engages in in terms of cyber warfare remains classified, the *Department of Defense Strategy for Operating in Cyberspaces* makes it clear that the department views cyber issues as a natural outgrowth of its regular military mission:

> Though the networks and systems that make up cyberspace are man-made, often privately owned, and primarily civilian in use, treating cyberspace as a domain is a critical organizing concept for DOD's national security missions. This allows DOD to organize, train, and equip for cyberspace as we do in air, land, maritime, and space to support national security interests.[42]

In light of this, and the specific vulnerabilities that DOD faces due to their own reliance on computer networks to conduct operations, the military established the **Cyber Command (USCYBERCOM)** under the United States Strategic Command (USSTRATCOM).[43] USCYBERCOM is specifically tasked with managing risk within DOD networks and making sure those networks are resilient in case of an attack, working with other agencies and organizations to ensure coordinated response to any attacks that occur, and to develop and deploy innovative capabilities in terms of the cyber-defensive environment.[44]

KEY TERM
USCYBERCOM—U.S. Cyber Command is specifically tasked with managing risk within DOD networks and making sure those networks are resilient in case of an attack.

Uniquely, USCYBERCOM is co-located in the National Security Agency (NSA), and the director of the NSA is also the commander of USCYBERCOM, underlying the importance of coordination across agencies, without which missions can easily fail.[45] This relationship also highlights the importance that intelligence, the NSA's specialty, plays in the realm of cybersecurity.

Courtesy of DOD.

National Security Agency

The NSA, in addition to housing USCYBERCOM, has an important role to play in the context of cyber defense. The agency is responsible for gathering intelligence from electronic signals, including computer networks, and responds directly to tasking from any executive agency, including both DOD and DHS.[46] Importantly, there are restrictions on the ability of the NSA to gather information on U.S. persons, as a way to safeguard citizen's privacy.

Like the DOD, much of what the NSA does in regards to cybersecurity is classified. The NSA does monitors suspect websites and occasionally renders them inaccessible.[47] Additionally, the NSA is a co-sponsor (with DHS) of the National Centers of Academic Excellence in Information Assurance Education, which allows colleges and universities to apply for a designation as a center of excellence, providing their students access to scholarships in related areas.[48]

Central Intelligence Agency

The Central Intelligence Agency's role in cyber defense is somewhat limited relative to homeland security. They are primarily responsible for identifying and evaluating foreign threats to domestic computer systems. Specifically, the Information Operations Center at the CIA has conducted a series of exercises to determine the nation's vulnerability to cyber attacks from both state and nonstate actors.[49] The results of these exercises have been helpful in identifying potential vulnerabilities and logistical issues, including the problem of coordination, as much of the nation's cyber infrastructure is controlled by private organizations.[50]

Federal Bureau of Investigation

The role of the Federal Bureau of Investigation's (FBI) role, as it relates to cyber attacks, is also limited. The FBI primarily deals with computer intrusion issues related to crime. The FBI Computer Intrusion Program provides support to field offices investigating computer crimes, though as mentioned previously, those crimes occasionally intersect with terrorism and other homeland security-relevant topics. The FBI's Deputy Assistant Director, Cyber Division, said this regarding the FBI's cyber capability:

> The FBI is expanding our efforts to address the rapidly growing cyber threat as it relates to both terrorism and national security. The number of individuals and groups with the ability to use computers for illegal, harmful, and possibly devastating purposes is on the rise. We are particularly concerned about terrorists and state actors wishing to exploit vulnerabilities in U.S. systems and networks … The FBI has a division dedicated to combating cyber crime and cyber-terrorism. We are committed to identifying and neutralizing those individuals or groups that

illegally access computer systems, spread malicious code, support terrorist or state sponsored computer operations, and steal trade secrets that present an economic and security threat to the U.S. (see **Box 14.3**).[51]

Hearing on cyberterrorism, 108 Cong. (2004) (Keith Lourdeau). Retrieved from http://www.fbi.gov/news/testimony/hearing-on-cyber-terrorism

Cybersecurity, though not a new realm of homeland security, is increasing in importance. Despite the difficulties in defining exactly what constitutes a cyber issue for homeland security, there is consensus that it poses a potential risk in a variety of areas including potentially critical infrastructure. While DHS is the lead agency in some respects, the response to cyber attacks is government-wide, with responsibility

---

BOX 14.3   Operation Aurora Attacks

Operation Aurora was a highly effective malware attack against private companies that took place over the course of 2010. The operation was geared towards stealing intellectual property and other valuable information such as user activity and usernames. The attacks targeted over 30 companies, ranging from Google to Lockheed Martin, and used a variety of types of attack to get the information. While there is no direct evidence of Chinese government involvement, the attacks have been traced to two large Chinese hacking groups who have been linked in the past to government operations.

How It Unfolded

The attacks were first publicly identified by Google, which released information that they had been hacked and had user information stolen. Google was quick to identify the type of information, in this case the search activity of Chinese dissidents, and suggested the Chinese government was involved. Shortly after Google identified the intrusion into its system, other companies, like Adobe and the security company RSA, also acknowledged that they had been attacked and had information stolen. In each case, the evidence suggested that the intrusions originated from China, though Chinese officials maintain that their government was not involved.

Code-named "Sneaky Panda," the Elderwood Gang (or the Beijing Group), the hacking organization based in China, steals information from companies based in the U.S. The software used for the attacks has been in development since at least 2006 and is very sophisticated. Aurora is unique in several respects, the most important of which is the scope of the attack—hitting a large number of companies essentially at the same time—and the sophistication of the intrusions, which use a variety of attack methods rather than a single "back-door" strategy.

Aurora's Relevance

Aside from the information stolen, Aurora represents a threat in several ways. First, it demonstrates the vulnerabilities of the nation's cyber infrastructure. The hackers were able to break into secure, technology-based organizations to get the information. Presumably, these organizations were aware of security concerns before the attack and were unable to adequately prevent their exploitation. This problem applies to government agencies as well, which frequently do not have the ability, or resources, to prevent intrusion into their systems.

Second, it shows that there are potentially hostile actors who are actively using the Internet and related technologies for political purposes. The hacking groups that engaged in Aurora's intrusions have been linked to the Chinese government. By utilizing these groups, the Chinese have been able to maintain plausible deniability, despite the U.S.'s ability to track the hackers down to an individual level.

Finally, it points to future threats. With organizations-for-hire potentially engaging in cyber attacks, it suggests we've reached the time when terrorists or other adversaries can hire groups to sabotage America's cyber infrastructure. Even if they are unable to do so, Aurora still remains a threat, for in the new technological environment, information is a powerful tool that can be used against American interests. Understanding this fact is essential to protecting the country against cyber threats into the future.

Data from: Clayton, M. (14 September 2012). "Stealing US Business Secrets: Experts ID Two Huge Cyber 'Gangs' in China. *The Christian Science Monitor*. Retrieved from http://www.csmonitor.com/USA/2012/0914/Stealing-US-business-secrets-Experts-ID-two-huge-cyber-gangs-in-China; Gary, H.B. (2010). *Operation Aurora*. Retrieved from http://hbgary.com/attachments/WhitePaper%20HBGary%20Threat%20Report,%20Operation%20Aurora.pdf on March 13, 2013.

falling to a variety of federal agencies. While the advent of a major cyber attack that, by itself, causes casualties is slim, the threat of a cyber attack in conjunction with other terrorist-related activities seem higher. In any event, the threat to our homeland security is significant enough that cybersecurity is clearly an area that cannot be ignored.

© AP Images/Charles Krupa.

Technology and Homeland Security

While homeland security has suffered threats resulting from the increasing amount of technology in society, it is clear that technology also presents opportunities to better safeguard the homeland.[52] From the advent of DHS, technological solutions to the problem of homeland security have been part of the overall department mission.[53] The Homeland Security Act of 2002 mandated that a counterpart to the Defense Department's Advanced Research Projects Agency (DARPA) be created in a homeland security context.[54] **The Homeland Security Advanced Research Projects Agency (HSARPA)**, housed within DHS's Directorate of Science and Technology, is responsible for the development of advanced technology for the protection of the nation's critical infrastructure and other important elements of homeland security.[55] HSARPA is, however, not the only technologically directed program within DHS, as other elements, such as the First Responder's Group (FRG), also have technologically relevant missions.[56]

HSARPA

HSARPA is the agency responsible for developing some of the most technologically advanced elements of homeland security. As part of their mission, HSARPA works directly with many of the lead stakeholders in homeland security, such as the Secret Service, bomb squads, transportation authorities and others, to develop technological solutions to real-world problems that these organizations face. HSARPA itself has several areas of focus, housed within divisions in DHS:

- Borders and Maritime Security Division
- Chemical and Biological Defense Division
- Cyber Security Division
- Explosives Division
- Human Factors and Behavioral Sciences Division
- Infrastructure Protection and Disaster Management Division

Each of these divisions is tasked with identifying gaps in the areas of need most relevant to the practitioners where technological solutions will have the most impact.[57] One example of these projects is the recently developed Imaging System for Immersive Surveillance (ISIS) system, a 360-degree camera with high resolution, which was developed under the Science and Technology Infrastructure and Geophysical Division for assistance with surveillance at public events.[58] Other, similar programs exist within each of HSARPA's areas (see **Box 14.4**).

> **KEY TERM**
> **HSARPA**—the Homeland Security Advanced Research Projects Agency, which is focused on providing security for critical infrastructure in the U.S.

BOX 14.4   Ground-Penetrating Radar to Detect Tunnels—HSARPA in Action

One of the challenges facing the U.S. Border Patrol is the increasing use of tunnels by smugglers on the U.S./Mexico border. While the tunnels have always been a problem, the number has gone up dramatically in recent years, with over 60% of the tunnels discovered being found in the past 7 years. These represent a significant threat to the homeland security of the United States, not only because of the drugs and illegal immigrants who are normally brought across the border, but because of the potential to use these tunnels to smuggle terrorists or WMDs into the country.

The Homeland Security Advanced Research Projects Agency (HSARPA) is working in conjunction with Lockheed Martin Advanced Technology Laboratories to develop technology to help the Border Patrol identify the location of these tunnels so they can be blocked. This is difficult because many of the tunnels are in urban areas, and can begin and end in buildings or behind structures, making it difficult to detect them from the air, the approach originally suggested. Instead, HSARPA is pursuing ground-penetrating radar technology, which can help map the tunnels from above ground.

How It Works

The new radar system will be attached to a vehicle and pulled across areas where there may be tunnels. Electromagnetic waves from the radar can be used to construct complete pictures of what appears underground. Tunnels will show up as red, yellow, and aquamarine dots against a neutral background, making identification of these threats relatively simple.

The technology being used for tunnel-detection is already field tested in the sense that engineers already use ground-penetrating radar for a variety of purposes. However, these uses tend to be confined to finding cables and other underground elements relatively near the surface. The tunnels being used for illegal activity frequently are dug much deeper, which requires a technological redevelopment by HSARPA and Lockheed Martin. The new radar will use frequencies much lower than those currently being used, allowing for additional depth of detection.

Conclusion

Technologies like the tunnel-detecting radar represent the utility of HSARPA for homeland security. Not only does it make it possible to detect and possibly deter threats from adversaries, it also represents a successful collaboration between the public and private sector to improve homeland security. Projects like this one also demonstrate the importance of primary research, which can propel the next generation of homeland security technologies.

Data from: Department of Homeland Security. (2009). *Tunnel-vision.* Retrieved from http://www.dhs.gov/tunnel-vision on March 13, 2013.

Support to the Homeland Security Enterprise and First Responders Group

In addition to the advanced research projects provided by HSARPA, a second high-technology group exists within the Directorate of Science and Technology. The Support to the Homeland Security Enterprise and First Responders Group (FRG) is tasked with the goals of making first responders safer as well as increasing the operational capacity of first responders through the adoption of technology that makes elements such as communication easier and more reliable.[59] Unlike HSARPA, however, the mission of the FRG is not to develop new technologies, but rather to assist with the deployment of existing technologies. The FRG accomplishes its mission through three divisions: the **National Urban Security Technology Laboratory (NUSTL)**, Office for Interoperability and Compatibility (OIC), and the Technology Clearinghouse/R-Tech (TCR).[60]

The NUSTL is focused, as its name suggests, on the adoption of technology primarily for a urban environments. Housed in New York City, the NUSTL serves as the technological authority for promoting and integrating useful technologies for end-users in homeland security—primarily first responders.[61] Additionally, the NUSTL conducts test programs and evaluations of new, homeland security-relevant technologies for first responders, while applying their knowledge of the

KEY TERM
NUSTL—National Urban Security Technology Laboratory focused on providing security for large cities and metropolitan areas.

first-responder environment for integration of these technologies. Further, the FRG plays a significant role in developing and establishing operations standards for homeland security equipment and technology.[62]

The OIC, on the other hand, is focused directly on the problems mentioned previously in this chapter. Specifically, they help with communications interoperability and operations for first responders.[63] This mission is particularly difficult, and particularly relevant, because the current first-responder landscape consists of over 60,000 state and local public safety agencies that have some homeland security responsibility. The OIC mission is to make communications among these agencies as seamless as possible, and they accomplish this mission through the development of technologies and standards for communications equipment and processes.[64]

The TCR is directed towards a different mission than either the OIC or the NUSTL. It has the mission of deploying technologies that are field-ready for first responders operating in the homeland security environment. It is a rapid-deployment program, with the goal of meeting 80% of requirements that fill an operational gap 12–15 months after that gap has been identified. The program received requests from active first responders rather than through an internal process of identification, ensuring that the technologies delivered meet the specific needs of those in the field.[65]

Courtesy of DHS.

Though technology represents a "double-edged sword," it is clear that DHS is relying on significant technological advancement and standardization to help in its mission. The goals of the Science and Technology Directorate, particularly in reference to HSARPA and the FRG, are essential given the ubiquity of technology across all critical domains. The technology developed by HSARPA implemented through the HRG provides first responders at all levels solutions they need to help fulfill their own respective homeland security missions. As it has been from the advent of DHS, technology will continue to be an essential part of defending the homeland.

Chapter Summary

Issues in communications and cyber defense are increasing in importance across the homeland security domain. With the increasing use of the Internet, and the use of networked systems for controlling much of our everyday lives, the risk of a cyber attack (of whatever type) has steadily increased. Additionally, and perhaps unsurprisingly, there has been an increase in the nexus of cyber crime and terrorist organizations. Meanwhile, communications issues identified after 9-11, though improved, still are not resolved. True interoperability and compatibility across the nation's 60,000 agencies remains somewhat distant.

However, even with the problems technology can present, it is clear that it can also provide solutions. The advent and promulgation of new technologies by organizations in homeland security such as HSARPA and the FRG have assisted first responders at all levels of government. Developments such as new surveillance options as well as communications equipment and explosive detection technology have assisted in helping secure the homeland from attack. Additional technologies being developed will most likely also assist in combating terrorism and aiding emergency response efforts.

In any event, technology is likely to remain both a focal point for future threats, particularly in cyberspace, and a method by which those threats can be neutralized. DHS and related agencies have devoted significant resources to studying the threat as well as developing appropriate responses.

■ Review/Discussion Questions

1. What role does communications technology play in homeland security, and what problems were identified by the 9/11 Commission as issues?

2. How many cyber attacks have there been that have physically damaged infrastructure in the United States? Does it represent a significant threat?

3. What are the problems with defining cyber-terrorism? How might that affect homeland security operations?

4. What do you think the role of HSARPA should be in regards to homeland security technology, and why is this role important?

5. Is there a good way to divide cyber defense issues between the Department of Defense and the Department of Homeland Security? How might these jurisdictions be defined?

■ Additional Readings

Arquilla, J. & Ronfeldt, D. (Eds.). *Networks and Netwar.* Santa Monica, CA: Rand.

The White House. (2009). *Cyberspace Policy Review.* Retrieved from http://www .dhs.gov/sites/default/files/publications/Cyberspace_Policy_Review_final_0 .pdf on March 13, 2013.

■ Endnotes

1. Misa, T.J., Brey, P., & Feenberg, A. (Eds.) (2004). *Modernity and Technology.* Boston, MA: MIT Press.

2. Wireless Quick Facts. (2013). Retrieved from http://www.ctia.org/advocacy/ research/index.cfm/aid/10323

3. Panetta, L. (2013). *Remarks by Secretary Panetta at Georgetown University, Washington, D.C.* Retrieved from http://www.defense.gov/transcripts/ transcript.aspx?transcriptid=5189

4. Jenkins, W.O. (2006). "Collaboration Over Adaptation: The Case for Interoperable Communications in Homeland Security." *Public Administration Review, 66,* 319–321.

5. National Commission on Terrorist Attacks Upon the United States. (2004). *The 9/11 Commission Report: Final Report of the National Commission on Terrorist Attacks Upon the United States (Authorized Ed.).* New York: W.W. Norton & Company, Inc.

6. National Commission on Terrorist Attacks Upon the United States. (2004). *The 9/11 Commission Report: Final Report of the National Commission on Terrorist Attacks Upon the United States (Authorized Ed.)*. New York: W.W. Norton & Company, Inc.

7. *Ten Years after 9/11: Improving Emergency Communications*, 112 Cong. (2011). (Susan Collins).

8. Moore, L.K. (2012). *The First Responder Network and Next-Generation Communications for Public Safety: Issues for Congress* (CRS report No. R42543). Retrieved from http://www.fas.org/sgp/crs/homesec/R42543.pdf

9. Moore, L.K. (2005). *Public Safety, Communications: Policy, Proposals, Legislation and Progress* (CRS report No. RL32594). Retrieved from http://www.fas.org/sgp/crs/homesec/R41842.pdf

10. Intelligence Reform and Terrorism Prevention Act of 2004. Pub. L. No. 108–458, §7303, 118 Stat. 3638.

11. Department of Homeland Security. *OEC Policy and Planning Branch*. Retrieved from http://www.dhs.gov/oec-policy-and-planning-branch

12. Department of Homeland Security. *Public Safety and National Security/ Emergency Preparedness (NS/EP) Partnerships*. Retrieved from http://www.dhs.gov/node/6018/

13. Department of Homeland Security. *Office of Emergency Communications Technical Assistance Program*. Retrieved from http://www.dhs.gov/office-emergency-communications-technical-assistance-program

14. Department of Homeland Security. *OEC Regional Coordination Program*. Retrieved from http://www.dhs.gov/oec-regional-coordination-program

15. Department of Homeland Security. *OEC Architecture and Advanced Technology Branch*. Retrieved from http://www.dhs.gov/oec-architecture-and-advanced-technology-branch

16. Department of Homeland Security. *OEC Communications Portfolio Management Branch*. Retrieved from http://www.dhs.gov/oec-communications-portfolio-management-branch

17. Office of the President (2010). *National Security Strategy*. Washington, DC: GPO.

18. Reese, S. (2012). *National Security and Emergency Preparedness Communications: A Summary of Executive Order 13618* (CRS report No. R24740). Retrieved from http://www.fas.org/sgp/crs/homesec/R42740.pdf

19. Department of Homeland Security. *GETS Program Information*. Retrieved from http://gets.ncs.gov/

20. Department of Homeland Security. *Telecommunications Service Priority*. Retrieved from http://tsp.ncs.gov/

21. "White House Gives Homeland Security Control of all Communications Systems." (13 July 2012). RT.com. Retrieved from http://rt.com/usa/news/white-house-systems-order-142/

22. Moore, L.K. (2012). *The First Responder Network and Next-generation Communications for Public Safety: Issues for Congress* (CRS report No. R42543). Retrieved from http://www.fas.org/sgp/crs/homesec/R42543.pdf

23. Department of Homeland Security (2011). *National Summary of Fiscal Year 2010: Statewide Communication Interoperability Plan Implementation Reports.* Retrieved from http://www.safecomprogram.gov/library/Lists/Library/Attachments/118/FY%202010%20Summary%20of%20SCIPs.pdf

24. Cavelty, M.D. (2007). "Cyber-terror—Looming Threat or Phantom Menace? The Framing of the US Cyber-threat Debate." *Journal of Information Technology & Politics, 4,* 19–36.

25. Rollins, J. & Wilson, C. (2007). Terrorist Capabilities for Cyberattack: Overview and Policy Issues (CRS report No. RL33123. Retrieved from http://www.fas.org/sgp/crs/homesec/RL33123.pdf

26. Wilson, C. (2008). *Botnets, Cybercrime and Cyberterrorism: Vulnerabilities and Policy Issues for Congress* (CRS report No. RL32114). Retrieved from http://www.fas.org/sgp/crs/homesec/RL32114.pdf

27. Cavelty, M.D. (2007). "Cyber-terror—Looming Threat or Phantom Menace? The Framing of the US Cyber-threat Debate." *Journal of Information Technology & Politics, 4,* 19-36.

28. Wilson, C. (2008). *Botnets, Cybercrime and Cyberterrorism: Vulnerabilities and Policy Issues for Congress* (CRS report No. RL32114). Retrieved from http://www.fas.org/sgp/crs/terror/RL32114.pdf

29. Weimann, G. (2008). "Cyber-terrorism: Are We Barking up the Wrong Tree?" *Harvard Asia Pacific Review, 9,* 41-46.

30. Denning, D. (2001). "Activism, Hactivism, and Cyberterrorism: The Internet as a Tool for Influencing Foreign Policy." In Arquilla, J., and Ronfeldt, D. (eds.). *Networks and Netwar.* Santa Monica, CA: Rand.

31. Weimann, G. (2008). "Cyber-terrorism: Are We Barking up the Wrong Tree?" *Harvard Asia Pacific Review, 9,* 41-46.

32. *Current and Projected National Security Threats to the United States,* 110 Cong. S. Hrg. 110-835. (2007). (Robert Mueller).

33. Krebs, B. (7 July 2007). "Three Worked the Web to Help Terrorists." *The Washington Post Online.* Retrieved from http://www.washingtonpost.com/wp-dyn/content/article/2007/07/05/AR2007070501945.html

34. Meserve, J. (2013). *Sources: Staged Cyber Attack Reveals Vulnerability in Power Grid.* Retrieved from http://articles.cnn.com/2007-09-26/us/power.at.risk_1_generator-cyber-attack-electric-infrastructure?_s=PM:US

35. Wilson, C. (2008). *Botnets, Cybercrime and Cyberterrorism: Vulnerabilities and Policy Issues for Congress* (CRS report No. RL32114). Retrieved from Retrieved from http://www.fas.org/sgp/crs/terror/RL32114.pdf

36. Wilson, C. (2003). *Computer Attacks and Cyber Terrorism: Vulnerabilities and Issues for Congress* (CRS report No. RL32114). Retrieved from https://opencrs.com/document/RL32114/2003-10-17/

37. Cavelty, M.D. (2007). "Cyber-terror—Looming Threat or Phantom Menace? The Framing of the US Cyber-threat Debate." *Journal of Information Technology & Politics, 4,* 19-36.

38. *Cybersecurity: Preventing Terrorist Attacks and Protecting Privacy in Cyberspace,* 111 Cong. S. Hrg. 111-664. (2007). (Steven Chabinsky).

39. Wilson, C. (2003). *Computer Attacks and Cyber Terrorism: Vulnerabilities and Issues for Congress* (CRS report No. RL32114). Retrieved from https://opencrs.com/document/RL32114/2003-10-17/

40. Department of Homeland Security. *National Cyber Security Division.* Retrieved from http://www.dhs.gov/national-cyber-security-division

41. Gjelten, T. (2013). *Pentagon Goes on the Offensive Against Cyberattacks.* Retrieved from http://www.npr.org/2013/02/11/171677247/pentagon-goes-on-the-offensive-against-cyber-attacks

42. Department of Defense. (2011). *Department of Defense Strategy for Operating in Cyberspace.* Retrieved from http://www.defense.gov/news/d20110714cyber.pdf

43. Department of Defense. (2011). *Department of Defense Strategy for Operating in Cyberspace.* Retrieved from http://www.defense.gov/news/d20110714cyber.pdf

44. Department of Defense. (2011). *Department of Defense Strategy for Operating in Cyberspace.* Retrieved from http://www.defense.gov/news/d20110714cyber.pdf

45. Nakashima, E. (19 March 2010). "Dismantling of Saudi-CIA Web Site Illustrates Clearer Need for Cyberwar Policies." *Washington Post Online.* Retrieved from http://www.washingtonpost.com/wp-dyn/content/article/2010/03/18/AR2010031805464.html?sid=ST2010031901063

46. National Security Agency. *Signals Intelligence.* Retrieved from http://www.nsa.gov/sigint/index.shtml

47. Nakashima, E. (19 March 2010). "Dismantling of Saudi-CIA Web Site Illustrates Clearer Need for Cyberwar Policies." *Washington Post Online.* Retrieved from http://www.washingtonpost.com/wp-dyn/content/article/2010/03/18/AR2010031805464.html?sid=ST2010031901063

48. National Security Agency. *National Centers for Academic Excellence.* Retrieved from http://www.nsa.gov/ia/academic_outreach/nat_cae/index.shtml

49. Bridis, T. (26 May 2005). "'Silent Horizon' War Games Wrap Up for the CIA." *USA Today.* Retrieved from http://usatoday30.usatoday.com/tech/news/techpolicy/2005-05-26-cia-wargames_x.htm

50. Rollins, J. & Wilson, C. (2007). Terrorist Capabilities for Cyberattack: Overview and Policy Issues (CRS report No. RL33123. Retrieved from Retrieved from http://www.fas.org/sgp/crs/homesec/RL33123.pdf

51. *Hearing on Cyberterrorism*, 108 Cong. (2004). (Keith Lourdeau). Retrieved from http://www.fbi.gov/news/testimony/hearing-on-cyber-terrorism

52. George Washington University Homeland Security Police Institute. (2008). *Technology in Homeland Security: A Double-edged Sword.* Retrieved from http://www.gwumc.edu/hspi/old/pubs/HSPI-IBM%20S&T%20in%20Homeland%20Security%20Hightlights%20-%20FINAL.pdf

53. Homeland Security Presidential Directive 7. Retrieved from http://www.dhs.gov/homeland-security-presidential-directive-7#1

54. Homeland Security Act of 2002, Pub. L. No. 107-296 § 307, 116 Stat. 2135.

55. Department of Homeland Security. *Science and Technology Directorate Homeland Security Advanced Research Projects Agency.* Retrieved from http://www.dhs.gov/st-hsarpa

56. Department of Homeland Security. *Science and Technology Directorate Support to the Homeland Security Enterprise and First Responders Group.* Retrieved from http://www.dhs.gov/st-frg

57. Department of Homeland Security. *Science and Technology Directorate Homeland Security Advanced Research Projects Agency.* Retrieved from http://www.dhs.gov/st-hsarpa

58. Department of Homeland Security. ISIS: *New Video Camera Sees It All.* Retrieved from http://www.dhs.gov/isis-new-video-camera-sees-it-all

59. Department of Homeland Security. *Science and Technology Directorate Support to the Homeland Security Enterprise and First Responders Group.* Retrieved from http://www.dhs.gov/st-frg

60. Department of Homeland Security. *Science and Technology Directorate Support to the Homeland Security Enterprise and First Responders Group.* Retrieved from http://www.dhs.gov/st-frg

61. Department of Homeland Security. *National Urban Security Technology Laboratory: Strategic Plan 2009-2013.* Retrieved from http://www.dhs.gov/xlibrary/assets/st_dhs_nustl_strategic_plan.pdf

62. Department of Homeland Security. *Science and Technology Directorate Support to the Homeland Security Enterprise and First Responders Group.* Retrieved from http://www.dhs.gov/st-frg

63. Department of Homeland Security. *Science and Technology Directorate Office for Interoperability and Compatibility.* Retrieved from https://www.dhs.gov/st-oic

64. National Public Safety Communications Council. *Office for Interoperability and Compatibility (OIC).* Retrieved from http://www.npstc.org/oic.jsp

65. Department of Homeland Security. *Science and Technology Directorate Technology Clearinghouse / R-tech.* Retrieved from http://www.dhs.gov/st-tcr

Domain Security and the Future of Homeland Security

Chapter Objectives

- To understand the importance of domain security, particularly airline security, port security, and border security

- To understand the role TSA plays in airline security and its additional oversight responsibilities in reference to other elements of domain security

- To identify the roles of the U.S. Border Patrol and Immigration and Customs Enforcement in terms of border security

- To understand the challenges faced by homeland security in the future

■ Introduction

The flight attendants did not notice the large man, at least 6'4" and 200 lbs, as he got on the plane.[1] He had an aisle seat, 29C, near the back of the Boeing 767 that was on its way from Paris's Charles De Gaulle Airport to Miami International Airport in Florida. Perhaps like many of the passengers, the man was jittery—after all, the 9-11 attacks on the World Trade Center and Pentagon had only happened about 3 months before.[2] The man, assumed to be on his way to a vacation, carried no luggage.[3]

As the flight took off and the attendants offered refreshments to the passengers, the man declined them all, including water—unusual for someone on a 10-hour transcontinental flight. One flight attendant tried to speak to the man in French, but he indicated that he spoke English. This piqued her curiosity, and she joked with the man about being on a diet, but her suspicions persisted. When asked where he was from, the man replied that he was from Sri Lanka, which the attendant didn't believe.[4]

Just after the 2-hour mark, the point at which it would be impossible for the plane to return to Paris,[5] some passengers complained of a smell of smoke in the cabin. Looking around, the attendant saw the man attempting to light a match. She reminded him that smoking on the flight was not allowed, and the man promised not to attempt it again. However, a few minutes later, she came by the man's seat again and found him bent over, apparently hiding something. Believing he was smoking a cigarette, she pulled him up after asking him what he was doing, and at that point saw that he was attempting to light another match—but this time, there was a shoe in his lap with what seemed like a fuse sticking out.[6]

Once the attendant realized what was happening, she tried to stop him, though he pushed her to the floor. With the help of other passengers, the flight crew subdued the man, and, using plastic handcuffs, seat belt extenders and other items, made sure he was immobile. A doctor on board the flight administered Valium to the man, to keep him calm.[7]

The man was Richard Reid, the now infamous "shoe bomber" and an Al Qaeda operative.[8]

While this act of heroism is deservedly celebrated as an instance of those in transportation thwarting a terrorist attack, the attempted bombing highlights one of the major issues that the homeland security community is still attempting to address today. While we place a premium on security in air transportation, the passenger system is designed for efficiency and convenience for the passengers—not to be perfectly secure.[9] At the time of Richard Reid's attempted attack, shoes—and other items that still make it through security without being completely inspected—could conceal weapons or bombs used against aircraft.[10] Importantly, other essential systems in the United States share a similar vulnerability—our shipping systems, immigrations systems, and our ports were all originally developed as commercial enterprises, making their security especially problematic.

© Plymouth County Jail/AP Images.

Sea, Land, Air

Homeland security is challenging, in part, because of the variety of environments the United States has to protect.[11] The challenges from adversaries are not limited to air transportation—what most people think of post-September 11th. Instead, homeland security in America deals with a variety of environments and threats, from protecting our land borders from a diverse range of actors (e.g., illegal immigrants and transnational criminals),[12] to protection of our maritime interests,[13] and of course, securing our airways for our public and cargo.

This chapter is focused around these three environments—air, land, and sea—as each represents some of the most pressing threats to homeland security today. The section dealing with aviation and transportation security examines specifically the issues of passenger transportation and cargo shipping by air and land in the U.S., while the following section focuses on **border security** and immigration issues. The third section examines maritime issues, particularly focusing on port security. Finally, this chapter examines the future of homeland security, examining the potential of future threats and what an appropriate response to these threats might be.

Though these sections are addressed individually, it is important to remember that they are not individual issues. Port security, for instance, is not simply a matter of **maritime security**, but also involves significant elements of the air-transport system in the United States, particularly cargo and individuals coming from abroad. Similarly, border security is not an issue confined only to the southern U.S./Mexico border, though many of the most significant threats from a homeland security perspective do come from that area.

In short, domain security is a challenging, multi-faceted area of homeland security with a variety of overlapping issues. Without securing each, the security of the other areas is jeopardized, and given the economic impact of each domain, it is essential they all remain as protected as possible.

KEY TERM
Border security—protecting the land borders of the United States from illegal movement.

KEY TERM
Maritime security—protecting the coastal waters of the United States from illegal movement.

KEY TERM
Transportation Security Administration—the federal department under Homeland Security responsible for transportation security in the U.S.

Aviation Security

While there have been many security changes in the post-9-11 homeland security environment, perhaps none of these changes are as familiar to most Americans as the changes to air security procedures. The additional requirements of taking off shoes,[14] instituted after the Richard Reid attempt, as well as the limitation on the amount of liquid-per-bottle, enforced after the failed "Operation Bojinka" plot was discovered,[15] have been widely mentioned in the press, and ridiculed by some.[16] These, mostly reactive, changes are only the public face of a large series of security changes that have taken place in aviation security post-9-11, the most important of which is the development of the **Transportation Security Administration (TSA).**

The TSA was created by virtue of the Aviation and Transportation Security Act of 2001,[17] passed just 2 months after the September 11th attacks. The agency was moved from the Department of Transportation

Courtesy of DHS.

and folded into the Department of Homeland Security upon the latter's creation in 2003.[18] As of 2010, the agency had approximately 52,000 employees and a budget of about $7.66 billion.[19] The TSA has a wide range of responsibilities related to homeland security and transportation, the most visible of which is the screening of all passengers and baggage for commercial flights originating in the United States. The TSA's aviation responsibilities include, in addition to the security obligations for commercial flights, the security of recreational aviation, and primary responsibility for the security of air-freight and cargo (see **Box 15.1**).[20]

TSA, in its role as the organization primarily responsible for airline security, has had several statutory mandates placed upon it. Chief among these is the mandate to screen all passengers and cargo placed on passenger aircraft, particularly those aircraft coming to the United States from outside the country, as well as eventually screening 100% of the shipments on all-cargo aircraft, though TSA has argued that a risk-based screening process is more effective.[21] In addition, the TSA is responsible for the development and deployment of new

---

BOX 15.1   Passenger Screening Technology

There are few who dispute the need for the Transportation Security Administration (TSA) to physically screen passengers for dangerous items. There has been, however, much debate about appropriate methods of screening and screening technologies. TSA has made revisions in its screening policy to try and adapt to these complaints, with particular modifications to screening policy focused on children under the age of 12 and passengers over the age of 75. In addition to these changes, and partially as a response to complaints about invasive pat-downs by TSA employees, the agency has developed new, advanced imaging technologies to assist with passenger screening.

Screening Technologies

TSA began testing advanced screening methods beginning in 2007 and had deployed some units by 2008. Two types of technology are being used to screen passengers in the new, more advanced systems. Millimeter wave and backscatter technologies allow for fast and complete scans of individuals, allowing TSA to identify contraband items quickly and effectively. The new technologies are, however, not without detractors. Many individuals are concerned about the potential long-term effects of the x-rays used in the process and the sometimes detailed pictures that result from the backscatter machines, particularly. So far, there have been over 800 units deployed at over 200 airports nationwide.

General Acceptance

Despite the controversy surrounding these technologies, there seems to be a general consensus on their use. According to the TSA, more than 99% of passengers choose the new screening process over the alternative screening procedures offered by the TSA. Also, a *CBS* poll suggests that a high percentage of Americans support the use of advanced imaging technology at airports. There is also some evidence to suggest that passengers with particular issues, such as knee replacements and other medical devices that would set of a regular metal detector, may prefer the newer technologies.

Conclusion

While the technology used in TSA's new, advanced imaging systems is controversial, there seems to be a general acceptance of the technology as necessary. The adoption of any new screening technology is likely to be controversial, as there are changes in the way passengers interact with the airport security system. Privacy issues notwithstanding, the new imaging technologies tend to be faster and provide for a more secure environment in the commercial passenger airline system.

Data from: Transportation Security Administration. (2013). *Advanced Imaging Technology (AIT)*. Retrieved from http://www.tsa.gov/traveler-information/advanced-imagingx-technology-ait; Wald, M.L. (2010). "Cancer Risks Debated for Type of X-ray Scan." *The New York Times*. Retrieved from http://www.nytimes.com/2010/01/09/health/09scanner.html?_r=0.

technologies and procedures for screening passengers.[22] Interestingly, the TSA is also required to examine the possibility of privatizing airport screening operations through the Screening Partnership Program[23] and manage the security of large, general-aviation aircraft. In their aviation security role, the TSA has been responsible for some of the more controversial processes that have been put in place since September 11, 2001. These include the new, arguably more invasive, screening procedures at airport checkpoints[24] as well as the use of the consolidated terrorist watch list, against which TSA checks all passengers who have an American destination.[25]

Commercial Passenger Aviation

The TSA carries out its aviation security mission in what it describes as a "layered approach."[26] The layers identified by the TSA begin with an appropriate collection of intelligence on potential threats and range through every layer of the aviation process and ending with passengers as the last line of defense as occurred on 9-11 on United Flight 93 (see Prologue).[27] The first layer is tied to compliance with the International Civil Aviation Organization—established to govern international aviation security standards. Perhaps the most significant aspect of the next layer is the screening processes, which involves the checking of names against the terrorist watch list maintained by the Terrorist Screening Center[28] and the physical screening of passengers considered "high risk."[29] The third layer involves the physical screening of passengers and their baggage, as well as the procedures developed to keep dangerous items off planes. The final layer involves stopping attacks in progress during flights, through on-board security (U.S. Air Marshals), armed pilots, and, as a last resort, the crew and passengers themselves.[30]

All Cargo Aircraft and General Aviation Security

While TSA obviously gets attention for its work on commercial passenger aviation, the organization is also responsible for the security of both commercial shipping and general aviation.[31] These two areas represent a significant percentage of the aircraft in the air at any given time, and perhaps more importantly, represent at least 25% of the commercial value of the aviation industry.[32] Unlike commercial passenger aviation, however, general aviation aircraft do not necessarily have to file flight plans, and until fairly recently, those traveling on these aircraft did not go through a significant vetting process.[33]

In addition to their aviation responsibilities and in conjunction with state and local partners, TSA is also responsible for the security of the nation's railway systems and other transportation networks, though the bulk of their operations are focused in the aviation arena with state, local, and private organizations taking larger roles in the other transportation sectors.

Maritime Security

The attacks on September 11, 2001, while focused on commercial aviation, suggested vulnerabilities in all modes of transportation. Since 9-11, port security has been highlighted as one of the areas of importance for dealing with terrorist threats of a number of types including smuggling of terrorist personnel, weapons of mass destruction, or other types of dangerous material into the country. These threats, however, do not only extend to the movement of arms or personnel, but include the ports themselves as a target, as much of the nation's commercial activity originates in ports. The *9/11 Commission Report* stated,

> While commercial aviation remains a possible target, terrorists may turn their attention to other modes. Opportunities to do harm are as great, or greater, in maritime and surface transportation. Initiatives to secure shipping containers have just begun.[34]

The threat of attack is complicated by the nature of port systems, as well as the number of organizations involved in both port security and managing the commercial activity of the ports.[35] The U.S. maritime port system includes more than 300 sea and river ports and has more than 3,700 cargo and passenger terminals. Additionally, there are more than 1,000 harbor channels spread along the country's vast coastlines. The scope of the commercial activity in these ports is enormous. The top 50 ports in the U.S. account for 90% of all cargo tonnage, and 25 U.S. ports account for 98% of all container shipments. Ships carry approximately 80% of world trade by volume, and the U.S. is the world's leading maritime trading nation, responsible for 20% of the worldwide shipping volume.[36]

There are a range of threat scenarios that have been identified in a maritime context. The smuggling scenario, mentioned previously, is one of the more benign, with other scenarios including using a ship as a collision weapon,[37] using a ship to cause a massive in-port explosion, or causing an offshore discharge of oil and fire. While some of these offer the possibility of high levels of civilian casualties, much of the danger also stems from the loss of commercial activity these attacks could entail.[38]

There are a number of federal agencies involved in port security. The Coast Guard, Bureau of Customs and Border Protection, the TSA, and all DHS agencies have some responsibility, and other organizations such as the Maritime Administration, the Department of State and the Department of Defense also have significant roles.[39] Each of these agencies has a specific role to play in the overlapping system of port security in the United Sates, and each plays a significant role in the security of maritime activity.[40]

The U.S. Coast Guard (USCG) is the principal agency in charge of maritime homeland security and operates under the auspices of the Department of Homeland Security.[41] Rolled into the department in 2003, the USCG is responsible for boarding, inspecting, and evaluating the threat of any commercial ships entering the territorial waters of the U.S. and for countering threats at U.S. ports.[42] In addition to their general homeland security responsibilities, the USCG has developed the concept of maritime domain awareness, which assists in giving a more complete picture of the maritime threat environment.

The Bureau of Customs and Border Protection (CBP) has a different role in maritime homeland security. It is responsible for inspecting cargo and containers that commercial ships bring into U.S. ports. Additionally, the CBP inspects crew manifests and cruise-ship passenger lists from any foreign port.[43] This combines the functions previously performed by two separate agencies, U.S. Customs Service and Immigration and Naturalization Service, which were combined into the CBP after the advent of DHS. CBP has several initiatives related to maritime homeland security, including the Container Security Initiative (CSI)[44] and the Customs-Trade Partnership Against Terrorism (C-TPAT).[45] These are designed to expand the United States' "zone of security" to foreign ports, so that a container's cargo can be verified through pre-screening before ever making it to the shores of the United States.[46]

The TSA also has a significant maritime security role, though it is not as large as its aviation role, as it is not the lead agency. The TSA has maritime security responsibility for, among other things, tracking containers through ports for security purposes and creating a transportation worker identification system—DHS's Transportation Worker Identification Credential system, which will help ensure that those employed by ports are not threats to U.S. homeland security.[47] The TSA works in conjunction with the FBI in some cases to assess whether individuals working at port authorities around the nation appear on the terrorism watch list.

In addition to those agencies having a role at the federal, state, and in particular local level, port authorities also have important responsibilities for maritime homeland security. Port authorities, responsible for managing day-to-day operations at ports, have to work very closely with those agencies responsible for maritime homeland security. In the event of an incident at a port, the first responders are local port authority fire and police agencies.[48] Additionally, given the fact that the vast majority of maritime activity is commercial, there is substantial cooperation required on the part of commercial organizations who engage in maritime trade.

While port security is probably the most directly relevant area of maritime homeland security, there are other significant elements that come into play in a maritime environment. The risk to ships that are not actually in port is significant, particularly container ships and oil tankers, as they are slow-moving and vulnerable to attack by smaller, faster vessels particularly when at anchor in a harbor or coming into port.[49] This scenario is particularly frightening considering that attempts have already been made, such as the attack on the French oil tanker *Limberg* in 2002 (see **Box 15.2**).[50] Further, ships are at risk for piracy, which some believe has a significant fundraising link to terrorism.

Maritime crimes are also problematic from a homeland security perspective. Like piracy, these activities can be used to finance terrorist activities. Additionally, the threat of smuggling individuals in through the cargo system is a significant vulnerability, considering the tremendous amount of cargo passing through U.S. ports.[51]

Maritime homeland security issues are some of the most significant facing the nation. Given the economic importance of the country's ports, and the unique vulnerabilities that they represent, protecting these assets is one of the most important elements of a homeland security strategy. Further, given the complex nature of a port, and its consistent contact with international trade, maritime homeland security requires a great deal more cooperation, from locally to internationally, than perhaps any other area contained within homeland security. The primary responsible agencies, the USCG, CBP, and the TSA, all have large-scale programs to address this complex area of homeland security.

BOX 15.2   The *Limburg* Attack

On October 6, 2002 the double-hull oil tanker *Limburg* was attacked in the Gulf of Aden off the Yemeni coast. The tanker was carrying 400,000 gallons of oil when it was attacked by a small vessel, killing one crew member, injuring 12 others, and rupturing both of the ship's hulls. Ninety-thousand gallons of oil leaked into the gulf from the breach caused by the attack. Though originally denying that the blast was the result of an attack, Yemeni officials eventually acknowledged that the ship was attacked after French investigators found traces of TNT in the *Limburg's* hull. The attack was similar to the suicide bombing of the *USS Cole* in a Yemeni harbor in 2000 that killed 17 Americans.

The Threat

The *Limburg* attack, like the attack on the *USS Cole* before it, represents a significant threat to the maritime security interests of the United States. While neither attack was enough to sink the ships, the fact that a small boat can be used to attack a much larger ship and do significant damage is a problem for all larger ships. Even the differences in the attacks suggest the scope of the threat. While the *USS Cole* was in port, the *Limburg* was on the move when it was attacked.

Aftermath

Though the attack was not against American interests, the United States has been involved in pursuing the terrorists responsible for the attack, in part because at least one of the terrorists was also involved in the bombing of the *USS Cole* and was an Al Qaeda operative. In August of 2012, the United States launched drone attacks against eight terrorists driving in the Hawra district in Yemen. One of the terrorists killed was Khaled Batis, the mastermind of the *Limburg* attack, who had escaped from a Yemeni prison in 2011. Abdul Mun'im Salim al Fatahani, another terrorist involved in the plot against the *Limburg*, was killed in a drone attack in January of 2012.

Conclusion

The attack on the *Limburg* represents the manifestation of one of the most significant maritime threats facing American interests. In many ways it represents the *best* case scenario, as the vessel did not sink, and there was no accompanying fire. If a similar attack were carried out in a port, the resulting issues—fire, casualties, damage to the facility—could be much greater. In addition, aside from the specific threat that the *Limburg* attack demonstrated, it also points to greater maritime threats, such as the hijacking of a liquefied petroleum gas tanker for use as a weapon of mass destruction.

Data from: *BBC News*. (2002). "Yemen Ship Attack 'Was Terrorism.'" Retrieved from http://news.bbc.co.uk/2/hi/middle_east/2324431.stm.; Roggio, B. (2012). *US Drone Strike Kills AQAP Operative Involved in Limburg Tanker Attack*. Retrieved from http://www.longwarjournal.org/archives/2012/09/us_drone_strike_kill_13.php.

■ Other Transportation Sectors

While airline security understandably has been the primary focus of transportation security since 9-11, other methods of transportation are also vulnerable to attack. Notably, the rail system in the United States, particularly subways in major cities, carries about five times as many passengers as airlines do on a given day. This high-volume of passenger traffic makes it a particularly significant potential target for terrorists.[52]

The daily volume of passengers also makes individual-level screening a virtual impossibility.[53] The focus of transit security has therefore been risk mitigation and consequence management in the event of an attack. Combined with a large grant program to assist rail systems to improve their security, these efforts have helped make the system more secure.

The problem with busing systems dwarfs the threat to the rail transportation system. Even more passengers use public busing systems or private passenger buses than use commuter rails. Up to 19 million people a day (during the week) utilize the nation's busing systems. Some efforts have been made to help secure these systems, primarily in the form of increased surveillance at stations and on buses, but the system remains vulnerable to a variety of potential attacks.[54]

◼ Border Security

Border security has long been an issue for the United States. Well before 9-11, the country faced a variety of problems threatening its security stemming from the border domain, and laws were made to exclude individuals who were perceived as affecting national security. Anarchists, communists, and terrorists have all been excluded from immigrating at different points in our history. Smuggling, too, has a long history on the border, with laws in place at least since the Prohibition Era of the 1920s and early 1930s meant to stop contraband from coming into the country.[55]

However, like port and maritime security, border security is a complex issue. There is an increasing diversity of threats emerging at the border, from illegal smuggled goods and persons[56] to spill-over violence from drug cartels, and managing these risks is a difficult problem for DHS as legitimate trade needs to continue efficiently while the threats to security are stopped.[57] Border risks are, by in large, linked to the flow of goods and people across the border and any item (or individual) crossing the border without appropriate permission represents a potential threat to U.S. security.[58]

More specifically, DHS's border security mission has three primary foci. The first, unauthorized migration, is perhaps the largest-scale problem. The second, criminal networks, is also important, particularly in regards to the contraband those networks attempt to bring into the country. Finally, potential terrorists represent a third threat to border security, primarily in illegal attempts at immigration.[59] There is also, obviously, overlap between these three threats as well. The complete border security picture is outlined in FIGURE 15.1.

Transnational terrorist activity, especially post 9-11, is one of the major security concerns that deal with border issues. The difficulty of carrying out the border control mission in a terrorist context was summed up well by the *9/11 Commission Report*:

> When Doris Meissner became INS [Immigration and Naturalization Service—now part of Customs and Border Patrol] Commissioner in 1993, she found an agency seriously hampered by outdated technology and insufficient human resources. Border Patrol agents were still using manual typewriters; inspectors at ports of entry were using a paper watch-list; and the asylum and other benefit systems did not effectively deter fraudulent applications.[60]

The primary concern regarding borders is the illegal movement of terrorists into the country. This is statutorily prohibited by the Immigration and Nationality Act,[61] but unsurprisingly, there have been documented instances of terrorists attempting to cross the border at legal points of entry.[62] Additionally, smuggling of contraband helpful to terrorists such as weapons of mass destruction (WMDs) remains a threat as well, especially considering the failure of DHS to actively screen all cargo coming into the U.S. over land borders, particularly cargo carried by trucks.[63]

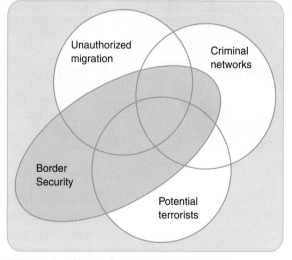

FIGURE 15.1 Border Threats and DHS Mission

Reproduced from: Peterman, D.R., Elias, B., and Frittelli, J. (2011). *Border Security: Understanding Threats at U.S. Borders* (CRS No. R42969), p. 4. Retrieved from www.fas.org/sgp/crs/homesec/R42969.pdf.

Immigration

As with terrorists, the INA prohibits the movements of certain people into the country; specifically, those with particular health concerns, those who raise foreign policy concerns, and those who are likely to become a public charge are prohibited from entering the country.[64] Most important, though, are those aliens who simply migrate without proper vetting or authorization. While most likely moving simply for better economic opportunity, those individuals, because they are unknown, pose a potential threat to homeland security.

This is, of course, not to equate illegal immigrants with terrorists. The motivations of the two groups differ dramatically, and the threat the former poses is usually negligible. However, because there is no simple way to separate out those undocumented immigrants who are here simply to seek a better life from those who wish to do the country harm, illegal immigration remains a significant homeland security problem.

There are two agencies responsible for immigration in a homeland security context. The CBP is responsible for securing the borders, both checkpoints where individuals can cross borders legally as well as patrols where individuals may cross illegally (though the patrols are carried out by the U.S. Border Patrol, a component of CBP).[65] This is made difficult by the sheer scope of the problem. CBP, in addition to its charge of dealing with illegal immigrants, is also responsible for stopping terrorists (as mentioned previously), preventing illegal contraband from entering the country (including drugs), as well as protecting the country's agriculture system from harmful pests and diseases.[66]

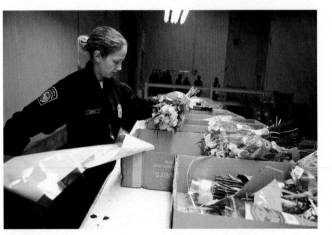

Courtesy of James Tourtellotte/DHS.

Complicating the issue further is the geographical size of the U.S. borders. The country's northern border with Canada is over 5,000 miles long and covers a range of ecosystems, including mountains and forests, as well as urban border crossings.[67] The U.S.'s southern border with Mexico is about 2,000 miles long and includes Texas, Arizona, New Mexico, and California. Both borders present significant challenges with illegal entry, smuggling, and criminal activity, making it virtually impossible to prevent all such instances from occurring.[68]

When someone dangerous enters the country, it becomes the responsibility of Immigration and Customs Enforcement (ICE). ICE is the primary investigative arm of DHS and is responsible for intelligence and investigation on terrorists who have entered the country, criminal migrants, and any illicit material that has crossed the borders into the U.S. used for support of criminal or terrorist activities. Unlike CBP, which is limited to border activities, ICE is responsible for investigations throughout the United States pertaining to immigrations and customs violations.[69]

Criminal Networks

Criminal networks, particularly along the southern border of the United States, represent one of the larger challenges to U.S. homeland security. Transnational criminal gangs, like Mara Salvatrucha (MS-13), represent a threat because of their connection to specific criminal activity, such as smuggling weapons, drugs, and even individuals across the border.[70] There is also significant danger presented by drug cartels who, even aside from their smuggling activities, pose a threat because of the violence that occurs between cartels and with law enforcement that sometimes spills across the border into the United States (see **Box 15.3**).[71]

There is also an additional concern that comes when terrorism and criminal networks meet. While it is unlikely that a criminal network would seek to carry out an act of terrorism for its own purposes, there is much concern that they could do so if they were paid for their activity.

Though border security and immigration—particularly in the areas of criminal networks, terrorist activity, and illegal immigration—present significant dangers respectively, it is perhaps most concerning where these threats overlap. The cooperation between criminal networks and terrorist organizations to smuggle terrorists, or weapons to be used by terrorists, into the country is one of a number of challenging threat scenarios that has to be addressed by DHS. However, given the size of the borders of the United States and the volume of traffic that legally comes across these borders, the scope of this problem makes it difficult to implement. CBP and ICE

BOX 15.3 The Border Violence Debate

Over the past several years, there has been an increase in the level of violence among drug cartels on the U.S./Mexico border. This, in turn, has led to increasing concerns among policymakers in the U.S. that this violence will "spill over" to the U.S. side of the border. This concern has been amplified by the concerns of many citizens who live on the border, who are convinced that their lives are becoming less safe. While federal officials have thus far denied any spill-over violence, there is tacit acknowledgment that this possibility exists as a future threat.

The Violence

While there are conflicting reports, the death toll from drug trafficking-related violence in Mexico since 2007 may be as high as 55,000 people. The death toll for 2012 alone has been estimated at over 9,575. The violence stems from ongoing conflict between the Mexican government and the drug trafficking organizations (DTOs). The DTOs, because of the pressure put on their markets by the Mexican government, are competing with one another for increasingly limited market space. This leads to violence on two fronts: violence among the DTOs themselves and violence between the DTOs and Mexican law enforcement agencies.

The Question of Spill Over

Whether or not this violence has spilled over into the United States is a difficult question to answer. Much of the problem stems from the fact that there is no agreed-upon definition of what constitutes spill-over violence. Some definitions include violence against civilians that seems unrelated to drug trafficking, with other definitions suggest that only violence between cartels, but on the U.S. side of the border, "count" as spill-over violence. These problems are exacerbated by the general lack of data on the topic as the UCR, the primary source for criminal justice data in the U.S., does not make a distinction between drug-related violence and violence unrelated to trafficking.

Conclusion

Despite the importance of the topic, there are few concrete answers to the question of whether or not the drug-related violence in Mexico has spilled into the United States. While many individuals on the border feel more threatened, and the level of violence in parts of Mexico remains high, the U.S. federal government maintains that there are historically low levels of violence on the border. Both sides lack sufficient data to make a credible argument, but both also agree that regardless of whether the violence has yet spilled over, the potential for it to do so remains a significant threat to American homeland security.

Data from: Finklea, K.M. (2013). *Southwest Border Violence: Issues in Identifying and Measuring Spillover Violence* (CRS No. R41075). Retrieved from http://www.fas.org/sgp/crs/homesec/R41075.pdf.

are the agencies with primary responsibility for combatting these threats, though there are additional federal resources being brought to bear on the problem. With political change such as immigration reform now possible, it is difficult to know whether the security situation on the border will change and how.

Future of Homeland Security

One of the most difficult challenges of homeland security is the fact that the environment in which homeland security professionals operate is not static.[72] The threat environment changes on a regular basis due to a variety of circumstances, the vast majority of which are totally outside the control of the homeland security community. Three things, in particular, can affect the homeland security threat environment—as well as the potential responses that homeland security professionals can provide in the event of an incident. These three areas are international threats, domestic threats, and the political climate in which decisions on how to address threats are (or are not) made.

International Threats

As one of the primary missions of homeland security deals with terrorism, and much of the terrorist threat is determined by factors outside of the United States, it is essential to understand the international environment.[73] Unfortunately, as is often the case, the international context is quite dynamic, making threats to homeland security difficult to pin down.

This, perhaps, has never been truer than now. The international political context has changed dramatically in the past 3 years, with the occurrence of the Arab Spring,[74] the replacement of the leadership in Libya,[75] and the current civil war in Syria; many of these are countries with some previous connection to terrorism. Additionally, North Korea, and perhaps Iran, have developed capacities that could be used to aid terrorists, particularly if those countries continue to feel threatened by increasing international pressure, generally led by the United States.

Domestic Threats

Like the international threat context, it is unclear where the domestic security situation lies at the moment. While the U.S. is undoubtedly more secure than before the September 11th attacks, there remain significant domestic terrorism threats, primarily in the guise of right-wing and racist terrorist activity and eco-terrorism.[76] However, these threats are, in part, determined by political issues. Immigration reform, for instance, has the potential to impact nativist organizations in the U.S. who might pose a potential threat.[77] In addition, the increasing focus on income inequality may stimulate activity among certain left-wing political organizations.

And vulnerabilities remain throughout the homeland security system. As discussed previously, there is a persistent threat to port security and our land borders are not 100% secure. All of these factors make threat prediction quite difficult.[78]

Natural Disasters

As with terrorist activity, there is much uncertainty when it comes to natural disasters. Aside from the fact that there is little ability for advanced prediction of many of these threats, there is increasing concern that natural disasters are getting worse because of global climate change (see **Box 15.4**).[79] Super-storm Sandy, the recent severe hurricane in the northeast, is an example of the type of disaster that many believe we must be better prepared for in the future. While it has been long contested whether storms are increasing in number and intensity due to climate change, regardless, natural disasters will always pose a threat to our homeland security.[80]

© Charles Sykes/AP Images.

Not only are major storms becoming more frequent, but other weather conditions such as droughts, flooding, and wildfires are also of great concern,[81] particularly in highly popu-lated areas.[82] First responders at the local level will be bearing the brunt of these weather sys-tems, and it is unlikely that there will be many additional changes to support those first responders in reacting to these events.

Changing Political Environment

Perhaps the most important development for homeland security's future will occur on the political front. While September 11, 2001, and then shortly afterwards Hurricane Katrina, provided the political motivation necessary to institute the sig-nificant changes that led to the current homeland security system, there has not been an event domestically approaching the magnitude of those incidents since. While, on one level, this may represent a success of our homeland security system, it also means that there is little impetus to provide additional resources or support for that system.

Anthony Downs, a political scientist, referenced this idea in what was called the Issue Attention Cycle.[83] This was adapted by a homeland security theorist Christopher Bellavita in 2005, and he suggested that there was difficulty in deal-ing with homeland security issues in the long term because the public would lose interest over time without an increasing numbers of events to keep their attention.[84]

Equally important to the future of homeland security in the U.S. are domestic issues that have little immediate relevance to the topic of security. In brief, the cur-rent economic climate is one where additional appropriations for security are not easily made, without the driving force of another significant event. In fact, along with other scheduled cuts, the sequester that went into effect in 2013 includes $4 billion in cuts to DHS.[85] This means that not only DHS itself is suffering cutbacks, but so too are those many state and local agencies on the receiving end of grants.[86]

The future of homeland security is difficult to predict. There are many moving pieces, and much of the risk that homeland security seeks to mitigate is difficult to assess in the best of circumstances. The international threat context is perhaps more dynamic that at any other point in recent time, and the domestic threat, particularly in regards to domestic terrorism, is in a state of flux because of the changing political situation. Similarly, the effects of global climate change remain to be seen, though it appears as if there will be an increasing number of severe weather events in the coming years.

BOX 15.4   Climate Change and Homeland Security

DEPARTMENT OF HOMELAND SECURITY

CLIMATE CHANGE ADAPTATION ROADMAP

JUNE 2012

Courtesy of the DHS.

Though still occasionally challenged, global climate change is increasingly being recognized as a scientific fact. Among the impacts that climate change can have is an increase in the number of significant weather events, and the severity of the events when they do occur. This fact, in turn, demonstrates why climate change is an increasingly relevant problem for homeland security. In 2010, both the *Quadrennial Defense Review* and the *National Security Strategy for the United States* recognized global climate change as potential threats to national security.

The Threat

The threat from global climate change is relatively complex. While unlikely to directly generate conflict by itself, climate change can act as an "accelerant" of instability, and can indirectly tax defense agencies because they may have to support civil authorities for disaster relief. There is also a more direct threat from climate change. As stated in the *Quadrennial Defense Review*, "in 2008, the National Intelligence Council judged that more than 30 U.S. military installations were already facing elevated levels of risk from rising sea levels." In its report *Climate Change Adaptation Roadmap,* DHS suggests the threat from climate change is particularly relevant to the organization, as it deals with the federal emergency management aspects of climate change.

Perhaps most important is the domestic political situation in regards to homeland security, which, as September 11th recedes in memory, may result in less money and political influence to support the homeland security system. This issue is exacerbated by continuing economic and social problems facing the country. Because of these many factors, it is unclear what the future holds for homeland security in the United States. Barring another catastrophic attack or disaster on American soil, the future of homeland security remains an open question.

■ Chapter Summary

KEY TERM
Domain security—securing the environments of air, land, and sea.

Domain security—or securing the environments of air, land, and sea—remains one of the most important elements of homeland security. With issues ranging from air passenger transport to port security, the threats faced by this area of homeland security are complex, and solutions require high levels of interaction between homeland security agencies. Moreover, these areas represent some of the largest segments of the U.S. economy, making them desirable targets for terrorists and criminals.

The Response

As a direct response to the challenges posed by climate change to national and homeland security, President Obama issued Executive Order 13514, charging the Interagency Climate Change Adaptation Task Force, made up from members of over 20 government agencies, with finding solutions to the challenges presented by climate change. The 2011 report produced by the task force, *Progress Report of the Interagency Climate Change Adaptation Task Force*, identifies several areas in which the government can make significant process in combating the effects of climate change. These include:

- Integrating adaptation into federal government planning and activities
- Building resilience to climate change in communities
- Improving accessibility and coordination of science for decision making
- Developing strategies to safeguard natural resources in a changing climate
- Enhancing efforts to lead and support international adaptation

This framework represents the tangible elements of a plan for coping with climate change at the federal level. One of the major recognitions of the task force, however, is that the majority of response to climate change will happen at the local level, so one of the primary responsibilities of the federal government is supporting local agencies.

Conclusion

With the inclusion of climate change as a significant element of the *Quadrennial Defense Review, Climate Change Adaptation Roadmap*, and *National Security Strategy*, the federal government is recognizing the fact that climate change presents significant dangers to the security of the United States. This recognition is most important in terms of homeland security, as any of the effects mentioned by the documents are likely to impact territories within the U.S. Additionally, the increasing scientific recognition of severe weather events as a consequence of global climate change illustrates the increasing importance of this topic to homeland security.

Data from: The White House. (2011). *Federal Actions for a Climate Resistant Nation.* Retrieved from http://www.whitehouse.gov/sites/default/files/microsites/ceq/2011_adaptation_progress_report.pdf; The White House. (2010). *National Security Strategy.* Retrieved from http://www.whitehouse.gov/sites/default/files/rss_viewer/national_security_strategy.pdf; United States Department of Defense. (2010). *Quadrennial Defense Review Report.* Retrieved from http://www.defense.gov/qdr/qdr%20as%20of%2026jan10%200700.pdf; Department of Homeland Security. (2012). *Climate ChangeAadaptation Roadmap.* Retrieved from http://www.dhs.gov/sites/default/files/publications/Appendix%20A%20DHS%20FY2012%20Climate%20Change%20Adaptation%20Plan_0.pdf.

While 9-11 understandably focused the U.S. on air passenger safety, other elements of domain security are also essential for the overall security of the country. The nexus of immigration, crime, and terrorism on the border represents one of the most significant threats to the homeland. Additionally, protecting the nations ports is one of the most difficult aspects of homeland security generally, and domain security specifically. With high numbers of targets and successful attacks taking place in the past, maritime security is still a significant issue in homeland security. This is not to mention the only partially solved issues of rail and other commuter transportation systems in the U.S.

Addressing these issues is the mission of several elements of DHS. The TSA is responsible for air cargo and passenger safety, as well as significant elements in other parts of domain security like the verification of transportation workers. The USCG is responsible for securing ports and maritime security while CBP secures the borders. ICE, as the investigative arm of DHS, examines cases of smuggling, terrorism, and other activities in the interior of the country. All of these agencies, along with other agencies outside of DHS like the FBI, must coordinate their efforts in the major areas of domain security in order to fulfill their individual missions.

This is all made more complicated by the changing nature of homeland security threats. Internationally, the system has changed dramatically in the past 4 years, and much of the current threat situation remains unknown. Domestically, the threat situation is also in flux, with the political landscape changing rapidly and influencing radicalized groups within the U.S. Other issues, such as global climate change, also may have unforeseen impact on homeland security in the U.S. as the number of natural disasters seems to be increasing, and severe weather events getting worse when they do occur.

However, despite all of these issues, what makes the future of homeland security most challenging to predict is the national political situation. With no catastrophic terrorist events or natural disasters occurring in the past 8 years, much of what brought homeland security to the forefront is receding in the public mind. This, combined with the slow economic recovery from the 2008 financial crisis and the potential effects of government-wide budget cuts, means homeland security will be vying for increasingly scarce resources.

Whatever changes happen to homeland security, however, it will remain an essential part of the security apparatus of the United States and will continue to be so for the foreseeable future.

■ Review/Discussion Questions

1. What role does the Transportation Security Administration play in the country's aviation system? What other roles does it play across other types of transportation?

2. Border security has been an issue in the U.S. for a long time. What elements of border security are most important and why?

3. What is the difference between the roles of the U.S. Border Patrol and Immigration and Customs Enforcement?

4. What future threats to homeland security are the most important? Why?

5. What role might climate change play in the future of homeland security in the United States?

■ Additional Readings

Department of Homeland Security. (2010). *Quadrennial Homeland Security Review*. Retrieved from http://www.dhs.gov/xlibrary/assets/qhsr_report.pdf

Peterman, D.R., Elias, B., & Frittelli, J. (2011). *Transportation Security: Issues for Congress* (CRS No. RL33512). Retrieved from http://www.fas.org/sgp/crs/homesec/RL33512.pdf

■ Endnotes

1. Booth, C.T. (2002). "The Flight Attendants. Courage in the Air." *Time*. Retrieved from http://www.time.com/time/magazine/article/0,9171,1003224-2,00.html

2. Fenton, B. & Ball, I. (2001). "Bomb on Flight 63." *The Telegraph*. Retrieved from http://www.telegraph.co.uk/news/worldnews/northamerica/usa/1366231/Bomb-on-Flight-63.html

3. Booth, C.T. (2002). "The Flight Attendants. Courage in the Air." *Time*. Retrieved from http://www.time.com/time/magazine/article/0,9171,1003224-2,00.html

4. Booth, C.T. (2002). "The Flight Attendants. Courage in the Air." *Time*. Retrieved from http://www.time.com/time/magazine/article/0,9171,1003224-2,00.html

5. Fenton, B. & Ball, I. (2001). "Bomb on Flight 63." *The Telegraph*. Retrieved from http://www.telegraph.co.uk/news/worldnews/northamerica/usa/1366231/Bomb-on-Flight-63.html

6. Booth, C.T. (2002). "The Flight Attendants. Courage in the Air." *Time*. Retrieved from http://www.time.com/time/magazine/article/0,9171,1003224-2,00.html

7. Booth, C.T. (2002). "The Flight Attendants. Courage in the Air." *Time*. Retrieved from http://www.time.com/time/magazine/article/0,9171,1003224-2,00.html

8. Ressa, M. (2003). "Sources: Reid is Al Qaeda Operative." Retrieved from http://www.cnn.com/2003/WORLD/asiapcf/southeast/01/30/reid.alqaeda/

9. Peterman, D.R., Elias, B., & Frittelli, J. (2011). *Transportation Security: Issues for Congress* (CRS No. RL33512). Retrieved from http://www.fas.org/sgp/crs/homesec/RL33512.pdf

10. Department of Homeland Security. (2011). *Congressional Budget Justification 2011*. Retrieved from http://www.dhs.gov/xlibrary/assets/dhs_congressional_budget_justification_fy2011.pdf

11. Peterman, D.R., Elias, B., & Frittelli, J. (2011). *Transportation Security: Issues for Congress* (CRS No. RL33512). Retrieved from http://www.fas.org/sgp/crs/homesec/RL33512.pdf

12. Department of Homeland Security. (2012). *Border Security Overview*. Retrieved from http://www.dhs.gov/border-security-overview

13. Frittelli, J.F. (2005). *Port and Maritime Security: Background and Issues for Congress* (CRS No. RL31733). Retrieved from http://www.fas.org/sgp/crs/homesec/RL31733.pdf

14. Transportation Security Administration. (n.d.). *Need for Shoe Removal at Checkpoints*. Retrieved from http://www.tsa.gov/press/news/2013/01/07/need-removal-shoes-checkpoint

15. Elias, B. (2010). *Screening and Securing Air Cargo: Background and Issues for Congress* (CRS No. R41515). Retrieved from http://www.fas.org/sgp/crs/homesec/R41515.pdf

16. Barro, J. (2012). "The TSA's Fake Liquid Rule." *Forbes*. Retrieved from http://www.forbes.com/sites/joshbarro/2012/05/02/the-tsas-fake-liquids-rule/

17. Aviation and Transportation Security Act of 2001, Public Law 107-71, 115 Stat. 597 (2001).

18. Transportation Security Administration. (n.d.). *TSA and 9/11*. Retrieved from http://www.tsa.gov/about-tsa/september-11-2001-and-tsa

19. Haddal, C.C. (2010). *Border Security: Key Agencies and Their Missions* (CRS No. RS21899). Retrieved from http://www.fas.org/sgp/crs/homesec/RS21899.pdf

20. Elias, B. (2010). *Screening and Securing Air Cargo: Background and Issues for Congress* (CRS No. R41515). Retrieved from http://www.fas.org/sgp/crs/homesec/R41515.pdf

21. Elias, B. (2010). *Screening and Securing Air Cargo: Background and Issues for Congress* (CRS No. R41515). Retrieved from http://www.fas.org/sgp/crs/homesec/R41515.pdf

22. Peterman, D.R., Elias, B., & Frittelli, J. (2011). *Transportation Security: Issues for Congress* (CRS No. RL33512). Retrieved from http://www.fas.org/sgp/crs/homesec/RL33512.pdf

23. Transportation Security Administration. (n.d.). *Screening Partnership Program.* Retrieved from http://www.tsa.gov/stakeholders/screening-partnership-program

24. Rosen, J. (2010). "The TSA is Invasive, Annoying—and Unconstitutional." *The Washington Post Online.* Retrieved from http://www.washingtonpost.com/wp-dyn/content/article/2010/11/26/AR2010112604290.html

25. Krouse, W.J. & Elias, B. (2009). *Terrorist Watchlist Checks and Air Passenger Screening.* Retrieved from http://www.fas.org/sgp/crs/homesec/RL33645.pdf

26. Transportation Security Administration. (n.d.). *Layers of Security.* Retrieved from http://www.tsa.gov/about-tsa/layers-security

27. Transportation Security Administration. (n.d.). *Layers of Security.* Retrieved from http://www.tsa.gov/about-tsa/layers-security

28. Krouse, W.J. & Elias, B. (2009). *Terrorist Watchlist Checks and Air Passenger Screening.* Retrieved from http://www.fas.org/sgp/crs/homesec/RL33645.pdf

29. Peterman, D.R., Elias, B., & Frittelli, J. (2011). *Transportation Security: Issues for Congress* (CRS No. RL33512). Retrieved from http://www.fas.org/sgp/crs/homesec/RL33512.pdf

30. Transportation Security Administration. (n.d.). *Layers of Security.* Retrieved from http://www.tsa.gov/about-tsa/layers-security

31. Aviation and Transportation Security Act of 2001, Public Law 107-71, 115 Stat. 597 (2001).

32. Elias, B. (2007). *Air Cargo Security* (CRS No. RL32022). Retrieved from http://www.fas.org/sgp/crs/homesec/RL32022.pdf

33. Sauter, M. & Carafano, J.J. (2012). *Homeland Security* (2nd ed.). New York, NY: McGraw Hill.

34. National Commission on Terrorist Attacks Upon the United States. (2004). *The 9/11 Commission Report: Final Report of the National Commission on Terrorist Attacks Upon the United States* (Authorized Ed.). New York: W.W. Norton & Company, Inc.

35. United States Department of Transportation. (1999). *An Assessment of U.S. Marine Transportation Systems.* Retrieved from http://www.marad.dot.gov/documents/Assessmnt_of_the_US_MTS_-_Rpt_to_Congr_Sep_1999_combined.pdf

36. United States Department of Transportation. (1999). *An Assessment of U.S. Marine Transportation Systems.* Retrieved from http://www.marad.dot.gov/documents/Assessmnt_of_the_US_MTS_-_Rpt_to_Congr_Sep_1999_combined.pdf

37. Department of Homeland Security. (2005). *National Plan to Achieve Maritime Domain Awareness.* Retrieved from http://www.dhs.gov/xlibrary/assets/HSPD_MDAPlan.pdf

38. Department of Homeland Security. (2005). *National Plan to Achieve Maritime Domain Awareness.* Retrieved from http://www.dhs.gov/xlibrary/assets/HSPD_MDAPlan.pdf

39. Fritelli, J.F. (2005). *Port and Maritime Security: Background and Issues for Congress* (CRS No. RL31733). Retrieved from http://www.fas.org/sgp/crs/homesec/RL31733.pdf

40. Fritelli, J.F. (2005). *Port and Maritime Security: Background and Issues for Congress* (CRS No. RL31733). Retrieved from http://www.fas.org/sgp/crs/homesec/RL31733.pdf

41. Homeland Security Act of 2002, Public Law 107-296, 116 Stat. 2137 (2002).

42. O'Rourke, R. (2007). *Homeland Security: Coast Guard Operations—Background and Issues for Congress.* Retrieved from http://congressionalresearch.com/RS21125/document.php?study=Homeland+Security+Coast+Guard+Operations+-+Background+and+Issues+for+Congress

43. Fritelli, J.F. (2005). *Port and Maritime Security: Background and Issues for Congress* (CRS No. RL31733). Retrieved from http://www.fas.org/sgp/crs/homesec/RL31733.pdf

44. Customs and Border Protection. (n.d.). *CSI: Container Security Initiative.* Retrieved from http://www.cbp.gov/xp/cgov/trade/cargo_security/csi/

45. Customs and Border Protection. (n.d.). *C-TPAT: Program Overview.* Retrieved from http://www.cbp.gov/linkhandler/cgov/trade/cargo_security/ctpat/ctpat_program_information/what_is_ctpat/ctpat_overview.ctt/ctpat_overview.pdf

46. Peterman, D.R., Elias, B., & Frittelli, J. (2011). *Transportation Security: Issues for Congress* (CRS No. RL33512). Retrieved from http://www.fas.org/sgp/crs/homesec/RL33512.pdf

47. Department of Homeland Security. (n.d.). *Transportation Worker Identification Credential.* Retrieved from https://twicprogram.tsa.dhs.gov/TWICWebApp/AboutTWIC.do

48. Port of Houston. (n.d.). *Port Security Emergency Operations.* Retrieved from http://www.portofhouston.com/inside-the-port-authority/port-security-emergency-operations/

49. Fritelli, J.F. (2005). *Port and Maritime Security: Background and Issues for Congress* (CRS No. RL31733). Retrieved from http://www.fas.org/sgp/crs/homesec/RL31733.pdf

50. Global Security. (n.d.). "Limberg Oil Tanker Attacked." Retrieved from http://www.globalsecurity.org/security/profiles/limburg_oil_tanker_attacked.htm

51. Bakir, N.O. (2007). A Brief Analysis of Threats and Vulnerabilities in the Maritime Domain. Retrieved from http://research.create.usc.edu/cgi/viewcontent.cgi?article=1004&context=nonpublished_reports

52. Government Accountability Office. (2007). *Critical Infrastructure: Challenges Remain in Protecting Key Sectors.* Retrieved from http://www.gao.gov/assets/120/115905.pdf

53. Peterman, D.R., Elias, B., & Frittelli, J. (2011). Transportation Security: Issues for Congress (CRS No. RL33512). Retrieved from http://www.fas.org/sgp/crs/homesec/RL33512.pdf

54. Peterman, D.R., Elias, B., & Frittelli, J. (2011). *Transportation Security: Issues for Congress* (CRS No. RL33512). Retrieved from http://www.fas.org/sgp/crs/homesec/RL33512.pdf

55. Rosenblum, M.R., Bjelopera, J.P., & Finklea, K.M. (2013). *Border Security: Understanding Threats at U.S. Borders* (CRS No. R42969). Retrieved from http://www.fas.org/sgp/crs/homesec/R42969.pdf

56. Border Security Threats to the Homeland: DHS' Response to Innovative Tactics and Techniques. 113 Cong. (2012) (Donna Bucella). Retrieved from http://homeland.house.gov/sites/homeland.house.gov/files/Testimony-Bucella.pdf

57. Customs and Border Protection. (n.d.). *CBP.* Retrieved from http://www.cbp.gov/xp/cgov/about/

58. Rosenblum, M.R., Bjelopera, J.P., & Finklea, K.M. (2013). *Border Security: Understanding Threats at U.S. Borders* (CRS No. R42969). Retrieved from http://www.fas.org/sgp/crs/homesec/R42969.pdf

59. Rosenblum, M.R., Bjelopera, J.P., & Finklea, K.M. (2013). *Border Security: Understanding Threats at U.S. Borders* (CRS No. R42969). Retrieved from http://www.fas.org/sgp/crs/homesec/R42969.pdf

60. National Commission on Terrorist Attacks Upon the United States. (2004). *The 9/11 Commission Report: Final Report of the National Commission on Terrorist Attacks Upon the United States* (Authorized Ed.). New York: W.W. Norton & Company, Inc.

61. Immigration and Nationality Act § 12, 8 USC 12 (2012).

62. Anti-Defamation League. (2004). *Canada and Terrorism.* Retrieved from http://archive.adl.org/terror/tu/tu_0401_canada.asp

63. Rosenblum, M.R., Bjelopera, J.P., & Finklea, K.M. (2013). *Border Security: Understanding Threats at U.S. Borders* (CRS No. R42969). Retrieved from http://www.fas.org/sgp/crs/homesec/R42969.pdf

64. Immigration and Nationality Act § 12, 8 USC 12 (2012).

65. Department of Homeland Security. (n.d.). *Border Security Overview.* Retrieved from http://www.dhs.gov/border-security-overview

66. Haddal, C.C. (2010). *Border Security: Key Agencies and Their Missions* (CRS No. RS21899). Retrieved from http://www.fas.org/sgp/crs/homesec/RS21899.pdf

67. United States Census Bureau. (2012). *U.S., Canada and Mexico Border Lengths.* Retrieved from http://www.census.gov/compendia/statab/2012/tables/12s0363.pdf

68. Rosenblum, M.R., Bjelopera, J.P., & Finklea, K.M. (2013). *Border Security: Understanding Threats at U.S. Borders* (CRS No. R42969). Retrieved from http://www.fas.org/sgp/crs/homesec/R42969.pdf

69. Haddal, C.C. (2010). *Border Security: Key Agencies and Their Missions* (CRS No. RS21899). Retrieved from http://www.fas.org/sgp/crs/homesec/RS21899.pdf

70. Federal Bureau of Investigation. (2008). *MS-13 Threat: A National Assessment.* Retrieved from http://www.fbi.gov/news/stories/2008/january/ms13_011408

71. Archibold, R.C. (2009). "Mexican Drug Cartel Violence Spills over, Alarming US." *New York Times Online.* Retrieved from http://www.nytimes.com/2009/03/23/us/23border.html?pagewanted=all&_r=0

72. Department of Homeland Security. (2010). *Quadrennial Homeland Security Review.* Retrieved from http://www.dhs.gov/xlibrary/assets/qhsr_report.pdf

73. Building Secure Partnerships in Travel Commerce and Trade with the Asia-Pacific Region. 112th Cong. (2012) (Mark Koumans).

74. House Permanent Subcommittee on Intelligence. 112th Congress. (2011) (Matthew G. Olsen). Retrieved from http://www.nctc.gov/press_room/speeches/dnctc_testimony_before_hpsci_111006.pdf

75. Hauslohner, A. (2011). "Gaddafi's Abandoned Arsenals Raise Libya's Terror Threat." *Time.* Retrieved from http://www.time.com/time/world/article/0,8599,2092333,00.html

76. Federal Bureau of Investigation. (2012). *Testimony.* Retrieved from http://www.fbi.gov/news/testimony/the-domestic-terrorism-threat

77. Federal Bureau of Investigation. (2012). *Testimony.* Retrieved from http://www.fbi.gov/news/testimony/the-domestic-terrorism-threat

78. Department of Homeland Security. (2010). *Quadrennial Homeland Security Review.* Retrieved from http://www.dhs.gov/xlibrary/assets/qhsr_report.pdf

79. Rice, D.S. (2012). "Report: Climate Change Behind Rise in Weather Disasters." *USA Today.* Retrieved from http://www.usatoday.com/story/weather/2012/10/10/weather-disasters-climate-change-munich-re-report/1622845/

80. Broder, J.M. (2009). "Climate Change Seen as Threat to U.S. Security." *The New York Times.* Retrieved from http://www.nytimes.com/2009/08/09/science/earth/09climate.html?pagewanted=all

81. Intergovernmental Panel on Climate Change. (2012). *Managing the Risks of Extreme Events and Disasters to Advance Climate Change Adaptation.* Retrieved from http://ipcc-wg2.gov/SREX/images/uploads/SREX-SPMbrochure_FINAL.pdf

82. Cornish, A. (2012). "Climate Change may Spark more Wildfires in the Future." *National Public Radio.* Retrieved from http://www.npr.org/2012/06/13/154959089/climate-change-may-spark-more-wildfires-in-future

83. Downs, A. (1972). "Up and Down with Ecology: The 'Issue Attention' Cycle." *National Affairs 28*, 38-50.

84. Bellavita, C. (2005). "Changing Homeland Security: The Issue Attention Cycle." *Homeland Security Affairs, 1,* 1-4.

85. Office of Management and Budget. (2013). *OMB Report Pursuant to the Sequestration Transparency Act of 2012.* Retrieved from http://www.whitehouse.gov/sites/default/files/omb/assets/legislative_reports/stareport.pdf

86. Department of Homeland Security. (2012). *DHS Announces Grant Guidance for Fiscal Year (FY) 2012 Preparedness Grants.* Retrieved from http://www.dhs.gov/news/2012/02/17/dhs-announces-grant-guidance-fiscal-year-fy-2012-preparedness-grants

Glossary

Anti-terrorism   the defensive aspects of protection from terrorism and can range from academic study to "target-hardening"

Biological weapon   weapons that use a biologically derived or living microorganism, bacteria, virus, rickettsia, or fungi to deliberately harm people, animals, or crops through infections that can incapacitate or kill

Border security   protecting the land borders of the United States from illegal movement

Category A biological weapon   agents that can easily be disseminated over a large area and infect many people and could cause a public health catastrophe

Category B biological weapon   agents that are easily disseminated over a large area but have a lower mortality rate

Category C biological weapon   common pathogens that could potentially be used as terrorist weapons

CBRNE   Chemical, Biological, Radiological, Nuclear, and Explosive weapons

Chemical weapon   a device that uses poisonous liquids, solids, gases, and vapor agents to cause death or injury to humans, animals, and plants

Civil defense   an effort to protect the citizens of the United States from a military attack

Critical infrastructure key resources   Critical infrastructure protection is comprised of the activities meant to prevent, deter, neutralize, or mitigate the effects of a terrorist attack on the nation's critical infrastructure

Command staff   Incident Command's staff that provides information, liaison, and safety services for the entire Incident Command and reports directly to the Incident Commander

Counter-terrorism   all offensive activities dedicated to tracking and eradicating terrorists both domestically and internationally

Cyber attack   any type of attack on America carried out through computing

Cyber crime   criminal activity carried out through computing

Cybersecurity   measures taken to protect computers against criminal or unauthorized use of electronic data

Cyber-terrorism   an attack that is conducted for terroristic purposes against the United States and is carried out through computing

Department of Homeland Security   a federal cabinet-level agency created in 2002 by taking various pre-existing agencies and placing them under one federal bureaucracy charged with protecting America's homeland

Dirty bomb   a device that involves the use of conventional explosive material that also contains radioactive material

Disaster declaration   a major disaster declaration, issued after catastrophes occur, constitutes broader authority for federal agencies to provide supplemental assistance to help state and local governments, families and individuals, and certain nonprofit organizations recover from the incident

Domain security   securing the environments of air, land, and sea

Domestic terrorism   the use of violence and intimidation in the pursuit of political aims committed by those from within one's own state/country

Emergency declaration   declarations to trigger aid that protects property, public health, and safety and lessens or averts the threat of an incident becoming a catastrophic event

Emergency management   the preparation for and the carrying out of all emergency functions, other than functions for which military forces are primarily responsible, to minimize injury and repair damage resulting from emergencies or disasters caused by enemy attack, sabotage or other hostile action, by fire, flood, earthquake, storm or other natural causes, or by technological or man-made catastrophes

Emergency operations center (EOC)   a central command and control facility for carrying out emergency management

Enemy combatant   historically, it meant someone fighting against the United States military, but the Bush Administration used the term to mean someone who fighting the United States unlawfully and therefore did not have the protections of the Geneva Convention as a soldier fighting for a country

Executive order   a presidential order that directs the executive branch or a specific agency within the executive branch to take some form of action

Explosive weapon   conventional weapons that have explosive properties

FEMA   the Federal Emergency Management Agency is the agency within the Department of Homeland Security responsible for responding to catastrophes and issuing a disaster and/or emergency declaration, thereby allowing them to provide monetary assistance

Fusion centers   an information sharing center created by the U.S. Department of Homeland Security and the Department of Justice to assist state and local law enforcement

General staff   This staff focuses the key functions of incident command, operations, planning, logistics, and finance/administration and reports directly to the Incident Commander

GETS   Government Emergency Telecommunications Service designed to ensure calls go through when a national emergency creates a congested phone line system

Guantanamo Bay   a bay located in Cuba that the U.S. acquired in the 1960s, that was converted into a U. S. military prison in 2002

Hazard   a danger or risk

Homeland security   1) an effort to prevent, mitigate, respond, and recover from natural and man-made disasters, including terrorist attacks; 2) a department within the Federal Government focused on prevention, mitigation, responding to and recovering from both natural and man-made disasters

Homeland security areas of emphasis   various ways of perceiving homeland security as detailed by Homeland Security expert Christopher Bellavita

Homeland security bureaucracy   the various federal, state, and local agencies that are directly or indirectly involved in the protection of America's homeland

Homeland security concepts   fundamental aspects of homeland security that are common to all responses whether they are natural disasters or terrorist attacks, such as preparedness

Homeland security enterprise   the collective efforts and shared responsibilities of federal, state, local, tribal, territorial, nongovernmental, and private-sector partners—as well as individuals, families, and communities—to maintain critical homeland security capabilities

Homeland security goals   those key tasks that must be accomplished in order for the homeland security mission to be accomplished

Homeland security mission   those key items that must be achieved in order for the homeland to be secure and the homeland security strategy implemented

Homeland security policing   the local police role in protecting the homeland

Homeland Security Presidential Directives   presidential executive orders that are focused on Homeland Security and advise the federal bureaucracy on administrative requirements the president wants implemented

Homeland security strategy   the overarching plan for dealing with all hazards that focuses on shared goals and responsibilities for protecting and defending the homeland

HSARPA   the Homeland Security Advanced Research Projects Agency, which is focused on providing security for critical infrastructure in the U.S.

Incident Command Post (ICP)   the physical location of the Incident Commander and his or her staff

Incident command system   the Incident Command System (ICS) is a standardized, on-scene, all-hazards incident management approach

Intelligence community   a group of government agencies and organizations that carry out intelligence activities for the United States government; headed by the Director of Central Intelligence

Intelligence cycle   a five step process for intelligence that consists of planning and direction, collecting, processing, analysis and production, and dissemination

International terrorism   the use of violence and intimidation in the pursuit of political aims committed by those from outside of one's own state/country

Joint field office   when an incident is of such severity, magnitude, and/or complexity that it requires coordinated Federal assistance, the Secretary of Homeland Security, in coordination with other Federal departments and agencies, initiates actions to respond to and recover from the incident, including the establishment of the Joint Field Office to provide the Incident Commander Federal Resources

Joint Terrorism Task Force   a partnership between various American law enforcement agencies that is charged with taking action against terrorism

Maritime security   protecting the coastal waters of the United States from illegal movement

Mitigation   the effort to reduce loss of life and property by lessening the impact of disasters

Multiagency Coordination System(s) (MACS)   a process that allows all levels of government and all disciplines to work together more efficiently and effectively; coordination occurs across the different disciplines involved in incident management, across jurisdictional lines or across levels of government

National Incident Management System   the National Incident Management System (NIMS) identifies concepts and principles that answer how to manage emergencies from preparedness to recovery regardless of their cause, size, location or complexity

National Infrastructure Protection Plan   provides a unifying framework that integrates a range of efforts designed to enhance the safety of our nation's critical infrastructure

National Response Framework   part of the National Strategy for Homeland Security which provides the guiding principles enabling all levels of domestic response partners to prepare for and provide a unified national response to disasters and emergencies

National Response Plan   the National Response Plan (NRP) is an all-discipline, all-hazards plan that establishes a single, comprehensive framework for the management of domestic incidents; it provides the structure and mechanisms for the coordination of federal support to state, local, and tribal incident managers and for exercising direct federal authorities and responsibilities (replaced by the broader National Response Framework)

National Security Presidential Directives   similar to an executive order, these directives are focused on directing the various agencies in the executive branch focused on matters concerning national security

National Strategy for Counterterrorism   the federal government's approach to dealing with the terrorist threat; it identifies the range of tools that are critical to the strategy's success

National Strategy for Homeland Security   a strategic document which guides, organizes, and unifies our Nation's homeland security efforts

National Terrorism Advisory System   a new general threat level system that replaced the old color-coded system that was much derided by the public and the media

Natural disaster   an event that occurs in nature, not caused by humans, that affects the environment and results in financial and/or human loss

Nongovernmental organizations (NGOs)   legally constituted corporations by people that operate independently from any form of government, such as the American Red Cross

Nuclear weapon   an explosive device that derives its destructive force from nuclear reactions, either fission or a combination of fission and fusion

NUSTL   National Urban Security Technology Laboratory focused on providing security for large cities and metropolitan areas

Office of the Director of National Intelligence   the Director of National Intelligence serves as the head of the Intelligence Community, overseeing and directing the implementation of the National Intelligence Program and acting as the principal advisor to the President, the National Security Council, and the Homeland Security Council for intelligence matters related to national security

Office of Homeland Security   the office inside of the White House (executive branch) led by former Governor Tom Ridge, charged with securing the homeland, and which served as the nucleus for the Department of Homeland Security

Preparedness   a continuous cycle of planning, organizing, training, equipping, exercising, evaluating, and taking corrective action in an effort to ensure effective coordination during incident response

Prevention   the capabilities necessary to avoid, prevent, or stop a threatened or actual act of terrorism; as defined by PPD-8, the term "prevention" refers to preventing imminent threats

Recovery   the efforts taken to restore the infrastructure and the social and economic underpinnings of a community to a state of normalcy

Response   any measures taken at the onset of an emergence to save lives and protect property

Risk   the possibility of loss or injury

Strategy   a plan of action or policy designed to achieve a major overall goal

Terrorism   the use of violence and intimidation in the pursuit of political aims

Transportation Security Administration   the federal department under Homeland Security responsible for transportation security in the U.S.

Unified command (UC)   a structure that brings together the "Incident Commanders" of all major organizations involved in the incident in order to coordinate an effective response while at the same time carrying out their own jurisdictional responsibilities

USA PATRIOT Act   a ten-letter acronym for federal legislation formally titled Uniting and Strengthening America by Providing Appropriate Tools Required to Intercept and Obstruct Terrorism Act of 2001; an act of Congress passed in 2001, six weeks after the 9-11 terrorist attacks, that gave new tools to investigate potential terroristic threats in the United States

USCYBERCOM   U.S. Cyber Command is specifically tasked with managing risk within DOD networks and making sure those networks are resilient in case of an attack

9/11 Commission   formally named the National Commission on Terrorist Attacks Upon the United States, it was formed after the terrorist attacks on September 11, 2001 to investigate the attacks and to make recommendations for future preparations

Epilogue

Make no mistake: The United States will hunt down and punish those responsible for these cowardly acts.
– President G.W. Bush, September 11, 2001

Reproduced from: Bush, George W. (2001). "Remarks at Barksdale Air Force Base, Louisiana, on the Terrorist Attacks." Public Papers of the Presidents of the United States. Washington, D.C.: U.S.

■ May 1, 2011

Two stealth Black Hawks lifted off from an airbase in Jalalabad, Afghanistan.[1] The helicopters were fully loaded, calculated down to the last pound, and completely blacked out. Inside were members of the Joint Special Operations Command's U.S. Naval Special Warfare Development Group (DEVGRU) Red Squadron, known more famously as SEAL Team VI. They were flying in two "chalks," heading due east. Approximately 10–15 minutes later, they crossed up and over a series of rocky peaks and entered into Pakistan airspace.

"Crossing the border," crackled across the airwaves.[2] That was the signal for three Chinook helicopters to lift off from Jalalabad. One would land just along the border, while the other two would follow on to support the two chalks. SEAL Team VI had just initiated an invasion into neighboring Pakistan. Their destination was a compound in Abbottabad that, according to the best intelligence since September 11, 2001, was the current location of Al Qaeda leader Osama bin Laden. If everything went as planned, bin Laden would be dead or captured by Navy SEALs in no more than 40 minutes—the operational time limit for the mission.[3]

The SEALs received their 1-minute warning as the Black Hawks approached the compound from the northwest. The compound was easy to spot through the night-vision goggles, for it was triangular in shape with a concrete wall higher than any in the surrounding area, and the main compound was three stories. The first chopper approached, hovered, and the SEAL team chalk kicked the ropes out as they prepared to fast rope into the compound.[4] Unfortunately, as every soldier knows, the best-laid plans typically go awry, and this mission was no different. The helicopter could not maintain lift; it wheeled suddenly, and the rotor clipped the extra-high compound wall.[5] The fast reaction of the pilot saved the day, but not the helicopter—he intentionally put it down for a controlled crash. The pilot knew that if he had not deliberately crashed, the chopper would have pitched, and the rotating blades would have buried into the compound, flipping the aircraft and potentially injuring or killing everyone on board. He buried the nose hard, and the SEAL team bailed out and went to work.

The second Black Hawk pilot, observing the tragedy befalling the first, quickly diverted to the secondary landing site, just outside the compound. Originally he was to hover over the compound and drop some of the chalk, then move to hover over the three-story building and drop the rest of the team on the roof. Now the members of that chalk had to gain access through the concrete wall and assault from the ground up.

The SEAL team did not let the setback disturb them. The crashed helicopter team set charges to an interior gate and headed directly for the main building. The second chalk exited the aircraft, quickly approached the exterior gate, set charges, and after a brilliant explosion, entered the compound. By this time, members of the crashed helicopter had reached the double metal doors of the main building.

One member tested the door handle, finding it locked. One SEAL pulled out a sledgehammer with an extendable handle, while the other covered him. Several blows did nothing to the handle and another attempt on the window nearby was equally futile because of the metal bars. They decided to go with explosives. They set the charges and were about to blow them, when unsuppressed gunfire erupted.

The last of the SEAL team to enter the main compound had arrived, but he drew fire from someone inside the building. Rounds tore through a glass window set above the two metal doors. It was the distinct sound of an AK-47 being fired. The last SEAL made it to cover, and the one setting the charges on the door handle pushed back to take cover away from the doorway. As the sound of gunfire stopped, he reached to blow the charges, but then the door handle latch clicked—someone was coming out.

The team once again jumped back for cover as a woman with a baby exited the building. One of the SEAL team members called to her in Arabic to come to him, drawing her away from the door. She was patted down and quickly questioned. She claimed "he" was dead, but no one on the SEAL team believed a word until they saw it with their own eyes.[6]

On the other side of the building, another team of SEALs entered through the garage. They found another locked door to the compound, set charges, and blew it wide open. As the team entered, AK-47 rounds fired down the hallway toward them. They returned fire injuring the shooter (later identified as Abrar Al-Kuwaiti).[7] A woman (his wife) then ran to shield him, and the SEALs fired multiple shots, killing them both.

The other team now received the signal to blow their door, and they entered the compound heading for the stairs. The team, moving with both stealth and speed, took to the stairs when someone on the second floor landing peeked around the corner. The lead SEAL fired, and when they reached the second floor, found a slender man with a beard shot dead (he was later identified as bin Laden's son Khalid).[8] Lying next to him was an unfired AK-47.

The SEAL team then cleared the second floor and proceeded up the last flight of steps to the third floor. As they reached the last few steps, the point-man could see two doors, one to the left and one to the right. The night-vision goggles gave him a distinct advantage, so when a head peaked out from the right side doorway, he fired off two rounds. The man then ran down the hallway and into another room approximately 10 feet away.

The SEALs continued moving methodically, entering the hallway, clearing the two rooms, and then advancing toward the room into which the man had fled. They slowly approached the doorway and peered in. Two women in robes were looking down at a man on the floor and they were wailing in hysterics. One of the women saw the SEAL in the doorway and rushed him. The point-man grabbed her and pushed her, along with the other woman, into a corner of the room. The other SEAL fired two rapid shots into the prone man's chest. It was clear that the man had been hit in the head with the point-man's bullets when he had peered out of the doorway. He had then retreated to his room and collapsed. The last two bullets ensured he was no longer a threat.

Osama bin Laden was dead.

Despite the United States finally eliminating Osama bin Laden, the leader of Al Qaeda, for the terrorist attacks of September 11, 2001, Al Qaeda still remains a threat, and the importance of homeland security has not abated. While foiled attempts do not receive the same attention as actual attacks, there have been at least 50 terrorist plots foiled in the United States since 9-11.[9] These plots include planned bombings of New York's Brooklyn Bridge, Times Square, subway system, and stock exchange, as well as Chicago's Sears Tower, the Fort Dix military base, the Washington D.C. metropolitan subway, and the U.S. Capitol (see **Epilogue** Figure 1). In addition, terrorist attacks against the United States, its interests, and its people, continue overseas in places like Cairo, Benghazi, Mali, and the U.S. Embassy in Turkey. And, unfortunately, just as this text was being completed, the first successful terrorist attack since September 11, 2001 occurred on April 15, 2013, near the finish line of the Boston Marathon.

Although the investigation continues, what is known is that two brothers, Tamerlan and Dzhokhar Tsarnaev, learned how to build a bomb through an online Al Qaeda magazine. They placed two pressure cooker bombs in separate duffel bags and dropped them in the crowd very near the finish line of the Boston Marathon. They then used a cell phone to set off the bombs at 2:49 p.m., and the explosion ultimately killed three spectators, including an eight-year-old boy, and injured over 250 people. Images of the suspects were obtained by the FBI and a manhunt ensued. The suspects later carjacked an SUV and shortly thereafter killed MIT Police Officer Sean A. Collier. The police tracked the two suspects down (by tracking the SUV owner's cell phone left in the car) and after a firefight that killed one (Tamerlan), they found the other one wounded, hiding in a boat in a homeowner's backyard. The investigation into their background and connections continues.

All of these incidents highlight the continued need for protecting the homeland. All of them highlight the need for homeland security.

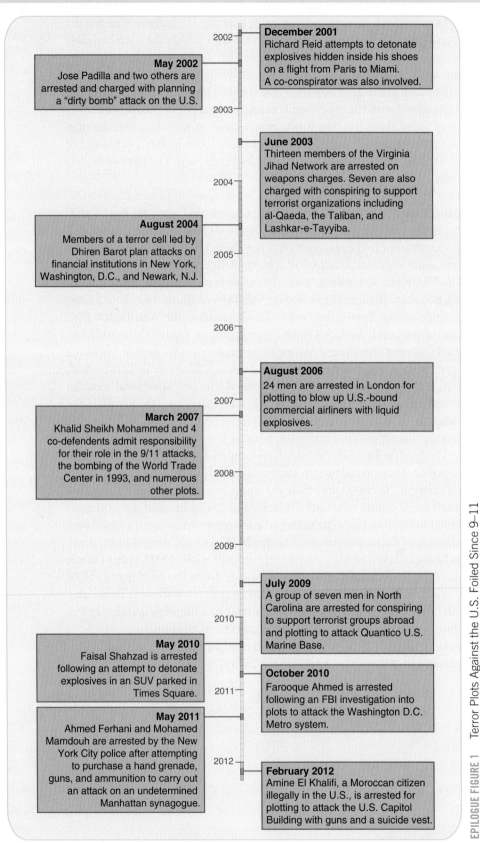

Reprinted and modified with permission from Carafano, James Jay, Steve Bucci, & Jessica Zuckerman. (2012). "Fifty Terror Plots Foiled Since 9/11: The Homegrown Threat and the Long War on Terrorism." The Heritage Foundation: Backgrounder, No. 2682. Washington, D.C.: The Heritage Foundation. The original timeline can be found here: http://www.heritage.org/research/reports/2012/04/fifty-terror-plots-foiled-since-9-11-the-homegrown-threat-and-the-long-war-on-terrorism

EPILOGUE FIGURE 1   Terror Plots Against the U.S. Foiled Since 9–11

■ Endnotes

1. This account of the death of Osama Bin Laden is based primarily on two sources: Bowden, M. (2012). *The Finish: The Killing of Osama bin Laden.* New York, NY: Atlantic Monthly Press; Owen, M. (2012). *No Easy Day: The Firsthand Account of the Mission that Killed Osama Bin Laden.* New York, NY: Dutton.

2. Owen, M. (2012). *No Easy Day: The Firsthand Account of the Mission that Killed Osama Bin Laden.* New York, NY: Dutton, p. 209.

3. Despite the setback of the Black Hawk crashing, the mission was still completed within the allotted time of 40 minutes (38 minutes to be precise). See Bowden, M. (2012). *The Finish: The Killing of Osama Bin Laden.* New York, NY: Atlantic Monthly Press; Owen, M. (2012). *No Easy Day: The Firsthand Account of the Mission that Killed Osama bin Laden.* New York, NY: Dutton.

4. Owen, M. (2012). *No Easy Day: The Firsthand Account of the Mission that Killed Osama Bin Laden.* New York, NY: Dutton.

5. Bowden, M. (2012). *The Finish: The Killing of Osama Bin Laden.* New York, NY: Atlantic Monthly Press.

6. Owen, M. (2012). *No Easy Day: The Firsthand Account of the Mission that Killed Osama Bin Laden.* New York, NY: Dutton.

7. Owen, M. (2012). *No Easy Day: The Firsthand Account of the Mission that Killed Osama Bin Laden.* New York, NY: Dutton.

8. Owen, M. (2012). *No Easy Day: The Firsthand Account of the Mission that Killed Osama Bin Laden.* New York, NY: Dutton.

9. Carafano, J.J., Bucci, S.P., & Zuckerman, J. (2012). *Fifty Terror Plots Foiled Since 9/11: The Homegrown Threat and the Long War on Terrorism.* The Heritage Foundation. Retrieved online at http://www.heritage.org/research/reports/2012/04/fifty-terror-plots-foiled-since-9-11-the-homegrown-threat-and-the-long-war-on-terrorism

Index

Note: Page numbers followed by *b*, *f*, and *t* indicate material in boxes, figures, and tables, respectively.